"Thank you! You have delivered upon me greatness!"

Comadres y Comics Podcast

"A genius fusion of Mesoamerican myth, Chicano culture, and American comics. Diego de la Muerte is the hero we need and deserve—his gritty and gripping adventures will keep you flipping the pages; his existential plight will linger with you long after you're done reading."

David Bowles, **Feathered Serpent, Dark Sky: Myths of Mexico**

"Javier Hernandez uses classic storytelling and detailed visceral artwork that takes the most interesting, important and fun things about Latino culture and rebirths it into a legendary tale of self discovery and self fulfillment. The visual imagery used in DAZE OF THE DEAD is intense as the drama that unfolds, taking the reader on a literary temazcal."

Chris C. Hernandez, **Cómix Latinx**

"El Muerto was one of the first comic books I was ever given. I looked at the pages and even before I could read, I was able to see characters who looked and spoke like everything and everyone around me. El Muerto is the supernatural super hero for *la gente* that we all need. The Special Edition is like discovering a hidden treasure all over again. *¡Que Viva El Muerto!*"

Xolo Maridueña, actor **Cobra Kai**

"DAZE OF THE DEAD brings together the familiarity of Mexican American life and Ancient Aztec gods in a way unlike I've ever seen. This new and improved release gives a whole new generation, including myself, the opportunity to experience this beautiful tale of family, loss, and sacrifice. This is exactly what I needed growing up and now I'm ready to dig into the next issues!"

Gonzalo Alvarez, **The Legend of Polloman**

Glossary of The Gods

This story contains characters based on Aztec mythology. Below is a pronounciation key. Please note that different scholars and historians use varying terms for the ancient Pre-Columbian culture commonly referred to as 'Aztecs'. Other names include 'Mexica (meh-hee-ka). For the purpose of my story I am using the Aztec label, with all due respect to differing opinions. Also, interpretations of the individual gods abound, so I end up creating my own version of the various identified deities.

Mictlan: *meek-tlan (Land of the Dead)*
Mictlantecuhtli: *meek-tlan-teh-coot-lee (Ruler of mictlan)*
Omecihuatli: *oh-meh-see-hwatl (Female nature/identity of creator god)*
Ometecuhtli: *oh-meh-teh-coot-lee (Male nature/identity of creator god)*
Tezcatlipoca: *tez-cat-lee-po-ka ("Smoking mirror", trickster god of dreams)*

DAZE Of The DEAD
by Javier Hernandez
HERE LIES DIEGO de la MUERTE
An EL MUERTO Graphic Novel

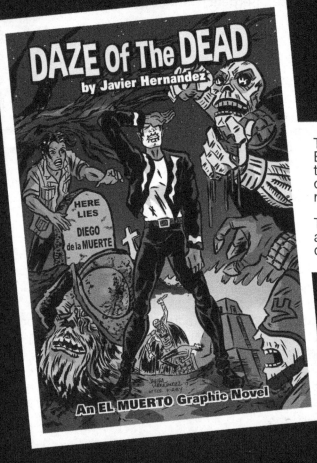

This Special "Dia de Los Muertos" Edition features the same story as the previous Advance Reader Edition of DAZE OF THE DEAD (originally released in Dec. 2017).

This edition features new cover art plus exclusive behind-the-scene content on the creation of El Muerto.

DAZE OF THE DEAD: Special Dia de Los Muertos Edition is published by Los Comex. P.O. Box 718, Whittier, CA 90608-0718. September 2018.

DAZE of The DEAD

¡SPECIAL DIA DE LOS MUERTOS EDITION!

by Javier Hernandez

Los COMEX

el Muerto
2O
ANIVERSARIO
1998-2018

CONTENTS

MAKING EL MUERTO

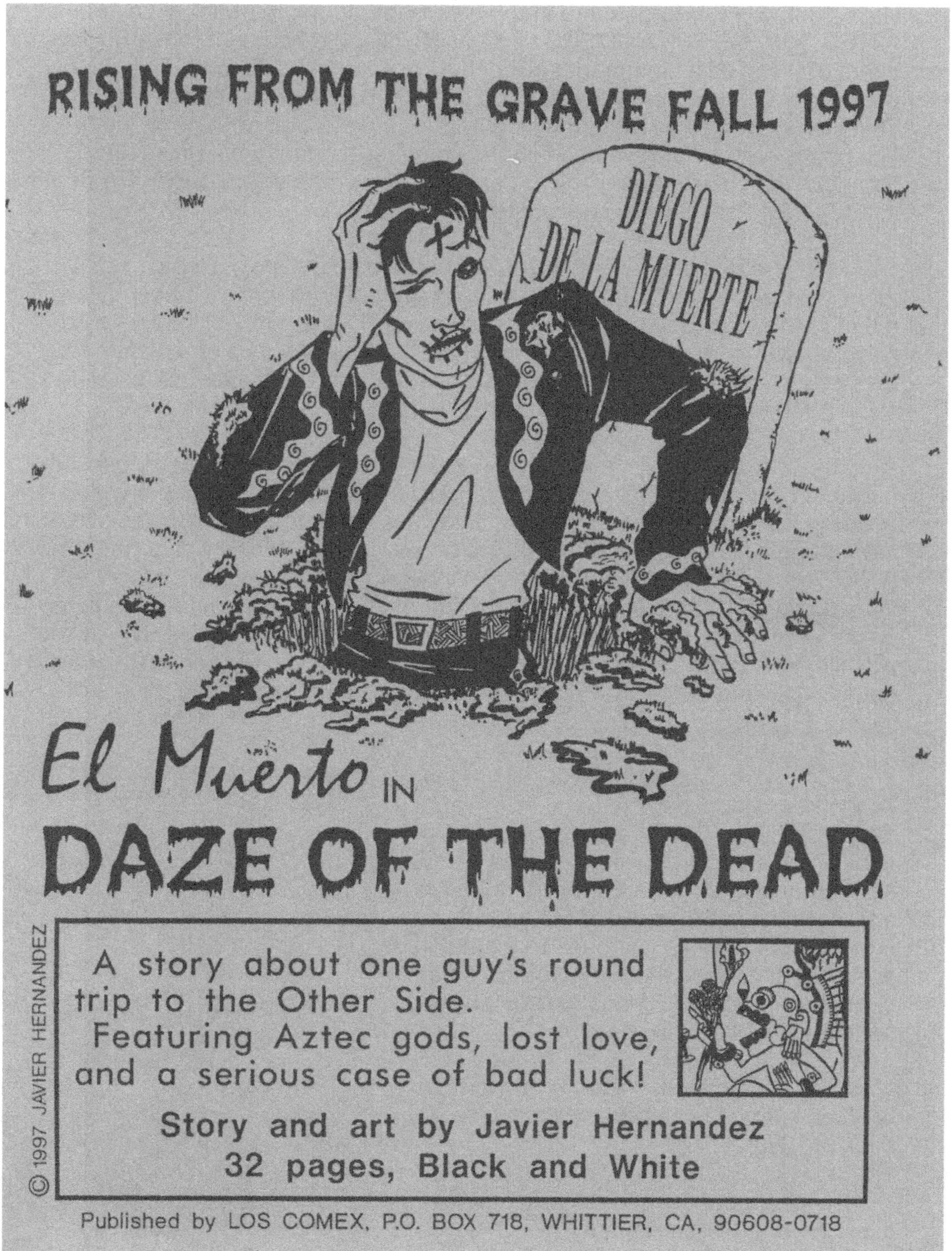

RISING FROM THE GRAVE FALL 1997
DIEGO DE LA MUERTE
El Muerto IN
DAZE OF THE DEAD
A story about one guy's round trip to the Other Side.
Featuring Aztec gods, lost love, and a serious case of bad luck!
Story and art by Javier Hernandez
32 pages, Black and White
© 1997 JAVIER HERNANDEZ
Published by LOS COMEX, P.O. BOX 718, WHITTIER, CA, 90608-0718

A flyer produced in early 1997 to promote the Fall release of the first issue of El Muerto. Only missed my release date by one season as the book didn't debut until February 1998!

If you're new to the world of El Muerto... Welcome! For those already, or somewhat familiar, allow me to make some introductions.

My name is Javier Hernandez and I'm a cartoonist. I both write and draw my own comics, which I've been publishing through my imprint Los Comex since 1998. El Muerto debuted in the b&w photocopied EL MUERTO- THE AZTEC ZOMBIE: THE NUMERO UNO EDITION. I did two print runs, totaling about 350 copies if I remember correctly. For sure less than 500. The book debuted at the Alternative Press Expo (APE) in San Jose in February, 1998. That first show was as nerve-racking and exciting as you could imagine. You're basically putting yourself on the stage for the first time, presenting the thing you've worked on (in my case) for well over a year. Longer if you actually count all the years dreaming about it.

At the end of this book, after you've read the actual story, I'll give you a more detailed account of the publishing history of El Muerto. It's been a small run of El Muerto stories over the past 20 years. The comic you'll be reading is basically both a reinvention of the original series as well as a completion to the previosly unfinished storyline. But all will be explained afterwards, so no skipping to the end of this book!

In those twenty years though I've had as full a life as one can being a self-published cartoonist. Traveled up and down every corner of the convention circuit in California plus trips across state lines. I had the good fortune of having had a film made from my comic book. Starring Wilmer Valderrama (THAT 70s SHOW) and produced by an independent production company, I scored myself both a cameo with our star as well as an Associate Producer credit. I was even asked to produce the artwork for the main titles. The movie was filmed in 2005, hit the independent film festival circuit in early 2007 then got a DVD release later that year. Quite a whirlwind for me, those couple of years!

Once filming was done (Feb. '05), I clearly remember settling back into my studio space. Sitting at my desk, with a sheet of paper in front of me and my drawing supplies at my side, I thought "Well, it was fun working with a team bringing the movie to life for the last 6 weeks, but now it's just back to me doing all the work!". While the crew worked on the film's post-production I was already back to to doing what I do: make comics.

So let me dig back a little further in time to when before I released the first issue way back in 1998...

I'm not sure of the exact moment when I came up with El Muerto, but it was after I had already decided that I wanted to create my own comic books.

By the early 90s, after having read comics regularly since the mid 1970s, I was actively creating characters and ideas for comics. I don't even think I gave much thought to how

With Wilmer Valderrama in East LA at Evergreen Cemetery where we filmed our scene for EL MUERTO.

Some of my earliest designs for El Muerto, from August and September 1994. About 3 and a half years before his first comic book appearance in February 1998. His basic design was established from the start, with subtle changes occuring before he eventually saw print.

those comics were going to be published, but "I wanna make comics!" was my mantra.

But I didn't necessarily want to work on Iron Man or Batman or The Hulk. I loved those characters, and I wasn't being a comics snob looking down my nose at superheroes. What I really wanted was to create my own ideas. Way back then long before the idea of hashtags like "#representation matters" were shared on something called the internet, I was interested in creating characters showcasing aspects of Latino culture, and specifically Mexican culture.

My siblings and I grew up in East Los Angeles in a bilingual home. Our parents were Spanish speakers. Mom was from Mexico and Dad, born in the U.S., was pretty much raised in Mexico as a small child. They met there, got married and moved to the U.S. to start a family.

Spanish was the household language. But amongst myself and my three siblings, we'd communicate in English. Spanish for our parents and to Mom's side of the family from Mexico, English to Dad's family in East LA and for our daily lives growing up in the U.S. At home the family would gather around the TV and watch "El Chavo del Ocho" or "Siempre en Domingo". My dad would play his Vicente Fernandez records. Mom fed us great Mexican dishes. On Wednesday nights I'd tune into the Spanish station to watch "Lucha Libre", listening to the commentators screaming in Spanish at the antics of a young Roddy Piper as he fueded with the hometown heroes, the Guerrero Family.

Then on Saturday afternoon I'd watch the English language wrestling show, also broadcast from the famed Olympic Auditorium, and listen to the American announcers call matches with Victor Rivera, Texas Red and that wrestler I loved to hate in any language, Roddy Piper. This was my childhood Golden Age. The rest of my 1970s was filled with comics I bought at the local 7-11, having previously gotten hooked on comics when my older brother Albert gave me his small collection of comics. He was hitting High School and his interests had changed. For the better, as far as I was concerned!

Moving so fluidly between English and Spanish entertainment wasn't even an issue to me. Just the way one grew up. At some point as an older child I'd take note when a Latino character appeared. Of course Speedy Gonzalez was clearly a Mexican mouse and Gomez Addams, the patriarch of the Addams Family, displayed Latino roots. And over in Marvel Comics, the Puerto Rican costumed martial artist White Tiger would fight alongside Spider-Man and the other heroes. Occasionally the writers would include some Spanish words among the Tiger's dialogue, causing me to wonder, with a bit of linguistic snobbery, if the other readers could figure out what he was saying!

Despite the overwhelming lack of identifiable Latinos in the majority of the American content I watched though, I don't remember being besieged by any feelings of being "marginalized", "underrepresented" or generally excluded. Perhaps I wasn't politcally self aware enough. But I don't know, I guess I had a very happy childhood and home life, and no shortage of exciting material to consume. I sure got plenty of enjoyment out of the Steve Ditko Spider-Man reprints I got a hold of. I was mesmerized by the adventures of Speed Racer, and completely engrossed in the drama of Bill Bixby's David Banner as he manuevered through the nightmare of living as the Hulk. The universality of those character's lives, and the storytelling excellence of their creative teams, transcended, to my young self anyway, any ethnic or cultural 'divide'.

Flash forward to the early/mid 90s. When I did start toying with the idea of creating my own stories, I instinctively felt, wanted to, create characters that reflected a Mexican background. It was admittedly a response to having not seen many of those type (if any) of characters in the comics and shows I loved as a kid. Not necessarily a defiant "I'll show them!" attitude, but more of a desire to show interesting new things that people were choosing not to tap into, the way they would with, for example, Greek or Norse mythology. I looked at it like, "I'm Mexican, my parents come from Mexico... Why not use this stuff?".

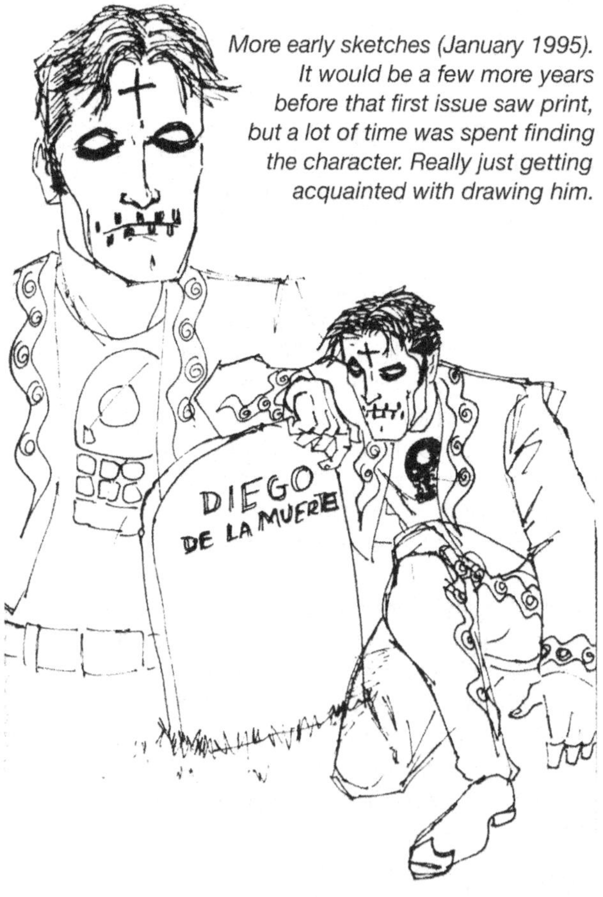
DIEGO
DE LA MUERTE

More early sketches (January 1995). It would be a few more years before that first issue saw print, but a lot of time was spent finding the character. Really just getting acquainted with drawing him.

So the first really concrete idea I came up with during this time was a group of Mexican superheroes, like the Avengers or JLA. The inevitable luchador. Some type of cosmic Aztec star god, like Captain Marvel but instead of hailing from the Kree Empire he sprang from ancient Mexico. There was a loose idea about some type of Latino Lone Ranger. Basically Zorro, to be honest. And the final member of the team was this Dia de Los Muertos inspired gothic looking character. Black mariachi suit, skull design on his face.

I had done a few sketches of the group before I decided that I didn't really want to draw a team book for my first effort. Too many people!

But also, there was something about that dead guy that drew my attention. Undead or unliving characters weren't a new idea, but basing an origin story on the Day of the Dead wasn't something I remember seeing in American comics. "El Muerto" was the obvious name for him. I just hadn't formulated much more about him at that time he was part of a group. But now that I had decided to focus on him exclusively I had to explore who and what he was, and how he came to be...

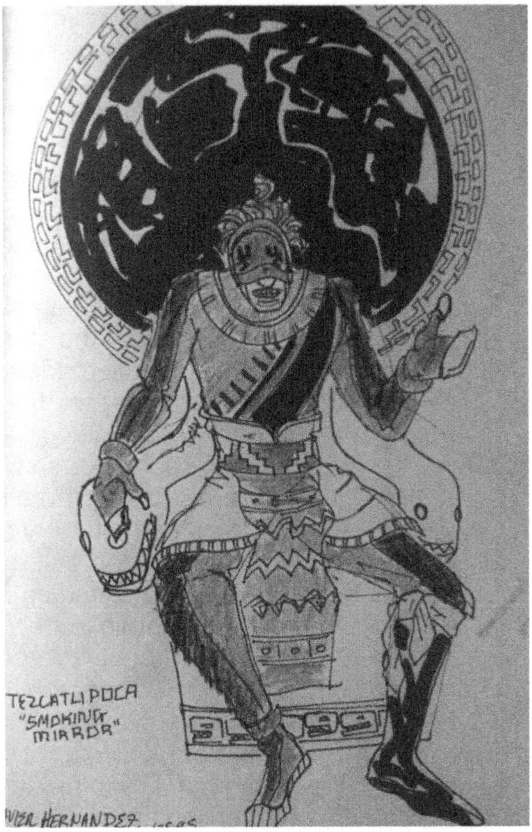
TEZCATLIPOCA
"SMOKING MIRROR"
One of my early interpretations of Tezcatlipoca, the god of destiny. I took elements from different images I saw in Aztec art. The large obsidian mirror above his throne, and the one shaped like his foot, were inspired by the what was shown in the various codices. From January 1995.

Comics, a visual medium, derive so much of their attraction from how a character looks. Giving El Muerto a black mariachi suit was an instinctual choice. I wanted something iconically Mexican, so instead of a traditional superhero costume made of spandex, I borrowed the attire of Mexico's singing cowboys. El Muerto's skull logo was taken from a design found in an Aztec history book. It was a carving on a wall, repeated multiple times in a pattern. I simplified it like the way they had done with Batman's bat logo. I always liked it when they gave a superhero a clearly recognizable logo, so El Muerto would fittingly have a stylized Aztec skull. And the reason I chose to place it on the back of his jacket was because I was inspired from that big red spider seen on the back of Spider-Man's costume. It seemed like a smart design choice to place the logo on the character's back as he would be easily identifiable from the front! For El Muerto, whose costume is mostly black from the back, the large white skull stands out boldly.

So I had this character, dressed in a stylized marciachi costume, a skull design adorning his face. From there I had to reverse engineer him: how did this happen to him and what does he do. I had already incorporated elements of Dia de Los Muertos in his visual identity. It seemd reasonable to me that a supernatural element would be needed to explain his powers and origin, so I looked to Aztec mythology for answers. Since my aim was to create a character with roots to Mexican culture, exploring the religion of the Mexico's ancestral people was the natural course to take. Like the rest of the public I was somewhat familar with the Roman & Greek myths. How many Hercules cartoons and movies have all of us seen? So I went to the library and bookstores and did some research. Over the years, I was exposed to Aztec art as well as some of their history. I was always fascinated by the elaborate visuals of the gods in their codices, the artistry of their storytelling and architecture. The mighty cities of pyramids and the colossal clash of civilations known as "The Conquest of Mexico".... But opening those books and studying their histories gave me a broader view of the Aztecs, and really a deeper and more personal connection to the people, artists and storytellers of those ancient times. My cultural and artistic roots.

I should explain something about my research and how I used what was learned. A favorite cartoonist of mine, Jack Kirby, used classic mythology in his comics quite often. His work with Stan Lee over at Marvel on THOR was a great example, to me, of how to take ancient myths and filter them through one's artistic eye and create something new. His Norse gods were a mixture of established notions of what they were like but also of that trademark Kirby trope of high-tech space gods. So in my survey of Aztec gods and myths, I freely took the liberty of visualizing designs and character traits based on existing examples but also formulating things based on my own ideas. Unless one is doing an actual faithful adaptation of a classic story or ancient text, why wouldn't you create the story as you need it? My hope was always that my work would entertain readers, but hopefully lead a few to want to study and explore even deeper the things I presented in my comics.

You'll find out soon enough what I came up with when you read "Daze of The Dead", but just a little more background here if you'll indulge me. Of course I needed a name for my character, before he became El Muerto. I think that the name Diego de La Muerte came about fairly quickly. I definitely wanted an interesting sounding name, but something just a little more memorable, more 'comic book' sounding. Dia de Los Muertos.... I looked at those words and thought "What name, visually and phonetically, reflects Dia de Los Muertos". Diego de La Muerte was the immediate answer. Juan Diego de La Muerte, his complete name. Juan Diego of course calls to mind the story of one of Mexico's most potent icons, La Virgen de Guadalupe. So from the beginning, Diego de La Muerte as a name was created to stand out and encompass a lot of story potential.

One last thing about the festival of Dia de Los Muertos. Back in the mid 90s when I was creating my character, my primary knowledge of the Day of the Dead came from the art of the great Mexican artist and printmaker Jose Guadalupe Posada. And also, believe it or not, the cover artwork from an album by the band Oingo Boingo! Dia de Los Muertos wasn't something

El Muerto meets his maker! When I launched the first issue of El Muerto I actually had a mariachi suit customized to use for promotional opportunities at conventions and such. I've had a few friends wear the suit in the early years. I did the face painting which was interesting because it was like I was drawing the character in 3D.

I grew up with as a kid. My mom told me that it wasn't something her family celebrated. I did find a book on the subject, "The Skeleton at The Feast", which did provide a treasure trove of information and imagery. And I was fortunate enough to catch a screening of MACARIO, a 1960 Mexican film that took place on Dia de Los Muertos (and was actually the the first Mexican film to be nominated for a Best Foreign Language Film Acadamy Award). I also found on VHS a film called ¡QUE VIVA MEXICO!. This was a project originally begun by Russian filmmaker Sergei Eisenstein in the 1930s, and was finally finished in 1979 by his co-director. The film was a series of shorts dealing with Mexico, with the final segment detailing a Dia de Los Muertos celebration. These films, and other works, provided some inspiring insights into the Day of the Dead, particularly as seen through the eyes of other artists.

At it's most basic, the core meaning of the Day of the Dead remains simple and beautiful: To honor and remember the lives and memories of loved ones who've passed on. The universality of of that, and the fact that it's a uniquely Mexican expression of love and art, really provided me the grounding for my comic book hero and his odyssey.

Today we see that Dia de Los Muertos has established itself far beyond Mexico's borders and into the world and popular culture. 2018's Academy Award-winning blockbuster Disney/Pixar film COCO is surely the great pop cultural highwater mark for the festival. This followed the release of an earlier animated film THE BOOK OF LIFE, by director Jorge Guiterrez. And years before those films I had started seeing Dia de Los Muertos party supplies and decorations on display at Target and Walmart during their Fall merchandising seasons. I'm not going to pull a Jeb Bush and ask anyone to "Please clap", but I take some pride that I got El Muerto onto the scene in February of '98 just before everyone finally realized, deservedly so, that Dia de Los Muertos is one of the world's great cultural celebrations. A true gift from my Mexico.

And now, I'm going stop here and let you get to the actual comic, if you haven't already. Step into the surreal world of Diego de La Muerte, courtesy of my mind's eye, and please enjoy. Afterwards, join me in the back of this book for another history lesson!

Javier Hernandez
September 2018

DAZE Of The DEAD

Story & Art by
JAVIER HERNANDEZ

PART ONE

DEAD MAN'S PARTY

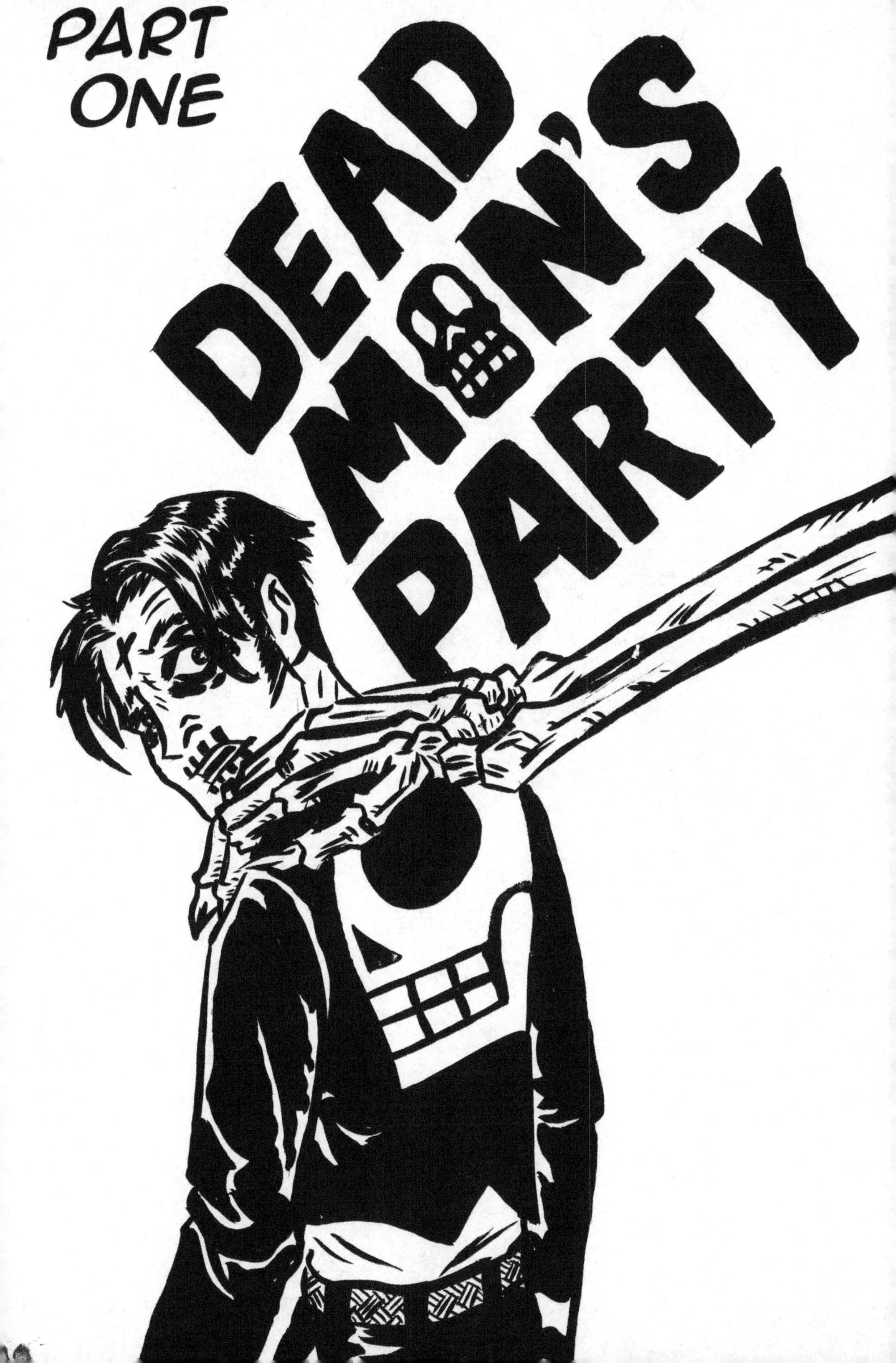

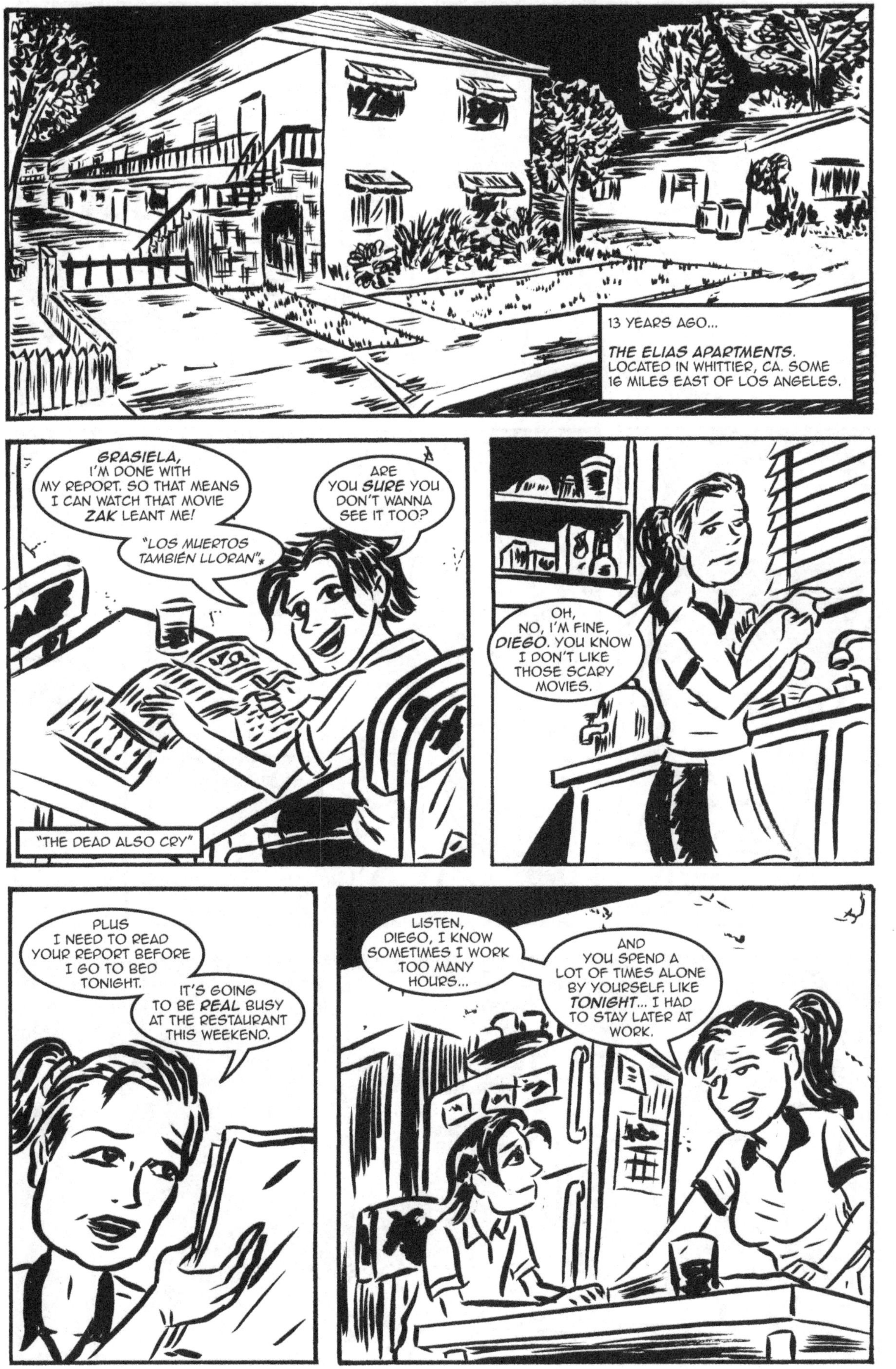
13 YEARS AGO...
THE ELIAS APARTMENTS. LOCATED IN WHITTIER, CA. SOME 16 MILES EAST OF LOS ANGELES.
GRASIELA, I'M DONE WITH MY REPORT. SO THAT MEANS I CAN WATCH THAT MOVIE ZAK LEANT ME!
"LOS MUERTOS TAMBIÉN LLORAN"*
ARE YOU SURE YOU DON'T WANNA SEE IT TOO?
"THE DEAD ALSO CRY"
OH, NO, I'M FINE, DIEGO. YOU KNOW I DON'T LIKE THOSE SCARY MOVIES.
PLUS I NEED TO READ YOUR REPORT BEFORE I GO TO BED TONIGHT.
IT'S GOING TO BE REAL BUSY AT THE RESTAURANT THIS WEEKEND.
LISTEN, DIEGO, I KNOW SOMETIMES I WORK TOO MANY HOURS...
AND YOU SPEND A LOT OF TIMES ALONE BY YOURSELF. LIKE TONIGHT... I HAD TO STAY LATER AT WORK.

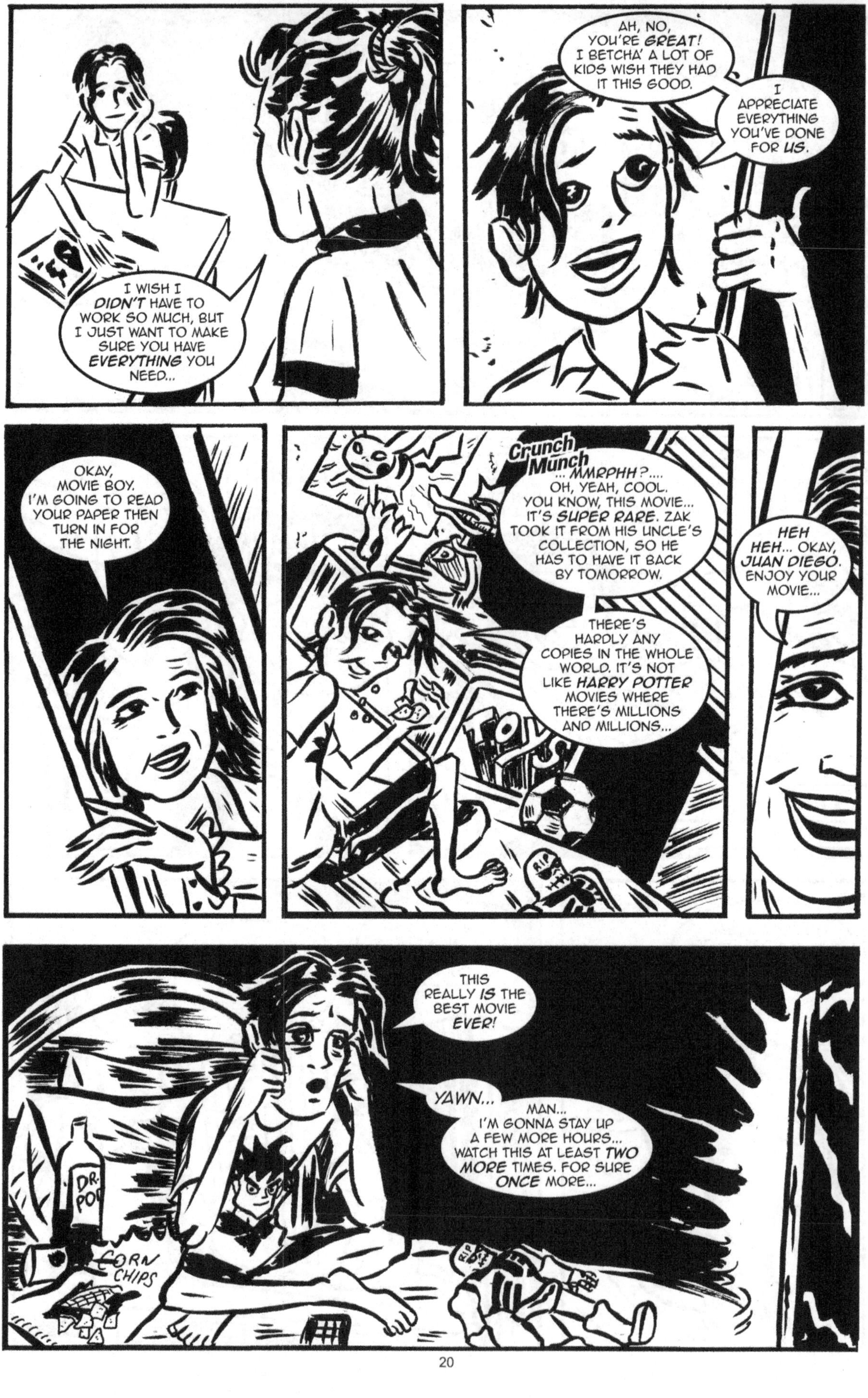
I WISH I DIDN'T HAVE TO WORK SO MUCH, BUT I JUST WANT TO MAKE SURE YOU HAVE EVERYTHING YOU NEED...
AH, NO, YOU'RE GREAT! I BETCHA' A LOT OF KIDS WISH THEY HAD IT THIS GOOD.
I APPRECIATE EVERYTHING YOU'VE DONE FOR US.
OKAY, MOVIE BOY. I'M GOING TO READ YOUR PAPER THEN TURN IN FOR THE NIGHT.
Crunch Munch
... MMRPHH?.... OH, YEAH, COOL. YOU KNOW, THIS MOVIE... IT'S SUPER RARE. ZAK TOOK IT FROM HIS UNCLE'S COLLECTION, SO HE HAS TO HAVE IT BACK BY TOMORROW.
THERE'S HARDLY ANY COPIES IN THE WHOLE WORLD. IT'S NOT LIKE HARRY POTTER MOVIES WHERE THERE'S MILLIONS AND MILLIONS...
TOYS
HEH HEH... OKAY, JUAN DIEGO. ENJOY YOUR MOVIE...
THIS REALLY IS THE BEST MOVIE EVER!
YAWN...
MAN... I'M GONNA STAY UP A FEW MORE HOURS... WATCH THIS AT LEAST TWO MORE TIMES. FOR SURE ONCE MORE...
DR. POP
CORN CHIPS
RIP

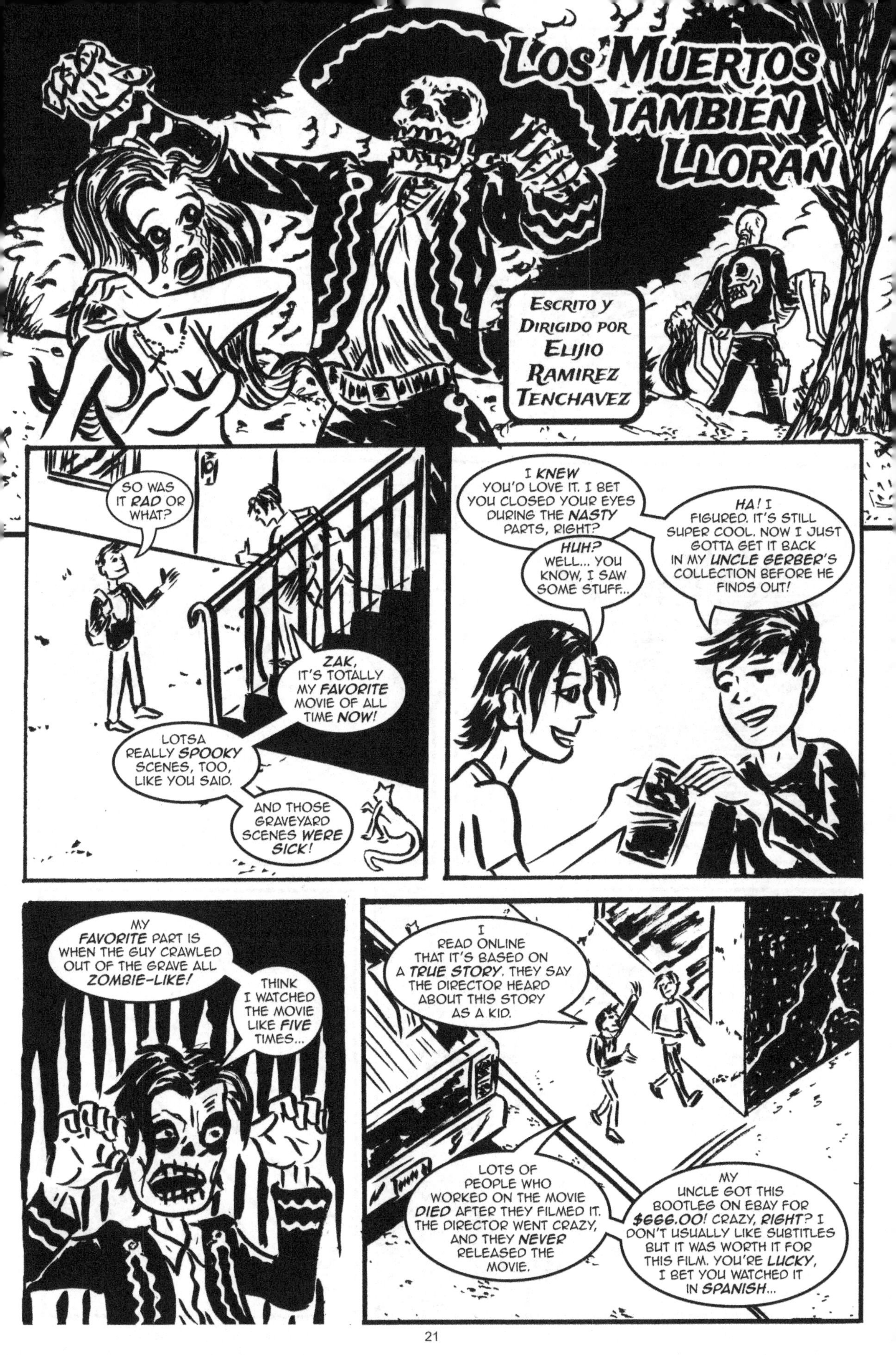
Los Muertos También Lloran
Escrito y Dirigido por Elijio Ramirez Tenchavez
SO WAS IT RAD OR WHAT?
ZAK, IT'S TOTALLY MY FAVORITE MOVIE OF ALL TIME NOW!
LOTSA REALLY SPOOKY SCENES, TOO, LIKE YOU SAID.
AND THOSE GRAVEYARD SCENES WERE SICK!
I KNEW YOU'D LOVE IT. I BET YOU CLOSED YOUR EYES DURING THE NASTY PARTS, RIGHT?
HUH? WELL... YOU KNOW, I SAW SOME STUFF...
HA! I FIGURED. IT'S STILL SUPER COOL. NOW I JUST GOTTA GET IT BACK IN MY UNCLE GERBER'S COLLECTION BEFORE HE FINDS OUT!
MY FAVORITE PART IS WHEN THE GUY CRAWLED OUT OF THE GRAVE ALL ZOMBIE-LIKE!
THINK I WATCHED THE MOVIE LIKE FIVE TIMES...
I READ ONLINE THAT IT'S BASED ON A TRUE STORY. THEY SAY THE DIRECTOR HEARD ABOUT THIS STORY AS A KID.
LOTS OF PEOPLE WHO WORKED ON THE MOVIE DIED AFTER THEY FILMED IT. THE DIRECTOR WENT CRAZY, AND THEY NEVER RELEASED THE MOVIE.
MY UNCLE GOT THIS BOOTLEG ON EBAY FOR $666.00! CRAZY, RIGHT? I DON'T USUALLY LIKE SUBTITLES BUT IT WAS WORTH IT FOR THIS FILM. YOU'RE LUCKY, I BET YOU WATCHED IT IN SPANISH...

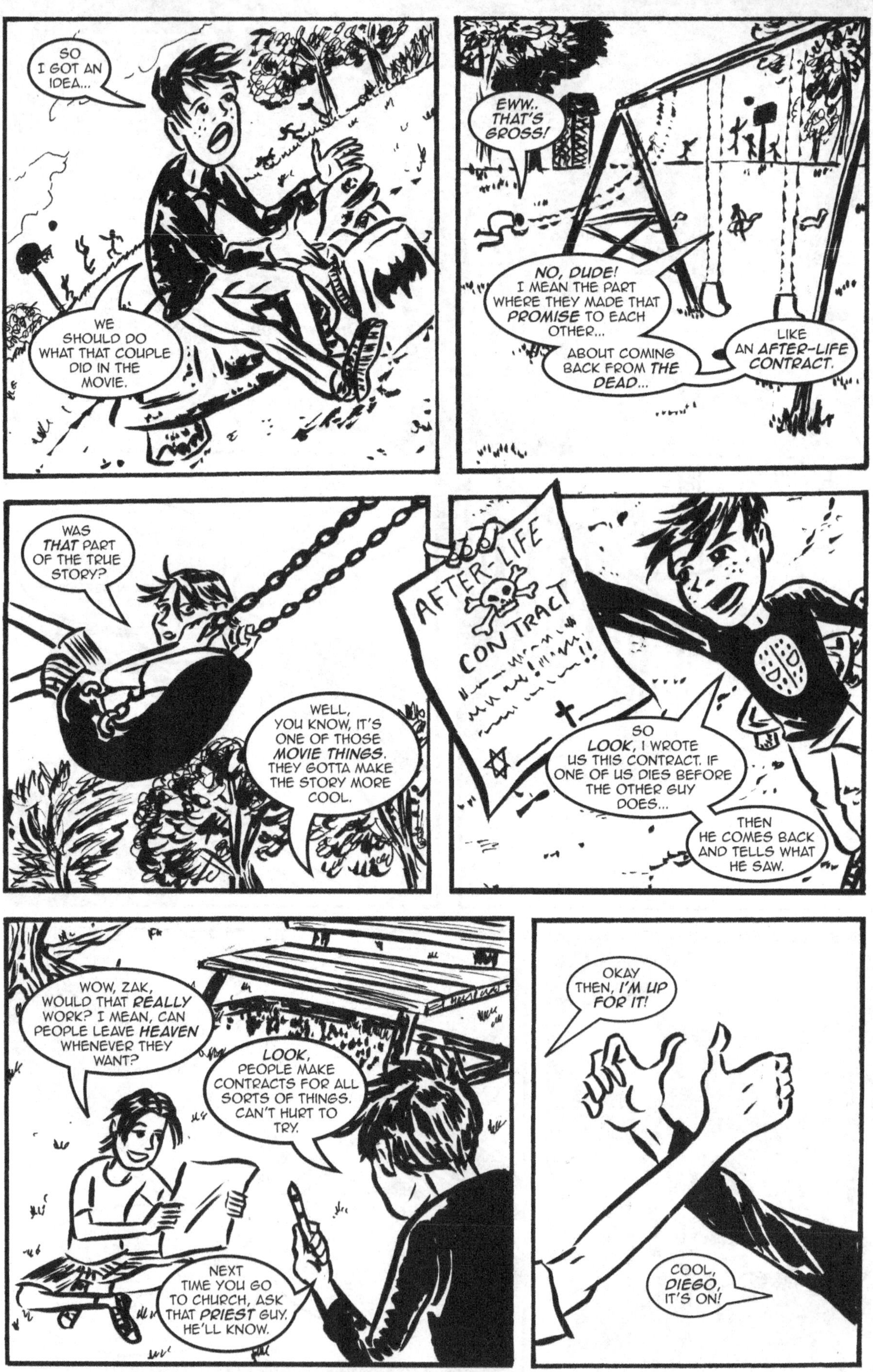
SO I GOT AN IDEA...
WE SHOULD DO WHAT THAT COUPLE DID IN THE MOVIE.
EWW.. THAT'S GROSS!
NO, DUDE! I MEAN THE PART WHERE THEY MADE THAT PROMISE TO EACH OTHER...
ABOUT COMING BACK FROM THE DEAD...
LIKE AN AFTER-LIFE CONTRACT.
WAS THAT PART OF THE TRUE STORY?
WELL, YOU KNOW, IT'S ONE OF THOSE MOVIE THINGS. THEY GOTTA MAKE THE STORY MORE COOL.
AFTER-LIFE CONTRACT
SO LOOK, I WROTE US THIS CONTRACT. IF ONE OF US DIES BEFORE THE OTHER GUY DOES...
THEN HE COMES BACK AND TELLS WHAT HE SAW.
WOW, ZAK, WOULD THAT REALLY WORK? I MEAN, CAN PEOPLE LEAVE HEAVEN WHENEVER THEY WANT?
LOOK, PEOPLE MAKE CONTRACTS FOR ALL SORTS OF THINGS. CAN'T HURT TO TRY.
NEXT TIME YOU GO TO CHURCH, ASK THAT PRIEST GUY. HE'LL KNOW.
OKAY THEN, I'M UP FOR IT!
COOL, DIEGO, IT'S ON!

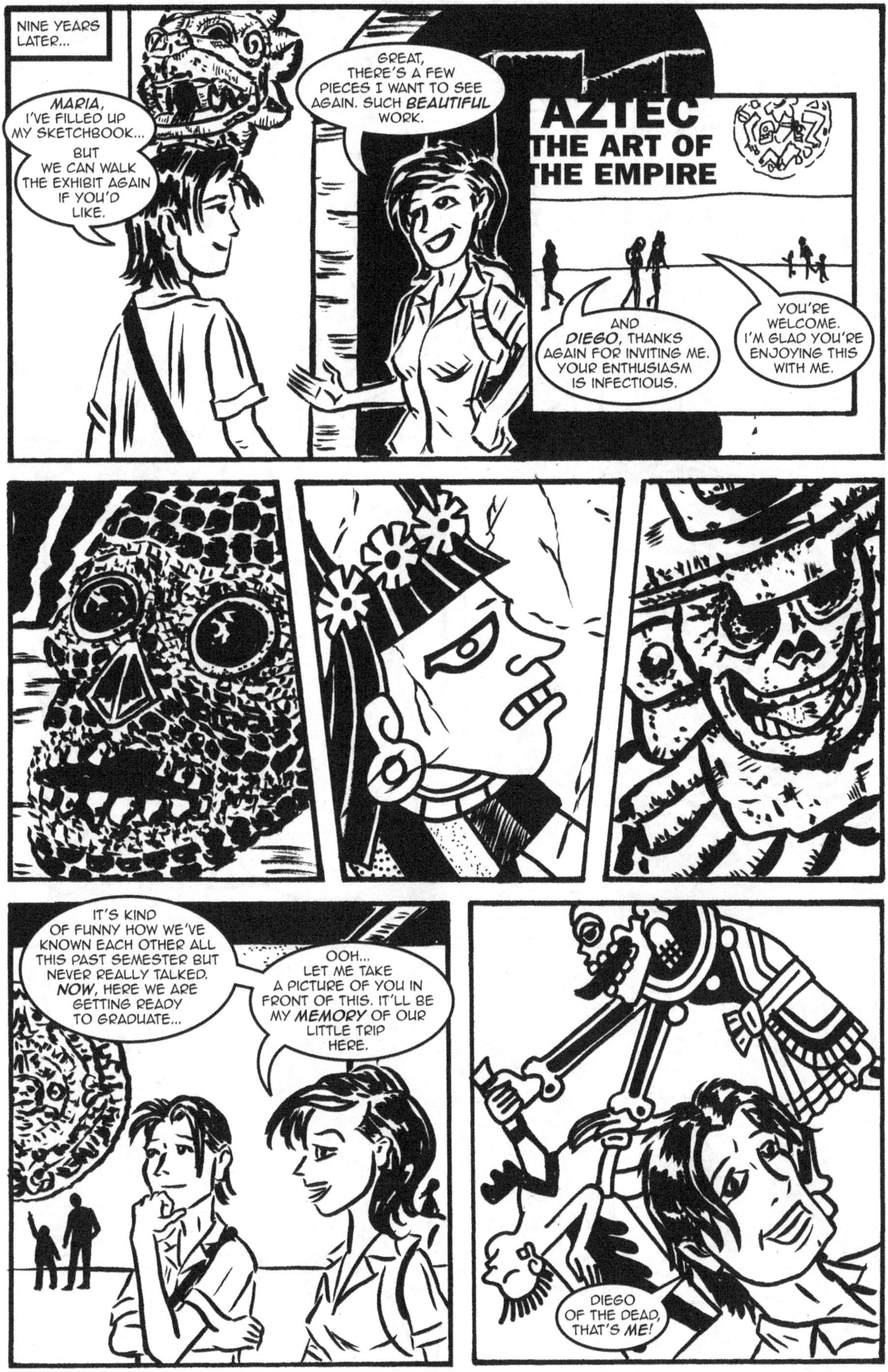
NINE YEARS LATER...
MARIA, I'VE FILLED UP MY SKETCHBOOK...
BUT WE CAN WALK THE EXHIBIT AGAIN IF YOU'D LIKE.
GREAT, THERE'S A FEW PIECES I WANT TO SEE AGAIN. SUCH BEAUTIFUL WORK.
AZTEC THE ART OF THE EMPIRE
AND DIEGO, THANKS AGAIN FOR INVITING ME. YOUR ENTHUSIASM IS INFECTIOUS.
YOU'RE WELCOME. I'M GLAD YOU'RE ENJOYING THIS WITH ME.
IT'S KIND OF FUNNY HOW WE'VE KNOWN EACH OTHER ALL THIS PAST SEMESTER BUT NEVER REALLY TALKED. NOW, HERE WE ARE GETTING READY TO GRADUATE...
OOH... LET ME TAKE A PICTURE OF YOU IN FRONT OF THIS. IT'LL BE MY MEMORY OF OUR LITTLE TRIP HERE.
DIEGO OF THE DEAD, THAT'S ME!

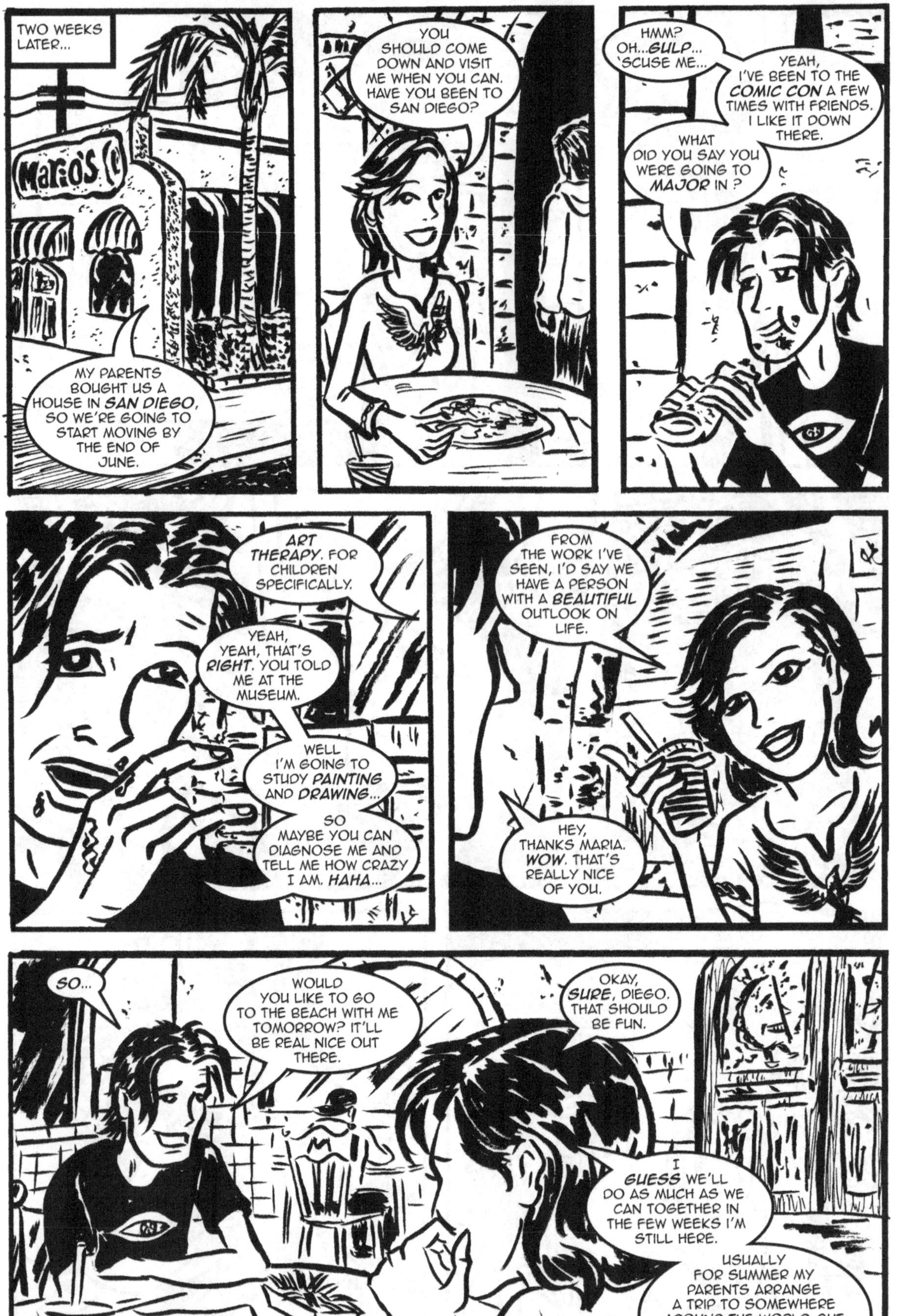
TWO WEEKS LATER...
MARIO'S
MY PARENTS BOUGHT US A HOUSE IN SAN DIEGO, SO WE'RE GOING TO START MOVING BY THE END OF JUNE.
YOU SHOULD COME DOWN AND VISIT ME WHEN YOU CAN. HAVE YOU BEEN TO SAN DIEGO?
HMM? OH...GULP... 'SCUSE ME...
YEAH, I'VE BEEN TO THE COMIC CON A FEW TIMES WITH FRIENDS. I LIKE IT DOWN THERE.
WHAT DID YOU SAY YOU WERE GOING TO MAJOR IN ?
ART THERAPY. FOR CHILDREN SPECIFICALLY.
YEAH, YEAH, THAT'S RIGHT. YOU TOLD ME AT THE MUSEUM.
WELL I'M GOING TO STUDY PAINTING AND DRAWING...
SO MAYBE YOU CAN DIAGNOSE ME AND TELL ME HOW CRAZY I AM. HAHA...
FROM THE WORK I'VE SEEN, I'D SAY WE HAVE A PERSON WITH A BEAUTIFUL OUTLOOK ON LIFE.
HEY, THANKS MARIA. WOW. THAT'S REALLY NICE OF YOU.
SO...
WOULD YOU LIKE TO GO TO THE BEACH WITH ME TOMORROW? IT'LL BE REAL NICE OUT THERE.
OKAY, SURE, DIEGO. THAT SHOULD BE FUN.
I GUESS WE'LL DO AS MUCH AS WE CAN TOGETHER IN THE FEW WEEKS I'M STILL HERE.
USUALLY FOR SUMMER MY PARENTS ARRANGE A TRIP TO SOMEWHERE AROUND THE WORLD, BUT IT'S NICE TO BE ABLE TO EXPLORE THE CITY WITH A NEW FRIEND.

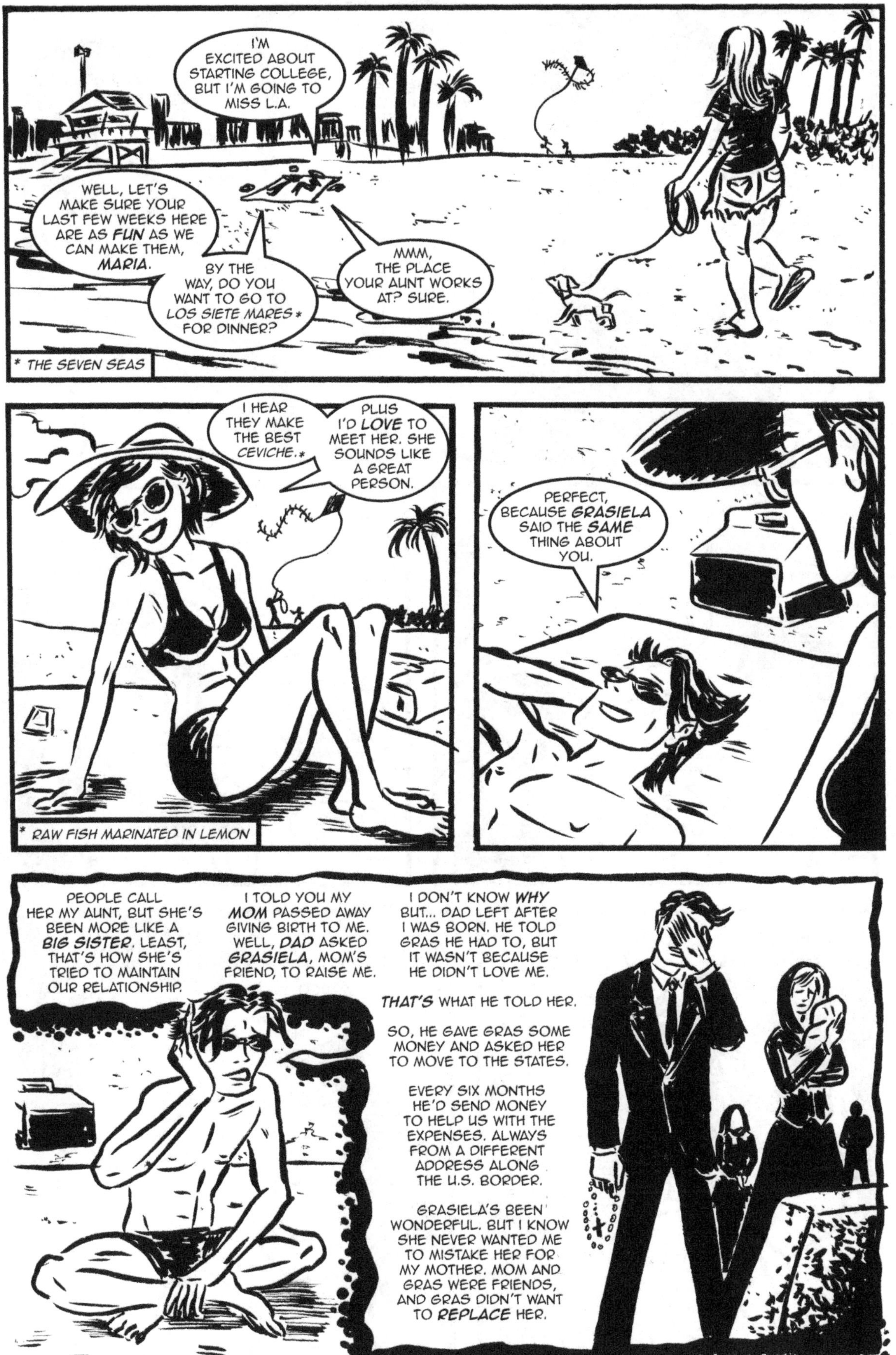

I'M EXCITED ABOUT STARTING COLLEGE, BUT I'M GOING TO MISS L.A.
WELL, LET'S MAKE SURE YOUR LAST FEW WEEKS HERE ARE AS **FUN** AS WE CAN MAKE THEM, ***MARIA***.
BY THE WAY, DO YOU WANT TO GO TO *LOS SIETE MARES** FOR DINNER?
MMM, THE PLACE YOUR AUNT WORKS AT? SURE.
* THE SEVEN SEAS
I HEAR THEY MAKE THE BEST *CEVICHE*.*
PLUS I'D ***LOVE*** TO MEET HER. SHE SOUNDS LIKE A GREAT PERSON.
* RAW FISH MARINATED IN LEMON
PERFECT, BECAUSE ***GRASIELA*** SAID THE ***SAME*** THING ABOUT YOU.
PEOPLE CALL HER MY AUNT, BUT SHE'S BEEN MORE LIKE A ***BIG SISTER***. LEAST, THAT'S HOW SHE'S TRIED TO MAINTAIN OUR RELATIONSHIP.
I TOLD YOU MY ***MOM*** PASSED AWAY GIVING BIRTH TO ME. WELL, ***DAD*** ASKED ***GRASIELA***, MOM'S FRIEND, TO RAISE ME.
I DON'T KNOW ***WHY*** BUT... DAD LEFT AFTER I WAS BORN. HE TOLD GRAS HE HAD TO, BUT IT WASN'T BECAUSE HE DIDN'T LOVE ME.
THAT'S WHAT HE TOLD HER.
SO, HE GAVE GRAS SOME MONEY AND ASKED HER TO MOVE TO THE STATES.
EVERY SIX MONTHS HE'D SEND MONEY TO HELP US WITH THE EXPENSES. ALWAYS FROM A DIFFERENT ADDRESS ALONG THE U.S. BORDER.
GRASIELA'S BEEN WONDERFUL. BUT I KNOW SHE NEVER WANTED ME TO MISTAKE HER FOR MY MOTHER. MOM AND GRAS WERE FRIENDS, AND GRAS DIDN'T WANT TO ***REPLACE*** HER.

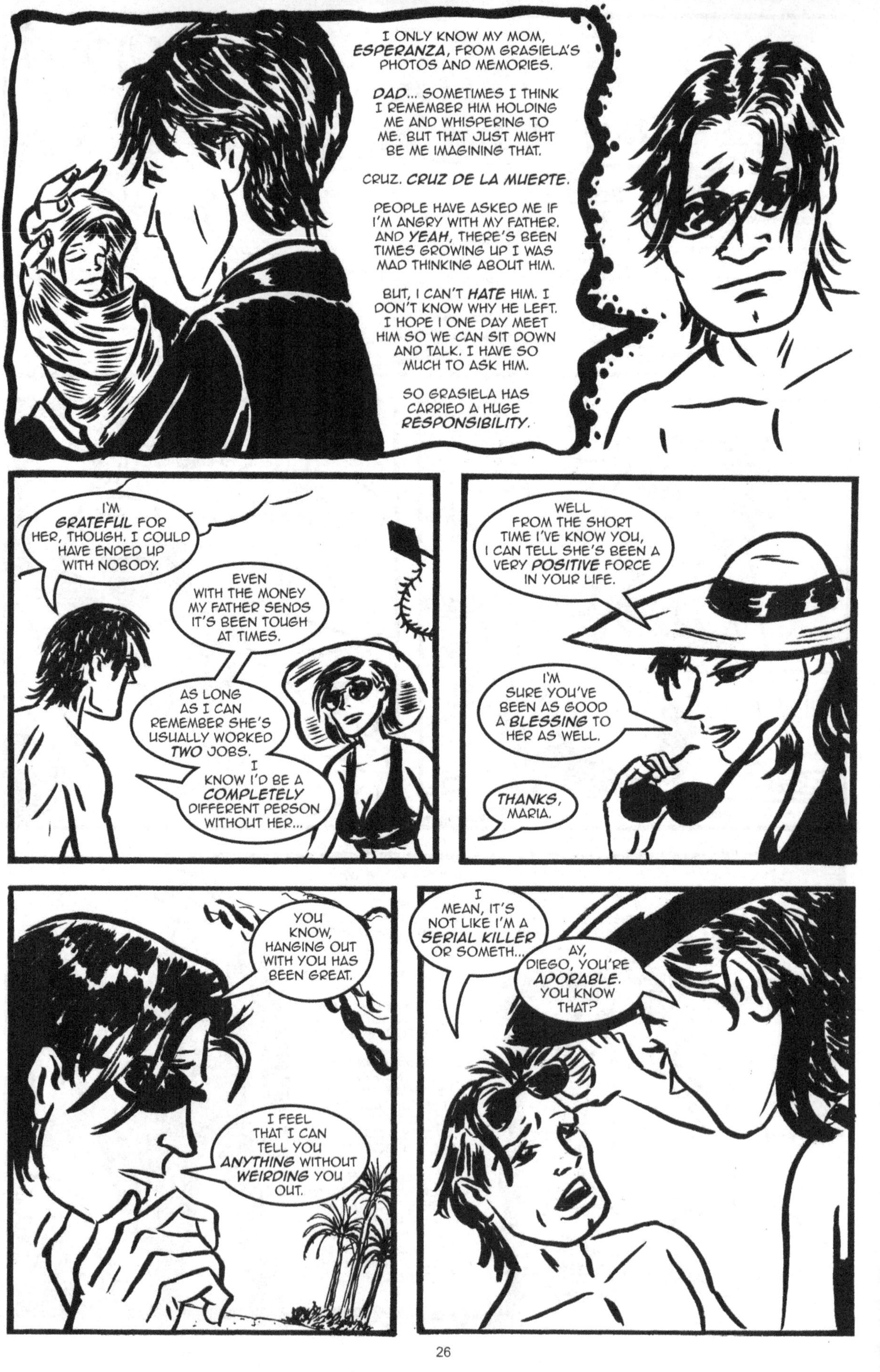
I ONLY KNOW MY MOM, ESPERANZA, FROM GRASIELA'S PHOTOS AND MEMORIES.
DAD... SOMETIMES I THINK I REMEMBER HIM HOLDING ME AND WHISPERING TO ME. BUT THAT JUST MIGHT BE ME IMAGINING THAT.
CRUZ. CRUZ DE LA MUERTE.
PEOPLE HAVE ASKED ME IF I'M ANGRY WITH MY FATHER. AND YEAH, THERE'S BEEN TIMES GROWING UP I WAS MAD THINKING ABOUT HIM.
BUT, I CAN'T HATE HIM. I DON'T KNOW WHY HE LEFT. I HOPE I ONE DAY MEET HIM SO WE CAN SIT DOWN AND TALK. I HAVE SO MUCH TO ASK HIM.
SO GRASIELA HAS CARRIED A HUGE RESPONSIBILITY.
I'M GRATEFUL FOR HER, THOUGH. I COULD HAVE ENDED UP WITH NOBODY.
EVEN WITH THE MONEY MY FATHER SENDS IT'S BEEN TOUGH AT TIMES.
AS LONG AS I CAN REMEMBER SHE'S USUALLY WORKED TWO JOBS.
I KNOW I'D BE A COMPLETELY DIFFERENT PERSON WITHOUT HER...
WELL FROM THE SHORT TIME I'VE KNOW YOU, I CAN TELL SHE'S BEEN A VERY POSITIVE FORCE IN YOUR LIFE.
I'M SURE YOU'VE BEEN AS GOOD A BLESSING TO HER AS WELL.
THANKS, MARIA.
YOU KNOW, HANGING OUT WITH YOU HAS BEEN GREAT.
I FEEL THAT I CAN TELL YOU ANYTHING WITHOUT WEIRDING YOU OUT.
I MEAN, IT'S NOT LIKE I'M A SERIAL KILLER OR SOMETH...
AY, DIEGO, YOU'RE ADORABLE. YOU KNOW THAT?

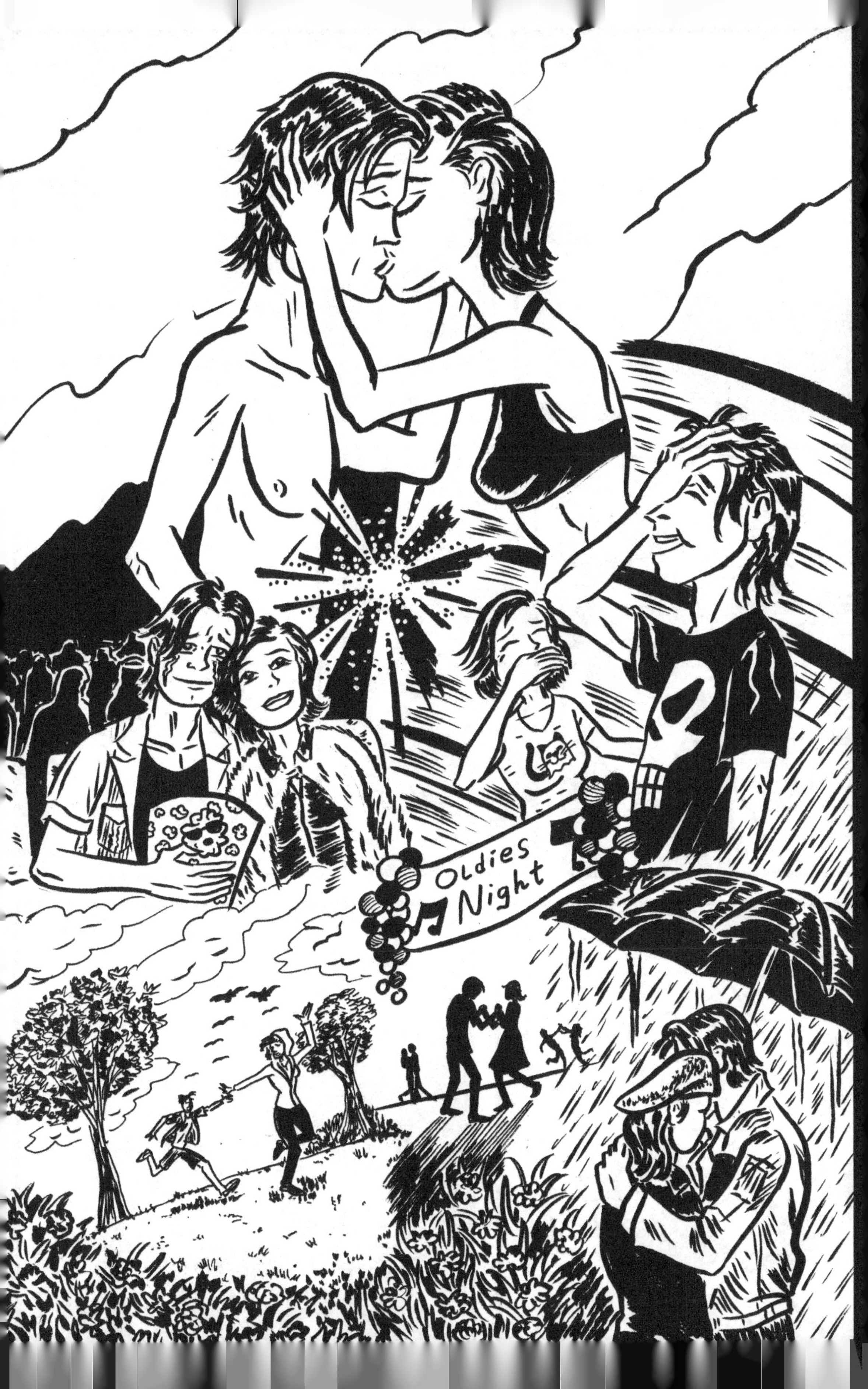
Oldies
Night

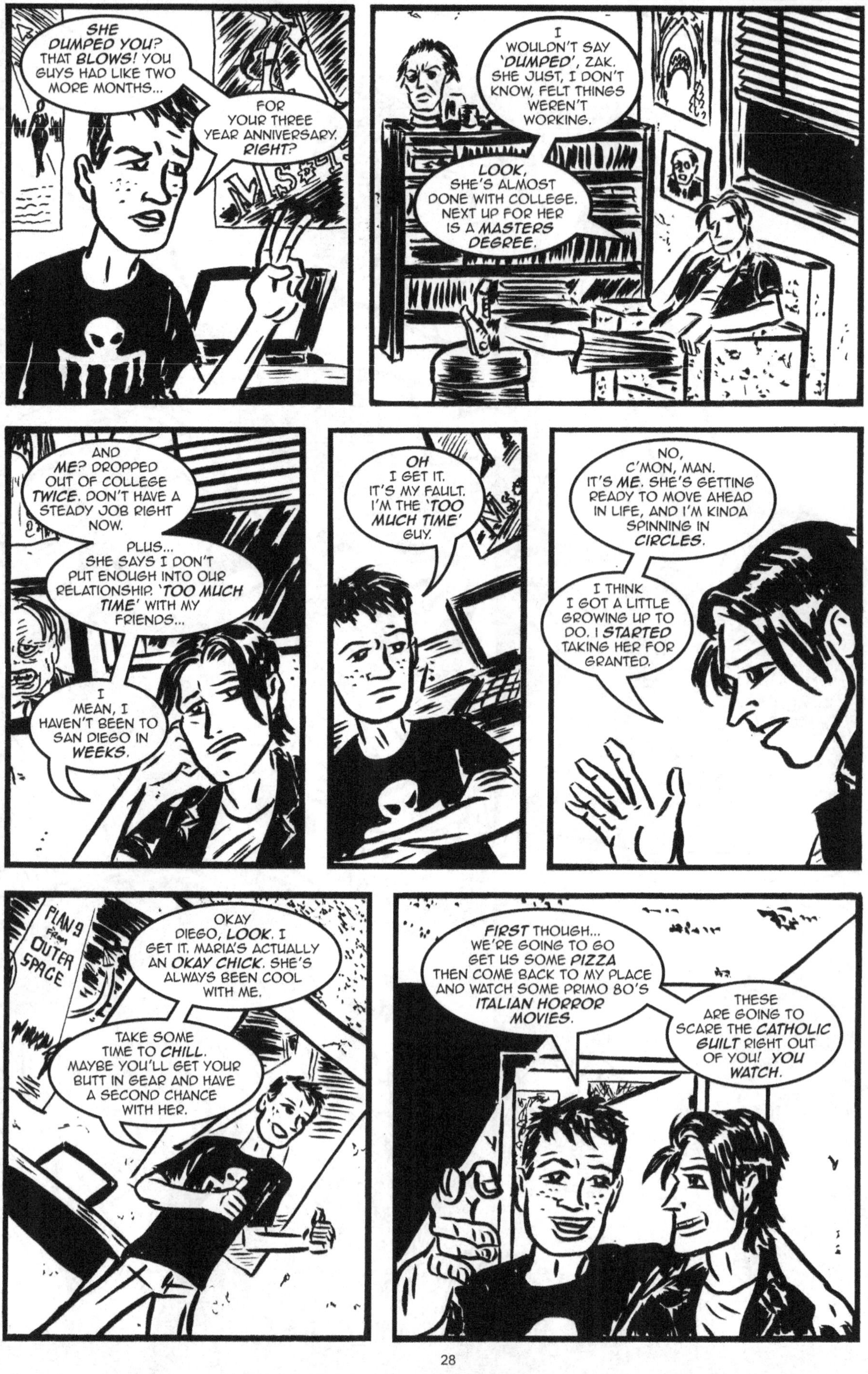
SHE DUMPED YOU? THAT BLOWS! YOU GUYS HAD LIKE TWO MORE MONTHS...
FOR YOUR THREE YEAR ANNIVERSARY. RIGHT?
I WOULDN'T SAY 'DUMPED', ZAK. SHE JUST, I DON'T KNOW, FELT THINGS WEREN'T WORKING.
LOOK, SHE'S ALMOST DONE WITH COLLEGE. NEXT UP FOR HER IS A MASTERS DEGREE.
AND ME? DROPPED OUT OF COLLEGE TWICE. DON'T HAVE A STEADY JOB RIGHT NOW.
PLUS... SHE SAYS I DON'T PUT ENOUGH INTO OUR RELATIONSHIP. 'TOO MUCH TIME' WITH MY FRIENDS...
I MEAN, I HAVEN'T BEEN TO SAN DIEGO IN WEEKS.
OH I GET IT. IT'S MY FAULT. I'M THE 'TOO MUCH TIME' GUY.
NO, C'MON, MAN. IT'S ME. SHE'S GETTING READY TO MOVE AHEAD IN LIFE, AND I'M KINDA SPINNING IN CIRCLES.
I THINK I GOT A LITTLE GROWING UP TO DO. I STARTED TAKING HER FOR GRANTED.
PLAN 9 FROM OUTER SPACE
OKAY DIEGO, LOOK. I GET IT. MARIA'S ACTUALLY AN OKAY CHICK. SHE'S ALWAYS BEEN COOL WITH ME.
TAKE SOME TIME TO CHILL. MAYBE YOU'LL GET YOUR BUTT IN GEAR AND HAVE A SECOND CHANCE WITH HER.
FIRST THOUGH... WE'RE GOING TO GO GET US SOME PIZZA THEN COME BACK TO MY PLACE AND WATCH SOME PRIMO 80'S ITALIAN HORROR MOVIES.
THESE ARE GOING TO SCARE THE CATHOLIC GUILT RIGHT OUT OF YOU! YOU WATCH.

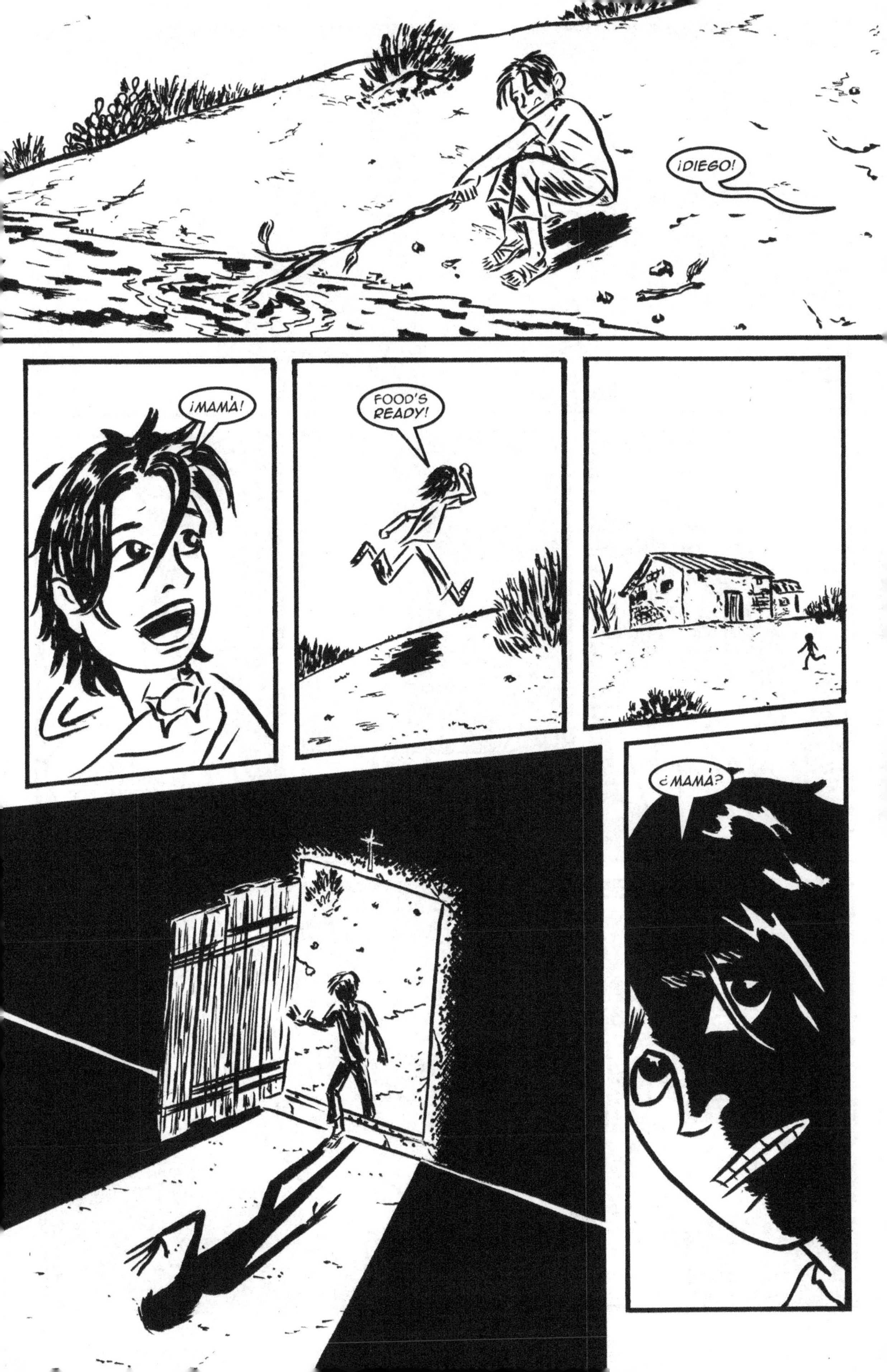
¡DIEGO!
¡MAMÁ!
FOOD'S READY!
¿MAMÁ?

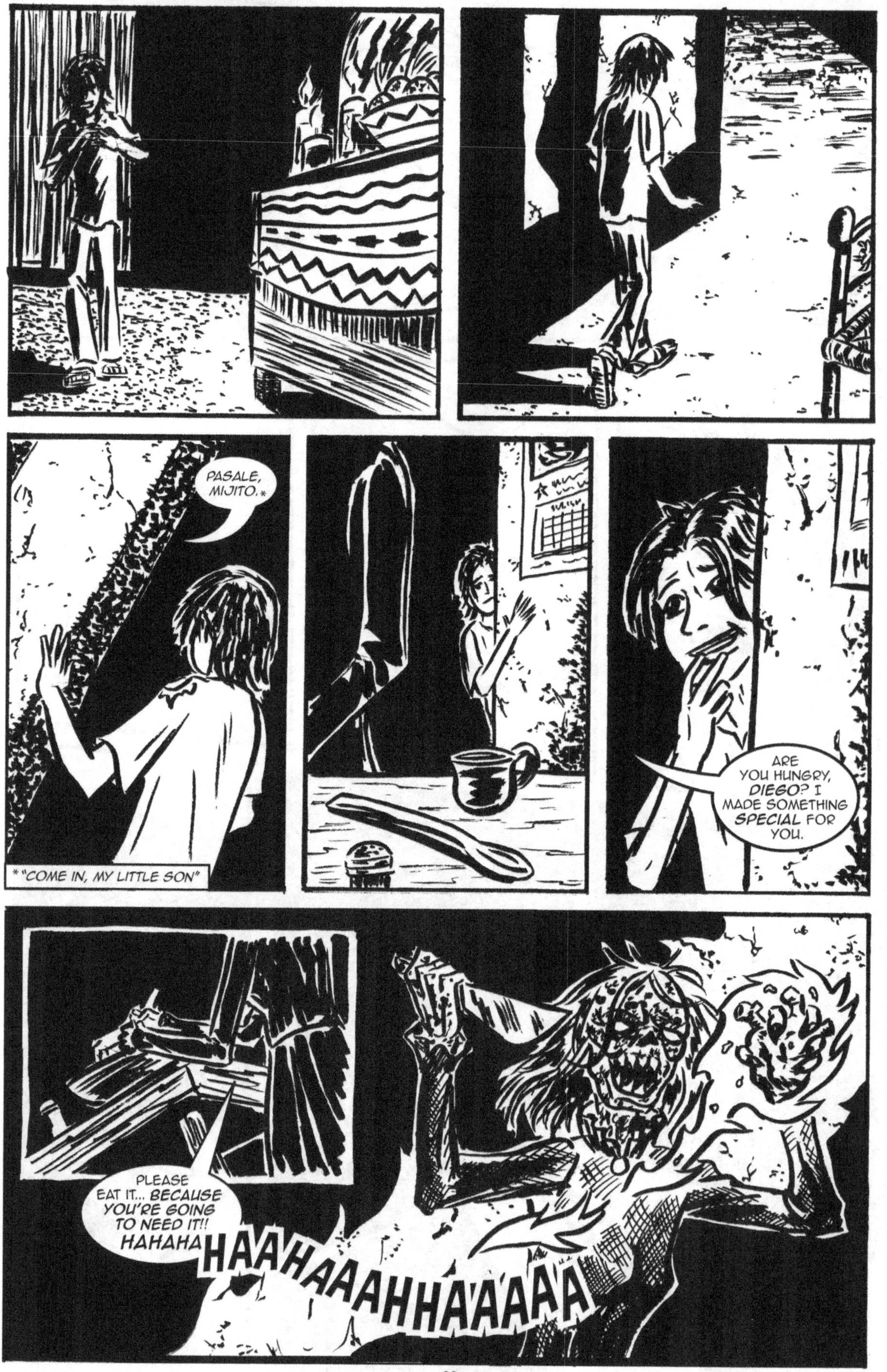
PASALE, MIJITO.*
*"COME IN, MY LITTLE SON"
ARE YOU HUNGRY, DIEGO? I MADE SOMETHING SPECIAL FOR YOU.
PLEASE EAT IT... BECAUSE YOU'RE GOING TO NEED IT!! HAHAHA
HAAHAAAHHAAAAA

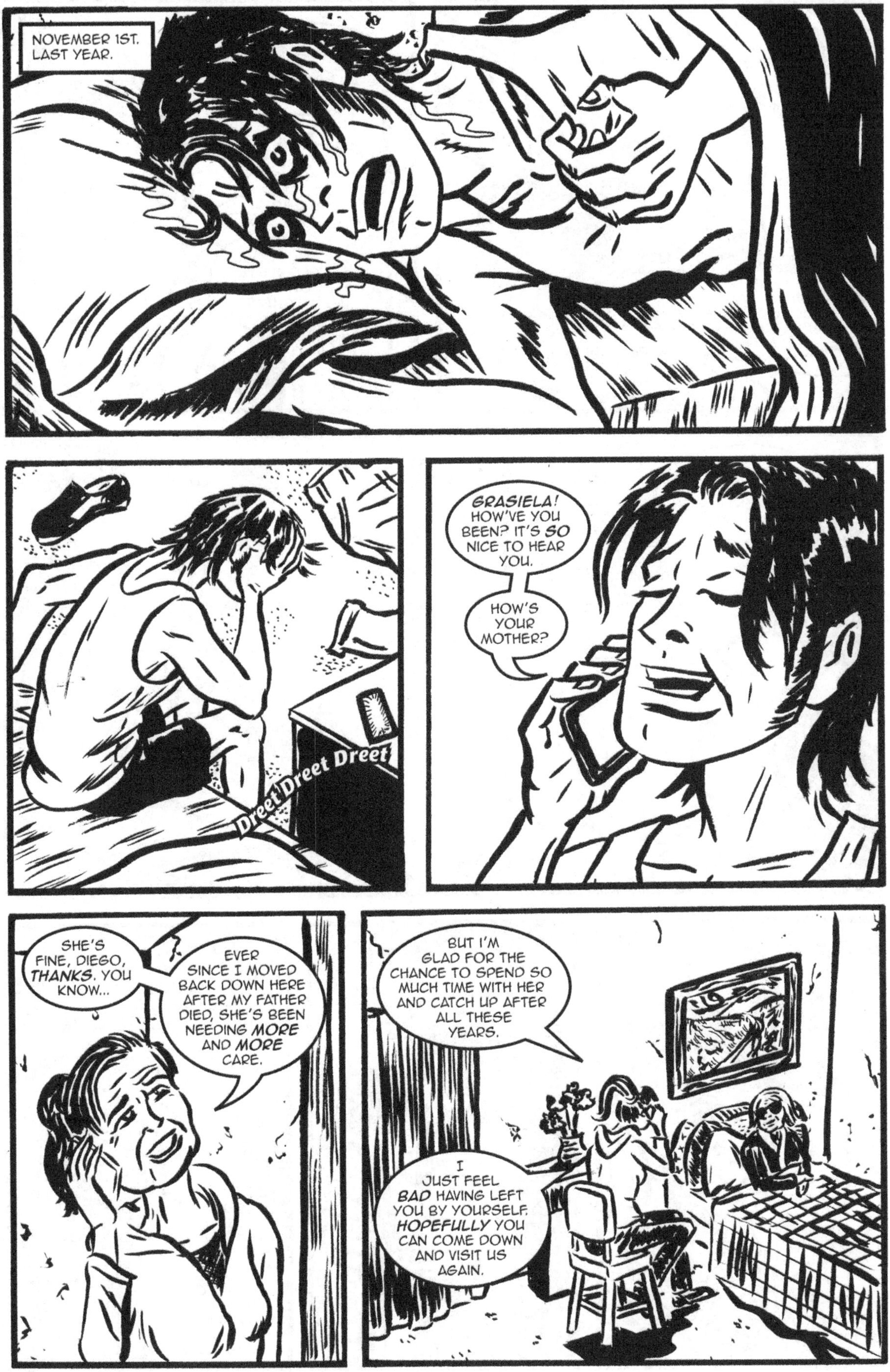
NOVEMBER 1ST. LAST YEAR.
Dreet Dreet Dreet
GRASIELA! HOW'VE YOU BEEN? IT'S SO NICE TO HEAR YOU.
HOW'S YOUR MOTHER?
SHE'S FINE, DIEGO, THANKS. YOU KNOW...
EVER SINCE I MOVED BACK DOWN HERE AFTER MY FATHER DIED, SHE'S BEEN NEEDING MORE AND MORE CARE.
BUT I'M GLAD FOR THE CHANCE TO SPEND SO MUCH TIME WITH HER AND CATCH UP AFTER ALL THESE YEARS.
I JUST FEEL BAD HAVING LEFT YOU BY YOURSELF. HOPEFULLY YOU CAN COME DOWN AND VISIT US AGAIN.

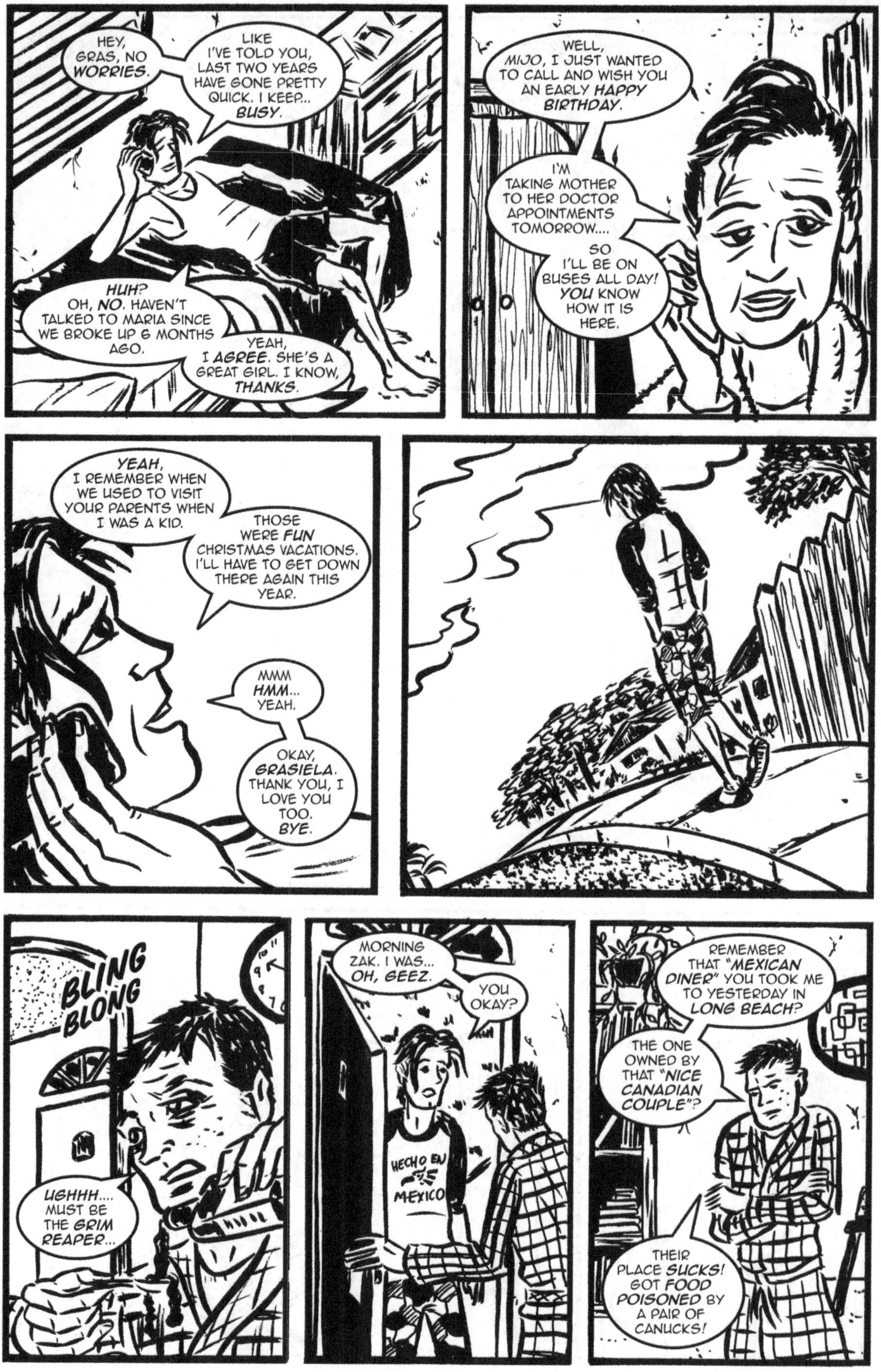
HEY, GRAS, NO WORRIES.
LIKE I'VE TOLD YOU, LAST TWO YEARS HAVE GONE PRETTY QUICK. I KEEP... BUSY.
HUH? OH, NO. HAVEN'T TALKED TO MARIA SINCE WE BROKE UP 6 MONTHS AGO.
YEAH, I AGREE. SHE'S A GREAT GIRL. I KNOW, THANKS.
WELL, MIJO, I JUST WANTED TO CALL AND WISH YOU AN EARLY HAPPY BIRTHDAY.
I'M TAKING MOTHER TO HER DOCTOR APPOINTMENTS TOMORROW....
SO I'LL BE ON BUSES ALL DAY! YOU KNOW HOW IT IS HERE.
YEAH, I REMEMBER WHEN WE USED TO VISIT YOUR PARENTS WHEN I WAS A KID.
THOSE WERE FUN CHRISTMAS VACATIONS. I'LL HAVE TO GET DOWN THERE AGAIN THIS YEAR.
MMM HMM... YEAH.
OKAY, GRASIELA. THANK YOU, I LOVE YOU TOO. BYE.
BLING BLONG
UGHHH.... MUST BE THE GRIM REAPER...
MORNING ZAK. I WAS... OH, GEEZ.
YOU OKAY?
HECHO EN MEXICO
REMEMBER THAT "MEXICAN DINER" YOU TOOK ME TO YESTERDAY IN LONG BEACH?
THE ONE OWNED BY THAT "NICE CANADIAN COUPLE"?
THEIR PLACE SUCKS! GOT FOOD POISONED BY A PAIR OF CANUCKS!

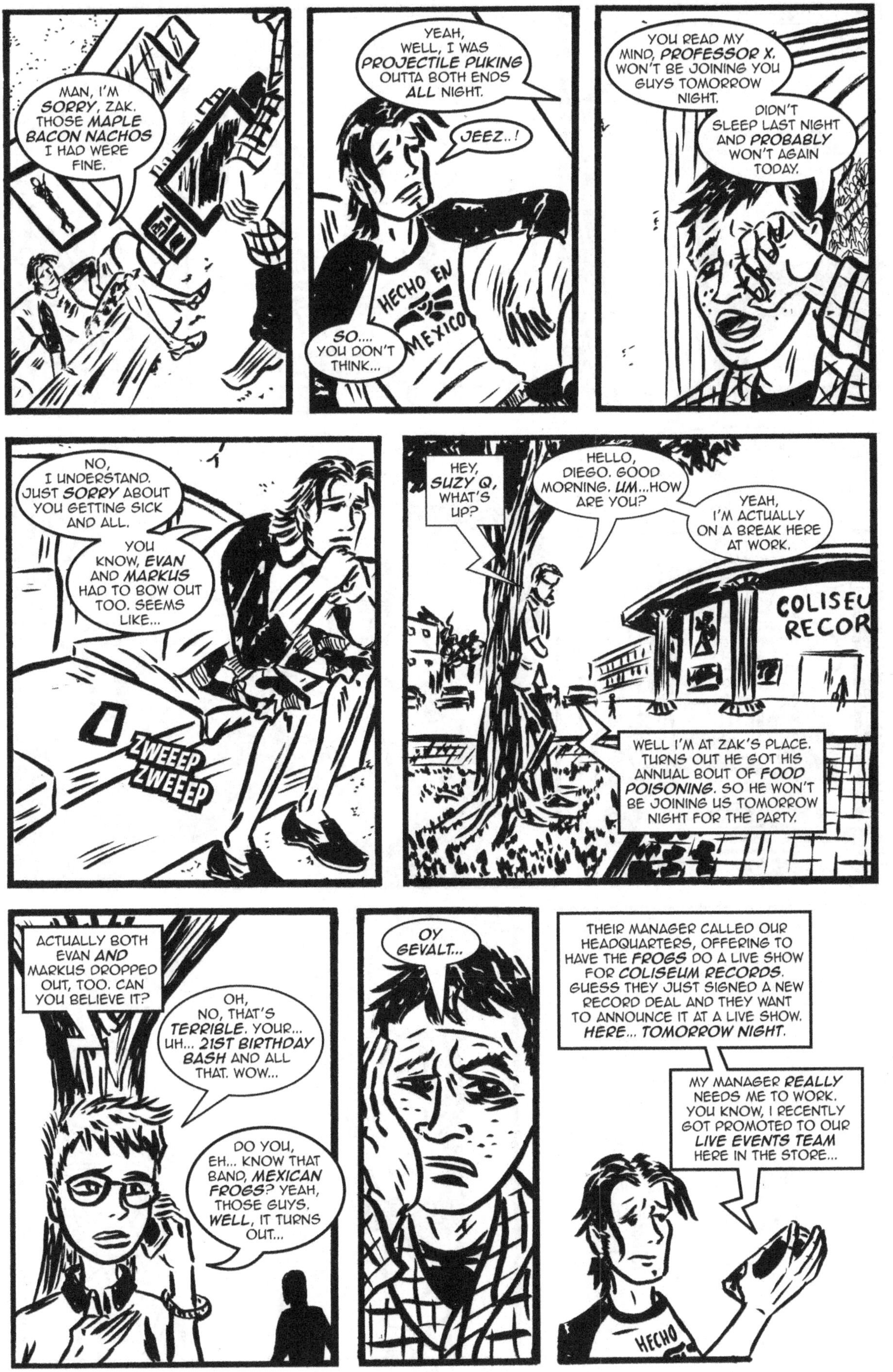
MAN, I'M SORRY, ZAK. THOSE MAPLE BACON NACHOS I HAD WERE FINE.
YEAH, WELL, I WAS PROJECTILE PUKING OUTTA BOTH ENDS ALL NIGHT.
JEEZ..!
HECHO EN MEXICO
SO.... YOU DON'T THINK...
YOU READ MY MIND, PROFESSOR X. WON'T BE JOINING YOU GUYS TOMORROW NIGHT.
DIDN'T SLEEP LAST NIGHT AND PROBABLY WON'T AGAIN TODAY.
NO, I UNDERSTAND. JUST SORRY ABOUT YOU GETTING SICK AND ALL.
YOU KNOW, EVAN AND MARKUS HAD TO BOW OUT TOO. SEEMS LIKE...
ZWEEEP ZWEEEP
HEY, SUZY Q, WHAT'S UP?
HELLO, DIEGO. GOOD MORNING. UM...HOW ARE YOU?
YEAH, I'M ACTUALLY ON A BREAK HERE AT WORK.
COLISEU RECOR
WELL I'M AT ZAK'S PLACE. TURNS OUT HE GOT HIS ANNUAL BOUT OF FOOD POISONING. SO HE WON'T BE JOINING US TOMORROW NIGHT FOR THE PARTY.
ACTUALLY BOTH EVAN AND MARKUS DROPPED OUT, TOO. CAN YOU BELIEVE IT?
OH, NO, THAT'S TERRIBLE. YOUR... UH... 21ST BIRTHDAY BASH AND ALL THAT. WOW...
DO YOU, EH... KNOW THAT BAND, MEXICAN FROGS? YEAH, THOSE GUYS. WELL, IT TURNS OUT...
OY GEVALT...
THEIR MANAGER CALLED OUR HEADQUARTERS, OFFERING TO HAVE THE FROGS DO A LIVE SHOW FOR COLISEUM RECORDS. GUESS THEY JUST SIGNED A NEW RECORD DEAL AND THEY WANT TO ANNOUNCE IT AT A LIVE SHOW. HERE... TOMORROW NIGHT.
MY MANAGER REALLY NEEDS ME TO WORK. YOU KNOW, I RECENTLY GOT PROMOTED TO OUR LIVE EVENTS TEAM HERE IN THE STORE...
HECHO

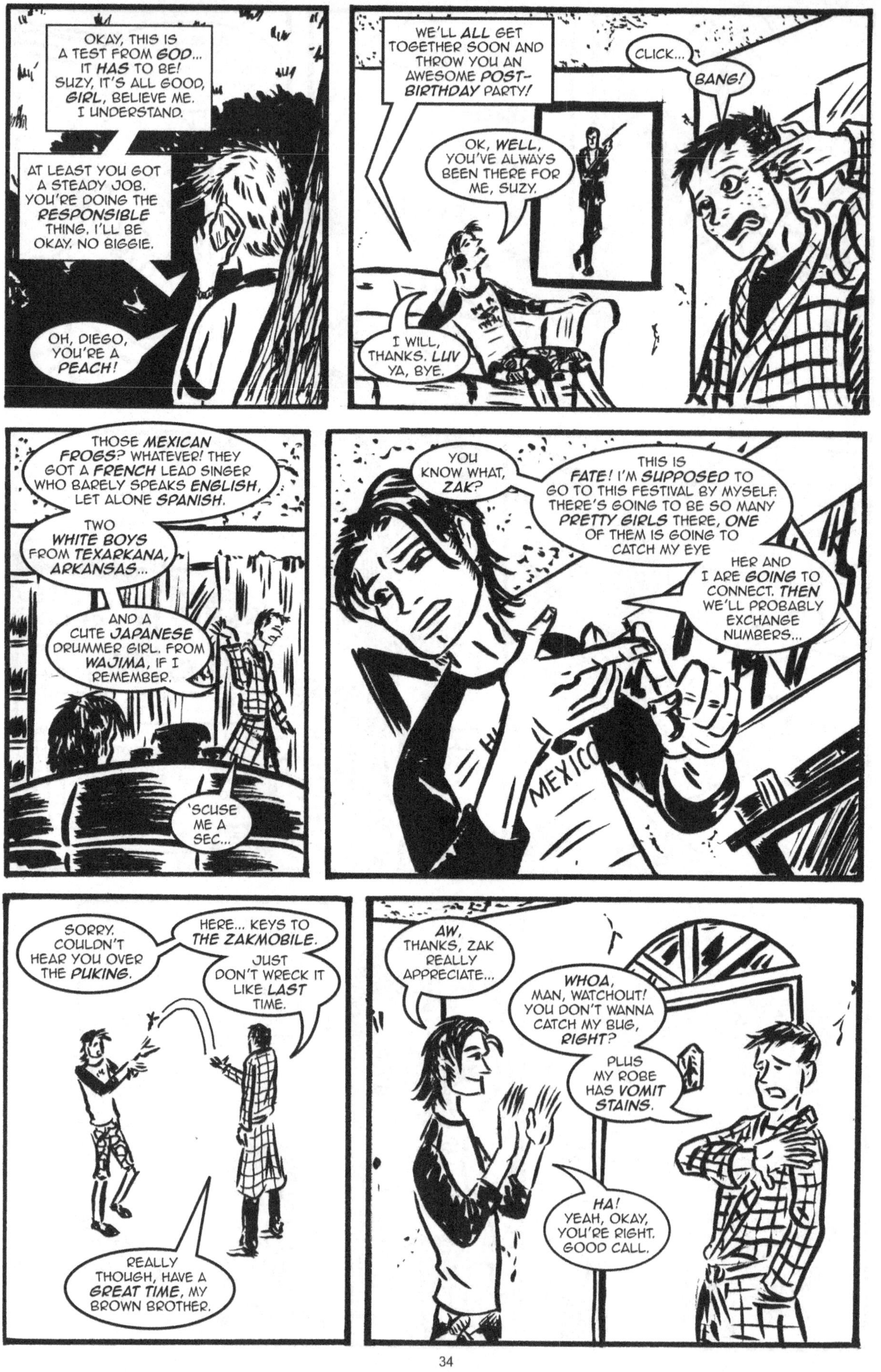
OKAY, THIS IS A TEST FROM GOD... IT HAS TO BE! SUZY, IT'S ALL GOOD, GIRL, BELIEVE ME. I UNDERSTAND.
AT LEAST YOU GOT A STEADY JOB. YOU'RE DOING THE RESPONSIBLE THING. I'LL BE OKAY. NO BIGGIE.
OH, DIEGO, YOU'RE A PEACH!
WE'LL ALL GET TOGETHER SOON AND THROW YOU AN AWESOME POST-BIRTHDAY PARTY!
OK, WELL, YOU'VE ALWAYS BEEN THERE FOR ME, SUZY.
I WILL, THANKS. LUV YA, BYE.
CLICK...
BANG!
THOSE MEXICAN FROGS? WHATEVER! THEY GOT A FRENCH LEAD SINGER WHO BARELY SPEAKS ENGLISH, LET ALONE SPANISH.
TWO WHITE BOYS FROM TEXARKANA, ARKANSAS...
AND A CUTE JAPANESE DRUMMER GIRL. FROM WAJIMA, IF I REMEMBER.
'SCUSE ME A SEC...
YOU KNOW WHAT, ZAK?
THIS IS FATE! I'M SUPPOSED TO GO TO THIS FESTIVAL BY MYSELF. THERE'S GOING TO BE SO MANY PRETTY GIRLS THERE, ONE OF THEM IS GOING TO CATCH MY EYE
HER AND I ARE GOING TO CONNECT. THEN WE'LL PROBABLY EXCHANGE NUMBERS...
MEXICO
SORRY. COULDN'T HEAR YOU OVER THE PUKING.
HERE... KEYS TO THE ZAKMOBILE.
JUST DON'T WRECK IT LIKE LAST TIME.
REALLY THOUGH, HAVE A GREAT TIME, MY BROWN BROTHER.
AW, THANKS, ZAK REALLY APPRECIATE...
WHOA, MAN, WATCHOUT! YOU DON'T WANNA CATCH MY BUG, RIGHT?
PLUS MY ROBE HAS VOMIT STAINS.
HA! YEAH, OKAY, YOU'RE RIGHT. GOOD CALL.

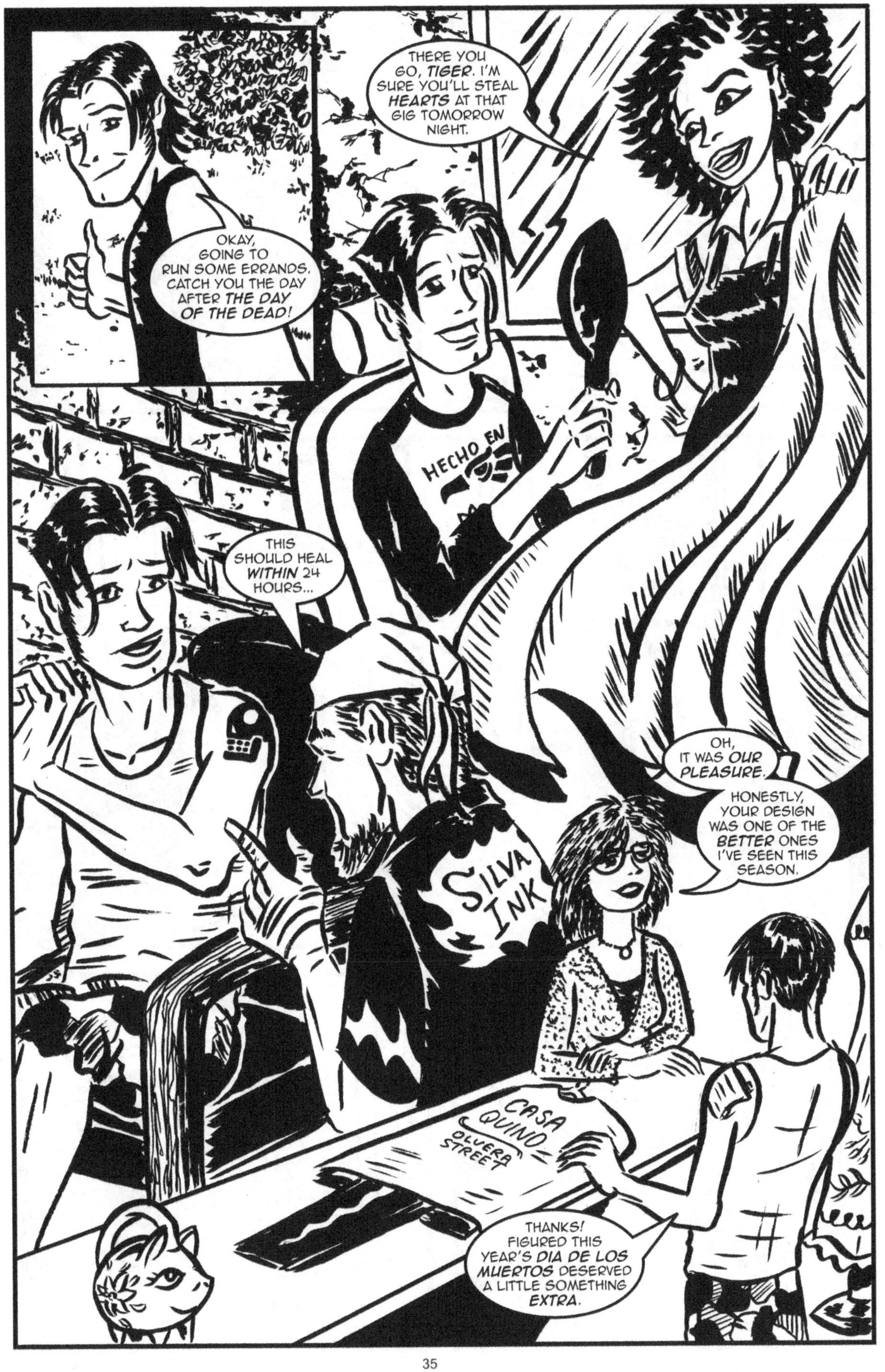
OKAY, GOING TO RUN SOME ERRANDS. CATCH YOU THE DAY AFTER THE DAY OF THE DEAD!
THERE YOU GO, TIGER. I'M SURE YOU'LL STEAL HEARTS AT THAT GIG TOMORROW NIGHT.
HECHO EN
THIS SHOULD HEAL WITHIN 24 HOURS...
OH, IT WAS OUR PLEASURE.
HONESTLY, YOUR DESIGN WAS ONE OF THE BETTER ONES I'VE SEEN THIS SEASON.
SILVA INK
CASA QUINO
OLVERA STREET
THANKS! FIGURED THIS YEAR'S DIA DE LOS MUERTOS DESERVED A LITTLE SOMETHING EXTRA.

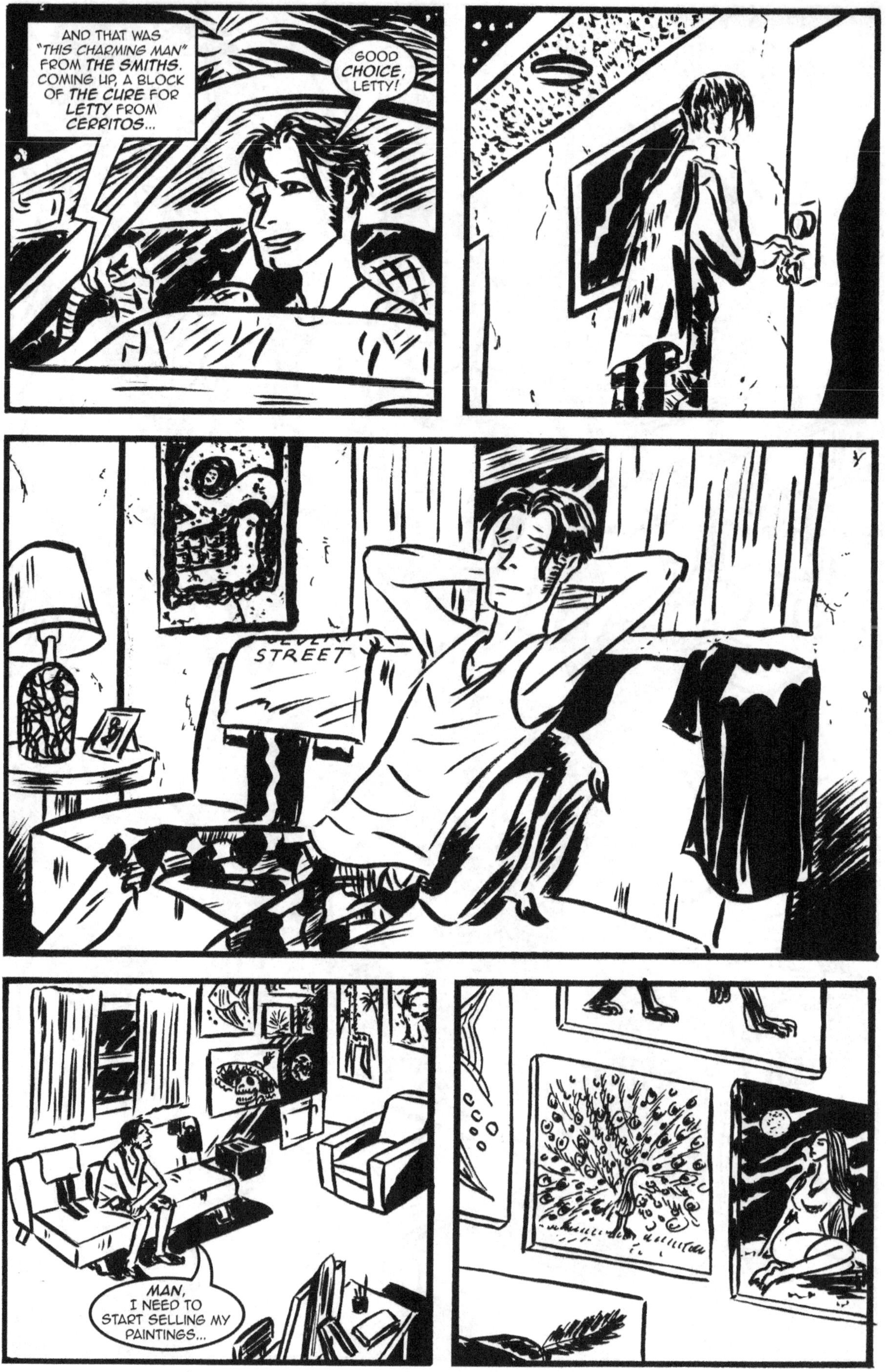
AND THAT WAS "THIS CHARMING MAN" FROM THE SMITHS. COMING UP, A BLOCK OF THE CURE FOR LETTY FROM CERRITOS...
GOOD CHOICE, LETTY!
STREET
MAN, I NEED TO START SELLING MY PAINTINGS...

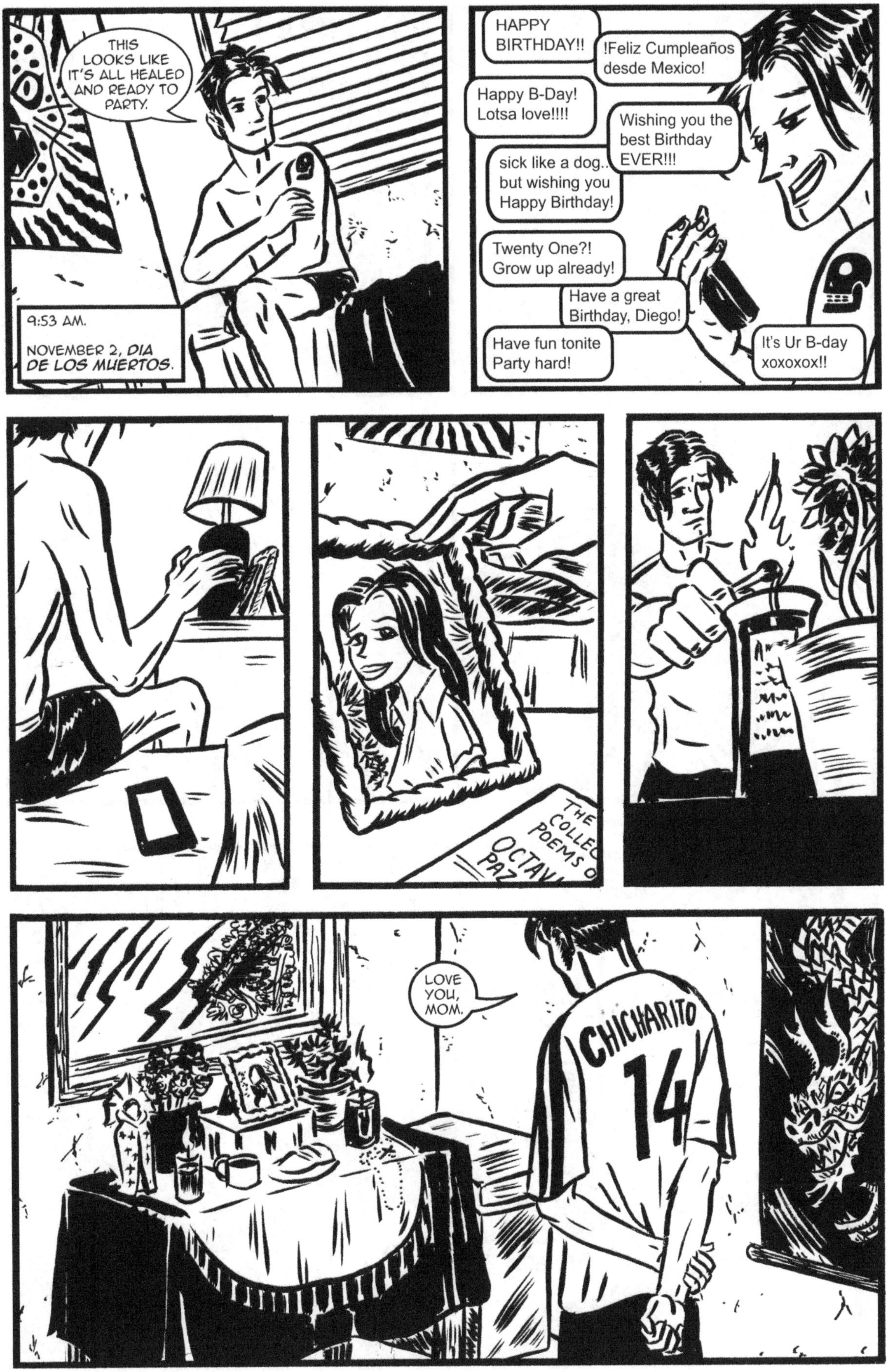
THIS LOOKS LIKE IT'S ALL HEALED AND READY TO PARTY.
9:53 AM.
NOVEMBER 2, DIA DE LOS MUERTOS.
HAPPY BIRTHDAY!!
!Feliz Cumpleaños desde Mexico!
Happy B-Day! Lotsa love!!!!
Wishing you the best Birthday EVER!!!
sick like a dog.. but wishing you Happy Birthday!
Twenty One?! Grow up already!
Have a great Birthday, Diego!
Have fun tonite Party hard!
It's Ur B-day xoxoxox!!
LOVE YOU, MOM.
CHICHARITO
14

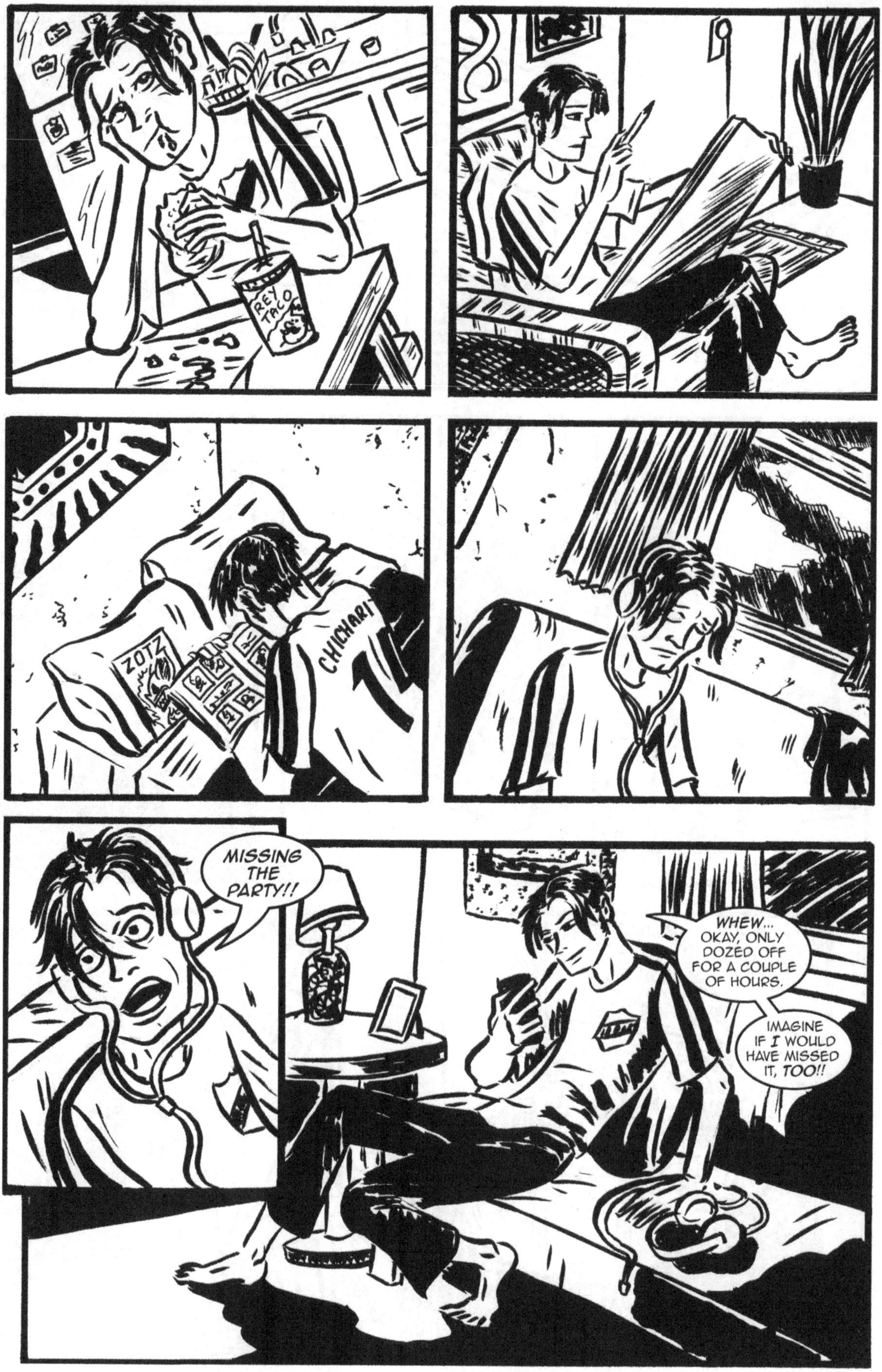

REY TACO
ZOTZ
CHICHARI
MISSING THE PARTY!!
WHEW... OKAY, ONLY DOZED OFF FOR A COUPLE OF HOURS.
IMAGINE IF I WOULD HAVE MISSED IT, TOO!!

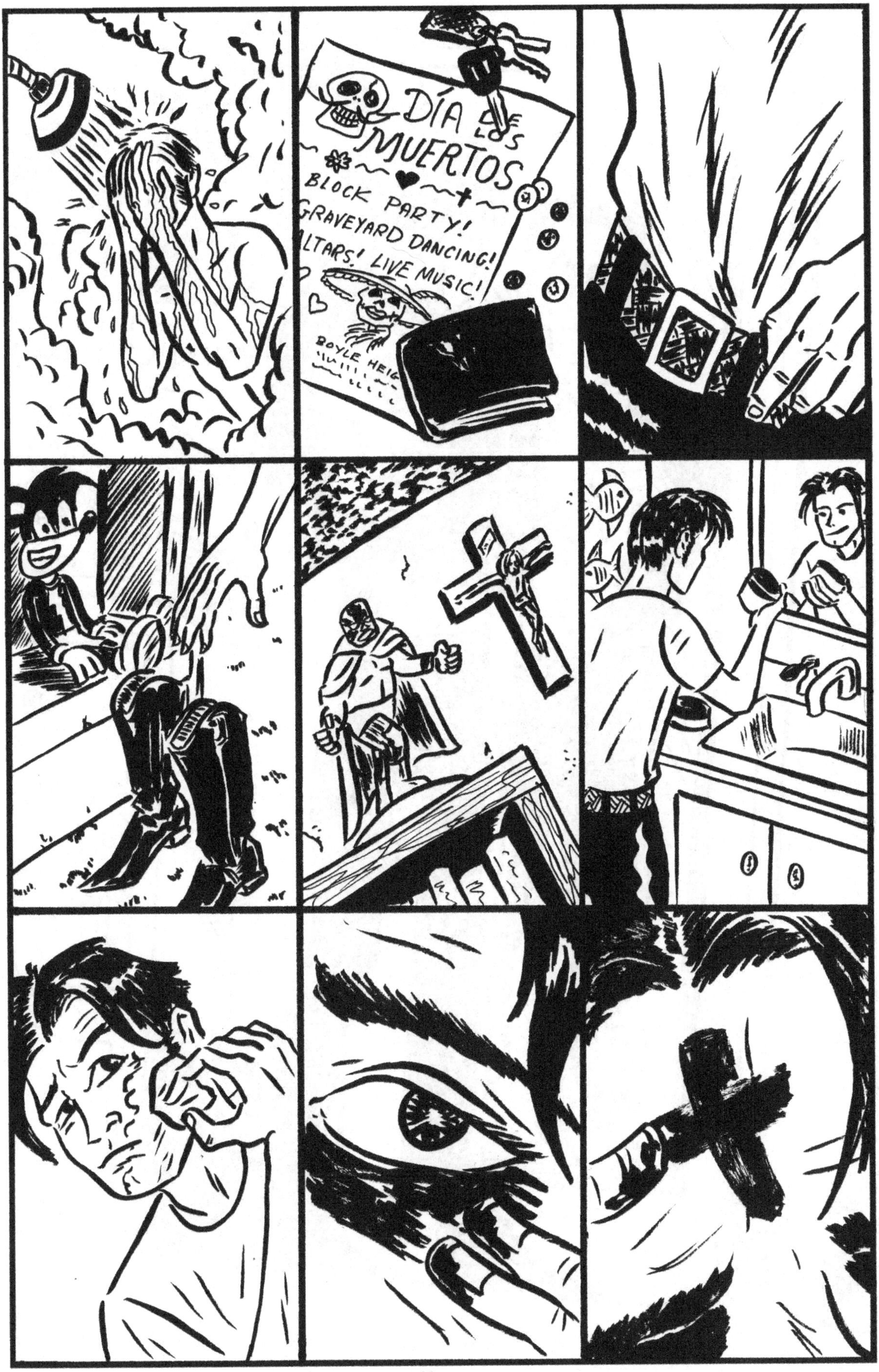
DÍA DE LOS MUERTOS
BLOCK PARTY!
GRAVEYARD DANCING!
LTARS! LIVE MUSIC!

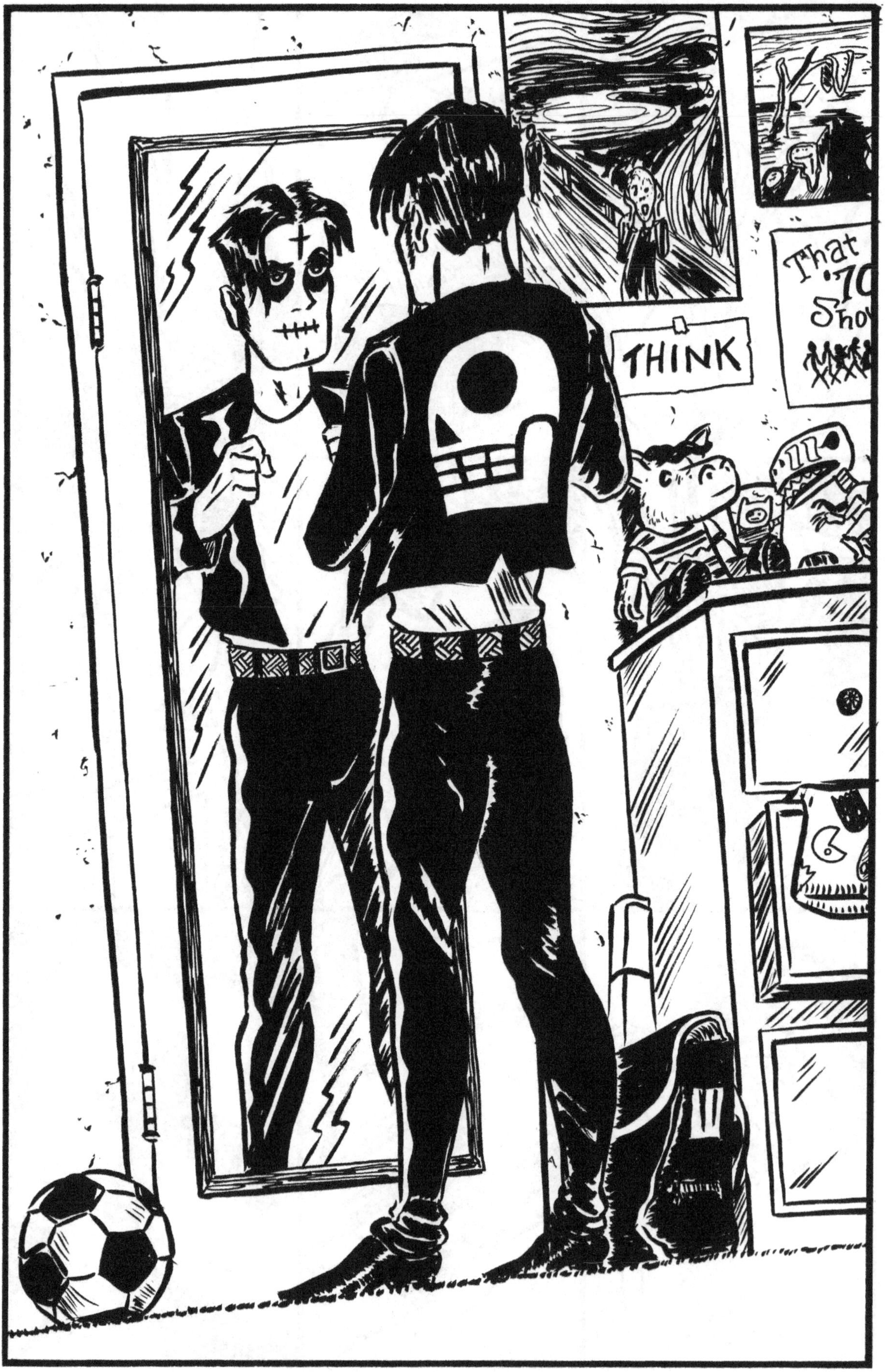
THINK

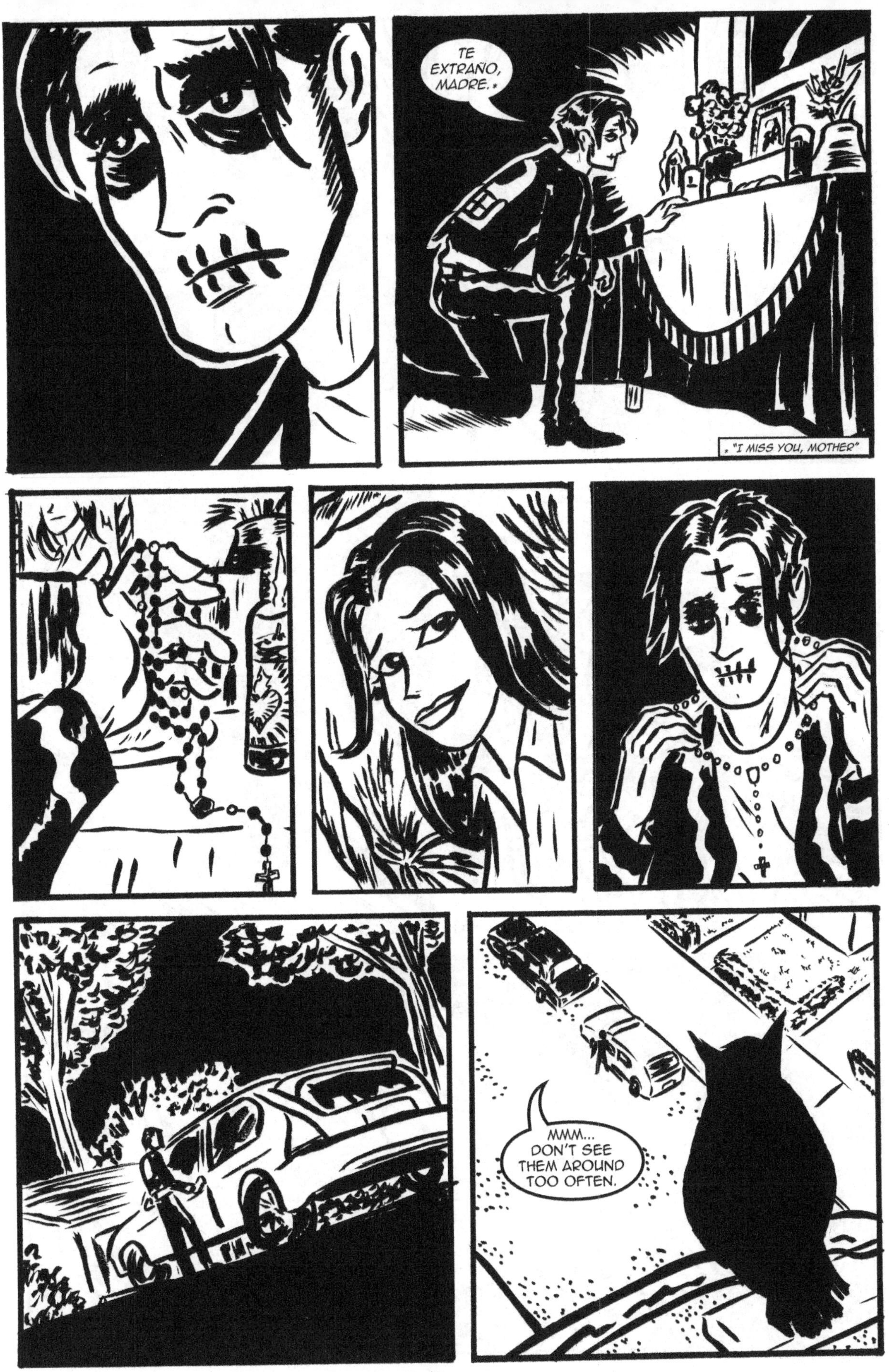
TE EXTRAÑO, MADRE.*
* "I MISS YOU, MOTHER"
MMM... DON'T SEE THEM AROUND TOO OFTEN.

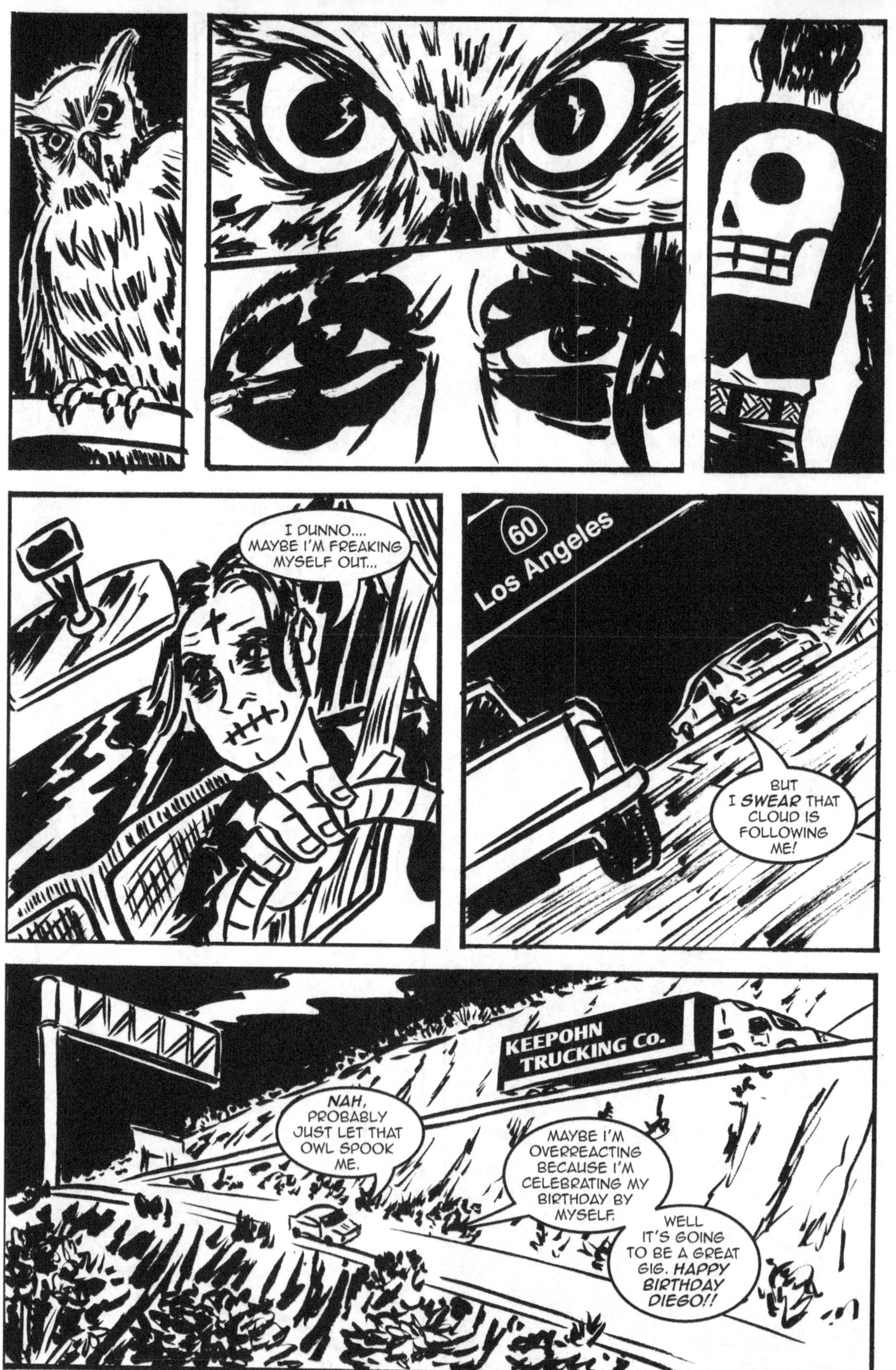
I DUNNO....
MAYBE I'M FREAKING
MYSELF OUT...
60
Los Angeles
BUT
I SWEAR THAT
CLOUD IS
FOLLOWING
ME!
KEEPOHN
TRUCKING Co.
NAH,
PROBABLY
JUST LET THAT
OWL SPOOK
ME.
MAYBE I'M
OVERREACTING
BECAUSE I'M
CELEBRATING MY
BIRTHDAY BY
MYSELF.
WELL
IT'S GOING
TO BE A GREAT
GIG. HAPPY
BIRTHDAY
DIEGO!!

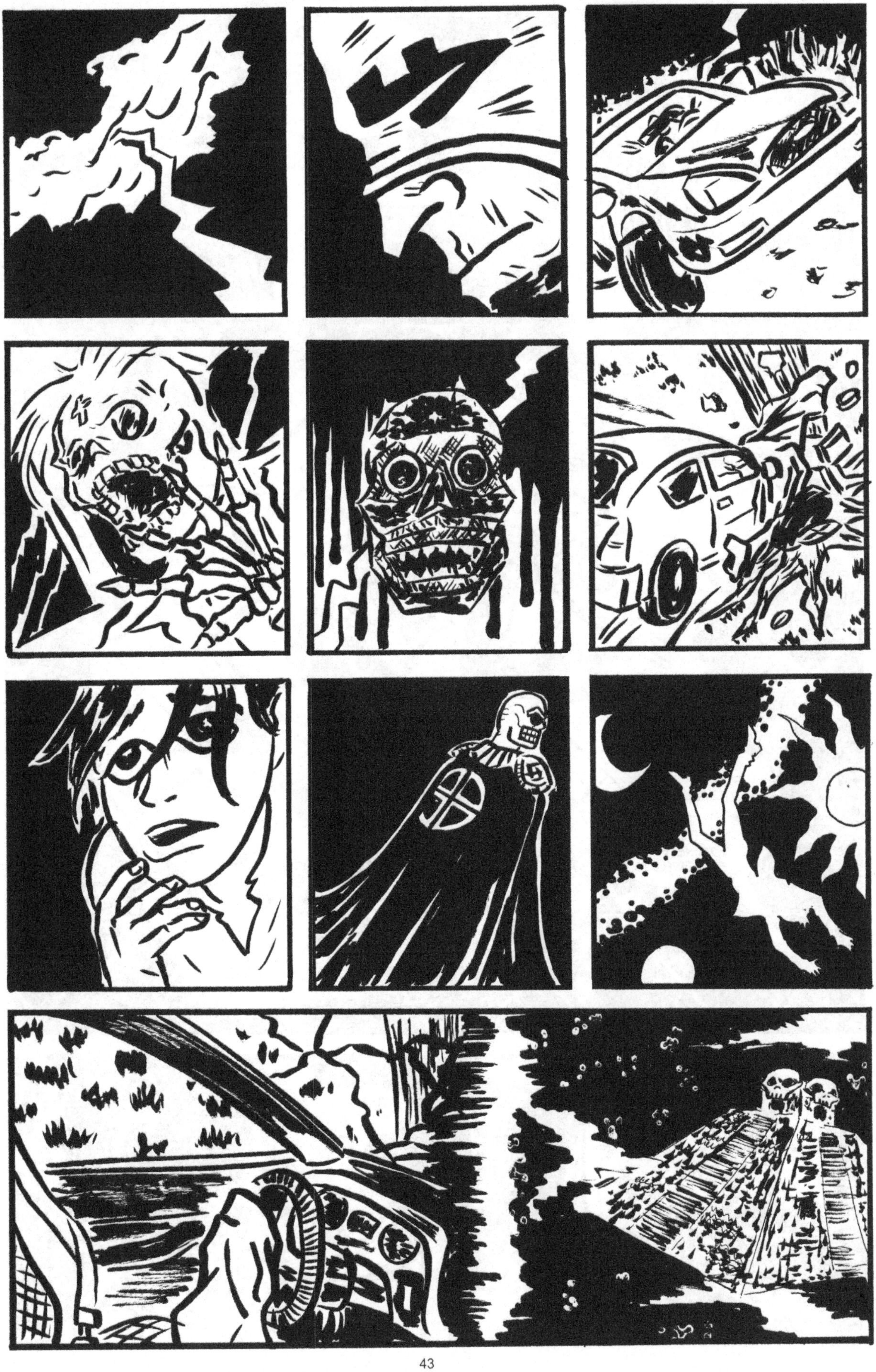

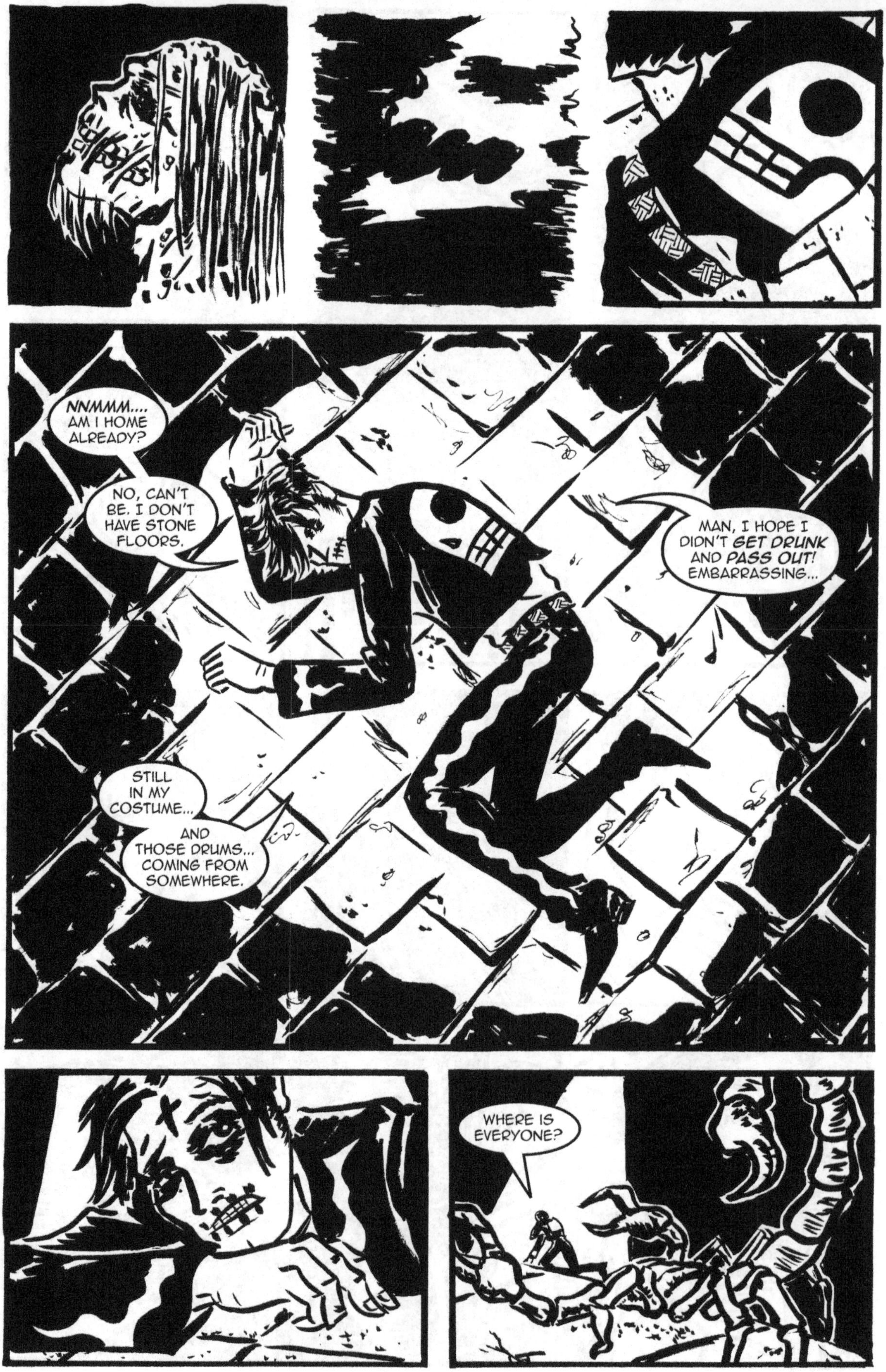
NNMMM.... AM I HOME ALREADY?
NO, CAN'T BE. I DON'T HAVE STONE FLOORS.
MAN, I HOPE I DIDN'T GET DRUNK AND PASS OUT! EMBARRASSING...
STILL IN MY COSTUME...
AND THOSE DRUMS... COMING FROM SOMEWHERE.
WHERE IS EVERYONE?

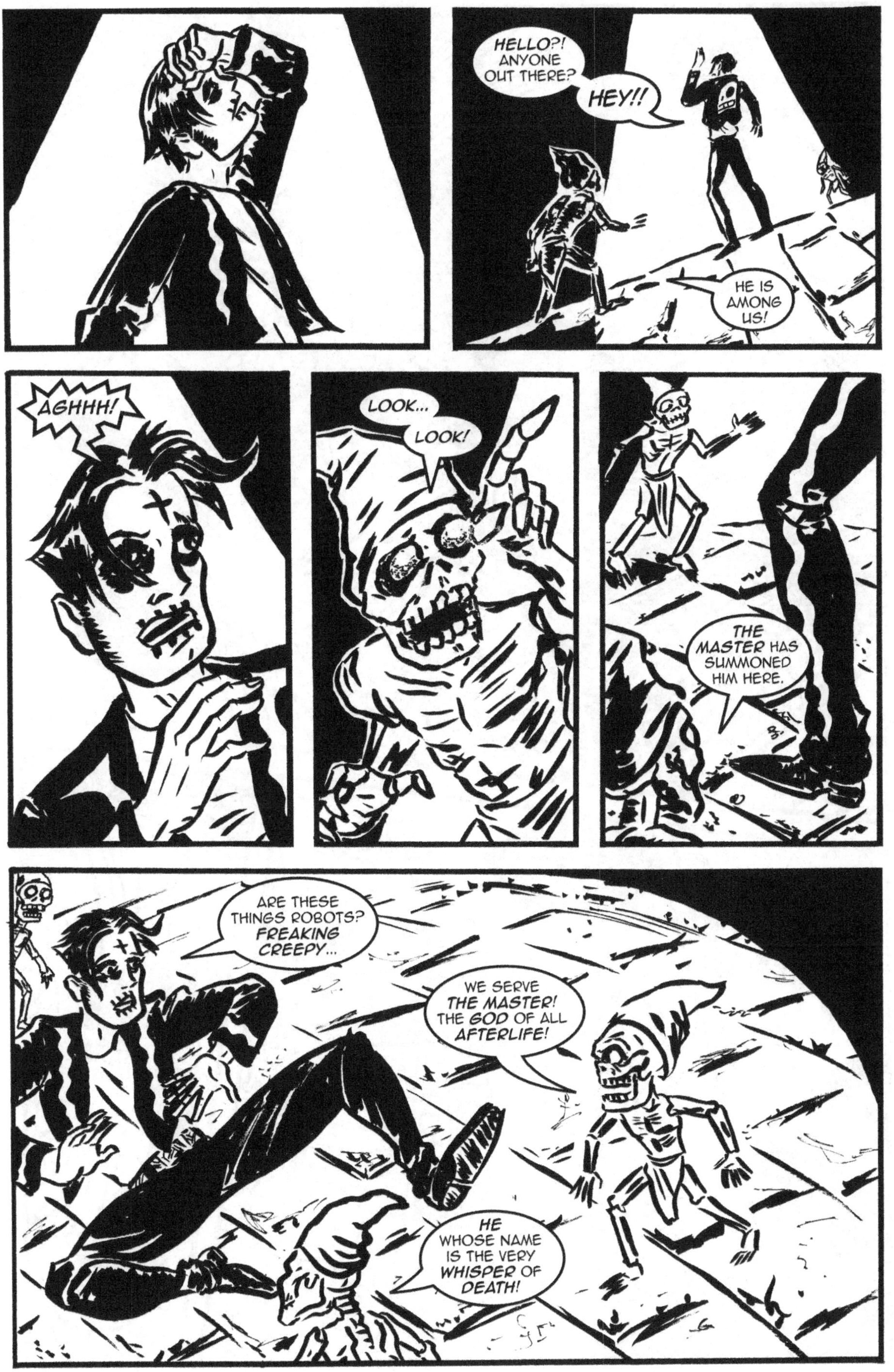
HELLO?! ANYONE OUT THERE?
HEY!!
HE IS AMONG US!
AGHHH!
LOOK...
LOOK!
THE MASTER HAS SUMMONED HIM HERE.
ARE THESE THINGS ROBOTS? FREAKING CREEPY...
WE SERVE THE MASTER! THE GOD OF ALL AFTERLIFE!
HE WHOSE NAME IS THE VERY WHISPER OF DEATH!

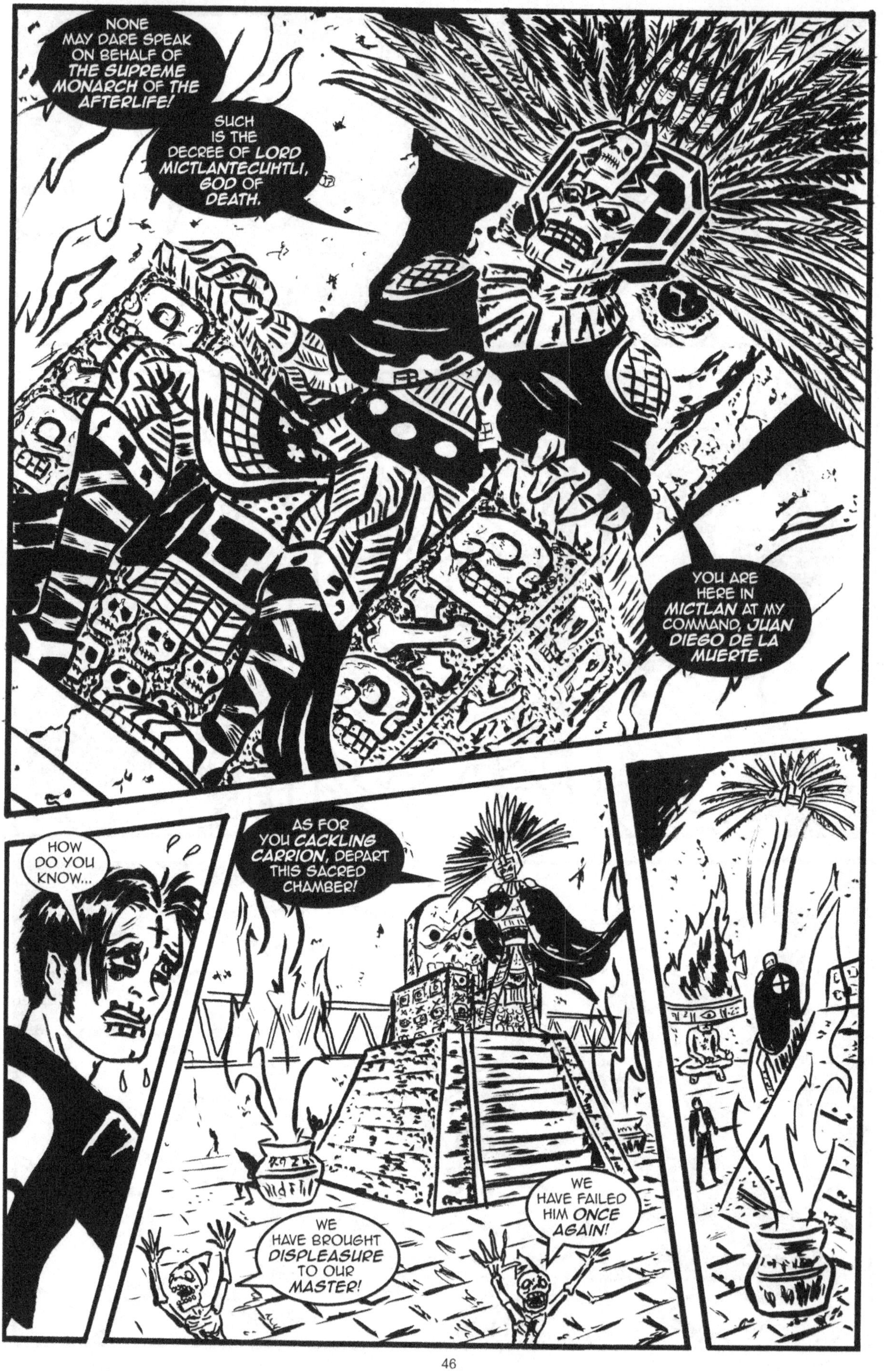
NONE MAY DARE SPEAK ON BEHALF OF THE SUPREME MONARCH OF THE AFTERLIFE!
SUCH IS THE DECREE OF LORD MICTLANTECUHTLI, GOD OF DEATH.
YOU ARE HERE IN MICTLAN AT MY COMMAND, JUAN DIEGO DE LA MUERTE.
HOW DO YOU KNOW...
AS FOR YOU CACKLING CARRION, DEPART THIS SACRED CHAMBER!
WE HAVE BROUGHT DISPLEASURE TO OUR MASTER!
WE HAVE FAILED HIM ONCE AGAIN!

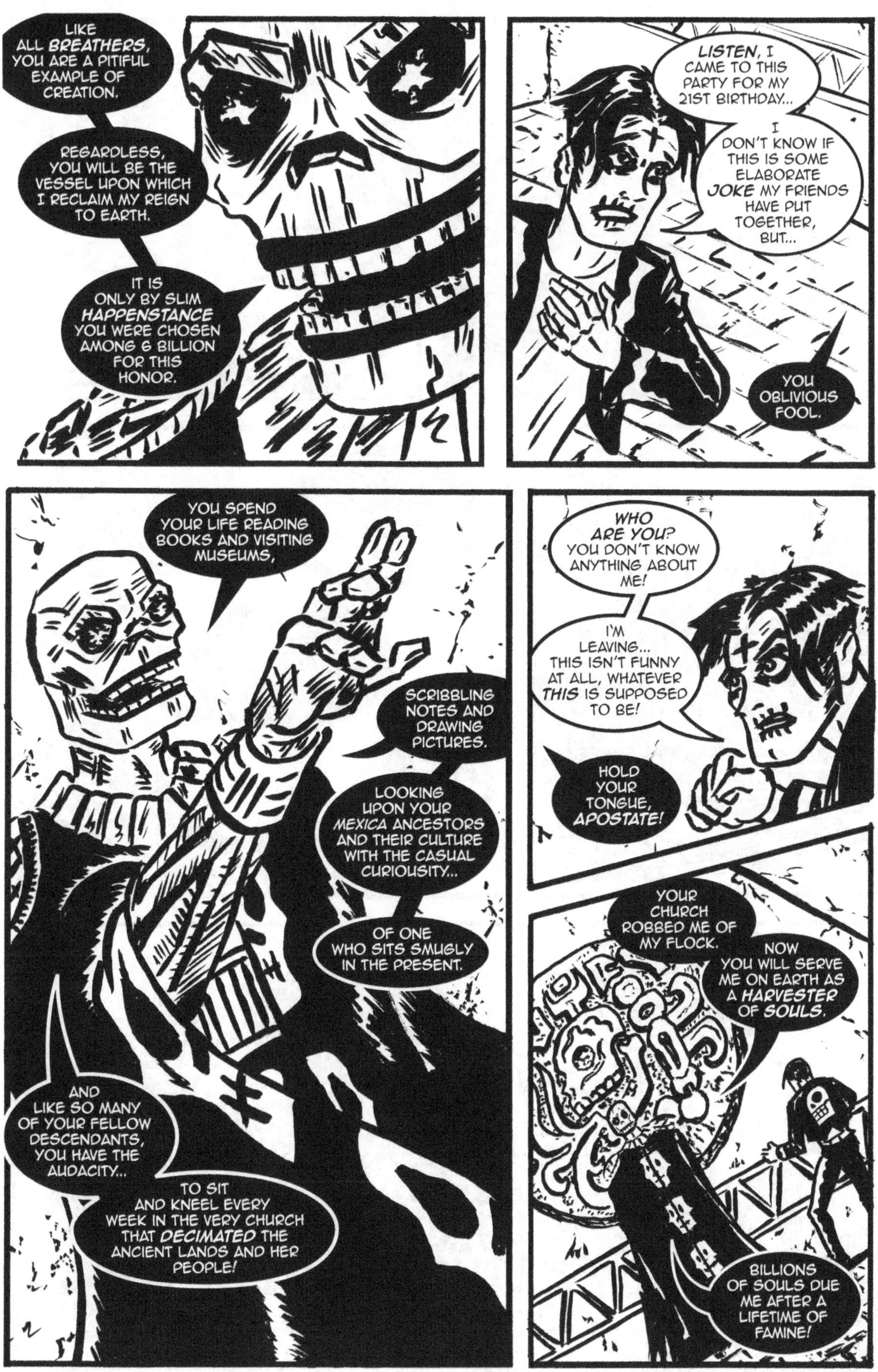
LIKE ALL BREATHERS, YOU ARE A PITIFUL EXAMPLE OF CREATION.
REGARDLESS, YOU WILL BE THE VESSEL UPON WHICH I RECLAIM MY REIGN TO EARTH.
IT IS ONLY BY SLIM HAPPENSTANCE YOU WERE CHOSEN AMONG 6 BILLION FOR THIS HONOR.
LISTEN, I CAME TO THIS PARTY FOR MY 21ST BIRTHDAY...
I DON'T KNOW IF THIS IS SOME ELABORATE JOKE MY FRIENDS HAVE PUT TOGETHER, BUT...
YOU OBLIVIOUS FOOL.
YOU SPEND YOUR LIFE READING BOOKS AND VISITING MUSEUMS,
SCRIBBLING NOTES AND DRAWING PICTURES.
LOOKING UPON YOUR MEXICA ANCESTORS AND THEIR CULTURE WITH THE CASUAL CURIOUSITY...
OF ONE WHO SITS SMUGLY IN THE PRESENT.
AND LIKE SO MANY OF YOUR FELLOW DESCENDANTS, YOU HAVE THE AUDACITY...
TO SIT AND KNEEL EVERY WEEK IN THE VERY CHURCH THAT DECIMATED THE ANCIENT LANDS AND HER PEOPLE!
WHO ARE YOU? YOU DON'T KNOW ANYTHING ABOUT ME!
I'M LEAVING... THIS ISN'T FUNNY AT ALL, WHATEVER THIS IS SUPPOSED TO BE!
HOLD YOUR TONGUE, APOSTATE!
YOUR CHURCH ROBBED ME OF MY FLOCK.
NOW YOU WILL SERVE ME ON EARTH AS A HARVESTER OF SOULS.
BILLIONS OF SOULS DUE ME AFTER A LIFETIME OF FAMINE!

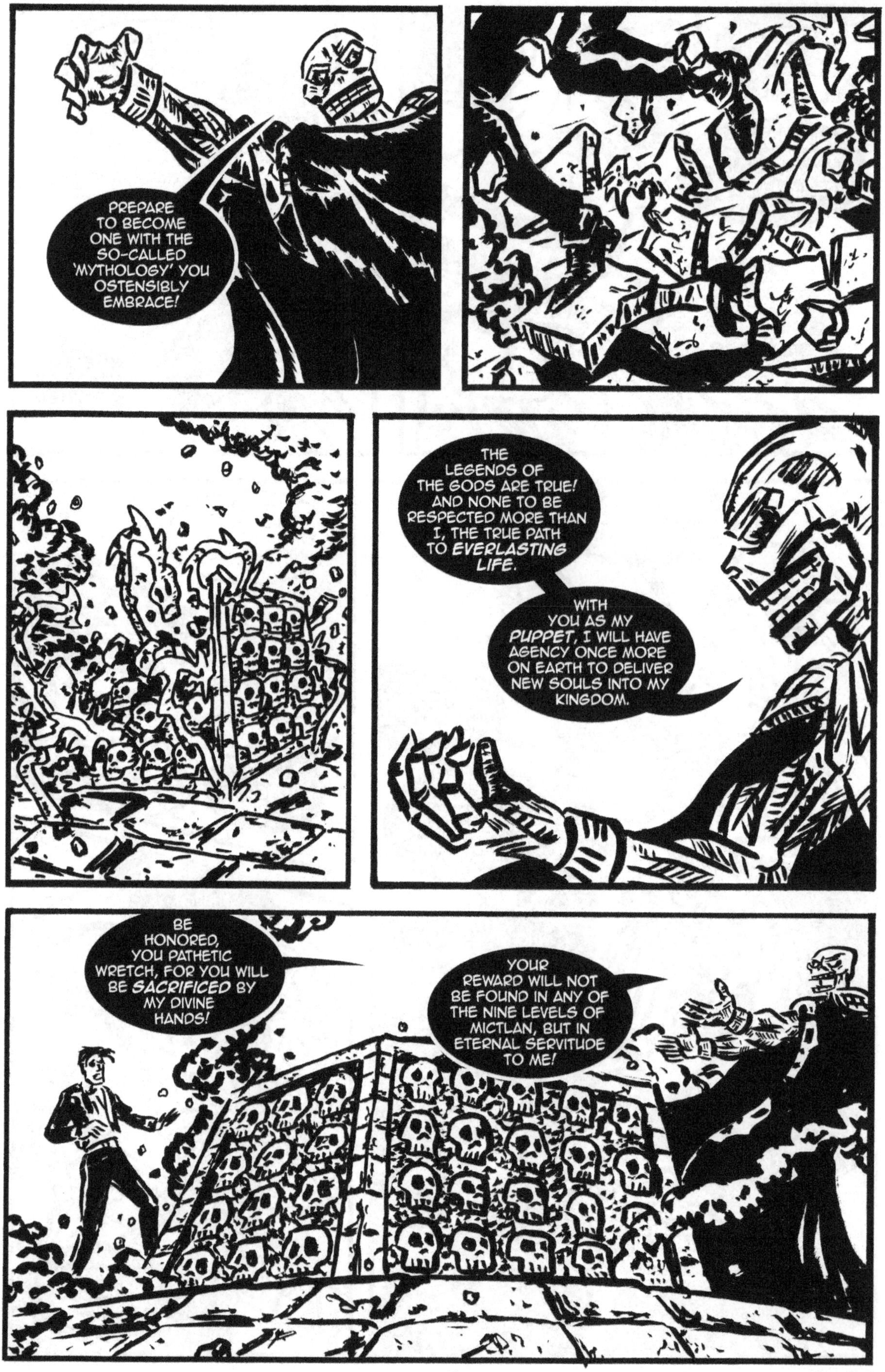
PREPARE TO BECOME ONE WITH THE SO-CALLED 'MYTHOLOGY' YOU OSTENSIBLY EMBRACE!
THE LEGENDS OF THE GODS ARE TRUE! AND NONE TO BE RESPECTED MORE THAN I, THE TRUE PATH TO EVERLASTING LIFE.
WITH YOU AS MY PUPPET, I WILL HAVE AGENCY ONCE MORE ON EARTH TO DELIVER NEW SOULS INTO MY KINGDOM.
BE HONORED, YOU PATHETIC WRETCH, FOR YOU WILL BE SACRIFICED BY MY DIVINE HANDS!
YOUR REWARD WILL NOT BE FOUND IN ANY OF THE NINE LEVELS OF MICTLAN, BUT IN ETERNAL SERVITUDE TO ME!

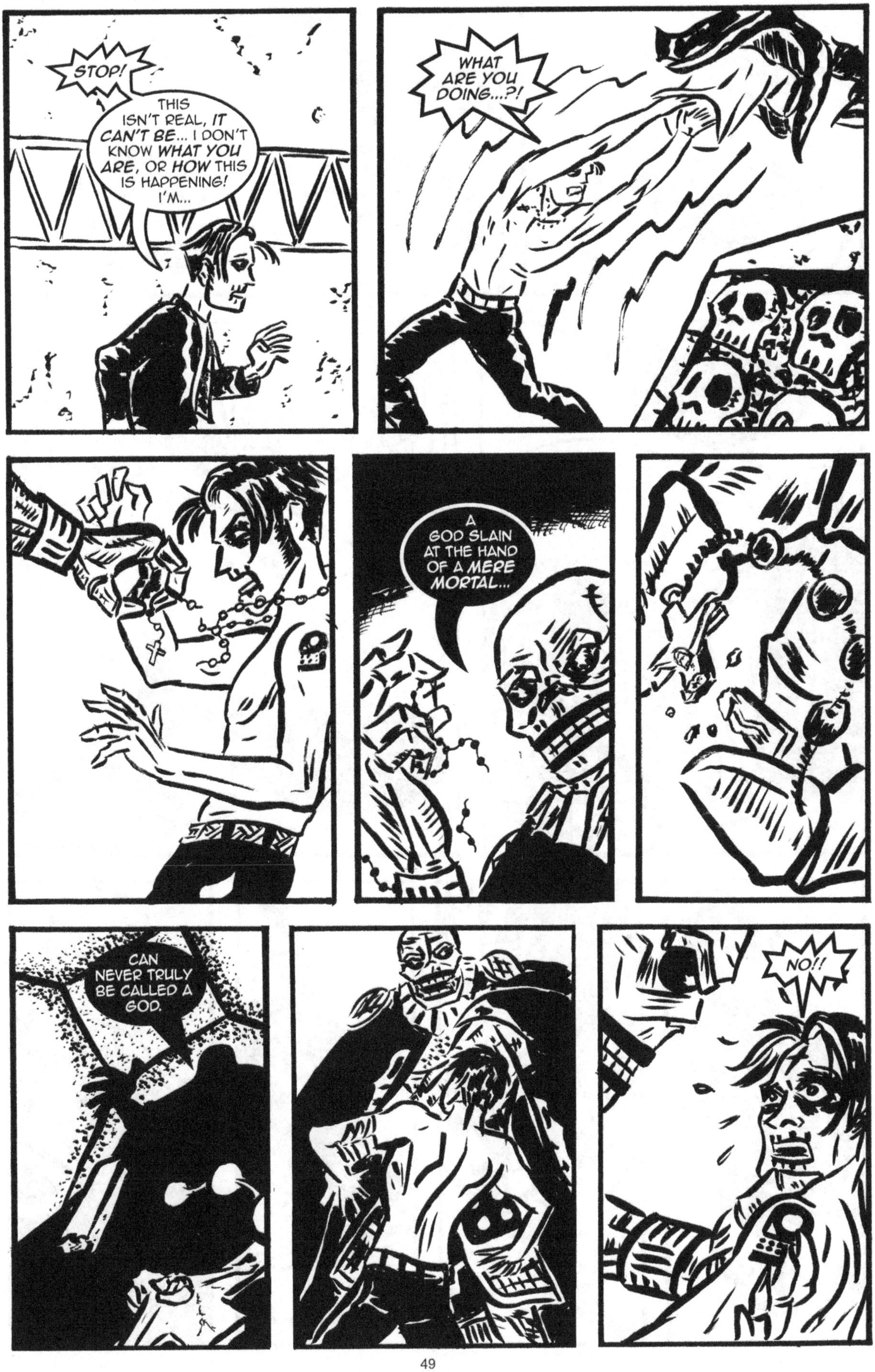
STOP!
THIS ISN'T REAL, *IT CAN'T BE*... I DON'T KNOW *WHAT YOU ARE*, OR *HOW* THIS IS HAPPENING! I'M...
WHAT ARE YOU DOING...?!
A GOD SLAIN AT THE HAND OF A *MERE MORTAL*...
CAN NEVER TRULY BE CALLED A GOD.
NO!!

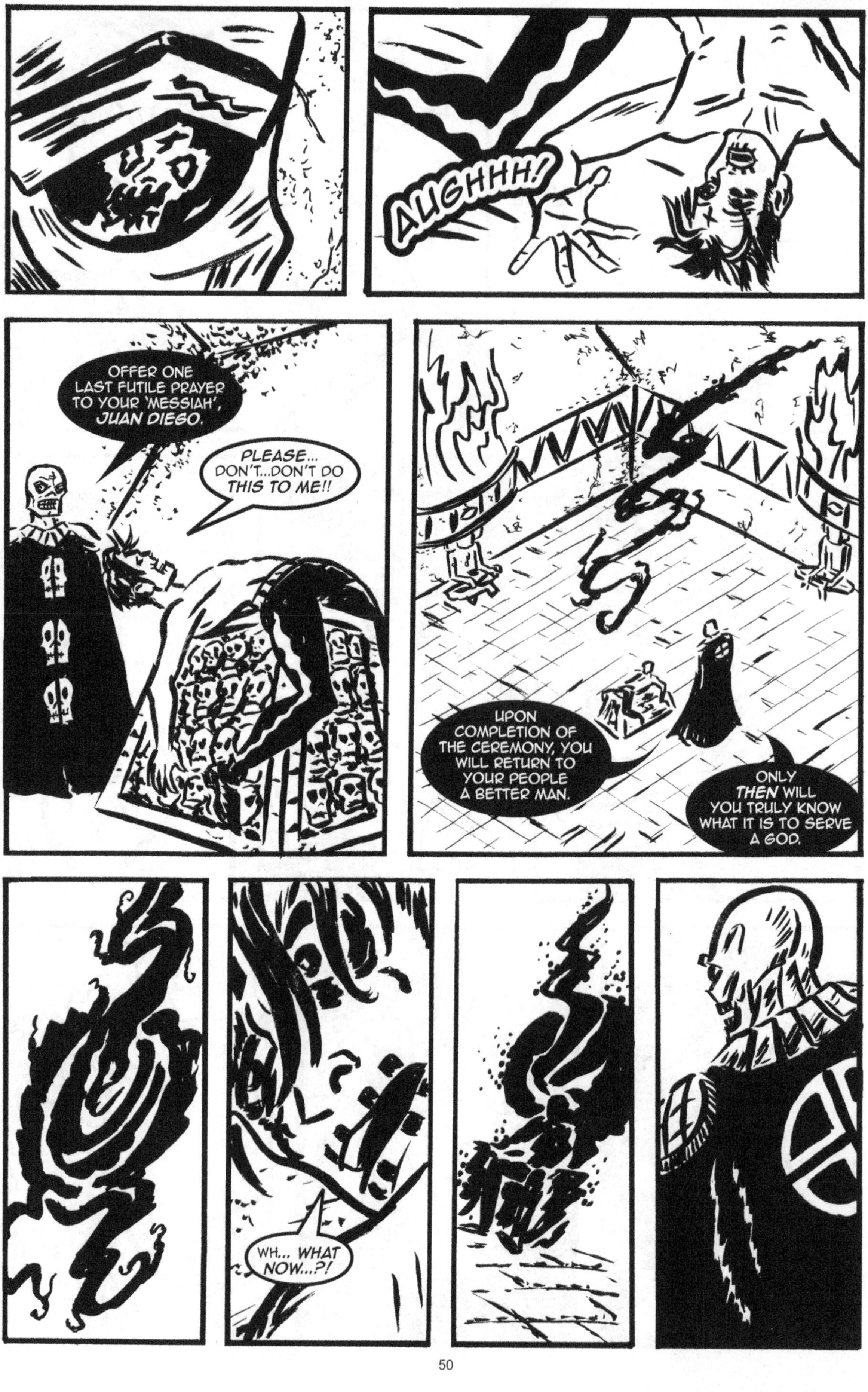
AUGHHH!
OFFER ONE LAST FUTILE PRAYER TO YOUR 'MESSIAH', JUAN DIEGO.
PLEASE... DON'T...DON'T DO THIS TO ME!!
UPON COMPLETION OF THE CEREMONY, YOU WILL RETURN TO YOUR PEOPLE A BETTER MAN.
ONLY THEN WILL YOU TRULY KNOW WHAT IT IS TO SERVE A GOD.
WH... WHAT NOW...?!

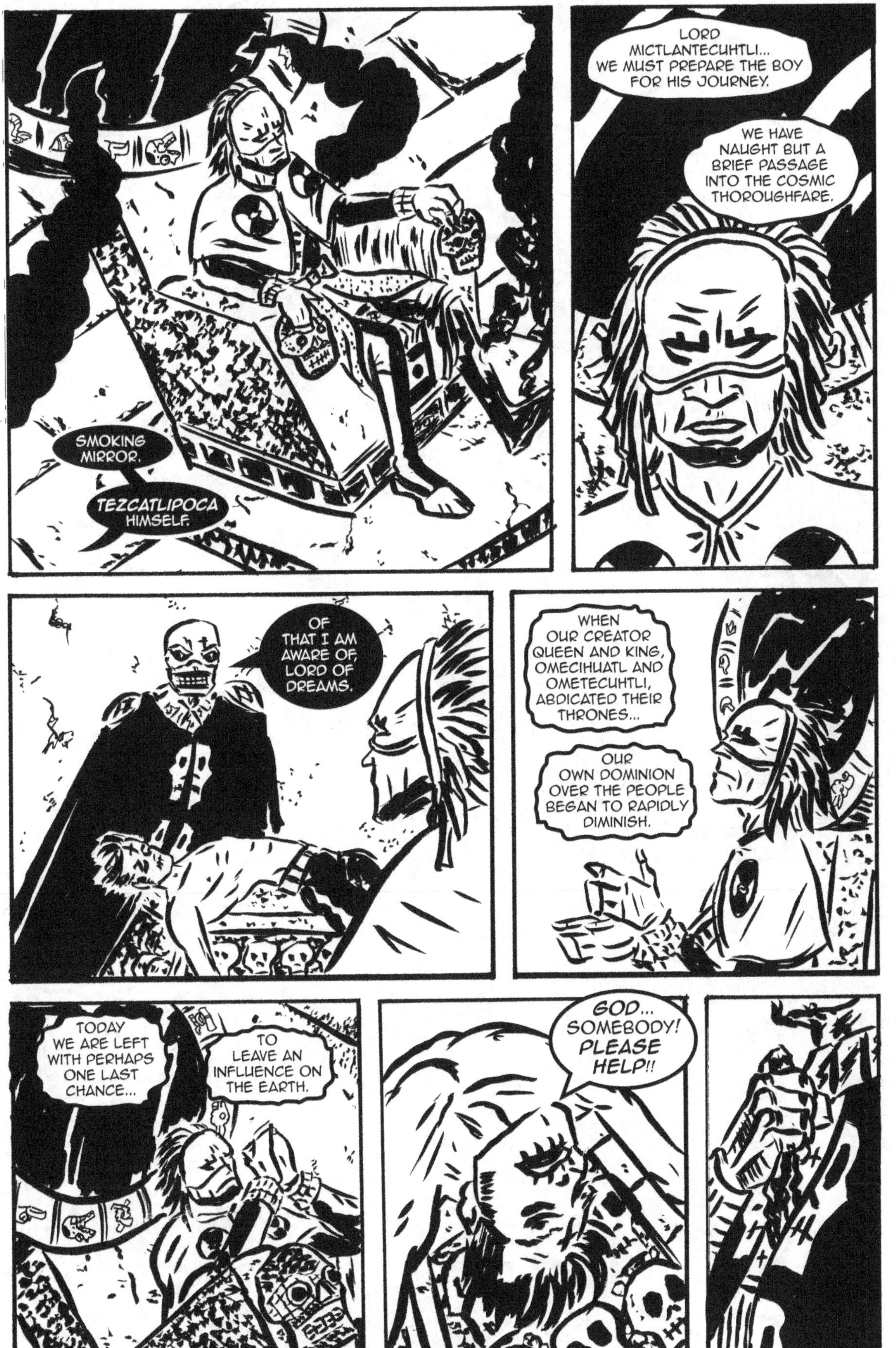
SMOKING MIRROR.
TEZCATLIPOCA HIMSELF.
LORD MICTLANTECUHTLI... WE MUST PREPARE THE BOY FOR HIS JOURNEY.
WE HAVE NAUGHT BUT A BRIEF PASSAGE INTO THE COSMIC THOROUGHFARE.
OF THAT I AM AWARE OF, LORD OF DREAMS.
WHEN OUR CREATOR QUEEN AND KING, OMECIHUATL AND OMETECUHTLI, ABDICATED THEIR THRONES...
OUR OWN DOMINION OVER THE PEOPLE BEGAN TO RAPIDLY DIMINISH.
TODAY WE ARE LEFT WITH PERHAPS ONE LAST CHANCE...
TO LEAVE AN INFLUENCE ON THE EARTH.
GOD... SOMEBODY! PLEASE HELP!!

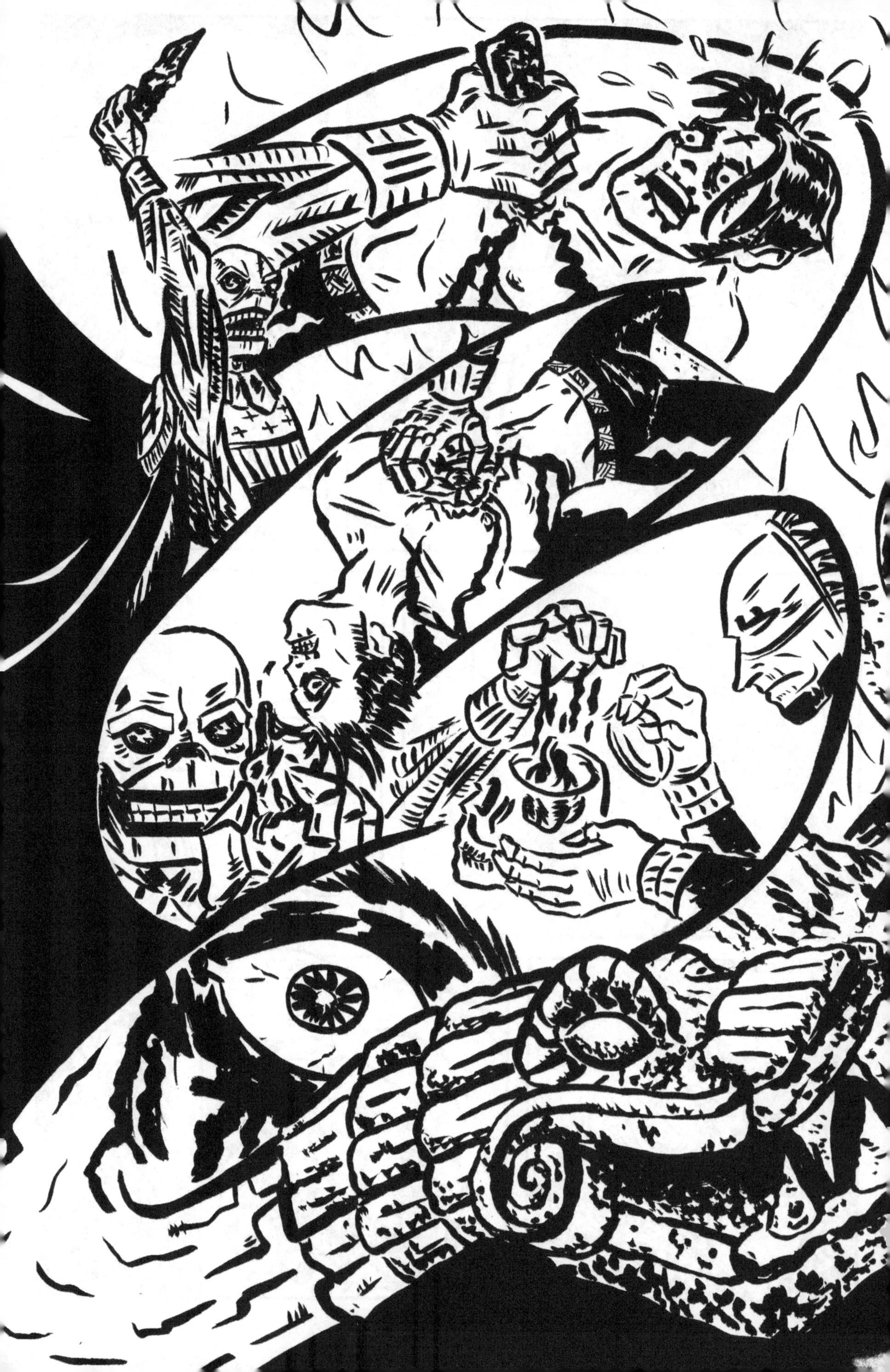

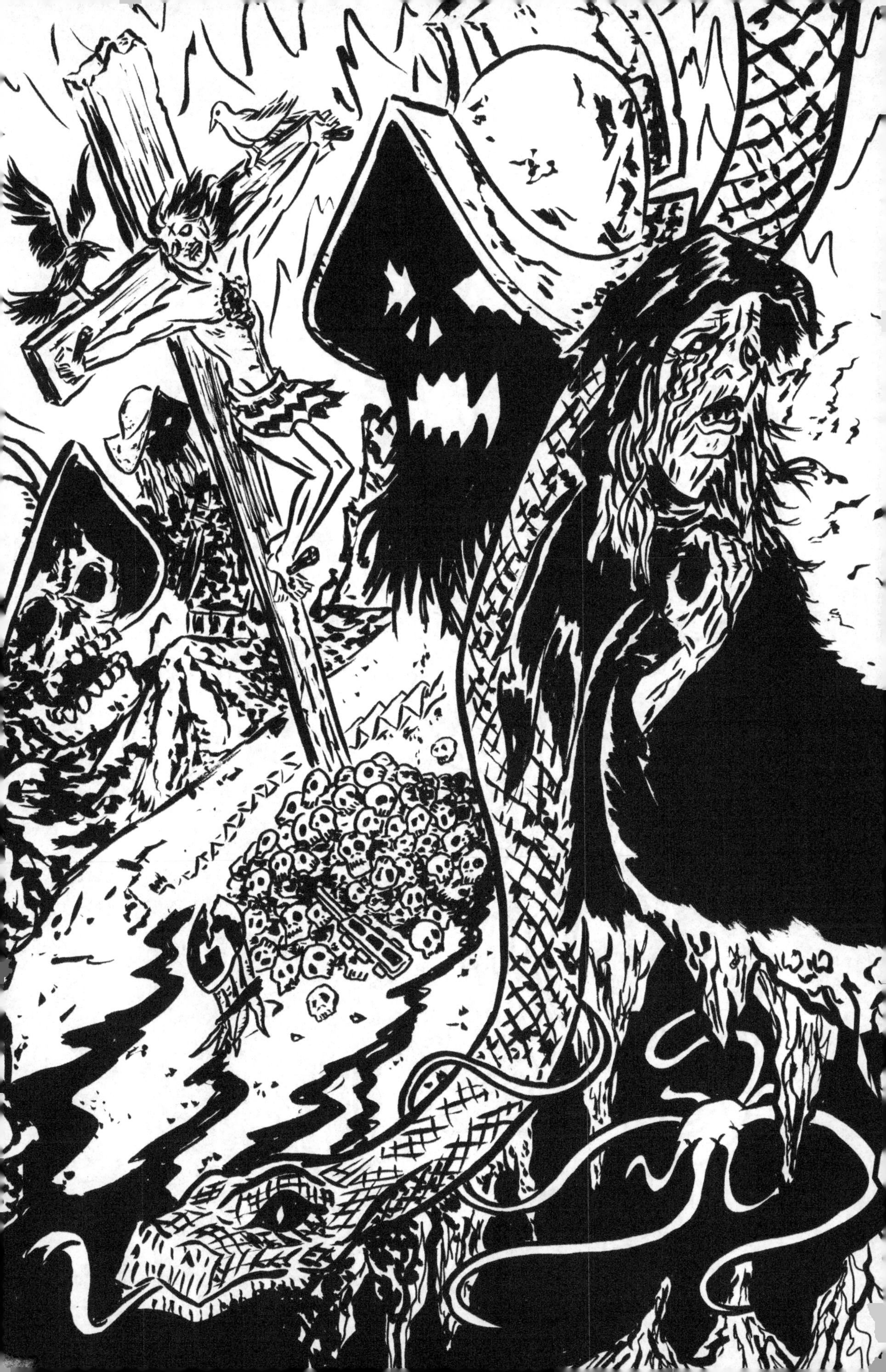

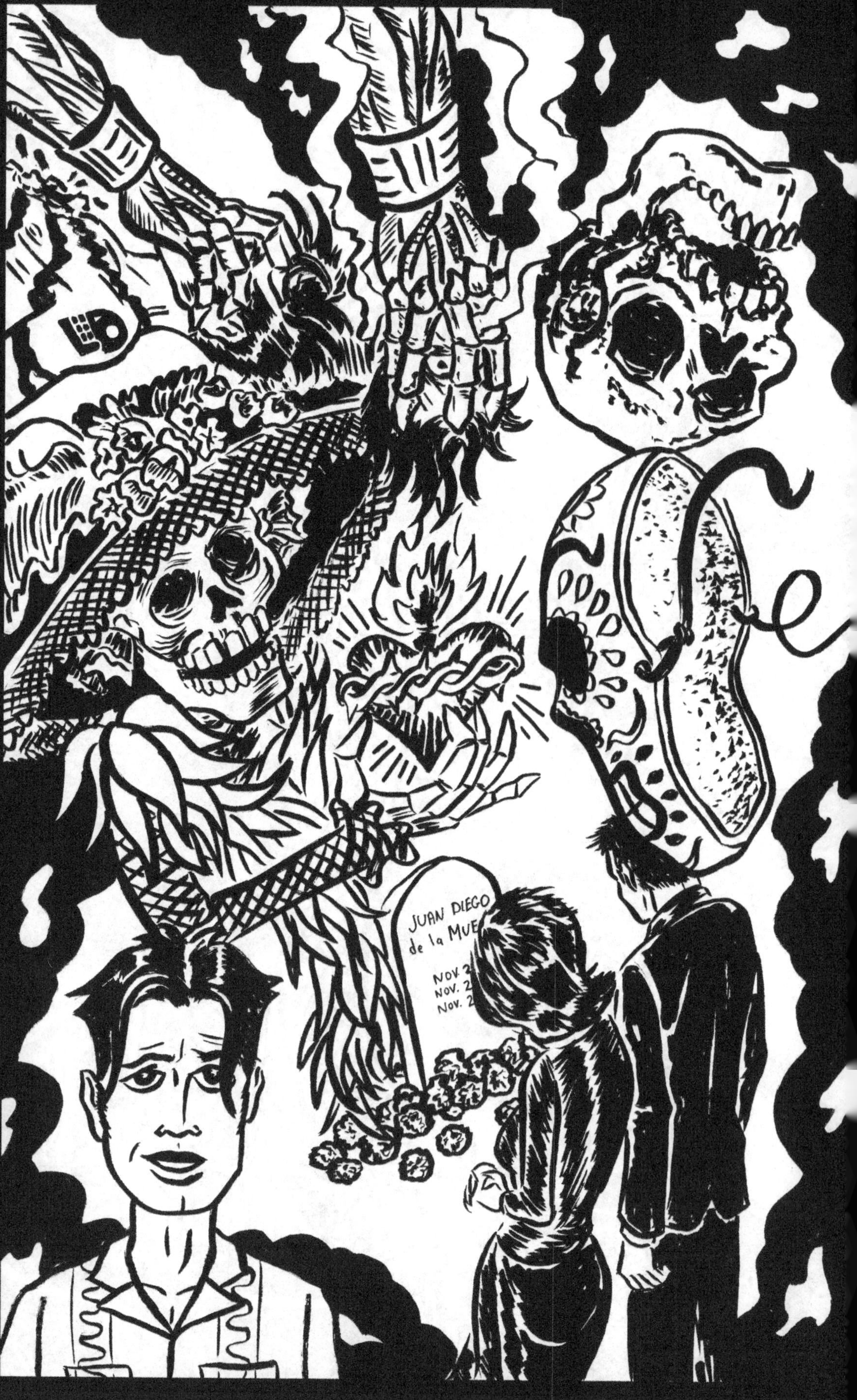
JUAN DIEGO
de la MUE
NOV. 2
NOV. 2
NOV. 2

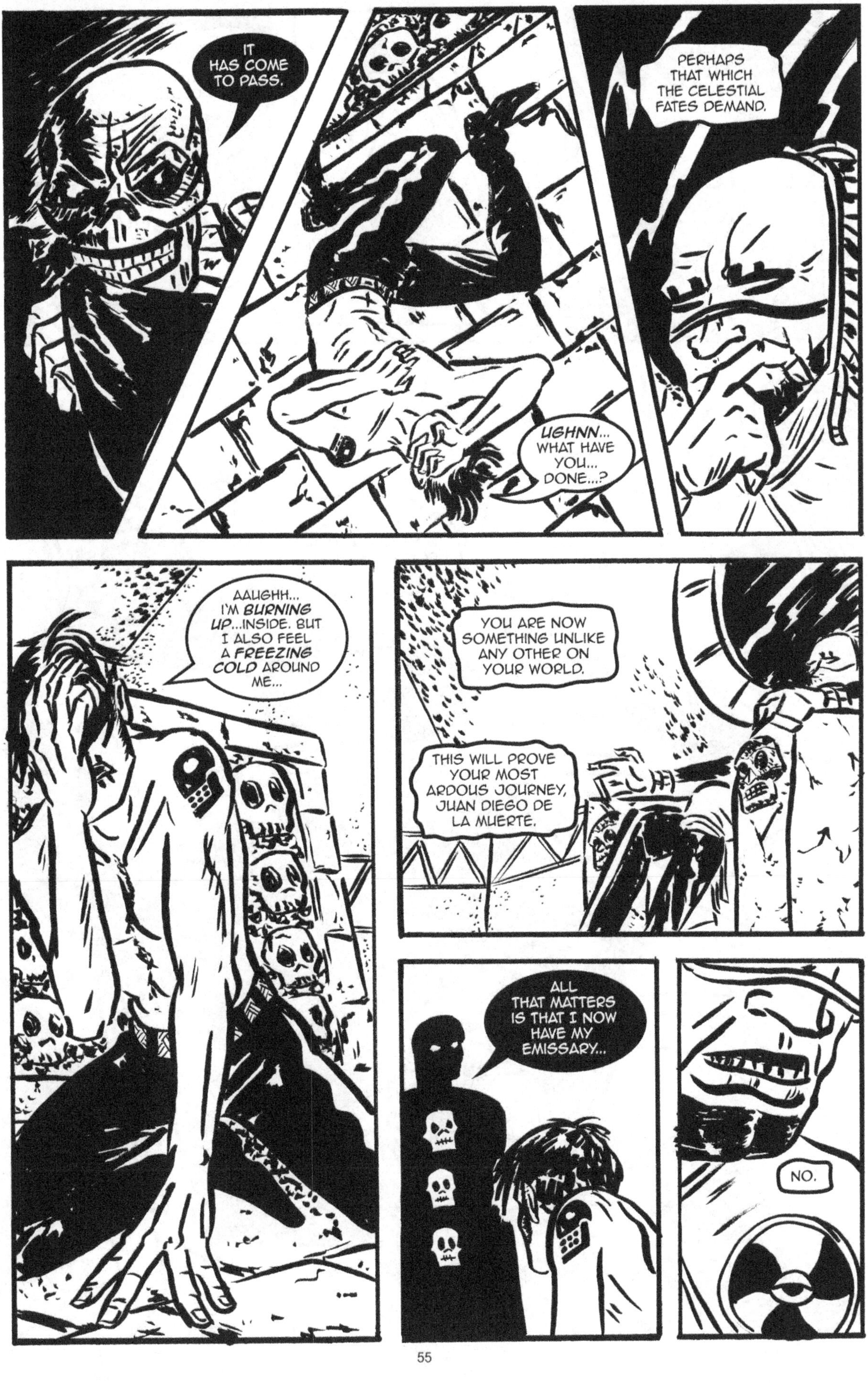
IT HAS COME TO PASS.
PERHAPS THAT WHICH THE CELESTIAL FATES DEMAND.
UGHNN... WHAT HAVE YOU... DONE...?
AAUGHH... I'M BURNING UP...INSIDE. BUT I ALSO FEEL A FREEZING COLD AROUND ME...
YOU ARE NOW SOMETHING UNLIKE ANY OTHER ON YOUR WORLD.
THIS WILL PROVE YOUR MOST ARDOUS JOURNEY, JUAN DIEGO DE LA MUERTE.
ALL THAT MATTERS IS THAT I NOW HAVE MY EMISSARY...
NO.

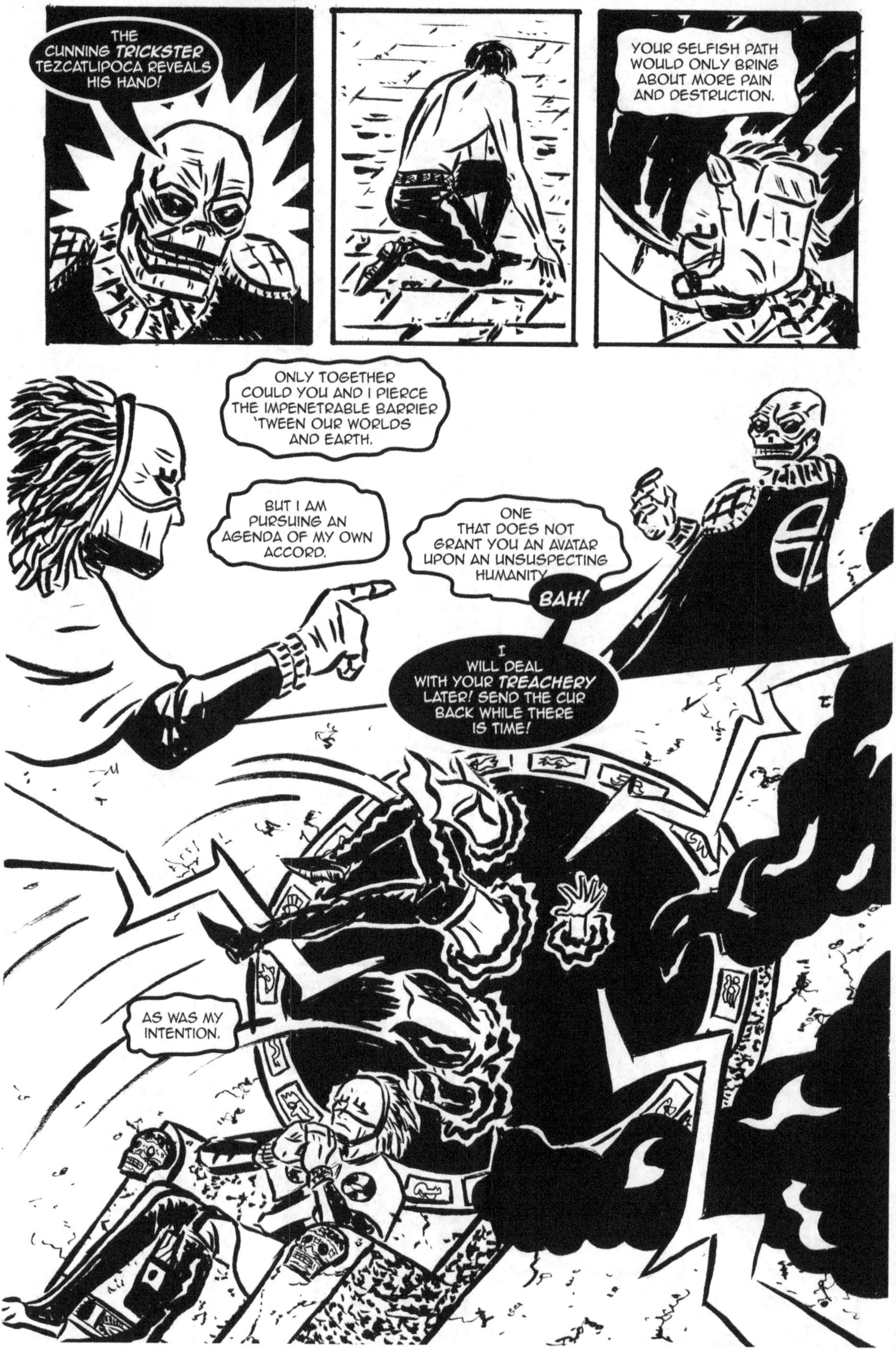
THE CUNNING TRICKSTER TEZCATLIPOCA REVEALS HIS HAND!
YOUR SELFISH PATH WOULD ONLY BRING ABOUT MORE PAIN AND DESTRUCTION.
ONLY TOGETHER COULD YOU AND I PIERCE THE IMPENETRABLE BARRIER 'TWEEN OUR WORLDS AND EARTH.
BUT I AM PURSUING AN AGENDA OF MY OWN ACCORD.
ONE THAT DOES NOT GRANT YOU AN AVATAR UPON AN UNSUSPECTING HUMANITY.
BAH!
I WILL DEAL WITH YOUR TREACHERY LATER! SEND THE CUR BACK WHILE THERE IS TIME!
AS WAS MY INTENTION.

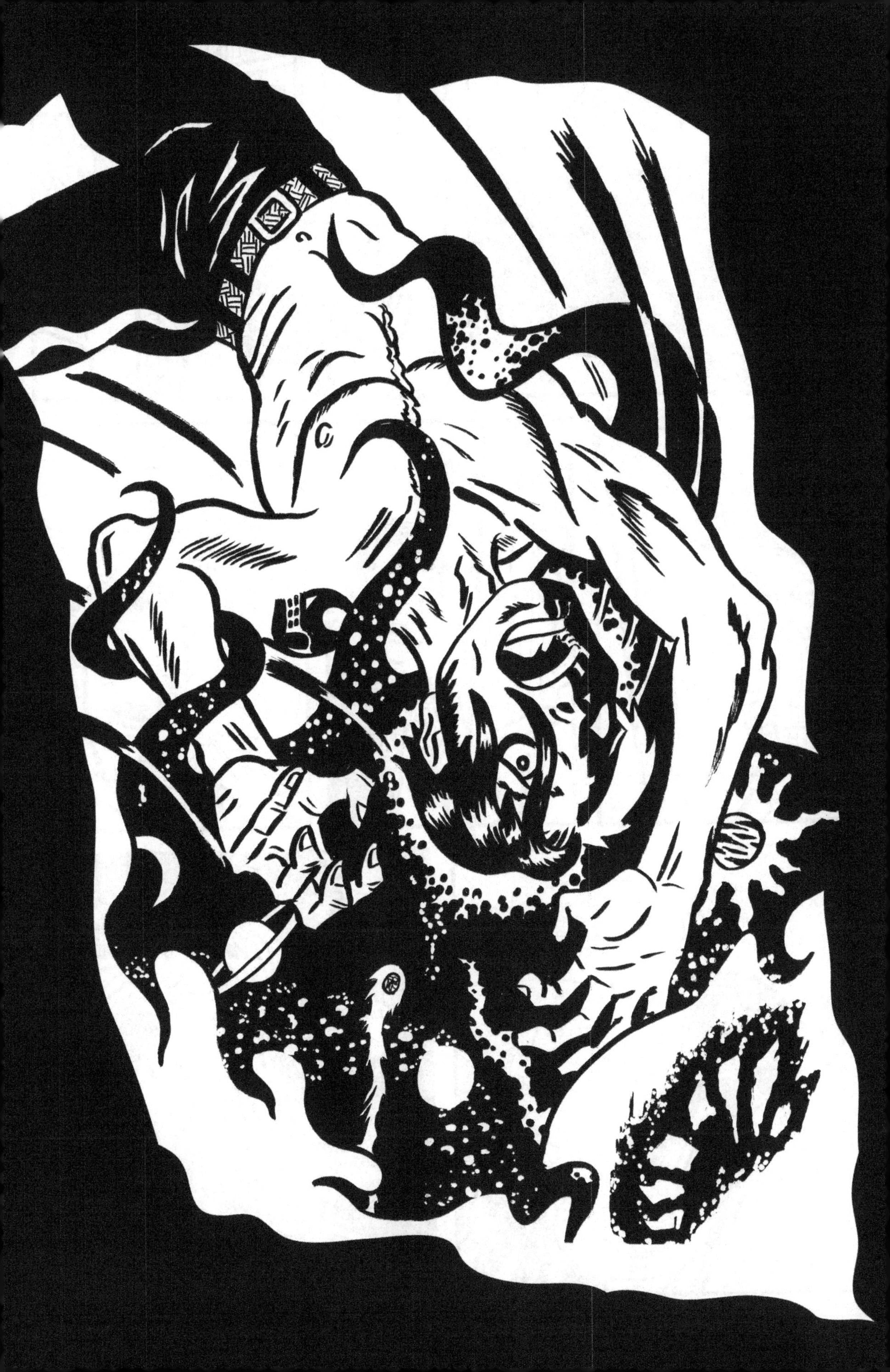

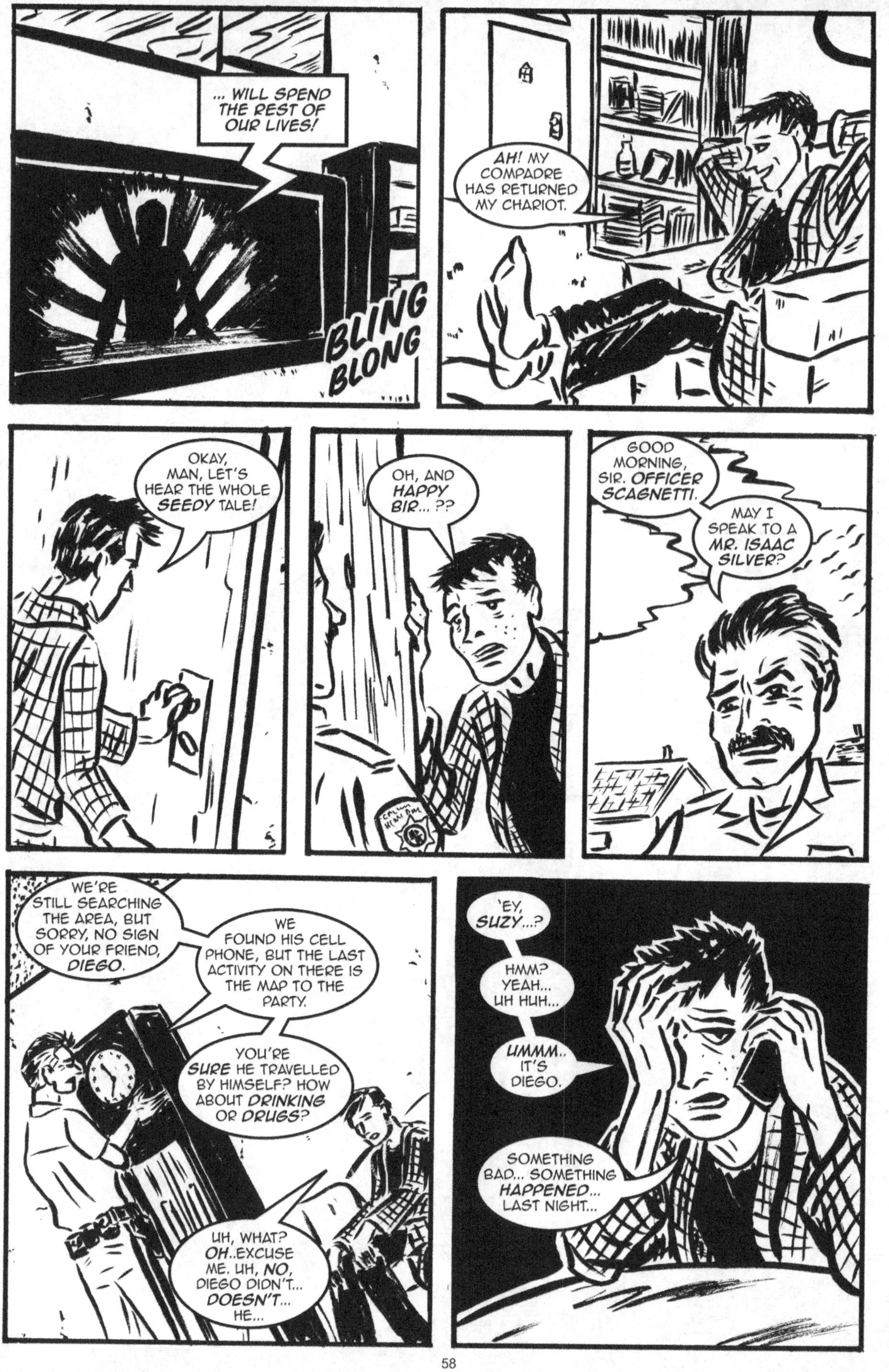

... WILL SPEND THE REST OF OUR LIVES!
BLING BLONG
AH! MY COMPADRE HAS RETURNED MY CHARIOT.
OKAY, MAN, LET'S HEAR THE WHOLE SEEDY TALE!
OH, AND HAPPY BIR... ??
GOOD MORNING, SIR. OFFICER SCAGNETTI.
MAY I SPEAK TO A MR. ISAAC SILVER?
WE'RE STILL SEARCHING THE AREA, BUT SORRY, NO SIGN OF YOUR FRIEND, DIEGO.
WE FOUND HIS CELL PHONE, BUT THE LAST ACTIVITY ON THERE IS THE MAP TO THE PARTY.
YOU'RE SURE HE TRAVELLED BY HIMSELF? HOW ABOUT DRINKING OR DRUGS?
UH, WHAT? OH..EXCUSE ME. UH, NO, DIEGO DIDN'T... DOESN'T... HE...
'EY, SUZY...?
HMM? YEAH... UH HUH...
UMMM.. IT'S DIEGO.
SOMETHING BAD... SOMETHING HAPPENED... LAST NIGHT...

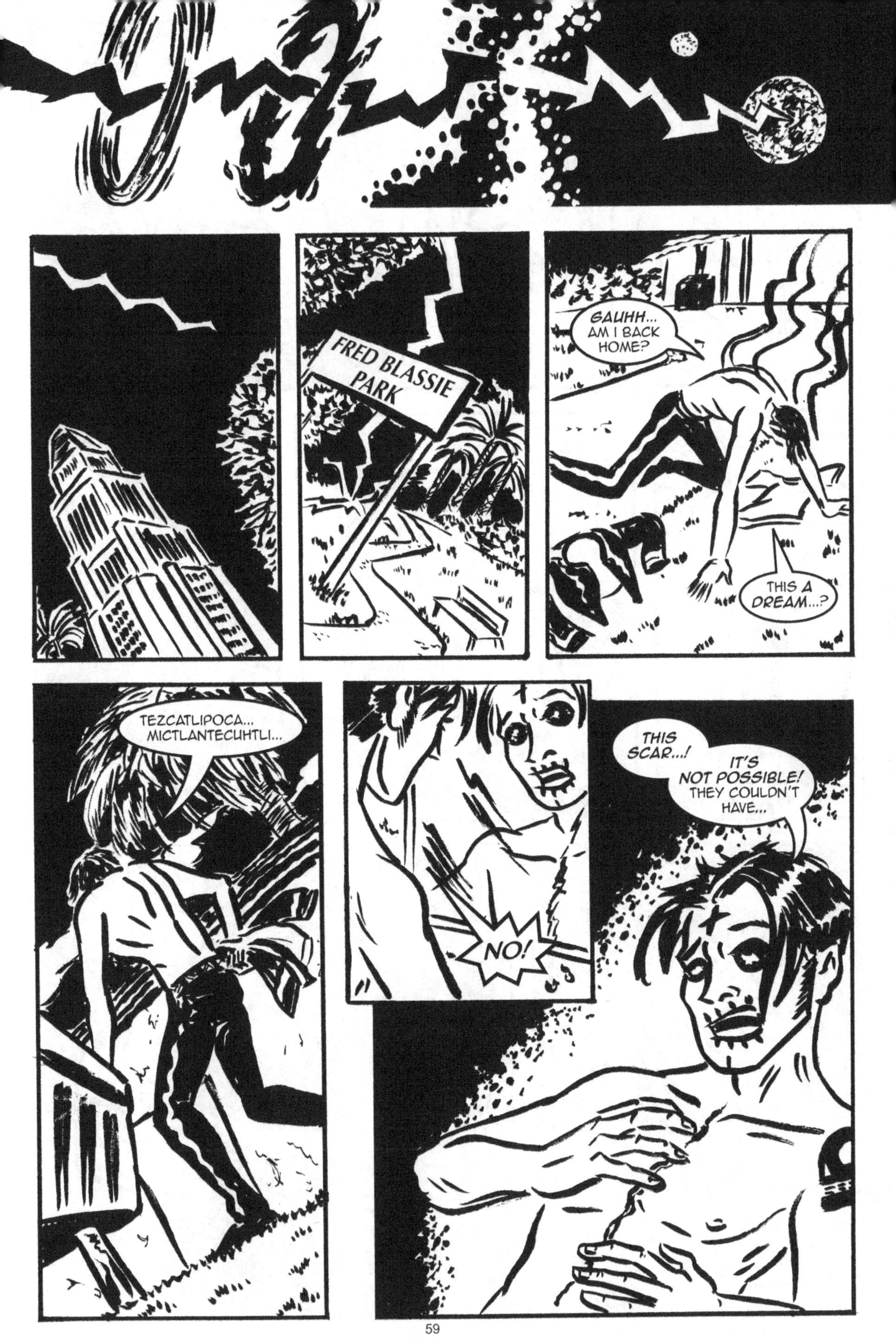
FRED BLASSIE PARK
GAUHH... AM I BACK HOME?
THIS A DREAM...?
TEZCATLIPOCA... MICTLANTECUHTLI...
NO!
THIS SCAR...!
IT'S NOT POSSIBLE! THEY COULDN'T HAVE...

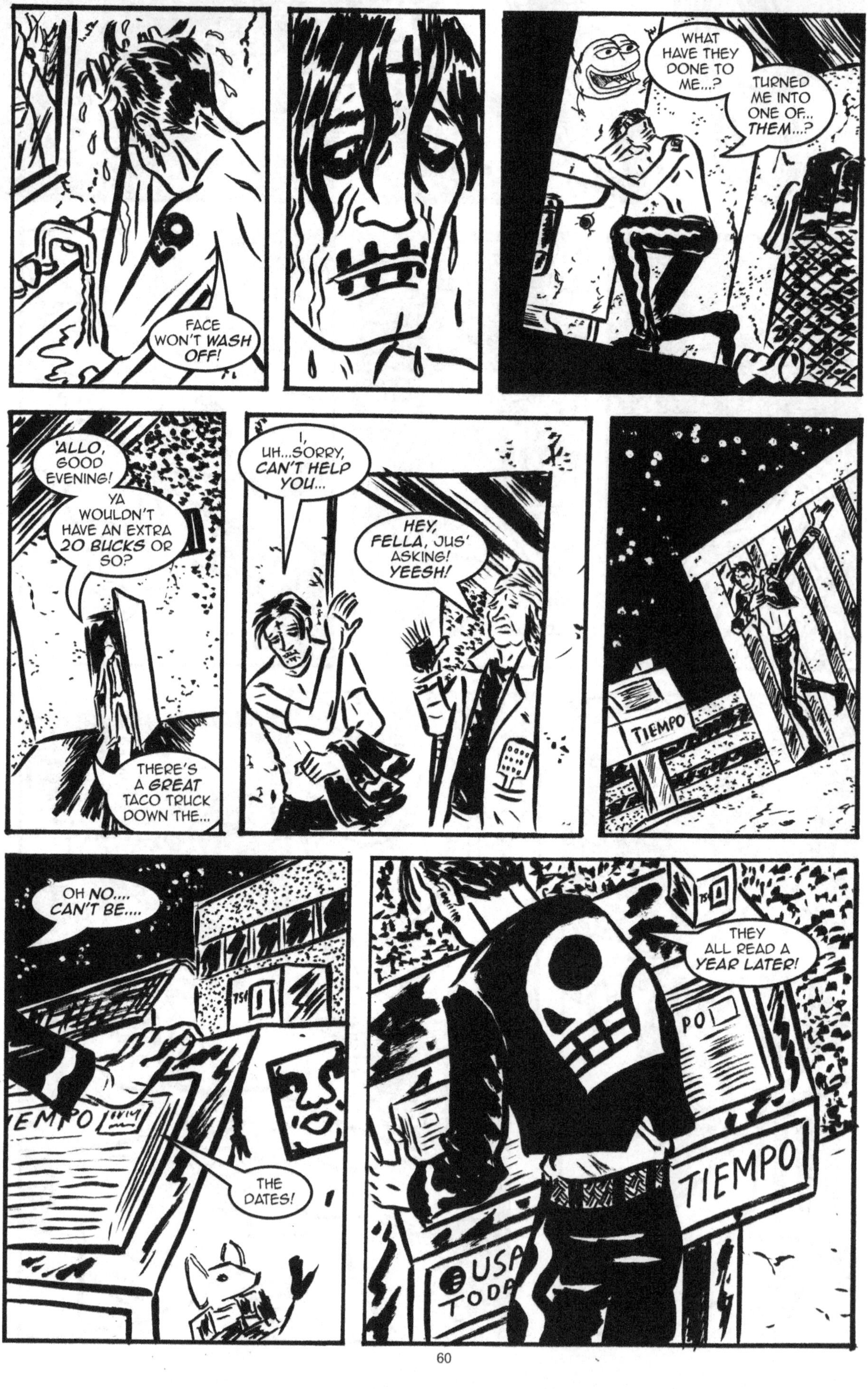
FACE WON'T WASH OFF!
WHAT HAVE THEY DONE TO ME...?
TURNED ME INTO ONE OF.. THEM...?
'ALLO, GOOD EVENING!
YA WOULDN'T HAVE AN EXTRA 20 BUCKS OR SO?
THERE'S A GREAT TACO TRUCK DOWN THE...
I, UH...SORRY, CAN'T HELP YOU...
HEY, FELLA, JUS' ASKING! YEESH!
TIEMPO
OH NO.... CAN'T BE....
THE DATES!
TIEMPO
THEY ALL READ A YEAR LATER!
TIEMPO
USA TODA

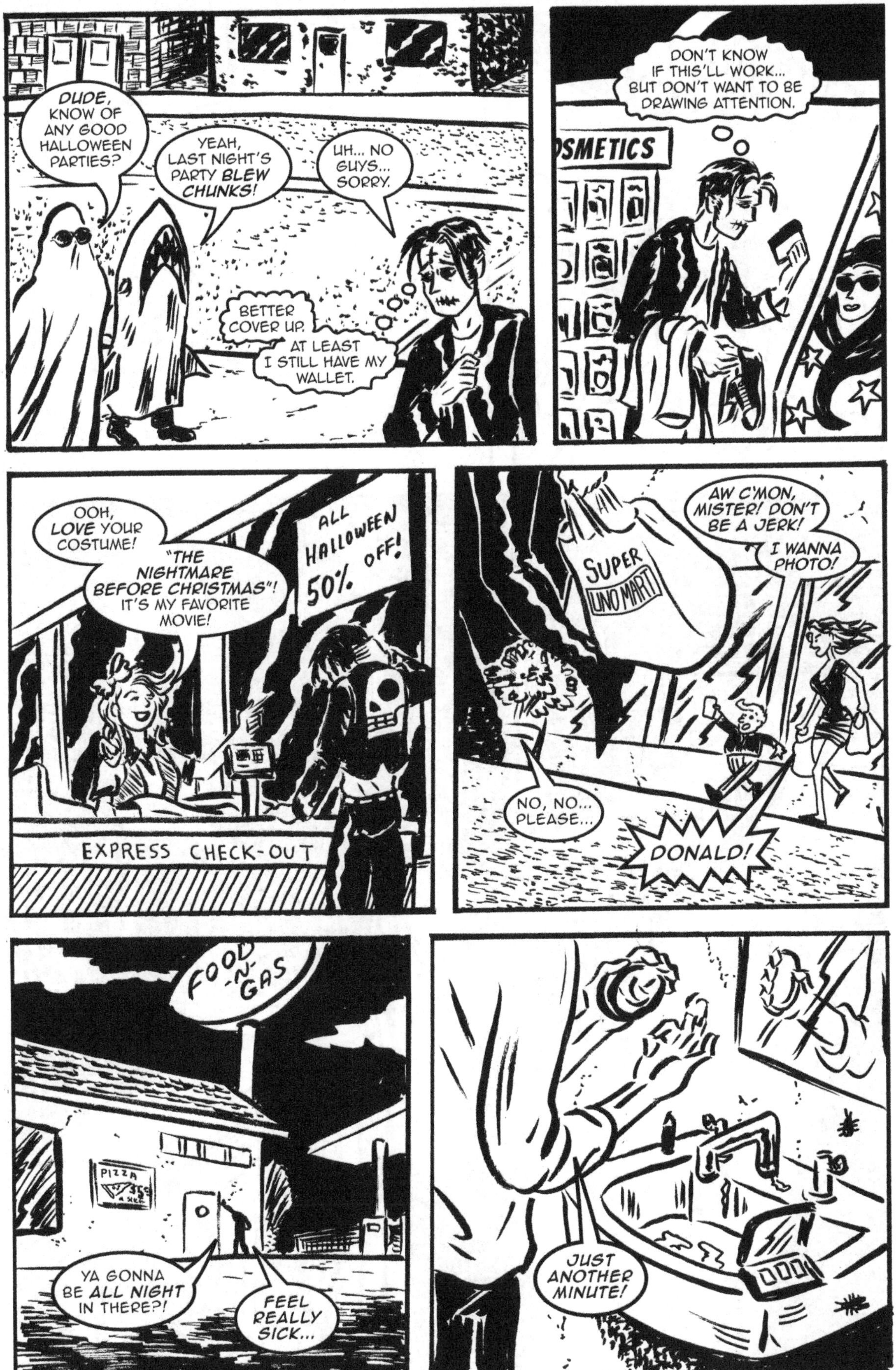
DUDE, KNOW OF ANY GOOD HALLOWEEN PARTIES?
YEAH, LAST NIGHT'S PARTY BLEW CHUNKS!
UH... NO GUYS... SORRY.
BETTER COVER UP.
AT LEAST I STILL HAVE MY WALLET.
DON'T KNOW IF THIS'LL WORK... BUT DON'T WANT TO BE DRAWING ATTENTION.
OSMETICS
OOH, LOVE YOUR COSTUME!
"THE NIGHTMARE BEFORE CHRISTMAS"! IT'S MY FAVORITE MOVIE!
ALL HALLOWEEN 50% OFF!
EXPRESS CHECK-OUT
AW C'MON, MISTER! DON'T BE A JERK!
I WANNA PHOTO!
SUPER UNO MART
NO, NO... PLEASE...
DONALD!
FOOD -N- GAS
PIZZA
YA GONNA BE ALL NIGHT IN THERE?!
FEEL REALLY SICK...
JUST ANOTHER MINUTE!

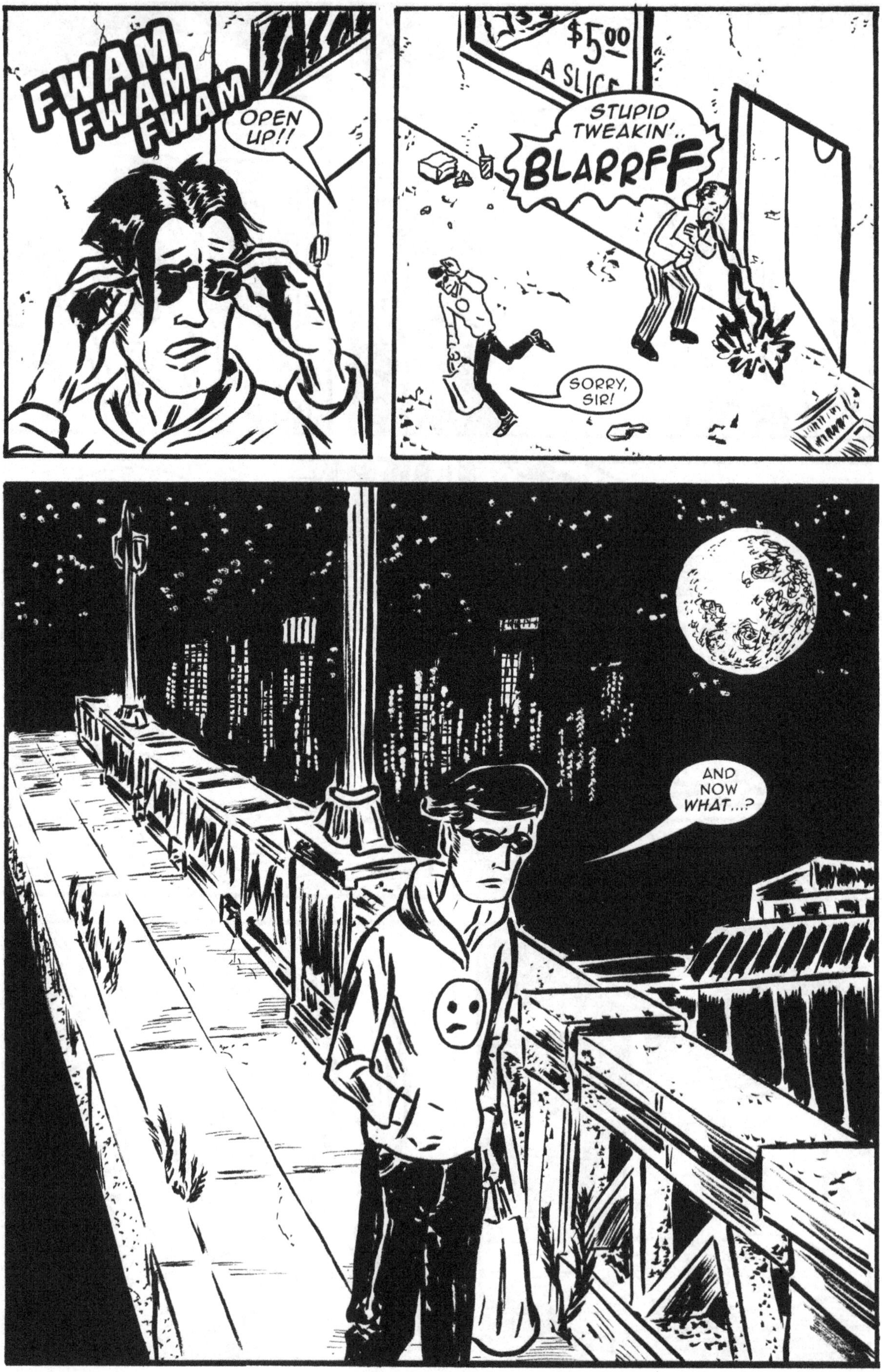

FWAM FWAM FWAM
OPEN UP!!
$5.00 A SLICE
STUPID TWEAKIN'..
BLARRFF
SORRY, SIR!
AND NOW WHAT...?

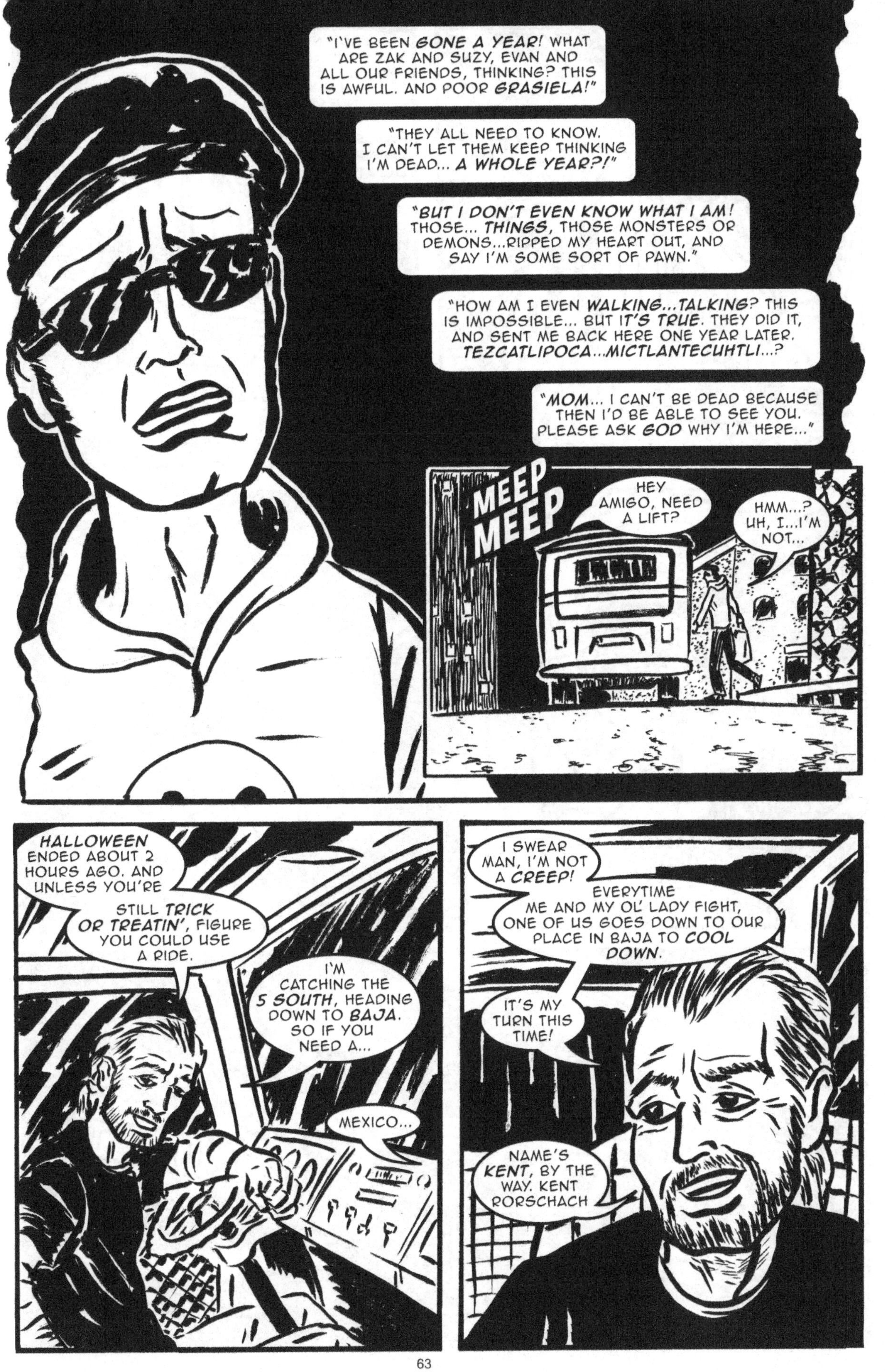
"I'VE BEEN GONE A YEAR! WHAT ARE ZAK AND SUZY, EVAN AND ALL OUR FRIENDS, THINKING? THIS IS AWFUL. AND POOR GRASIELA!"
"THEY ALL NEED TO KNOW. I CAN'T LET THEM KEEP THINKING I'M DEAD... A WHOLE YEAR?!"
"BUT I DON'T EVEN KNOW WHAT I AM! THOSE... THINGS, THOSE MONSTERS OR DEMONS...RIPPED MY HEART OUT, AND SAY I'M SOME SORT OF PAWN."
"HOW AM I EVEN WALKING...TALKING? THIS IS IMPOSSIBLE... BUT IT'S TRUE. THEY DID IT, AND SENT ME BACK HERE ONE YEAR LATER. TEZCATLIPOCA...MICTLANTECUHTLI...?
"MOM... I CAN'T BE DEAD BECAUSE THEN I'D BE ABLE TO SEE YOU. PLEASE ASK GOD WHY I'M HERE..."
MEEP MEEP
HEY AMIGO, NEED A LIFT?
HMM...? UH, I...I'M NOT...
HALLOWEEN ENDED ABOUT 2 HOURS AGO. AND UNLESS YOU'RE
STILL TRICK OR TREATIN', FIGURE YOU COULD USE A RIDE.
I'M CATCHING THE 5 SOUTH, HEADING DOWN TO BAJA. SO IF YOU NEED A...
MEXICO...
I SWEAR MAN, I'M NOT A CREEP!
EVERYTIME ME AND MY OL' LADY FIGHT, ONE OF US GOES DOWN TO OUR PLACE IN BAJA TO COOL DOWN.
IT'S MY TURN THIS TIME!
NAME'S KENT, BY THE WAY. KENT RORSCHACH

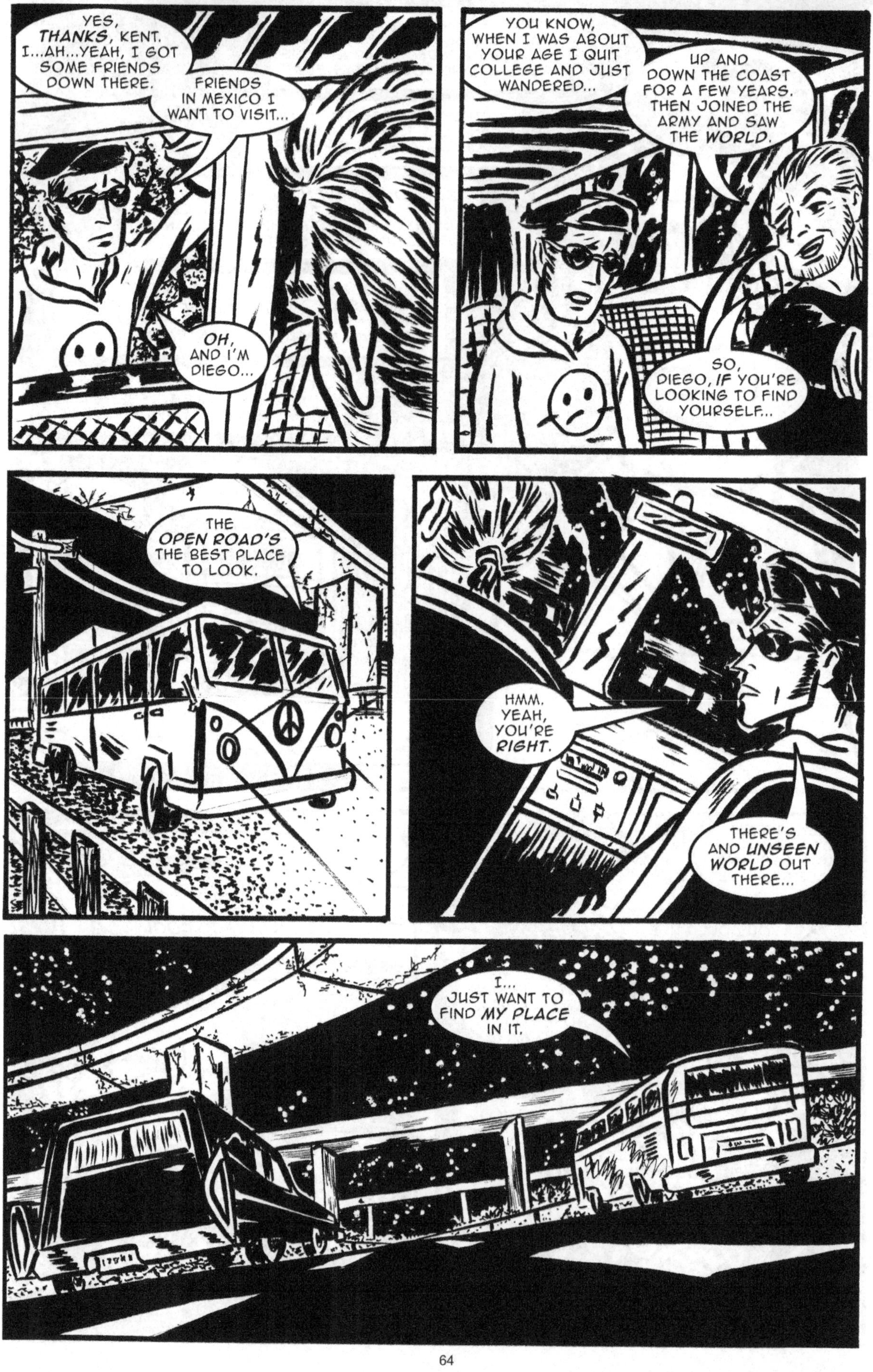
YES, THANKS, KENT. I...AH...YEAH, I GOT SOME FRIENDS DOWN THERE.
FRIENDS IN MEXICO I WANT TO VISIT...
OH, AND I'M DIEGO...
YOU KNOW, WHEN I WAS ABOUT YOUR AGE I QUIT COLLEGE AND JUST WANDERED...
UP AND DOWN THE COAST FOR A FEW YEARS. THEN JOINED THE ARMY AND SAW THE WORLD.
SO, DIEGO, IF YOU'RE LOOKING TO FIND YOURSELF...
THE OPEN ROAD'S THE BEST PLACE TO LOOK.
HMM. YEAH, YOU'RE RIGHT.
THERE'S AND UNSEEN WORLD OUT THERE...
I... JUST WANT TO FIND MY PLACE IN IT.

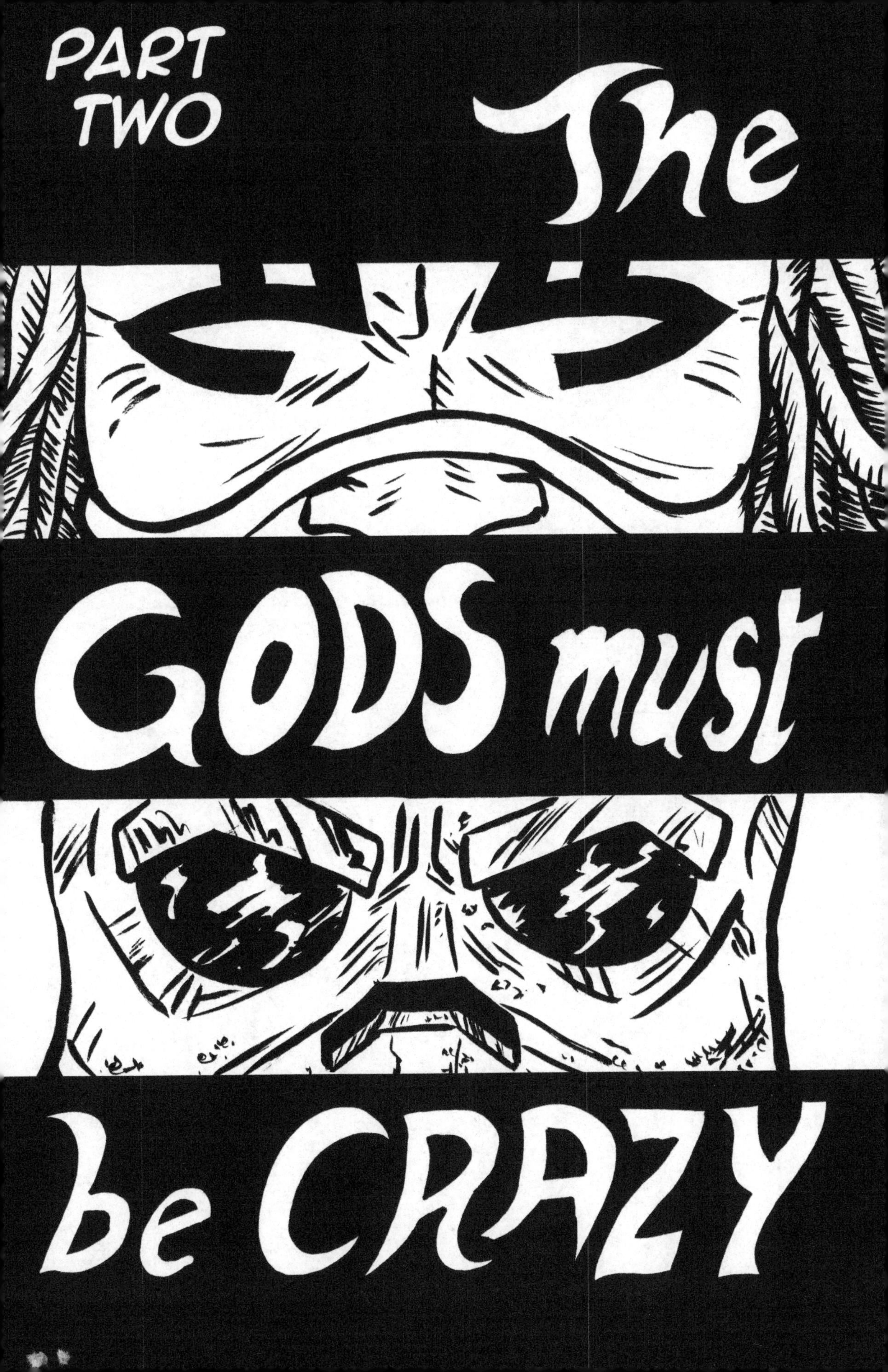
PART TWO
The
GODS must
be CRAZY

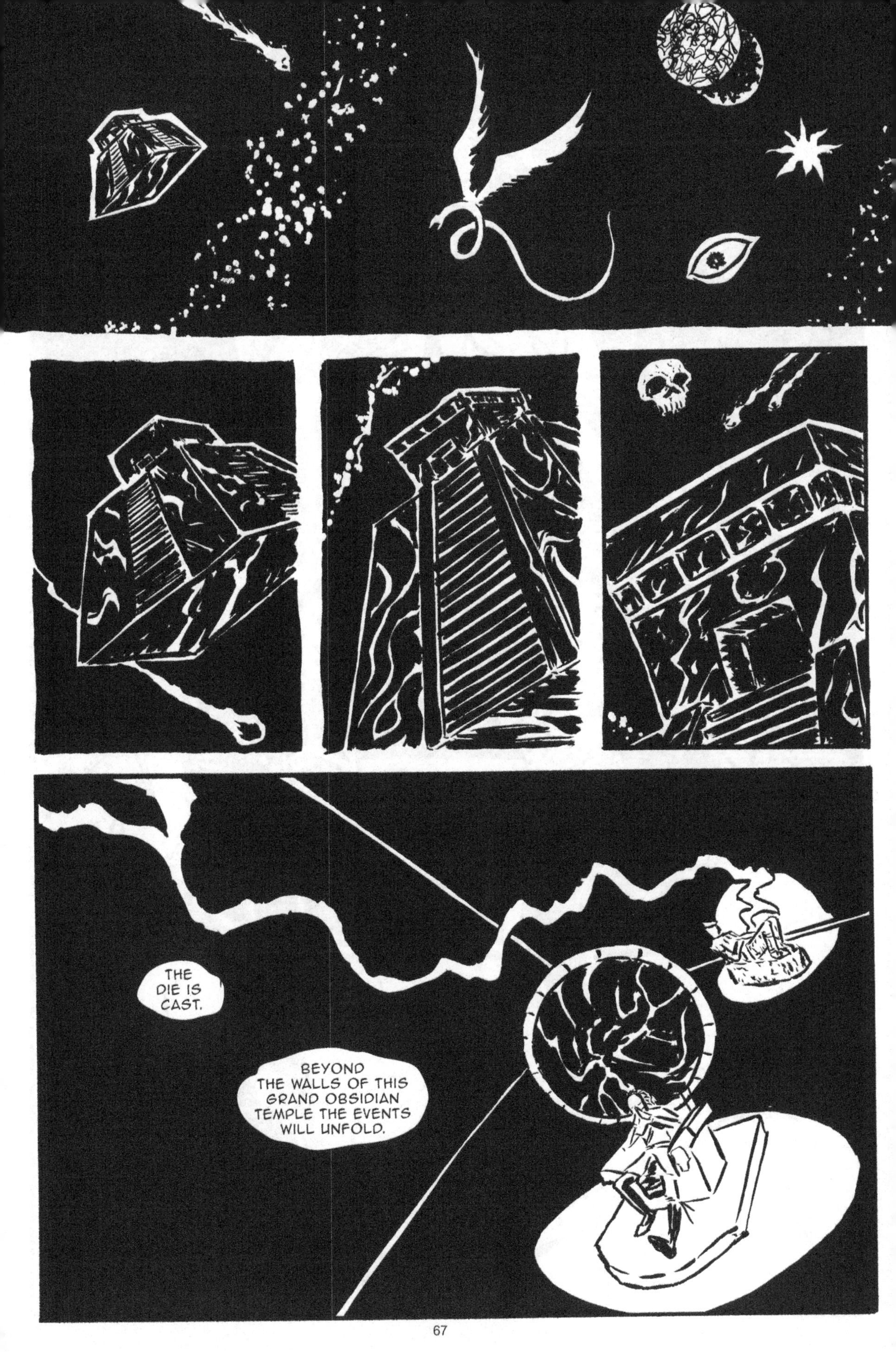
THE DIE IS CAST.
BEYOND THE WALLS OF THIS GRAND OBSIDIAN TEMPLE THE EVENTS WILL UNFOLD.

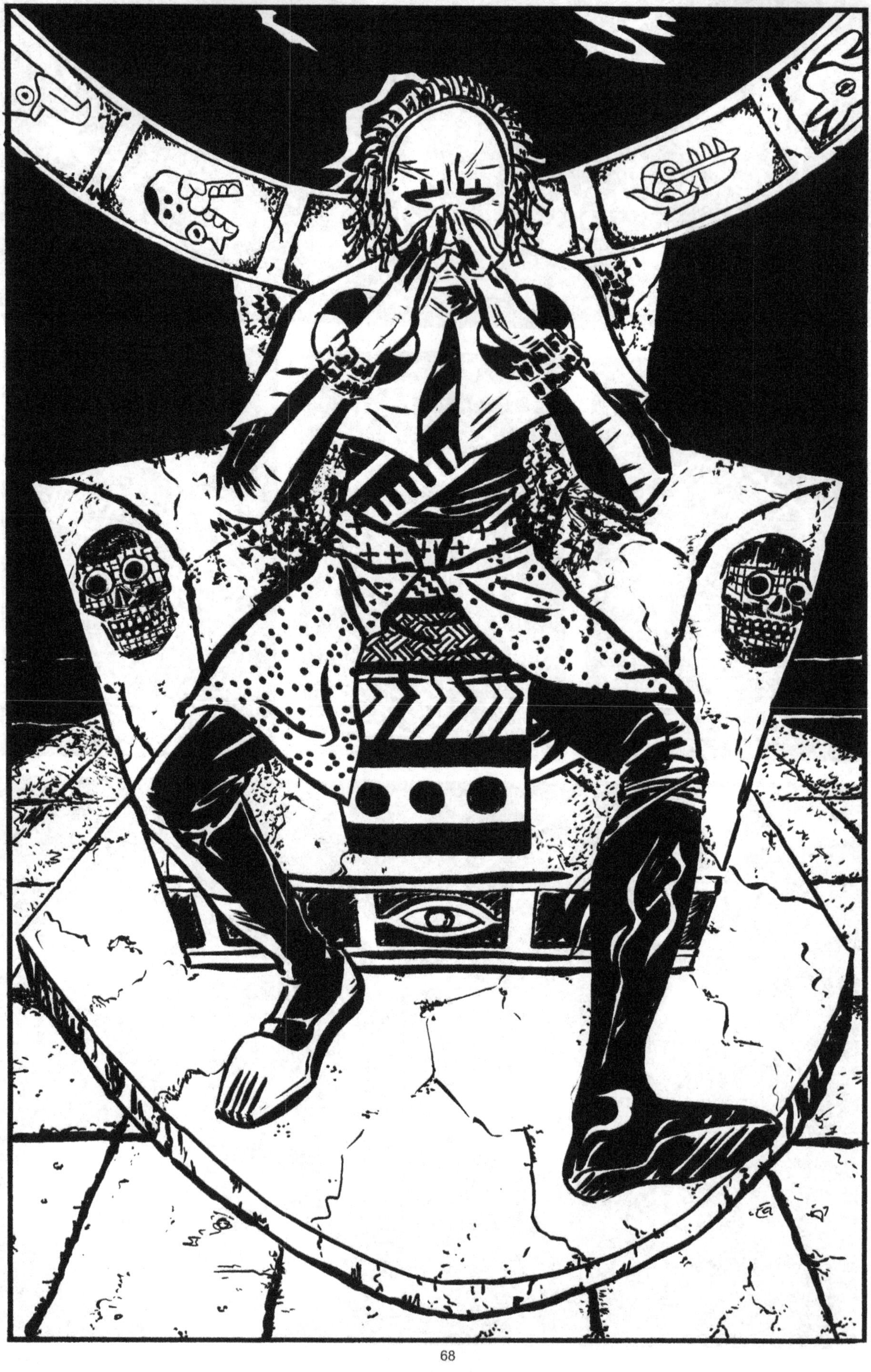

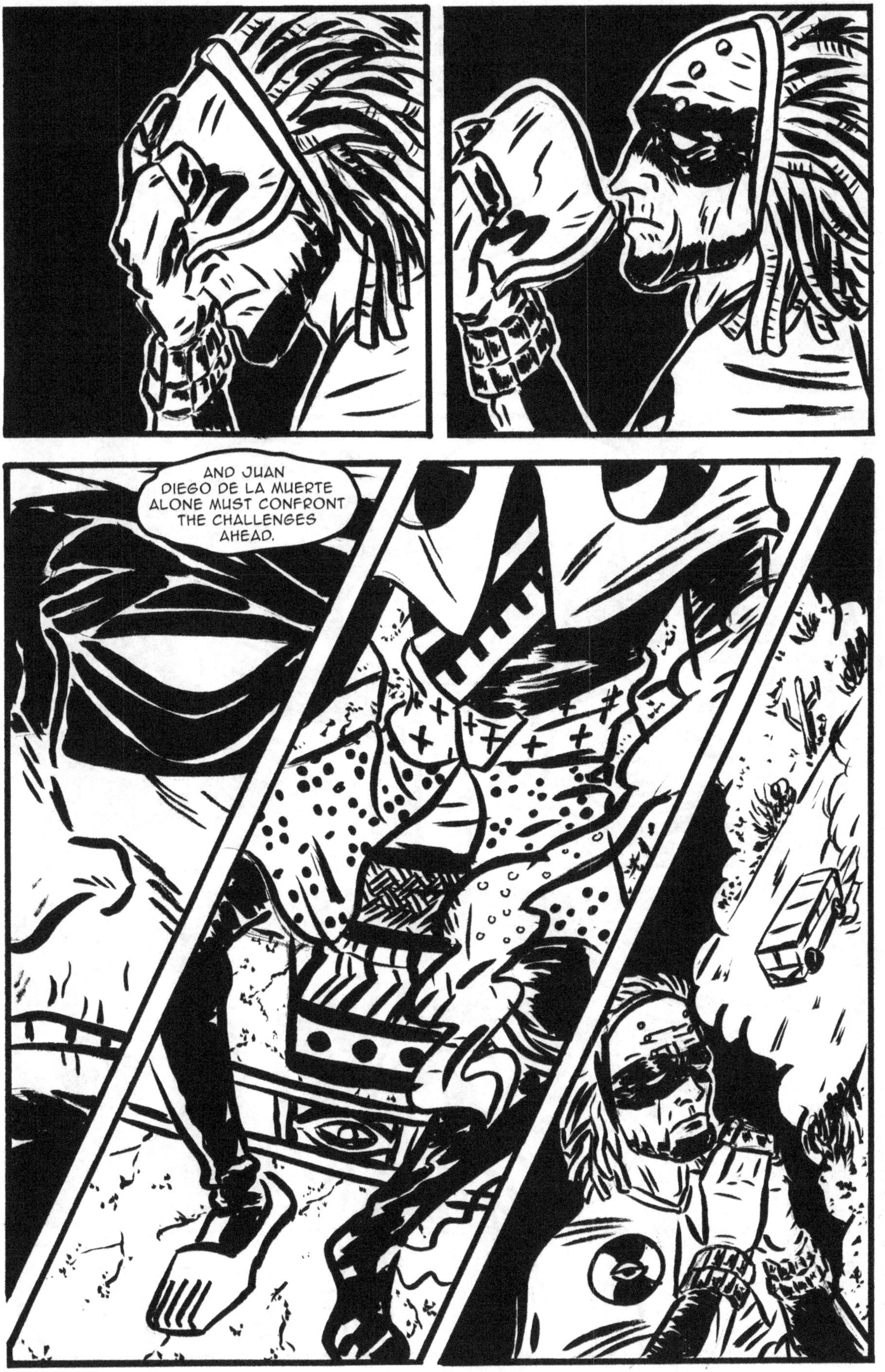
AND JUAN DIEGO DE LA MUERTE ALONE MUST CONFRONT THE CHALLENGES AHEAD.

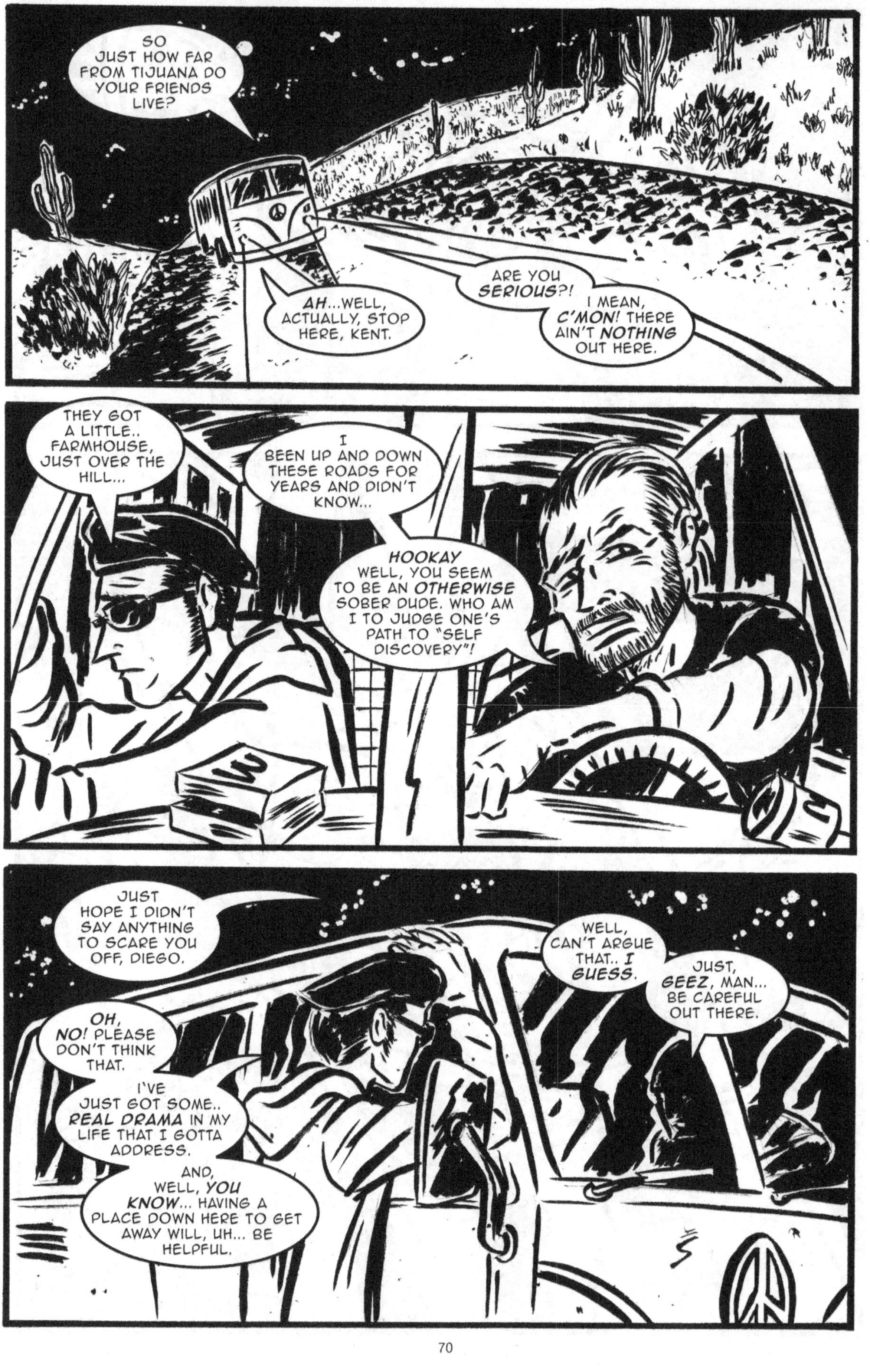
SO JUST HOW FAR FROM TIJUANA DO YOUR FRIENDS LIVE?
AH...WELL, ACTUALLY, STOP HERE, KENT.
ARE YOU SERIOUS?!
I MEAN, C'MON! THERE AIN'T NOTHING OUT HERE.
THEY GOT A LITTLE.. FARMHOUSE, JUST OVER THE HILL...
I BEEN UP AND DOWN THESE ROADS FOR YEARS AND DIDN'T KNOW...
HOOKAY WELL, YOU SEEM TO BE AN OTHERWISE SOBER DUDE. WHO AM I TO JUDGE ONE'S PATH TO "SELF DISCOVERY"!
JUST HOPE I DIDN'T SAY ANYTHING TO SCARE YOU OFF, DIEGO.
OH, NO! PLEASE DON'T THINK THAT.
I'VE JUST GOT SOME.. REAL DRAMA IN MY LIFE THAT I GOTTA ADDRESS.
AND, WELL, YOU KNOW... HAVING A PLACE DOWN HERE TO GET AWAY WILL, UH... BE HELPFUL.
WELL, CAN'T ARGUE THAT.. I GUESS.
JUST, GEEZ, MAN... BE CAREFUL OUT THERE.

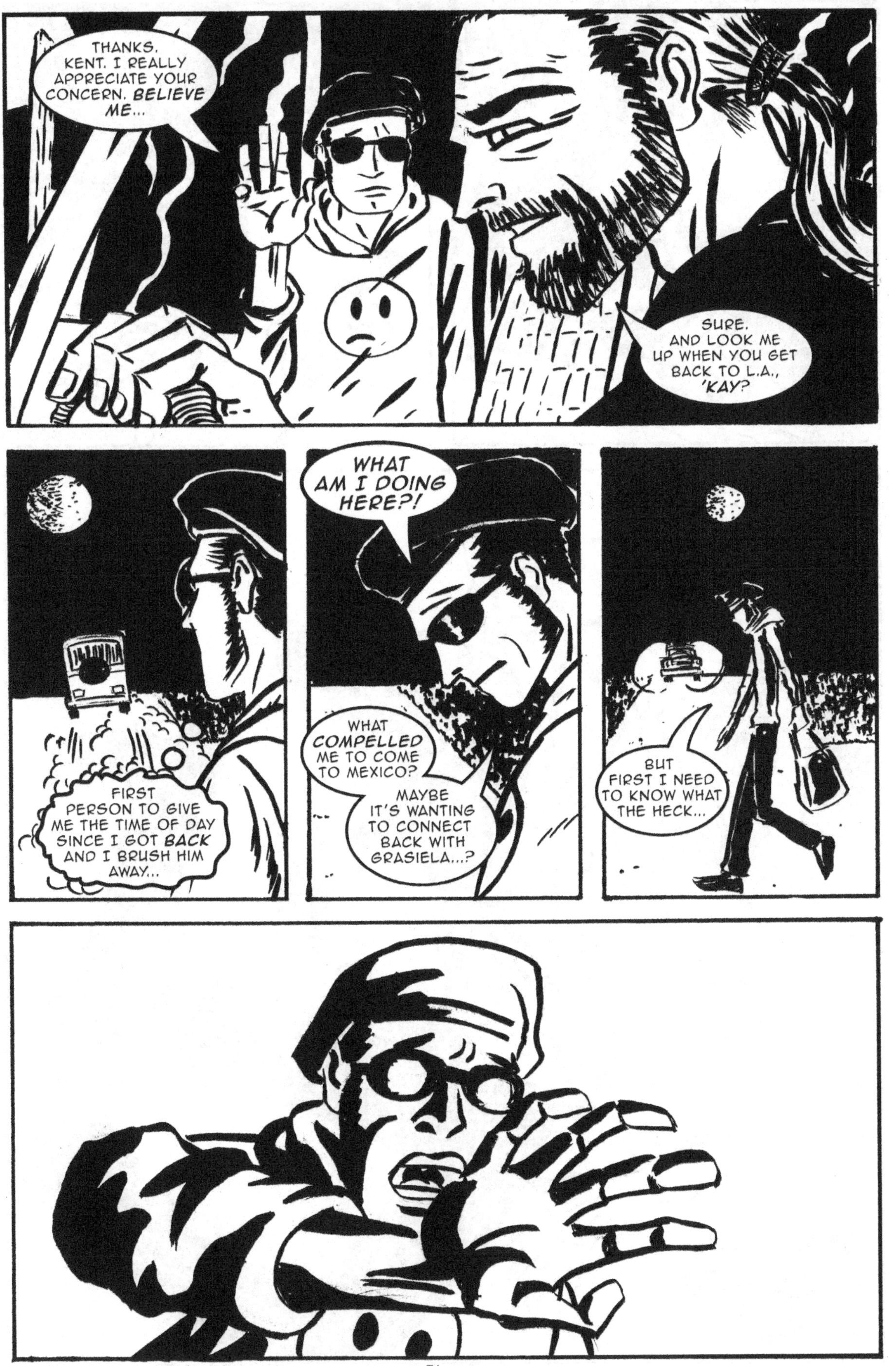
THANKS. KENT. I REALLY APPRECIATE YOUR CONCERN. BELIEVE ME...
SURE. AND LOOK ME UP WHEN YOU GET BACK TO L.A., 'KAY?
FIRST PERSON TO GIVE ME THE TIME OF DAY SINCE I GOT BACK AND I BRUSH HIM AWAY...
WHAT AM I DOING HERE?!
WHAT COMPELLED ME TO COME TO MEXICO?
MAYBE IT'S WANTING TO CONNECT BACK WITH GRASIELA...?
BUT FIRST I NEED TO KNOW WHAT THE HECK...

KA-THUMP!
¡POR DIOS!*
SKREECHHHH
* "DEAR GOD!"

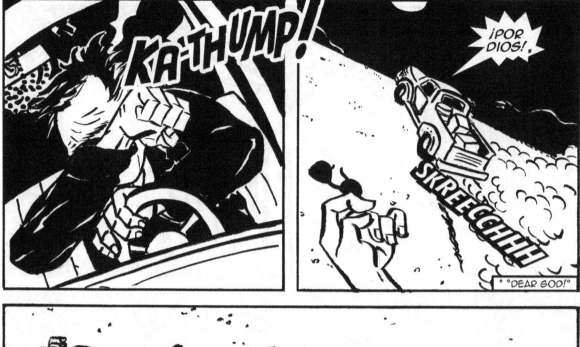

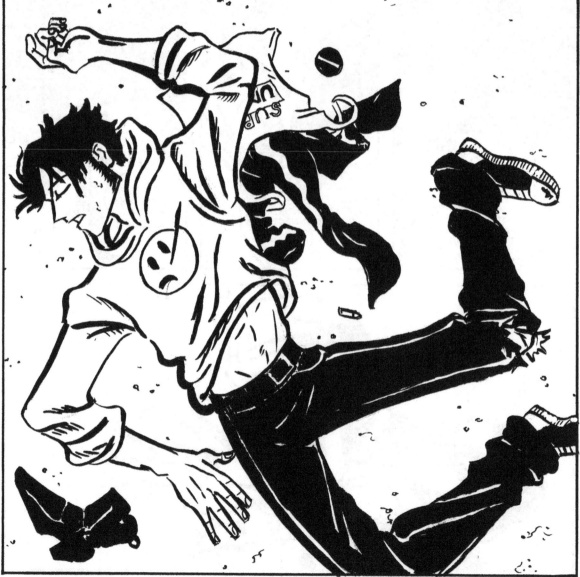

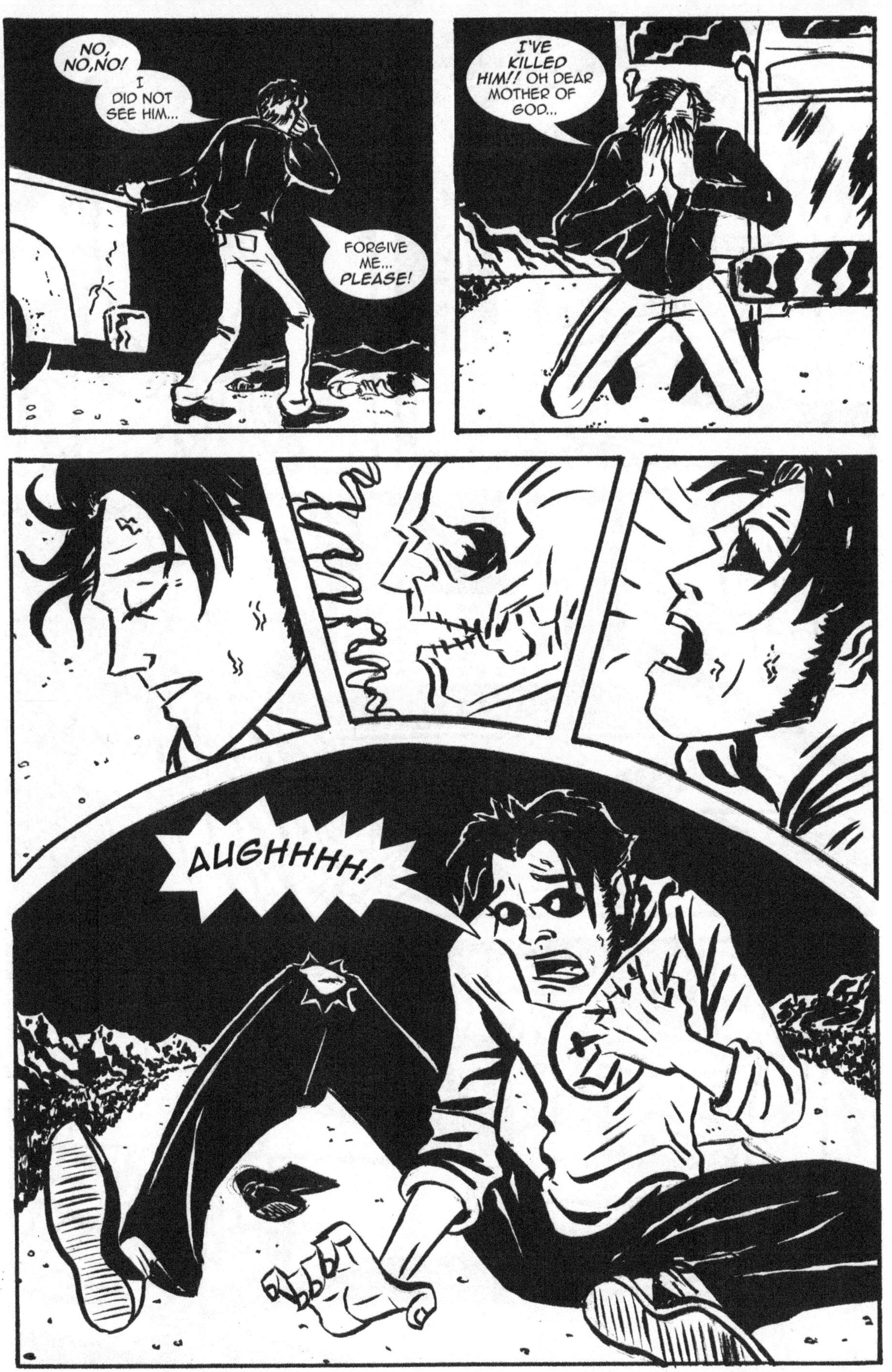
NO, NO,NO!
I DID NOT SEE HIM...
FORGIVE ME... PLEASE!
I'VE KILLED HIM!! OH DEAR MOTHER OF GOD...
AUGHHHH!

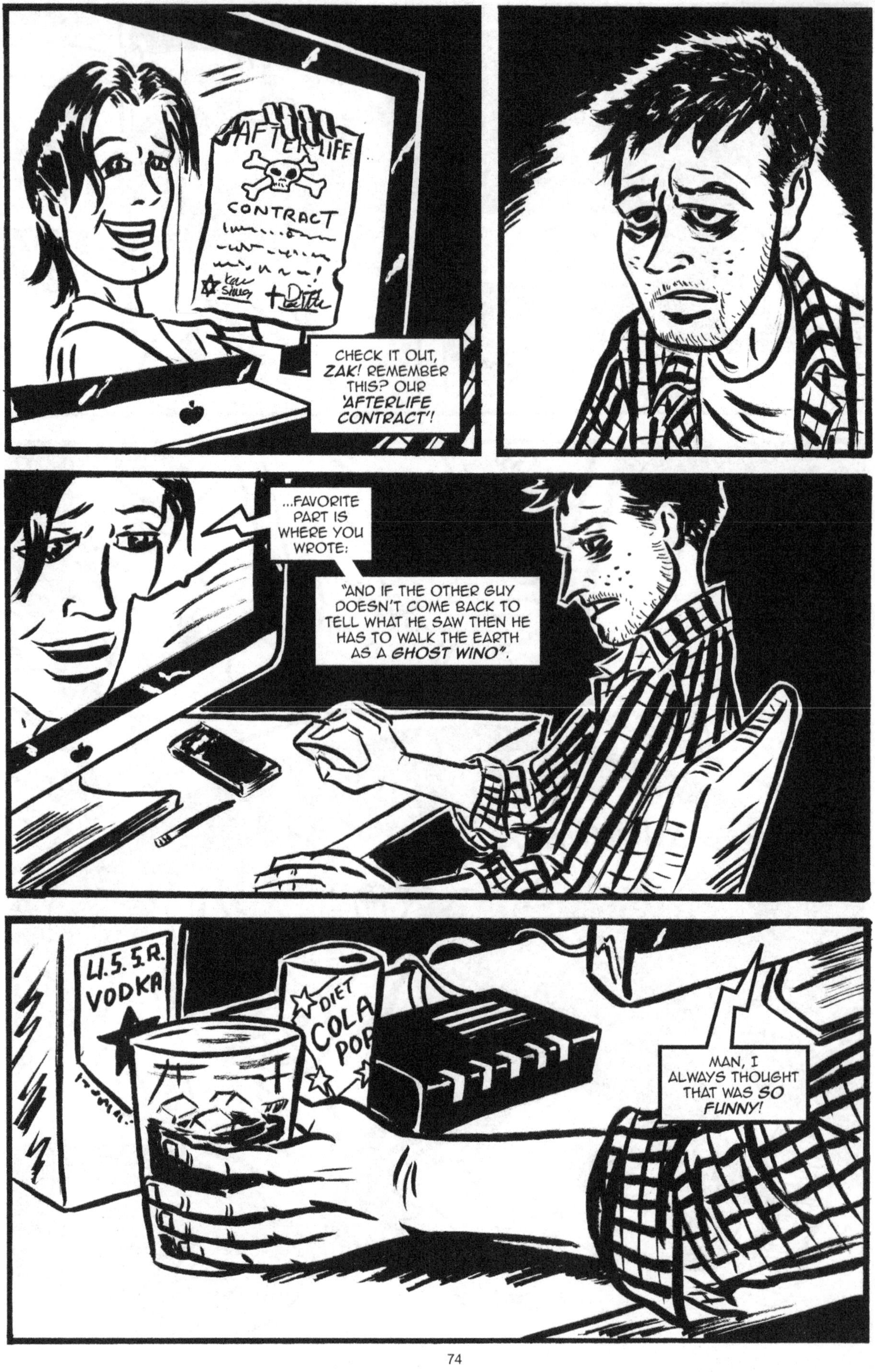
AFTERLIFE
CONTRACT
CHECK IT OUT, ZAK! REMEMBER THIS? OUR 'AFTERLIFE CONTRACT'!
...FAVORITE PART IS WHERE YOU WROTE:
"AND IF THE OTHER GUY DOESN'T COME BACK TO TELL WHAT HE SAW THEN HE HAS TO WALK THE EARTH AS A GHOST WINO".
U.S.S.R. VODKA
DIET COLA POP
MAN, I ALWAYS THOUGHT THAT WAS SO FUNNY!

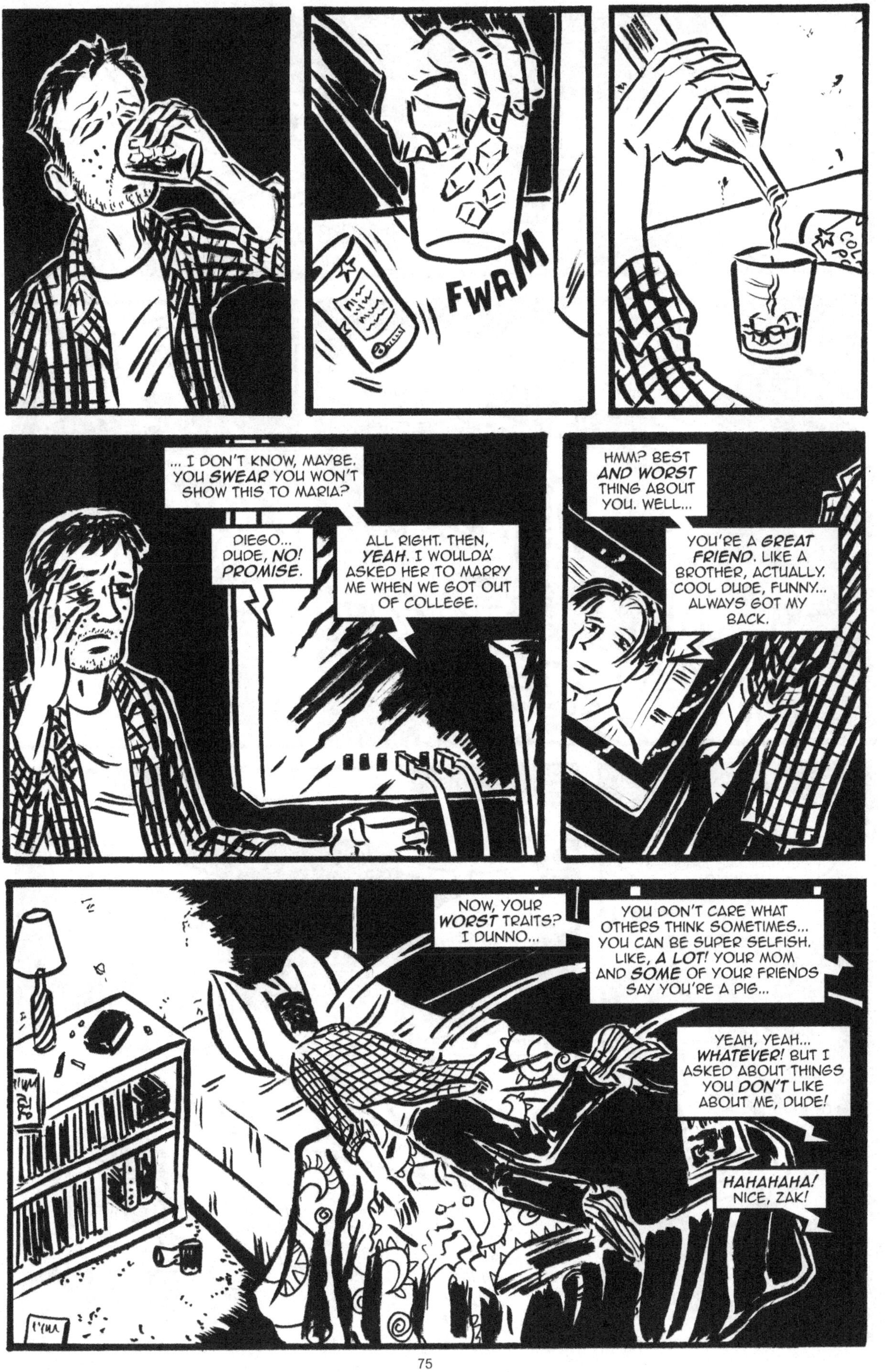
FWAM
... I DON'T KNOW, MAYBE. YOU SWEAR YOU WON'T SHOW THIS TO MARIA?
DIEGO... DUDE, NO! PROMISE.
ALL RIGHT. THEN, YEAH. I WOULDA' ASKED HER TO MARRY ME WHEN WE GOT OUT OF COLLEGE.
HMM? BEST AND WORST THING ABOUT YOU. WELL...
YOU'RE A GREAT FRIEND. LIKE A BROTHER, ACTUALLY. COOL DUDE, FUNNY... ALWAYS GOT MY BACK.
NOW, YOUR WORST TRAITS? I DUNNO...
YOU DON'T CARE WHAT OTHERS THINK SOMETIMES... YOU CAN BE SUPER SELFISH. LIKE, A LOT! YOUR MOM AND SOME OF YOUR FRIENDS SAY YOU'RE A PIG...
YEAH, YEAH... WHATEVER! BUT I ASKED ABOUT THINGS YOU DON'T LIKE ABOUT ME, DUDE!
HAHAHAHA! NICE, ZAK!

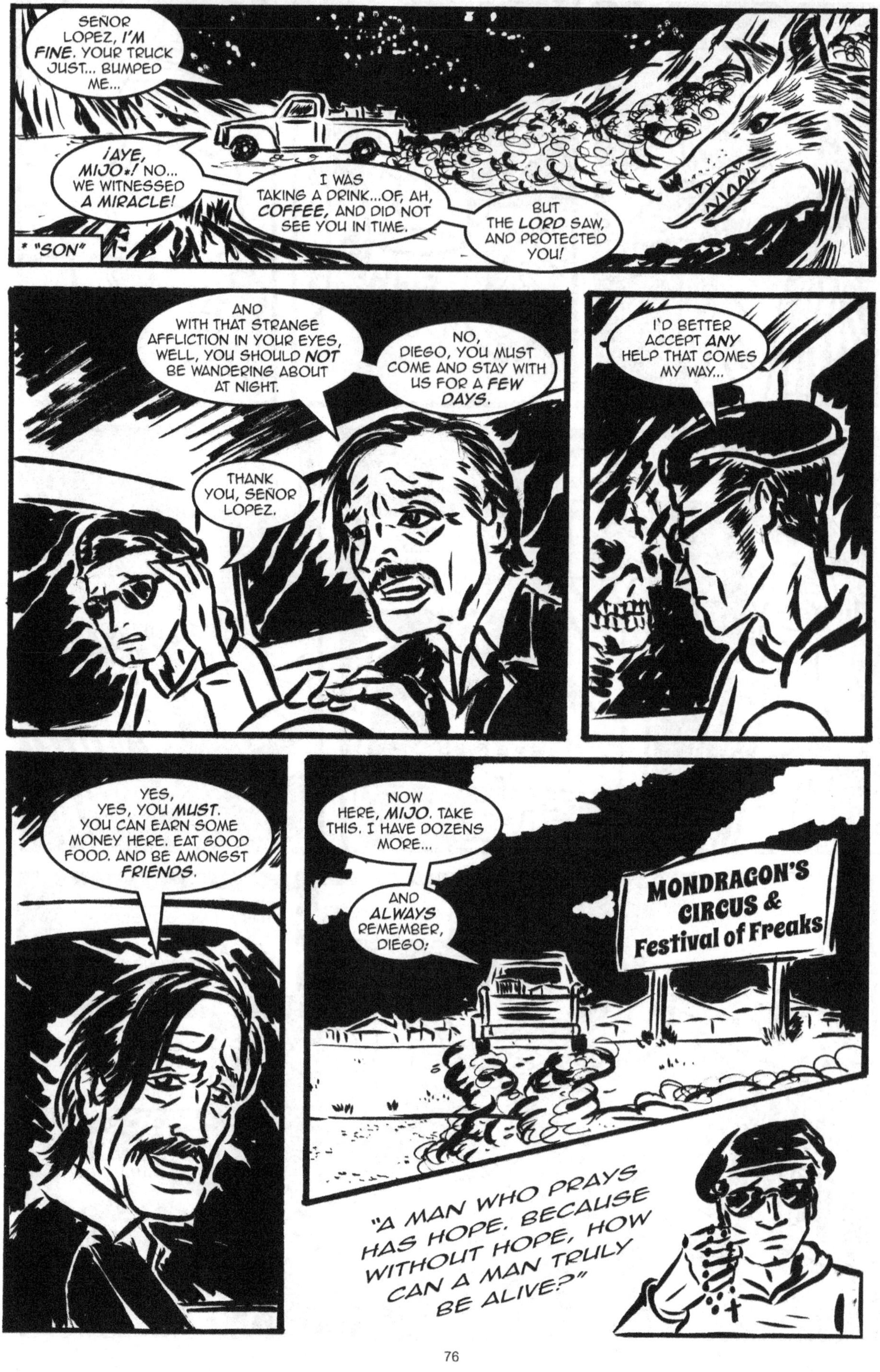
SEÑOR LOPEZ, I'M FINE. YOUR TRUCK JUST... BUMPED ME...
¡AYE, MIJO*! NO... WE WITNESSED A MIRACLE!
I WAS TAKING A DRINK...OF, AH, COFFEE, AND DID NOT SEE YOU IN TIME.
BUT THE LORD SAW, AND PROTECTED YOU!
* "SON"
AND WITH THAT STRANGE AFFLICTION IN YOUR EYES, WELL, YOU SHOULD NOT BE WANDERING ABOUT AT NIGHT.
NO, DIEGO, YOU MUST COME AND STAY WITH US FOR A FEW DAYS.
THANK YOU, SEÑOR LOPEZ.
I'D BETTER ACCEPT ANY HELP THAT COMES MY WAY...
YES, YES, YOU MUST. YOU CAN EARN SOME MONEY HERE. EAT GOOD FOOD. AND BE AMONGST FRIENDS.
NOW HERE, MIJO. TAKE THIS. I HAVE DOZENS MORE...
AND ALWAYS REMEMBER, DIEGO:
MONDRAGON'S CIRCUS & Festival of Freaks
"A MAN WHO PRAYS HAS HOPE. BECAUSE WITHOUT HOPE, HOW CAN A MAN TRULY BE ALIVE?"

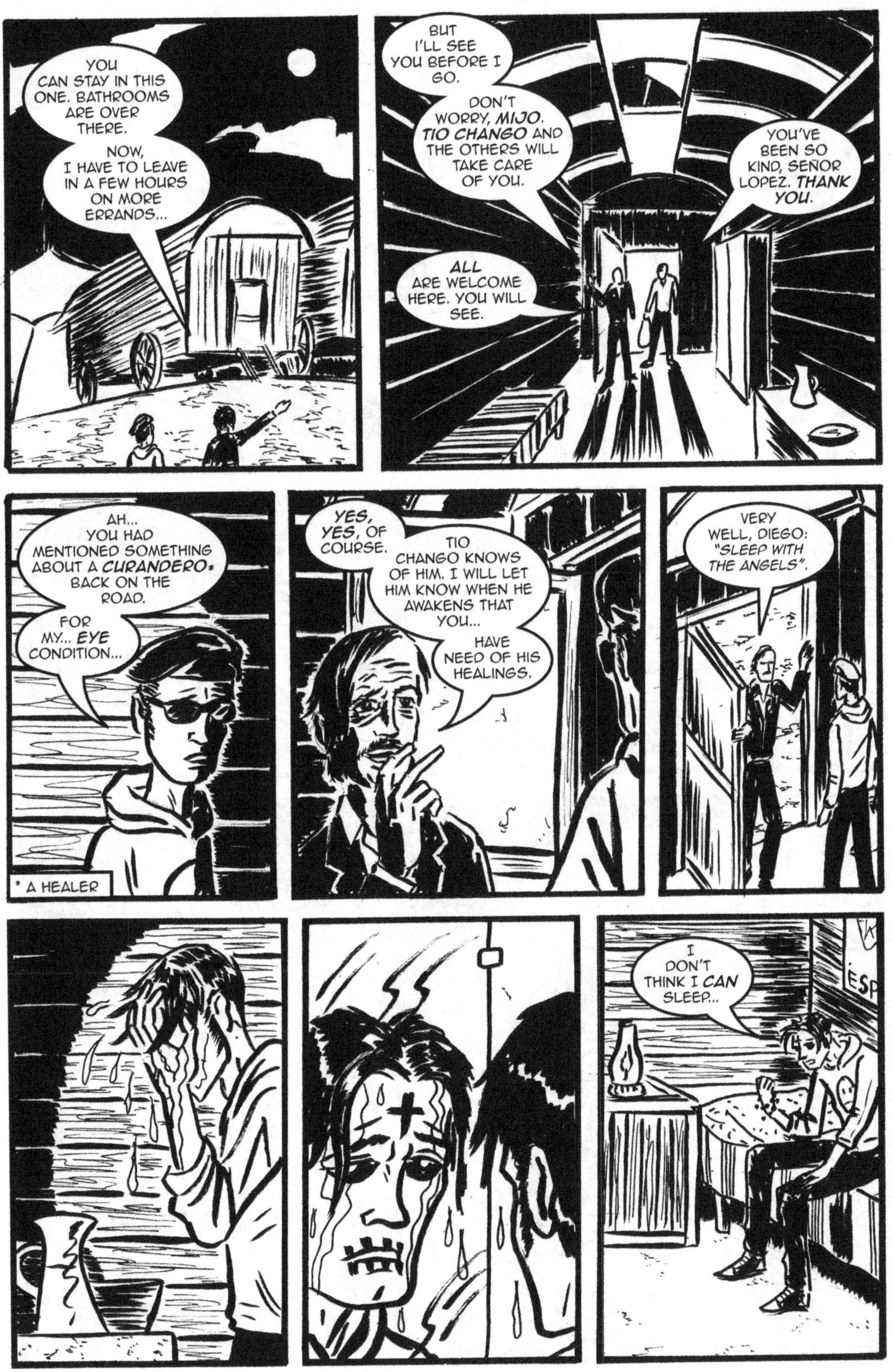
YOU CAN STAY IN THIS ONE. BATHROOMS ARE OVER THERE.
NOW, I HAVE TO LEAVE IN A FEW HOURS ON MORE ERRANDS...
BUT I'LL SEE YOU BEFORE I GO.
DON'T WORRY, MIJO. TIO CHANGO AND THE OTHERS WILL TAKE CARE OF YOU.
YOU'VE BEEN SO KIND, SEÑOR LOPEZ. THANK YOU.
ALL ARE WELCOME HERE. YOU WILL SEE.
AH... YOU HAD MENTIONED SOMETHING ABOUT A CURANDERO* BACK ON THE ROAD.
FOR MY... EYE CONDITION...
* A HEALER
YES, YES, OF COURSE.
TIO CHANGO KNOWS OF HIM. I WILL LET HIM KNOW WHEN HE AWAKENS THAT YOU...
HAVE NEED OF HIS HEALINGS.
VERY WELL, DIEGO: "SLEEP WITH THE ANGELS".
I DON'T THINK I CAN SLEEP...
ESP

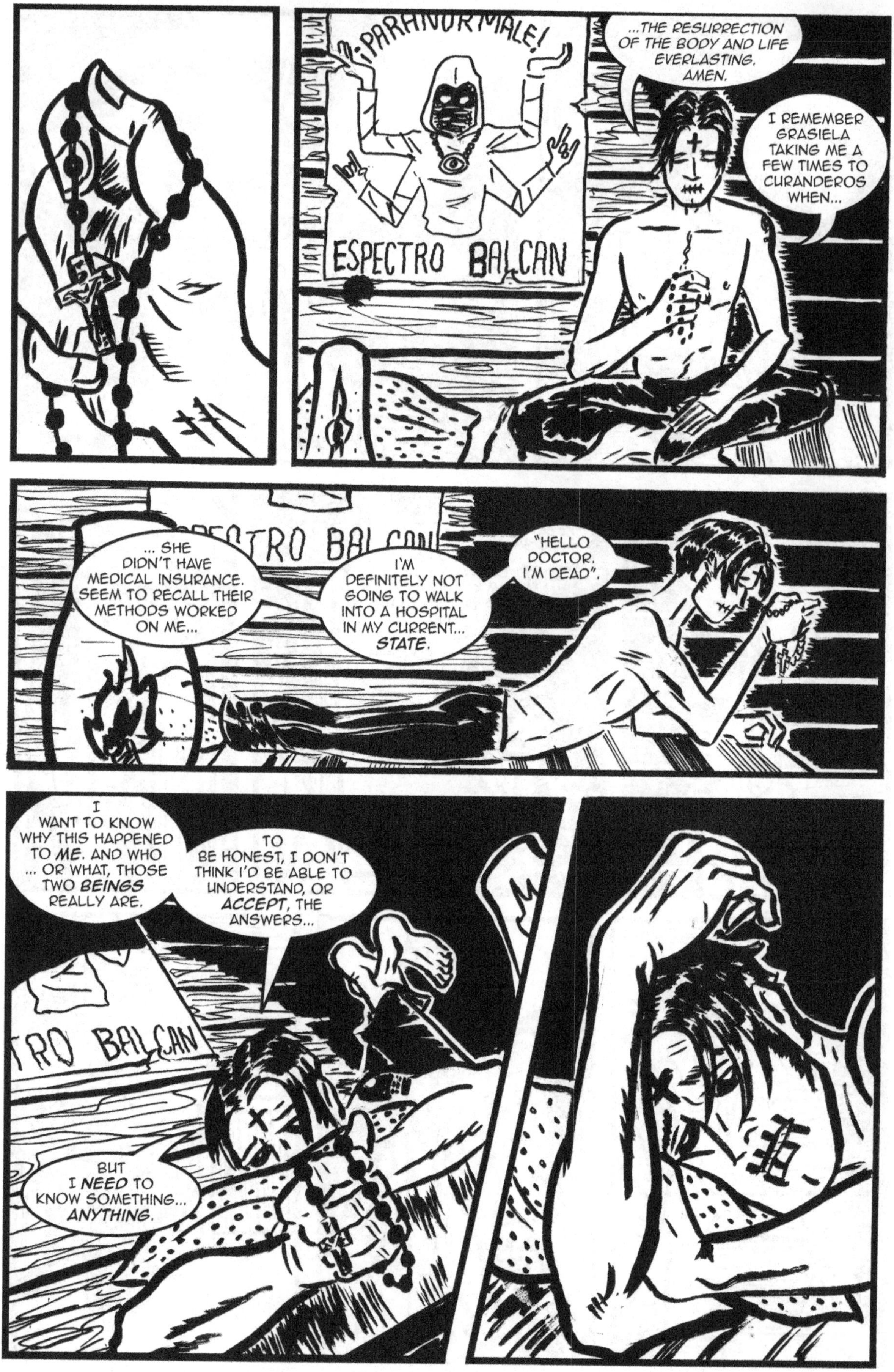
¡PARANORMALE!
ESPECTRO BALCAN
...THE RESURRECTION OF THE BODY AND LIFE EVERLASTING. AMEN.
I REMEMBER GRASIELA TAKING ME A FEW TIMES TO CURANDEROS WHEN...
... SHE DIDN'T HAVE MEDICAL INSURANCE. SEEM TO RECALL THEIR METHODS WORKED ON ME...
I'M DEFINITELY NOT GOING TO WALK INTO A HOSPITAL IN MY CURRENT... *STATE*.
"HELLO DOCTOR. I'M DEAD".
I WANT TO KNOW WHY THIS HAPPENED TO *ME*. AND WHO ... OR WHAT, THOSE TWO *BEINGS* REALLY ARE.
TO BE HONEST, I DON'T THINK I'D BE ABLE TO UNDERSTAND, OR *ACCEPT*, THE ANSWERS...
BUT I *NEED* TO KNOW SOMETHING... *ANYTHING*.

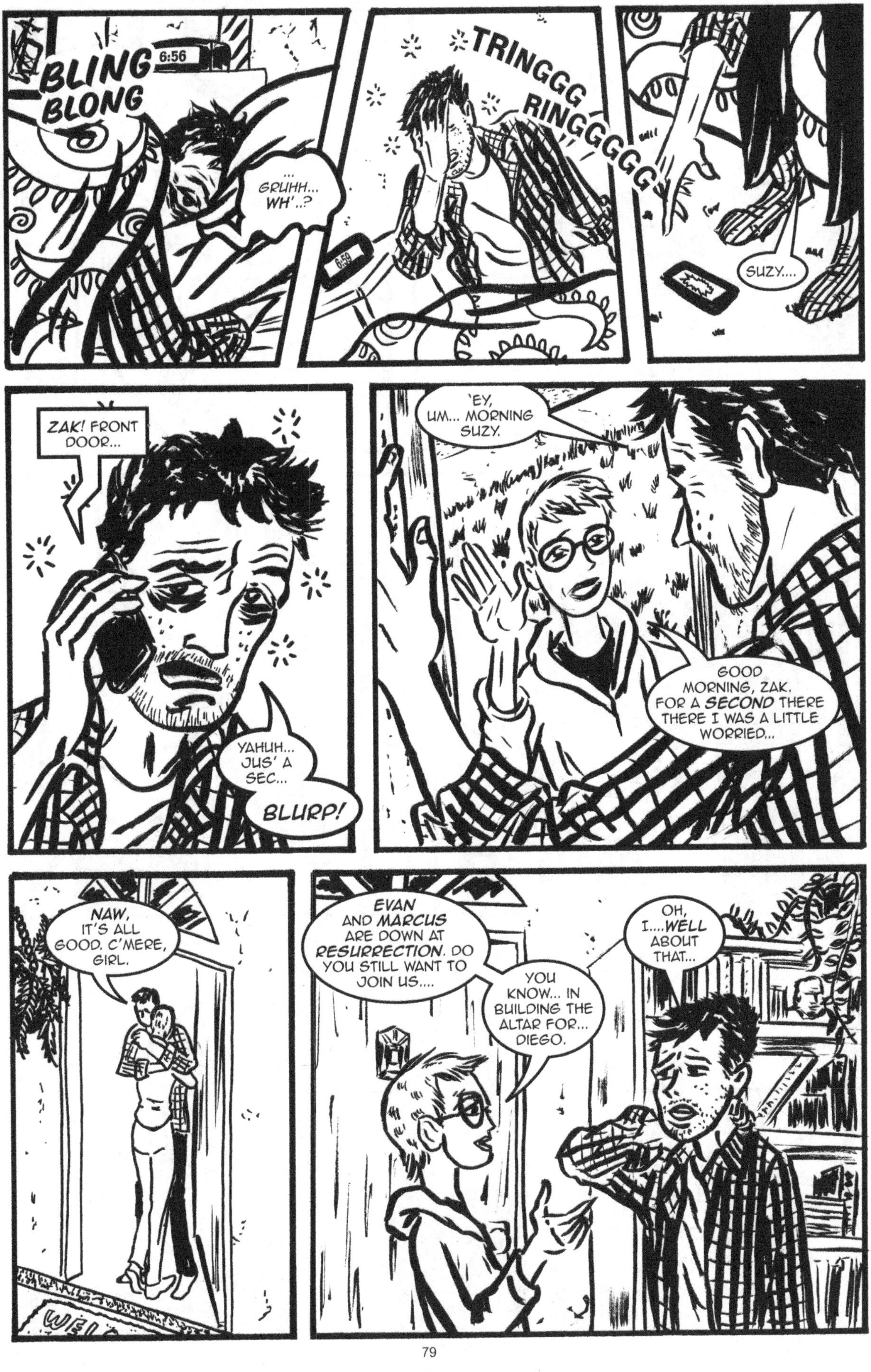
BLING
BLONG
6:56
... GRUHH... WH'..?
TRINGGG
RINGGGGGG
6:59
SUZY....
ZAK! FRONT DOOR...
YAHUH... JUS' A SEC...
BLURP!
'EY, UM... MORNING SUZY.
GOOD MORNING, ZAK. FOR A SECOND THERE THERE I WAS A LITTLE WORRIED...
NAW, IT'S ALL GOOD. C'MERE, GIRL.
EVAN AND MARCUS ARE DOWN AT RESURRECTION. DO YOU STILL WANT TO JOIN US....
YOU KNOW... IN BUILDING THE ALTAR FOR... DIEGO.
OH, I....WELL ABOUT THAT...

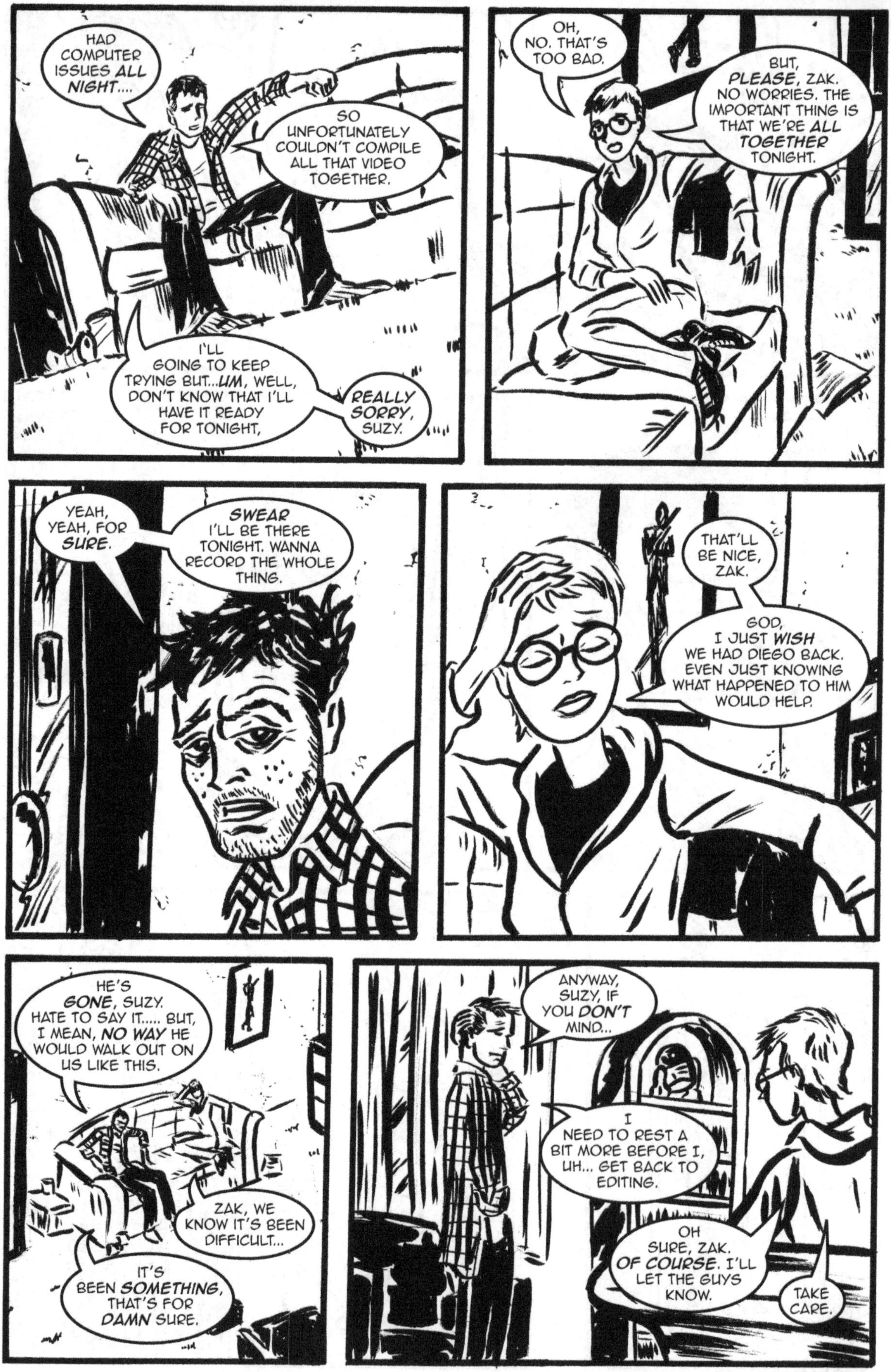
HAD COMPUTER ISSUES ALL NIGHT....
SO UNFORTUNATELY COULDN'T COMPILE ALL THAT VIDEO TOGETHER.
I'LL GOING TO KEEP TRYING BUT...UM, WELL, DON'T KNOW THAT I'LL HAVE IT READY FOR TONIGHT,
REALLY SORRY, SUZY.
OH, NO. THAT'S TOO BAD.
BUT, PLEASE, ZAK. NO WORRIES. THE IMPORTANT THING IS THAT WE'RE ALL TOGETHER TONIGHT.
YEAH, YEAH, FOR SURE.
SWEAR I'LL BE THERE TONIGHT. WANNA RECORD THE WHOLE THING.
THAT'LL BE NICE, ZAK.
GOD, I JUST WISH WE HAD DIEGO BACK. EVEN JUST KNOWING WHAT HAPPENED TO HIM WOULD HELP.
HE'S GONE, SUZY. HATE TO SAY IT..... BUT, I MEAN, NO WAY HE WOULD WALK OUT ON US LIKE THIS.
ZAK, WE KNOW IT'S BEEN DIFFICULT...
IT'S BEEN SOMETHING, THAT'S FOR DAMN SURE.
ANYWAY, SUZY, IF YOU DON'T MIND...
I NEED TO REST A BIT MORE BEFORE I, UH... GET BACK TO EDITING.
OH SURE, ZAK. OF COURSE. I'LL LET THE GUYS KNOW.
TAKE CARE.

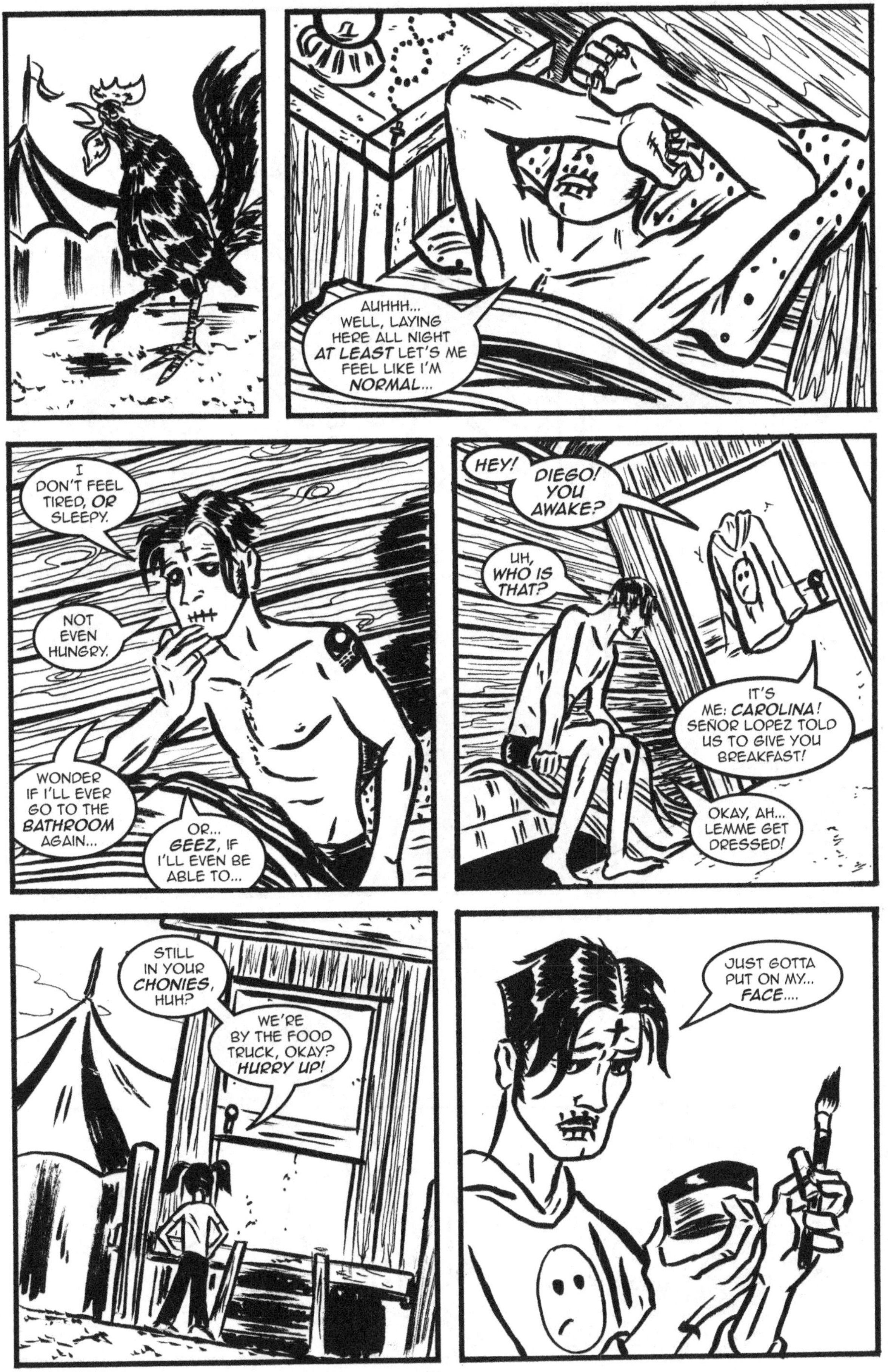
AUHHH... WELL, LAYING HERE ALL NIGHT AT LEAST LET'S ME FEEL LIKE I'M NORMAL...
I DON'T FEEL TIRED, OR SLEEPY.
NOT EVEN HUNGRY.
WONDER IF I'LL EVER GO TO THE BATHROOM AGAIN...
OR... GEEZ, IF I'LL EVEN BE ABLE TO...
HEY!
DIEGO! YOU AWAKE?
UH, WHO IS THAT?
IT'S ME: CAROLINA! SEÑOR LOPEZ TOLD US TO GIVE YOU BREAKFAST!
OKAY, AH... LEMME GET DRESSED!
STILL IN YOUR CHONIES, HUH?
WE'RE BY THE FOOD TRUCK, OKAY? HURRY UP!
JUST GOTTA PUT ON MY... FACE....

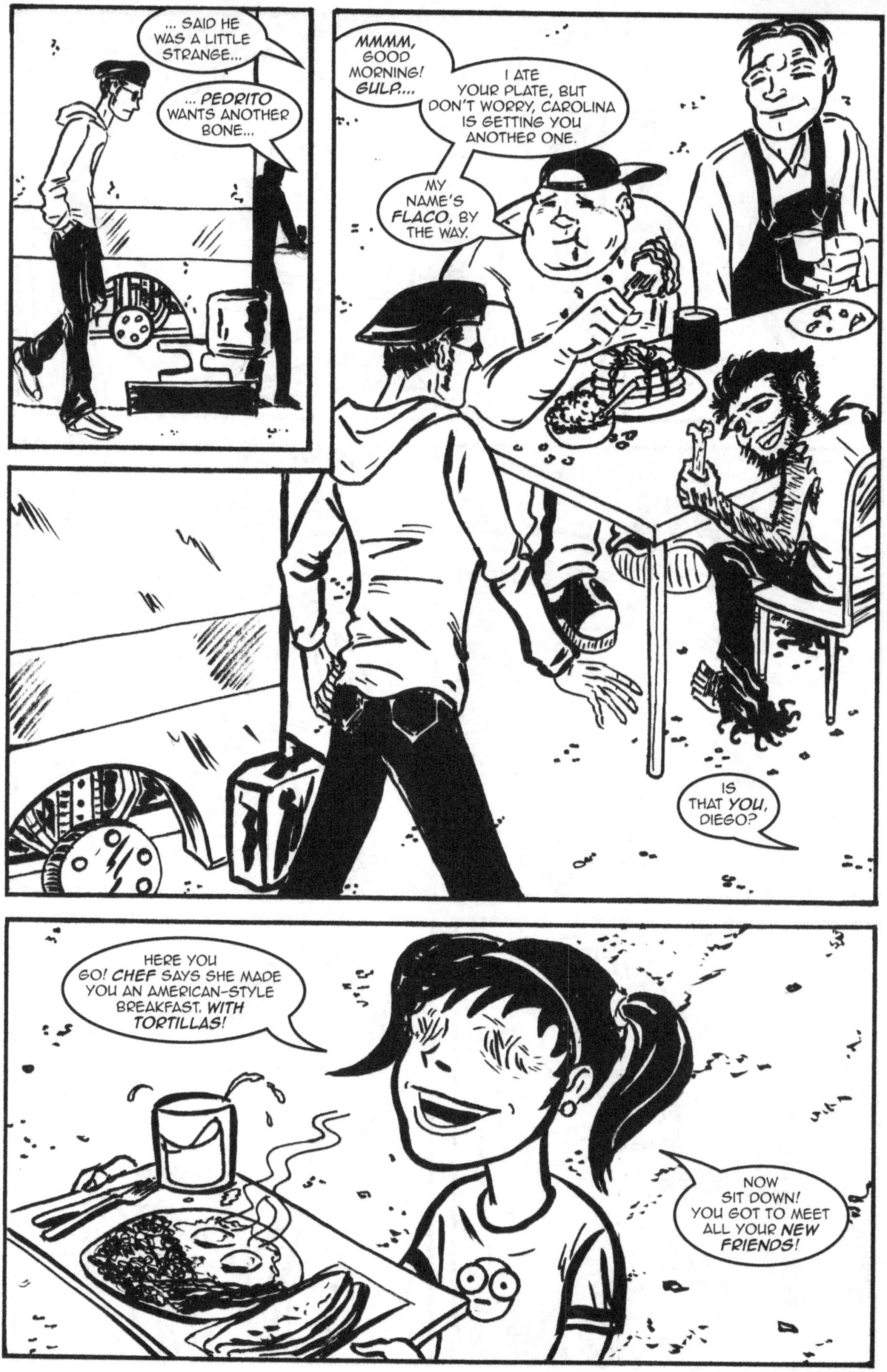
... SAID HE WAS A LITTLE STRANGE...
... PEDRITO WANTS ANOTHER BONE...
MMMM, GOOD MORNING! GULP....
I ATE YOUR PLATE, BUT DON'T WORRY, CAROLINA IS GETTING YOU ANOTHER ONE.
MY NAME'S FLACO, BY THE WAY.
IS THAT YOU, DIEGO?
HERE YOU GO! CHEF SAYS SHE MADE YOU AN AMERICAN-STYLE BREAKFAST. WITH TORTILLAS!
NOW SIT DOWN! YOU GOT TO MEET ALL YOUR NEW FRIENDS!

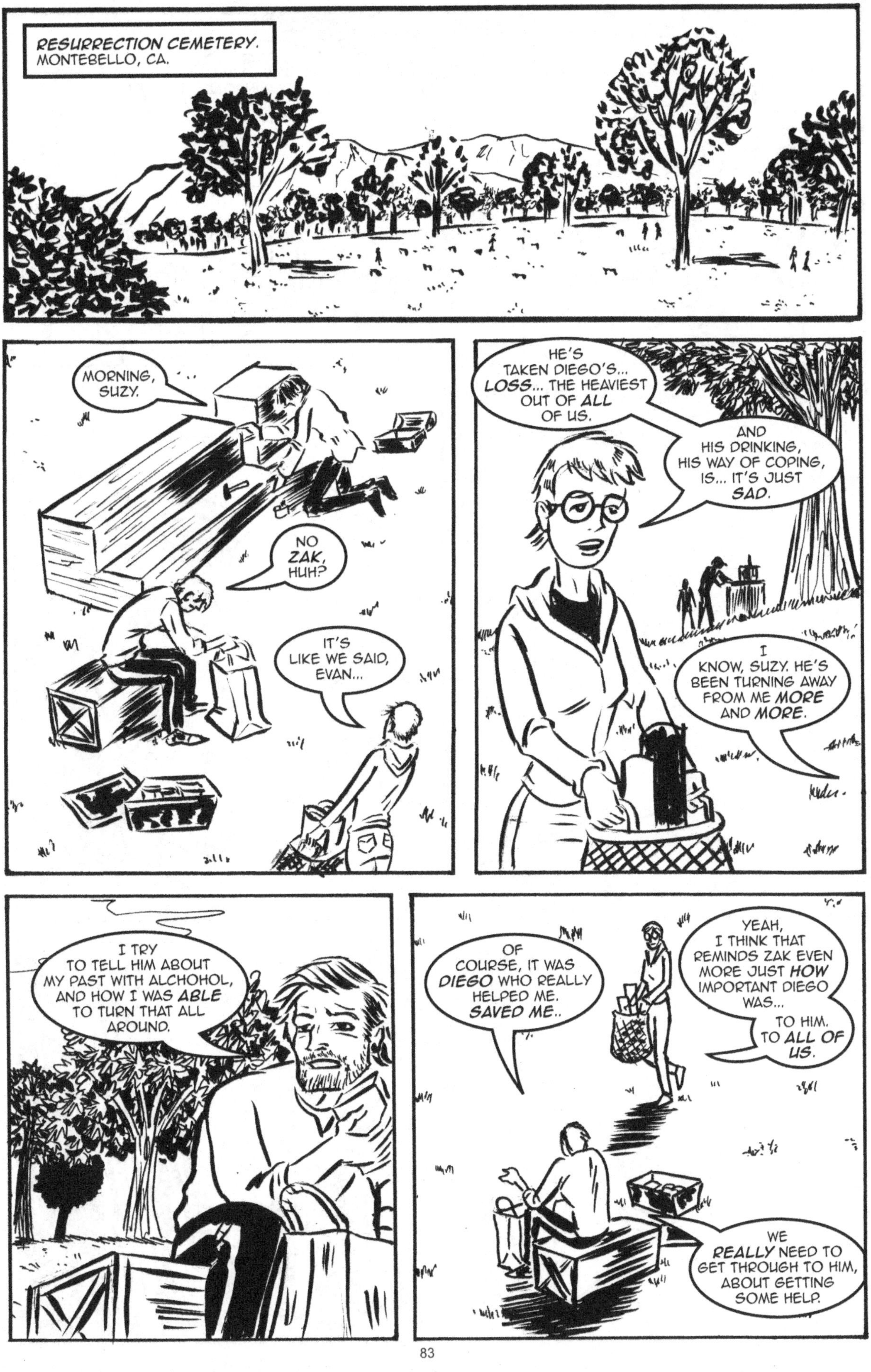

RESURRECTION CEMETERY.
MONTEBELLO, CA.
MORNING, SUZY.
NO ZAK, HUH?
IT'S LIKE WE SAID, EVAN...
HE'S TAKEN DIEGO'S... LOSS... THE HEAVIEST OUT OF ALL OF US.
AND HIS DRINKING, HIS WAY OF COPING, IS... IT'S JUST SAD.
I KNOW, SUZY. HE'S BEEN TURNING AWAY FROM ME MORE AND MORE.
I TRY TO TELL HIM ABOUT MY PAST WITH ALCHOHOL, AND HOW I WAS ABLE TO TURN THAT ALL AROUND.
OF COURSE, IT WAS DIEGO WHO REALLY HELPED ME. SAVED ME..
YEAH, I THINK THAT REMINDS ZAK EVEN MORE JUST HOW IMPORTANT DIEGO WAS...
TO HIM. TO ALL OF US.
WE REALLY NEED TO GET THROUGH TO HIM, ABOUT GETTING SOME HELP.

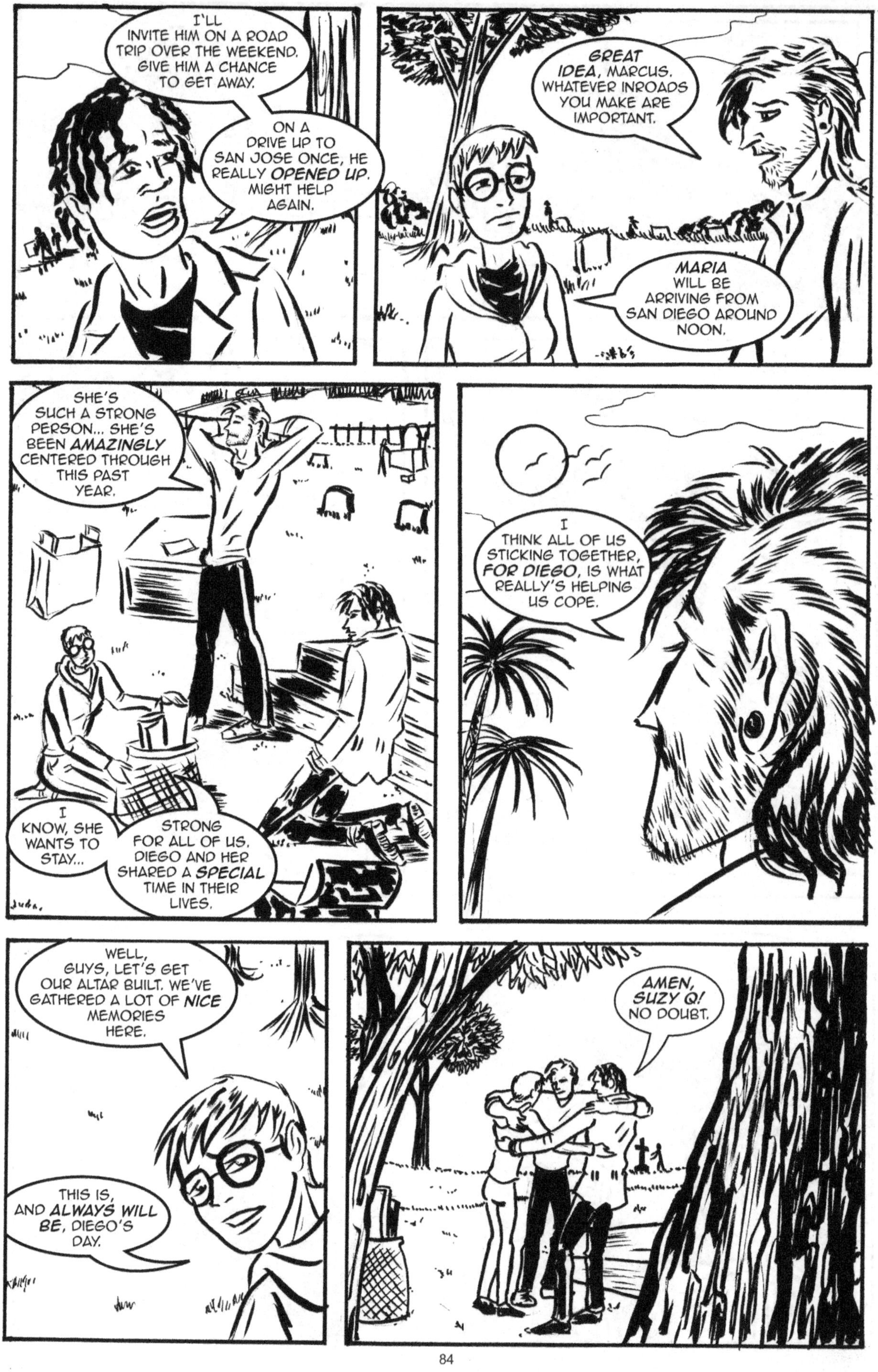
I'LL INVITE HIM ON A ROAD TRIP OVER THE WEEKEND. GIVE HIM A CHANCE TO GET AWAY.
ON A DRIVE UP TO SAN JOSE ONCE, HE REALLY OPENED UP. MIGHT HELP AGAIN.
GREAT IDEA, MARCUS. WHATEVER INROADS YOU MAKE ARE IMPORTANT.
MARIA WILL BE ARRIVING FROM SAN DIEGO AROUND NOON.
SHE'S SUCH A STRONG PERSON... SHE'S BEEN AMAZINGLY CENTERED THROUGH THIS PAST YEAR.
I KNOW, SHE WANTS TO STAY...
STRONG FOR ALL OF US. DIEGO AND HER SHARED A SPECIAL TIME IN THEIR LIVES.
I THINK ALL OF US STICKING TOGETHER, FOR DIEGO, IS WHAT REALLY'S HELPING US COPE.
WELL, GUYS, LET'S GET OUR ALTAR BUILT. WE'VE GATHERED A LOT OF NICE MEMORIES HERE.
THIS IS, AND ALWAYS WILL BE, DIEGO'S DAY.
AMEN, SUZY Q! NO DOUBT.

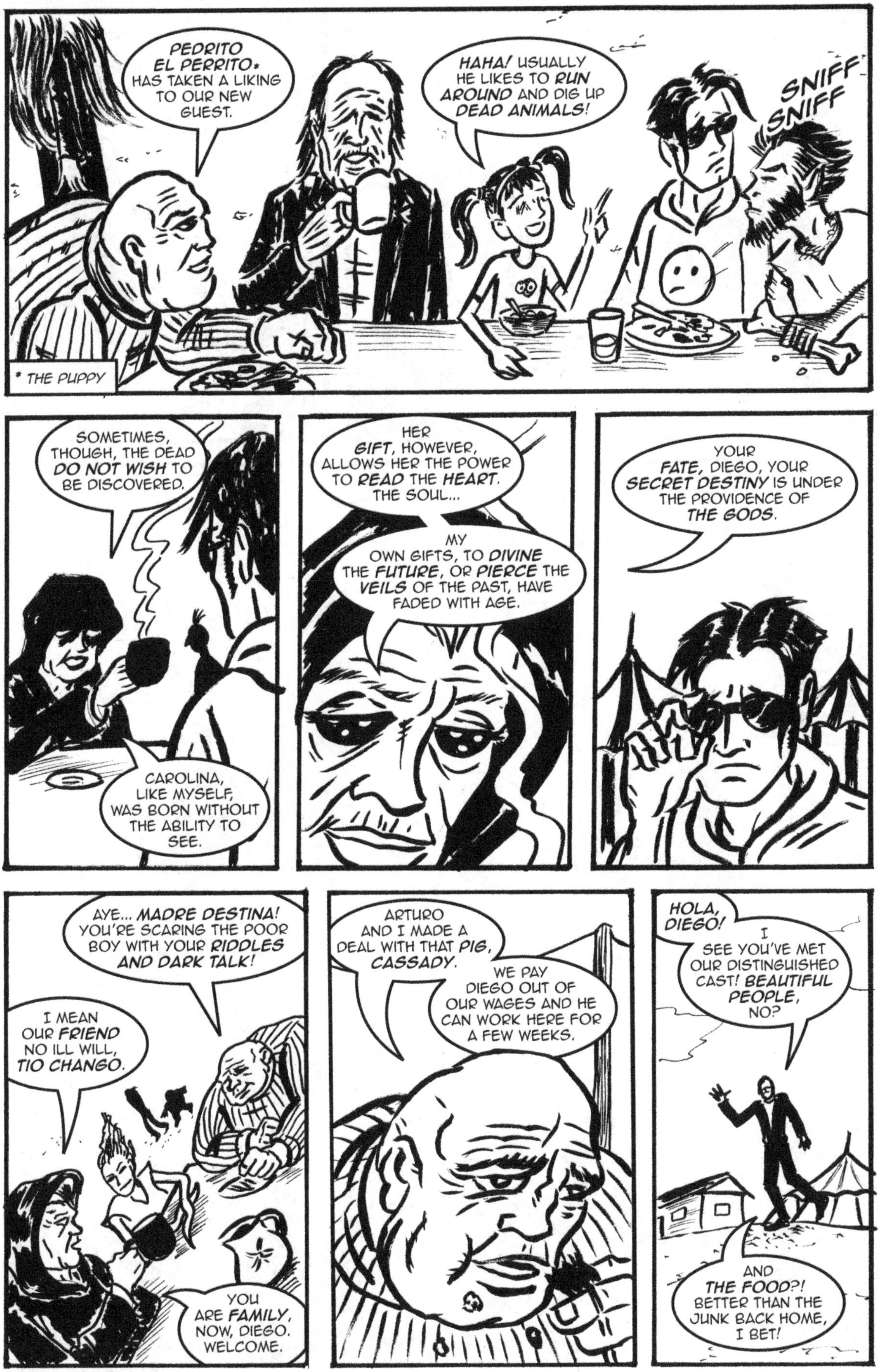
PEDRITO EL PERRITO* HAS TAKEN A LIKING TO OUR NEW GUEST.
HAHA! USUALLY HE LIKES TO RUN AROUND AND DIG UP DEAD ANIMALS!
SNIFF SNIFF
* THE PUPPY
SOMETIMES, THOUGH, THE DEAD DO NOT WISH TO BE DISCOVERED.
CAROLINA, LIKE MYSELF, WAS BORN WITHOUT THE ABILITY TO SEE.
HER GIFT, HOWEVER, ALLOWS HER THE POWER TO READ THE HEART. THE SOUL...
MY OWN GIFTS, TO DIVINE THE FUTURE, OR PIERCE THE VEILS OF THE PAST, HAVE FADED WITH AGE.
YOUR FATE, DIEGO, YOUR SECRET DESTINY IS UNDER THE PROVIDENCE OF THE GODS.
AYE... MADRE DESTINA! YOU'RE SCARING THE POOR BOY WITH YOUR RIDDLES AND DARK TALK!
I MEAN OUR FRIEND NO ILL WILL, TIO CHANGO.
YOU ARE FAMILY, NOW, DIEGO. WELCOME.
ARTURO AND I MADE A DEAL WITH THAT PIG, CASSADY.
WE PAY DIEGO OUT OF OUR WAGES AND HE CAN WORK HERE FOR A FEW WEEKS.
HOLA, DIEGO!
I SEE YOU'VE MET OUR DISTINGUISHED CAST! BEAUTIFUL PEOPLE, NO?
AND THE FOOD?! BETTER THAN THE JUNK BACK HOME, I BET!

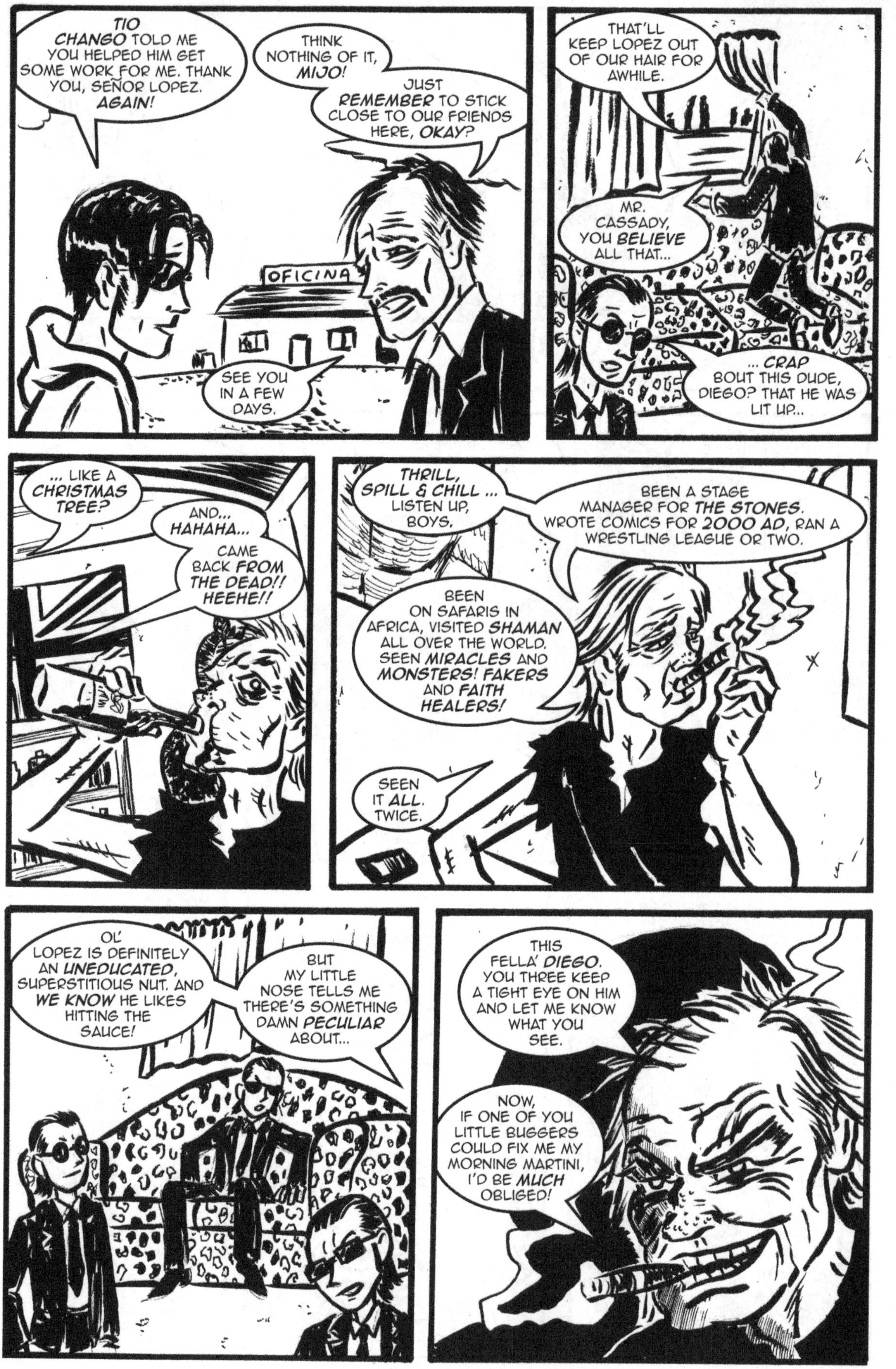

TIO CHANGO TOLD ME YOU HELPED HIM GET SOME WORK FOR ME. THANK YOU, SEÑOR LOPEZ. AGAIN!
THINK NOTHING OF IT, MIJO!
JUST REMEMBER TO STICK CLOSE TO OUR FRIENDS HERE, OKAY?
OFICINA
SEE YOU IN A FEW DAYS.
THAT'LL KEEP LOPEZ OUT OF OUR HAIR FOR AWHILE.
MR. CASSADY, YOU BELIEVE ALL THAT...
... CRAP BOUT THIS DUDE, DIEGO? THAT HE WAS LIT UP...
... LIKE A CHRISTMAS TREE?
AND... HAHAHA...
CAME BACK FROM THE DEAD!! HEEHE!!
THRILL, SPILL & CHILL ... LISTEN UP, BOYS.
BEEN A STAGE MANAGER FOR THE STONES. WROTE COMICS FOR 2000 AD, RAN A WRESTLING LEAGUE OR TWO.
BEEN ON SAFARIS IN AFRICA, VISITED SHAMAN ALL OVER THE WORLD. SEEN MIRACLES AND MONSTERS! FAKERS AND FAITH HEALERS!
SEEN IT ALL. TWICE.
OL' LOPEZ IS DEFINITELY AN UNEDUCATED, SUPERSTITIOUS NUT. AND WE KNOW HE LIKES HITTING THE SAUCE!
BUT MY LITTLE NOSE TELLS ME THERE'S SOMETHING DAMN PECULIAR ABOUT...
THIS FELLA' DIEGO. YOU THREE KEEP A TIGHT EYE ON HIM AND LET ME KNOW WHAT YOU SEE.
NOW, IF ONE OF YOU LITTLE BUGGERS COULD FIX ME MY MORNING MARTINI, I'D BE MUCH OBLIGED!

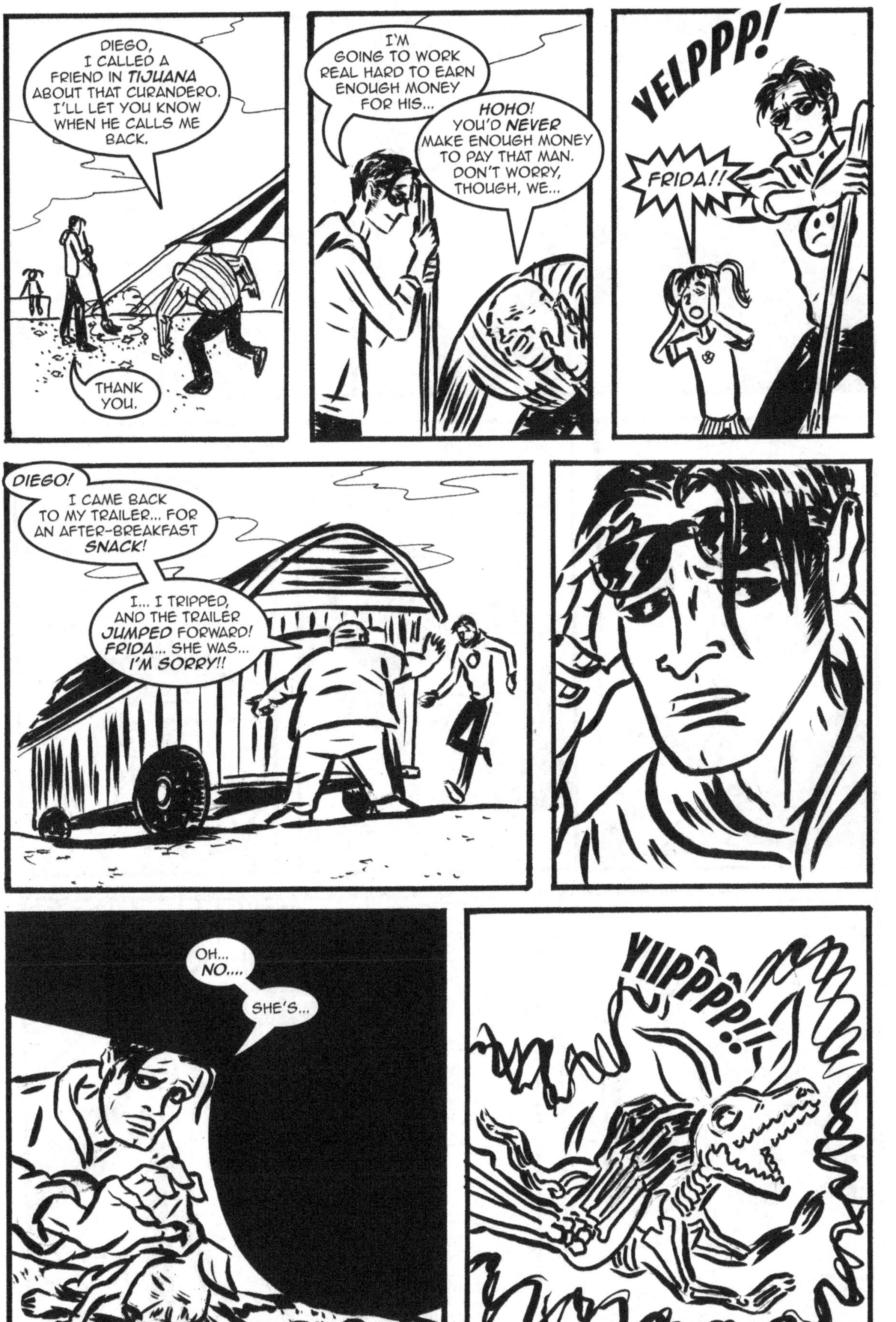
DIEGO, I CALLED A FRIEND IN TIJUANA ABOUT THAT CURANDERO. I'LL LET YOU KNOW WHEN HE CALLS ME BACK.
THANK YOU.
I'M GOING TO WORK REAL HARD TO EARN ENOUGH MONEY FOR HIS...
HOHO! YOU'D NEVER MAKE ENOUGH MONEY TO PAY THAT MAN. DON'T WORRY, THOUGH, WE...
YELPPP!
FRIDA!!
DIEGO!
I CAME BACK TO MY TRAILER... FOR AN AFTER-BREAKFAST SNACK!
I... I TRIPPED, AND THE TRAILER JUMPED FORWARD! FRIDA... SHE WAS... I'M SORRY!!
OH... NO....
SHE'S...
YIIPPPP!!!

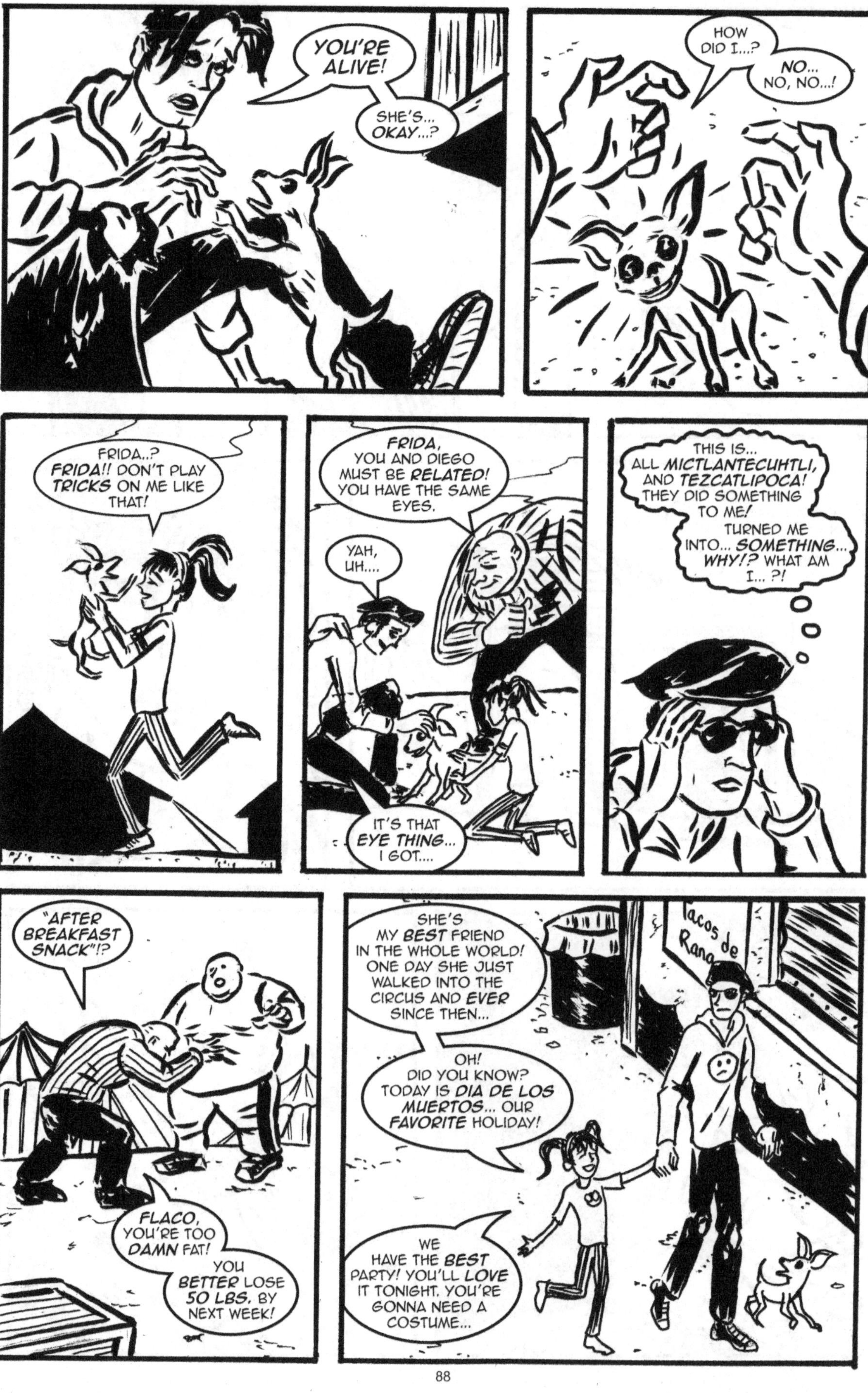

YOU'RE ALIVE!
SHE'S... OKAY...?
HOW DID I...?
NO... NO, NO...!
FRIDA..? FRIDA!! DON'T PLAY TRICKS ON ME LIKE THAT!
FRIDA, YOU AND DIEGO MUST BE RELATED! YOU HAVE THE SAME EYES.
YAH, UH....
IT'S THAT EYE THING... I GOT....
THIS IS... ALL MICTLANTECUHTLI, AND TEZCATLIPOCA! THEY DID SOMETHING TO ME! TURNED ME INTO... SOMETHING... WHY!? WHAT AM I... ?!
"AFTER BREAKFAST SNACK"!?
FLACO, YOU'RE TOO DAMN FAT!
YOU BETTER LOSE 50 LBS. BY NEXT WEEK!
Tacos de Rana
SHE'S MY BEST FRIEND IN THE WHOLE WORLD! ONE DAY SHE JUST WALKED INTO THE CIRCUS AND EVER SINCE THEN...
OH! DID YOU KNOW? TODAY IS DIA DE LOS MUERTOS... OUR FAVORITE HOLIDAY!
WE HAVE THE BEST PARTY! YOU'LL LOVE IT TONIGHT. YOU'RE GONNA NEED A COSTUME...

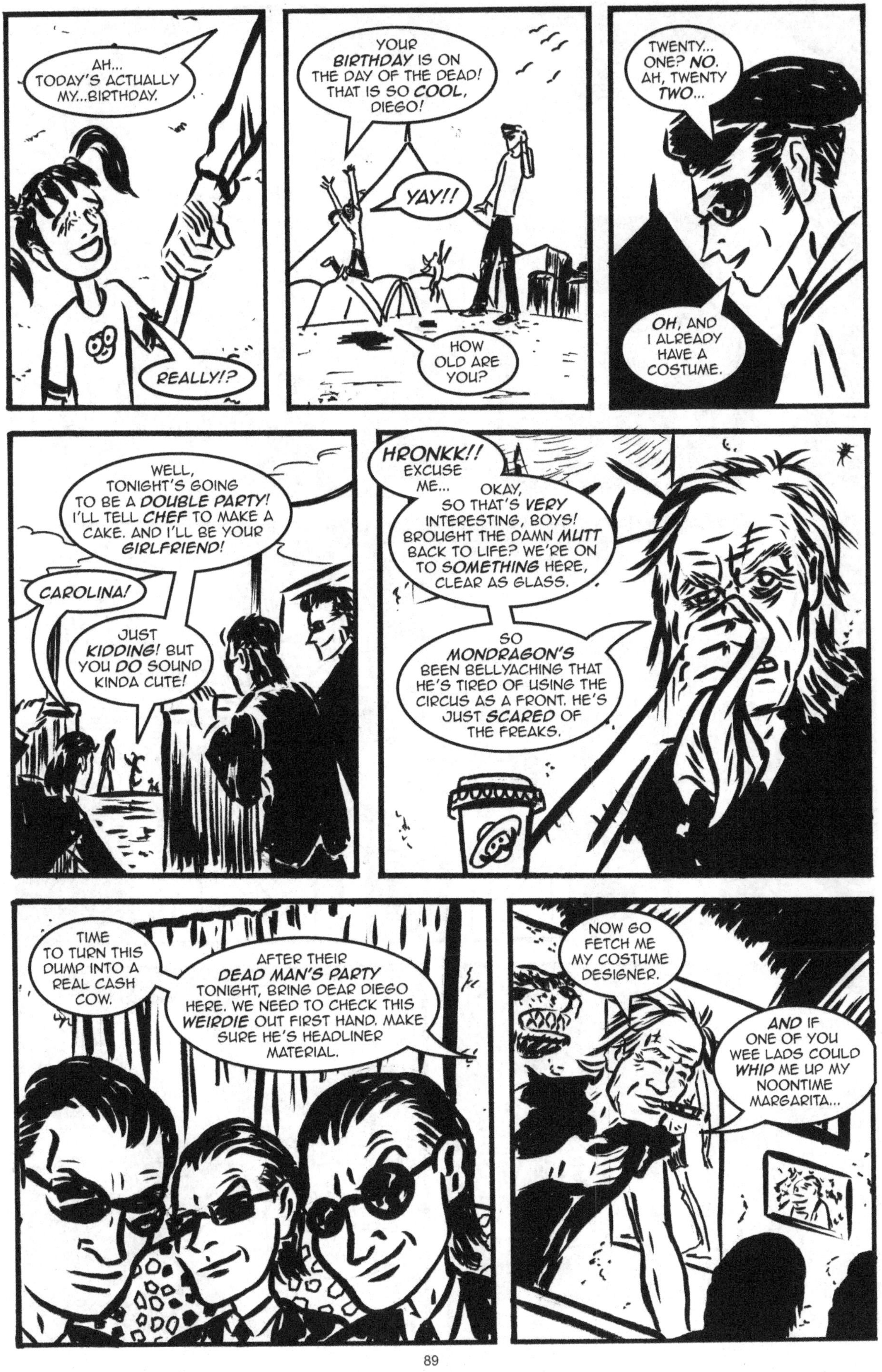
AH... TODAY'S ACTUALLY MY...BIRTHDAY.
REALLY!?
YOUR BIRTHDAY IS ON THE DAY OF THE DEAD! THAT IS SO COOL, DIEGO!
YAY!!
HOW OLD ARE YOU?
TWENTY... ONE? NO. AH, TWENTY TWO...
OH, AND I ALREADY HAVE A COSTUME.
WELL, TONIGHT'S GOING TO BE A DOUBLE PARTY! I'LL TELL CHEF TO MAKE A CAKE. AND I'LL BE YOUR GIRLFRIEND!
CAROLINA!
JUST KIDDING! BUT YOU DO SOUND KINDA CUTE!
HRONKK!! EXCUSE ME...
OKAY, SO THAT'S VERY INTERESTING, BOYS! BROUGHT THE DAMN MUTT BACK TO LIFE? WE'RE ON TO SOMETHING HERE, CLEAR AS GLASS.
SO MONDRAGON'S BEEN BELLYACHING THAT HE'S TIRED OF USING THE CIRCUS AS A FRONT. HE'S JUST SCARED OF THE FREAKS.
TIME TO TURN THIS DUMP INTO A REAL CASH COW.
AFTER THEIR DEAD MAN'S PARTY TONIGHT, BRING DEAR DIEGO HERE. WE NEED TO CHECK THIS WEIRDIE OUT FIRST HAND. MAKE SURE HE'S HEADLINER MATERIAL.
NOW GO FETCH ME MY COSTUME DESIGNER.
AND IF ONE OF YOU WEE LADS COULD WHIP ME UP MY NOONTIME MARGARITA...

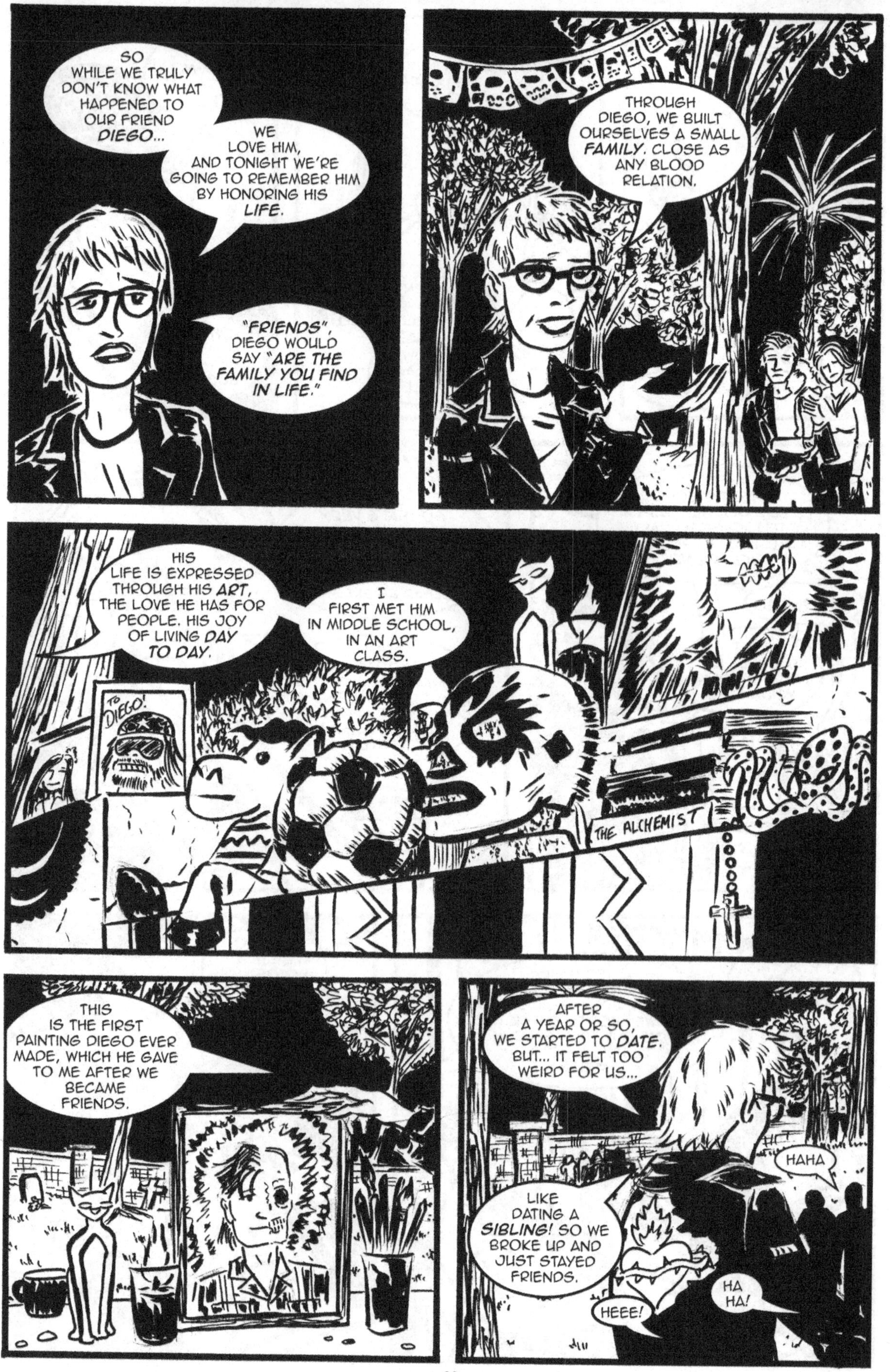
SO WHILE WE TRULY DON'T KNOW WHAT HAPPENED TO OUR FRIEND DIEGO...
WE LOVE HIM, AND TONIGHT WE'RE GOING TO REMEMBER HIM BY HONORING HIS LIFE.
"FRIENDS", DIEGO WOULD SAY "ARE THE FAMILY YOU FIND IN LIFE."
THROUGH DIEGO, WE BUILT OURSELVES A SMALL FAMILY. CLOSE AS ANY BLOOD RELATION.
HIS LIFE IS EXPRESSED THROUGH HIS ART, THE LOVE HE HAS FOR PEOPLE. HIS JOY OF LIVING DAY TO DAY.
I FIRST MET HIM IN MIDDLE SCHOOL, IN AN ART CLASS.
TO DIEGO!
THE ALCHEMIST
THIS IS THE FIRST PAINTING DIEGO EVER MADE, WHICH HE GAVE TO ME AFTER WE BECAME FRIENDS.
AFTER A YEAR OR SO, WE STARTED TO DATE. BUT... IT FELT TOO WEIRD FOR US...
HAHA
LIKE DATING A SIBLING! SO WE BROKE UP AND JUST STAYED FRIENDS.
HA HA!
HEEE!

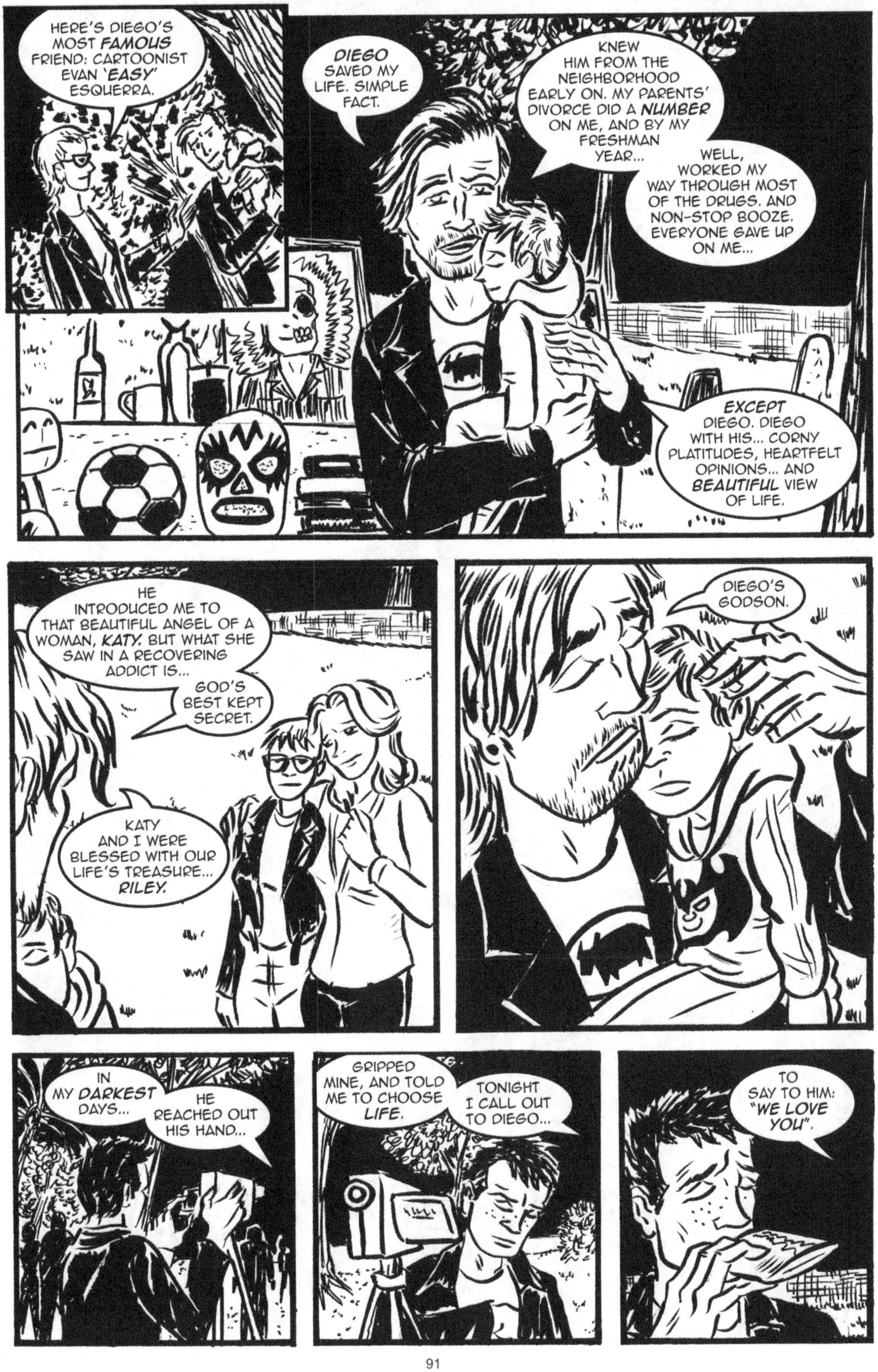
HERE'S DIEGO'S MOST FAMOUS FRIEND: CARTOONIST EVAN 'EASY' ESQUERRA.
DIEGO SAVED MY LIFE. SIMPLE FACT.
KNEW HIM FROM THE NEIGHBORHOOD EARLY ON. MY PARENTS' DIVORCE DID A NUMBER ON ME, AND BY MY FRESHMAN YEAR...
WELL, WORKED MY WAY THROUGH MOST OF THE DRUGS. AND NON-STOP BOOZE. EVERYONE GAVE UP ON ME...
EXCEPT DIEGO. DIEGO WITH HIS... CORNY PLATITUDES, HEARTFELT OPINIONS... AND BEAUTIFUL VIEW OF LIFE.
HE INTRODUCED ME TO THAT BEAUTIFUL ANGEL OF A WOMAN, KATY. BUT WHAT SHE SAW IN A RECOVERING ADDICT IS...
GOD'S BEST KEPT SECRET.
KATY AND I WERE BLESSED WITH OUR LIFE'S TREASURE... RILEY.
DIEGO'S GODSON.
IN MY DARKEST DAYS...
HE REACHED OUT HIS HAND...
GRIPPED MINE, AND TOLD ME TO CHOOSE LIFE.
TONIGHT I CALL OUT TO DIEGO...
TO SAY TO HIM: "WE LOVE YOU".

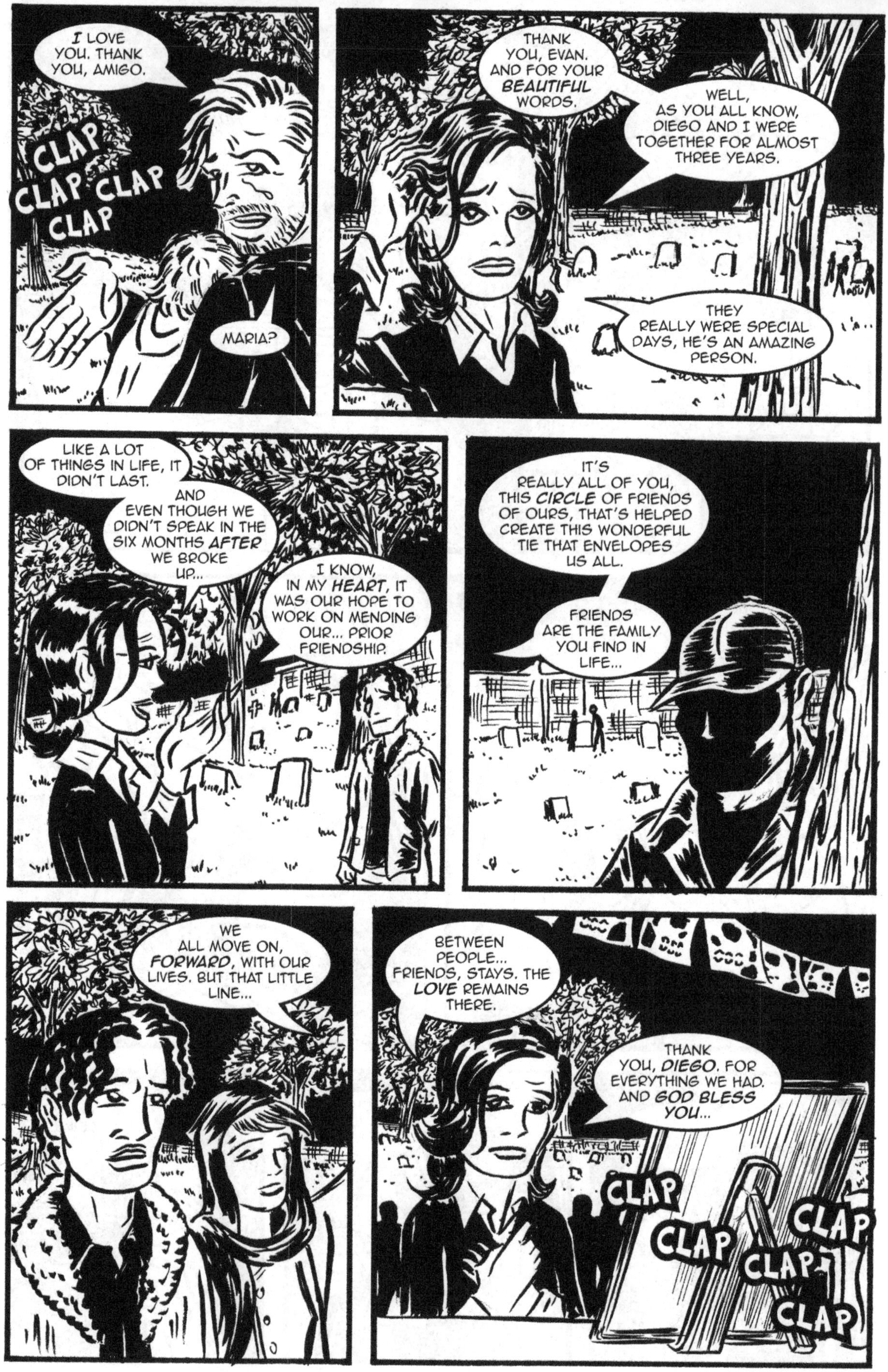
I LOVE YOU. THANK YOU, AMIGO.
CLAP CLAP CLAP CLAP
MARIA?
THANK YOU, EVAN. AND FOR YOUR BEAUTIFUL WORDS.
WELL, AS YOU ALL KNOW, DIEGO AND I WERE TOGETHER FOR ALMOST THREE YEARS.
THEY REALLY WERE SPECIAL DAYS, HE'S AN AMAZING PERSON.
LIKE A LOT OF THINGS IN LIFE, IT DIDN'T LAST.
AND EVEN THOUGH WE DIDN'T SPEAK IN THE SIX MONTHS AFTER WE BROKE UP...
I KNOW, IN MY HEART, IT WAS OUR HOPE TO WORK ON MENDING OUR... PRIOR FRIENDSHIP.
IT'S REALLY ALL OF YOU, THIS CIRCLE OF FRIENDS OF OURS, THAT'S HELPED CREATE THIS WONDERFUL TIE THAT ENVELOPES US ALL.
FRIENDS ARE THE FAMILY YOU FIND IN LIFE...
WE ALL MOVE ON, FORWARD, WITH OUR LIVES. BUT THAT LITTLE LINE...
BETWEEN PEOPLE... FRIENDS, STAYS. THE LOVE REMAINS THERE.
THANK YOU, DIEGO. FOR EVERYTHING WE HAD. AND GOD BLESS YOU...
CLAP CLAP CLAP CLAP CLAP

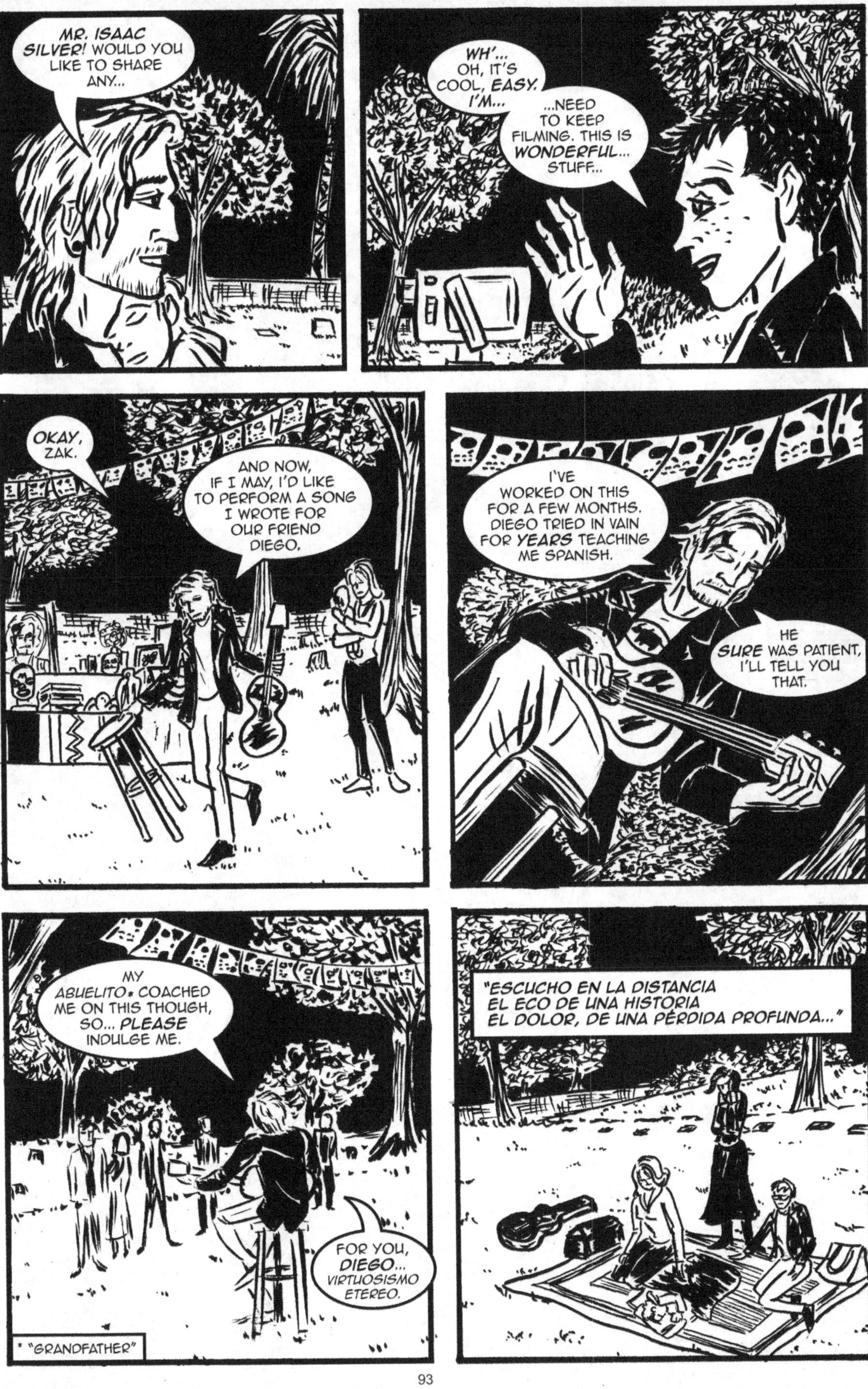
MR. ISAAC SILVER! WOULD YOU LIKE TO SHARE ANY...
WH'... OH, IT'S COOL, EASY. I'M...
...NEED TO KEEP FILMING. THIS IS WONDERFUL... STUFF...
OKAY, ZAK.
AND NOW, IF I MAY, I'D LIKE TO PERFORM A SONG I WROTE FOR OUR FRIEND DIEGO.
I'VE WORKED ON THIS FOR A FEW MONTHS. DIEGO TRIED IN VAIN FOR YEARS TEACHING ME SPANISH.
HE SURE WAS PATIENT, I'LL TELL YOU THAT.
MY ABUELITO* COACHED ME ON THIS THOUGH, SO... PLEASE INDULGE ME.
FOR YOU, DIEGO... VIRTUOSISMO ETEREO.
* "GRANDFATHER"
"ESCUCHO EN LA DISTANCIA
EL ECO DE UNA HISTORIA
EL DOLOR, DE UNA PÉRDIDA PROFUNDA..."

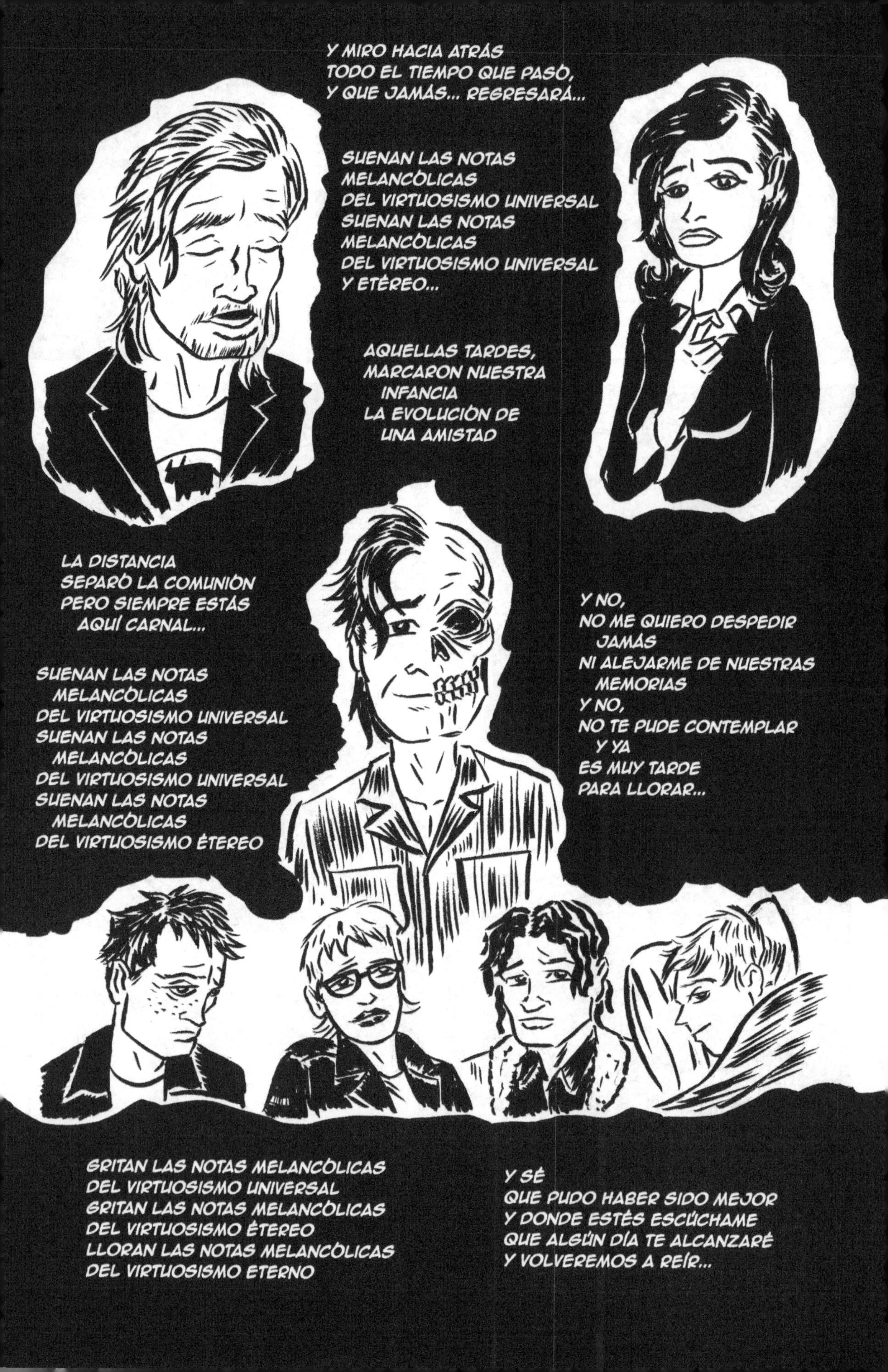
Y MIRO HACIA ATRÁS
TODO EL TIEMPO QUE PASÓ,
Y QUE JAMÁS... REGRESARÁ...
SUENAN LAS NOTAS
MELANCÓLICAS
DEL VIRTUOSISMO UNIVERSAL
SUENAN LAS NOTAS
MELANCÓLICAS
DEL VIRTUOSISMO UNIVERSAL
Y ETÉREO...
AQUELLAS TARDES,
MARCARON NUESTRA
INFANCIA
LA EVOLUCIÓN DE
UNA AMISTAD
LA DISTANCIA
SEPARÓ LA COMUNIÓN
PERO SIEMPRE ESTÁS
AQUÍ CARNAL...
SUENAN LAS NOTAS
MELANCÓLICAS
DEL VIRTUOSISMO UNIVERSAL
SUENAN LAS NOTAS
MELANCÓLICAS
DEL VIRTUOSISMO UNIVERSAL
SUENAN LAS NOTAS
MELANCÓLICAS
DEL VIRTUOSISMO ÉTEREO
Y NO,
NO ME QUIERO DESPEDIR
JAMÁS
NI ALEJARME DE NUESTRAS
MEMORIAS
Y NO,
NO TE PUDE CONTEMPLAR
Y YA
ES MUY TARDE
PARA LLORAR...
GRITAN LAS NOTAS MELANCÓLICAS
DEL VIRTUOSISMO UNIVERSAL
GRITAN LAS NOTAS MELANCÓLICAS
DEL VIRTUOSISMO ÉTEREO
LLORAN LAS NOTAS MELANCÓLICAS
DEL VIRTUOSISMO ETERNO
Y SÉ
QUE PUDO HABER SIDO MEJOR
Y DONDE ESTÉS ESCÚCHAME
QUE ALGÚN DÍA TE ALCANZARÉ
Y VOLVEREMOS A REÍR...

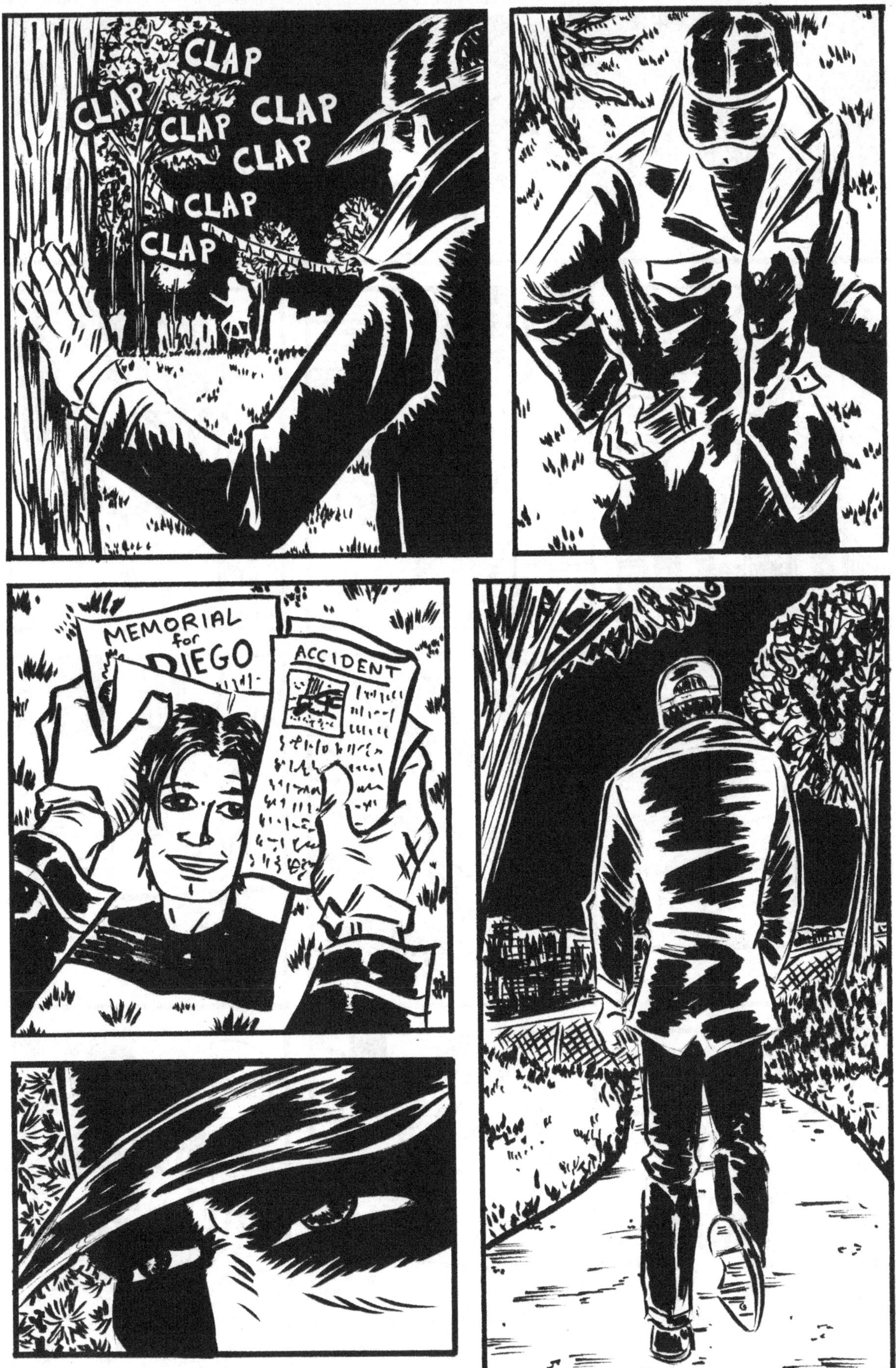
CLAP
CLAP
CLAP
CLAP
CLAP
CLAP
CLAP
MEMORIAL for DIEGO
ACCIDENT

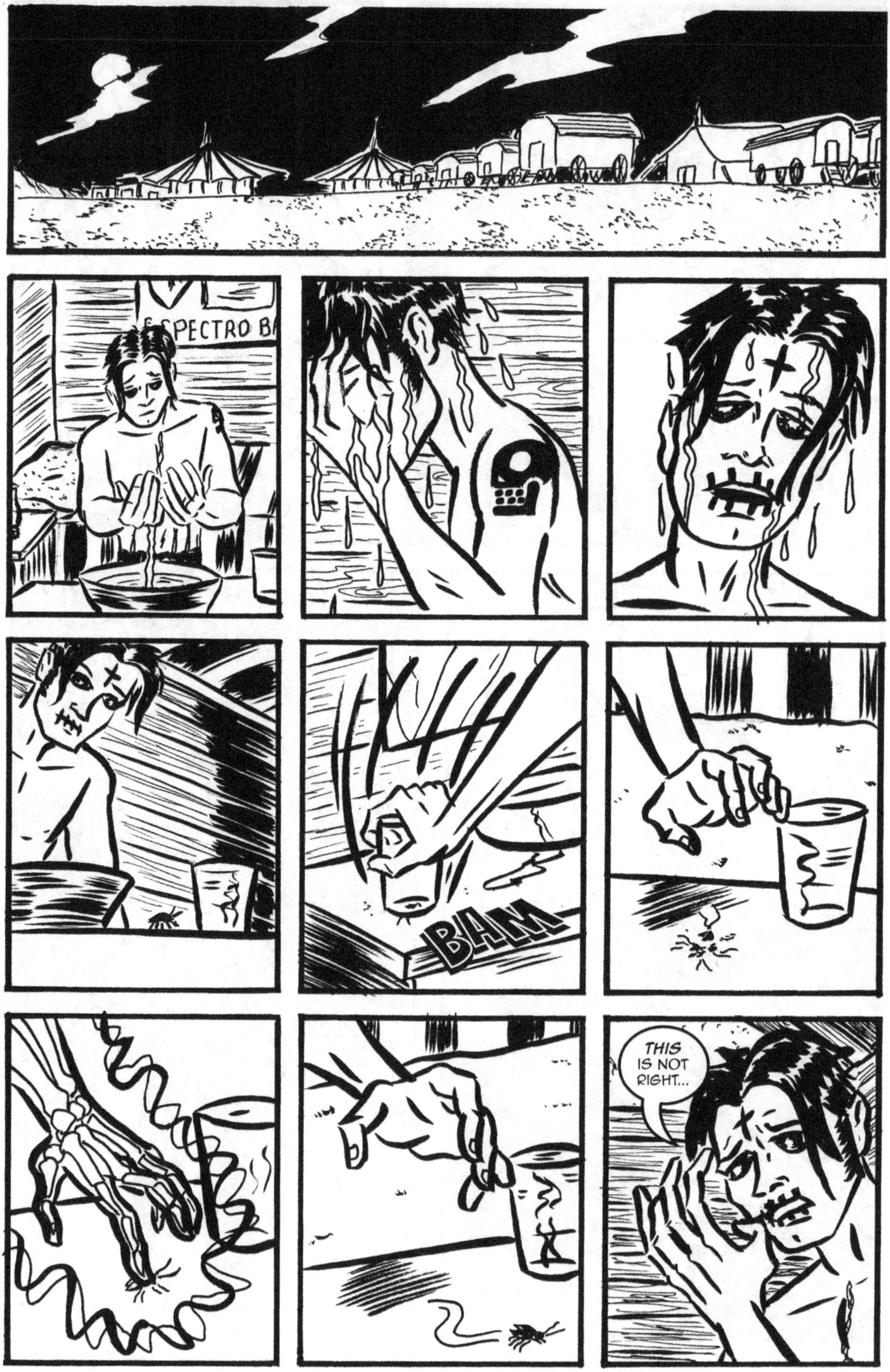
ESPECTRO B
BAM
THIS IS NOT RIGHT...

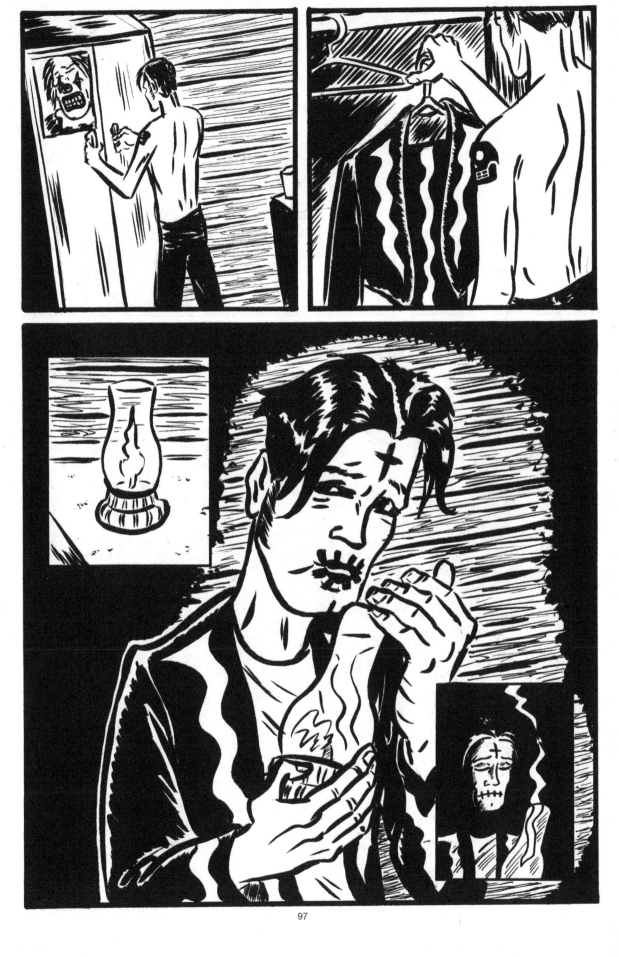

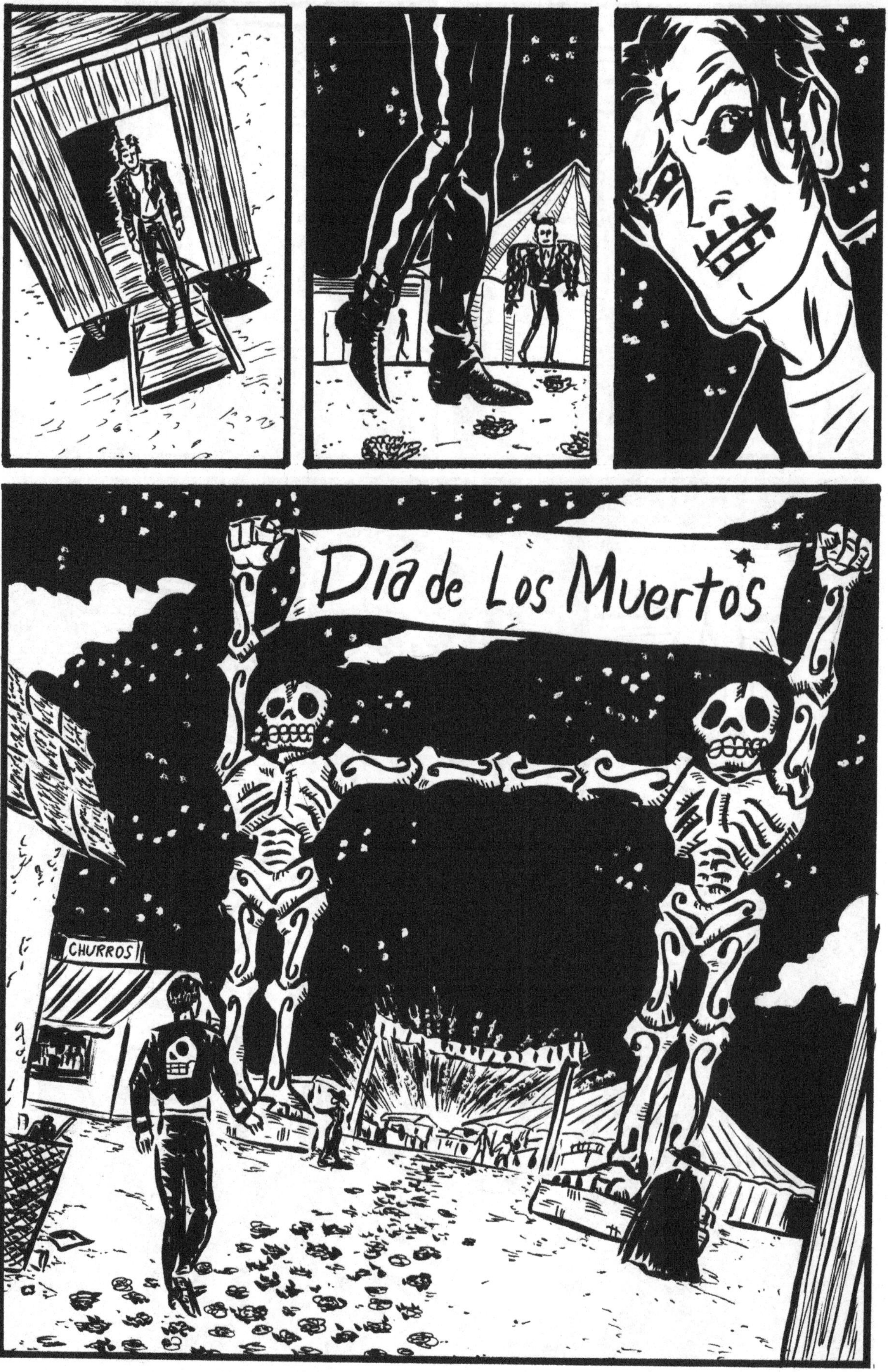
Día de Los Muertos
CHURROS

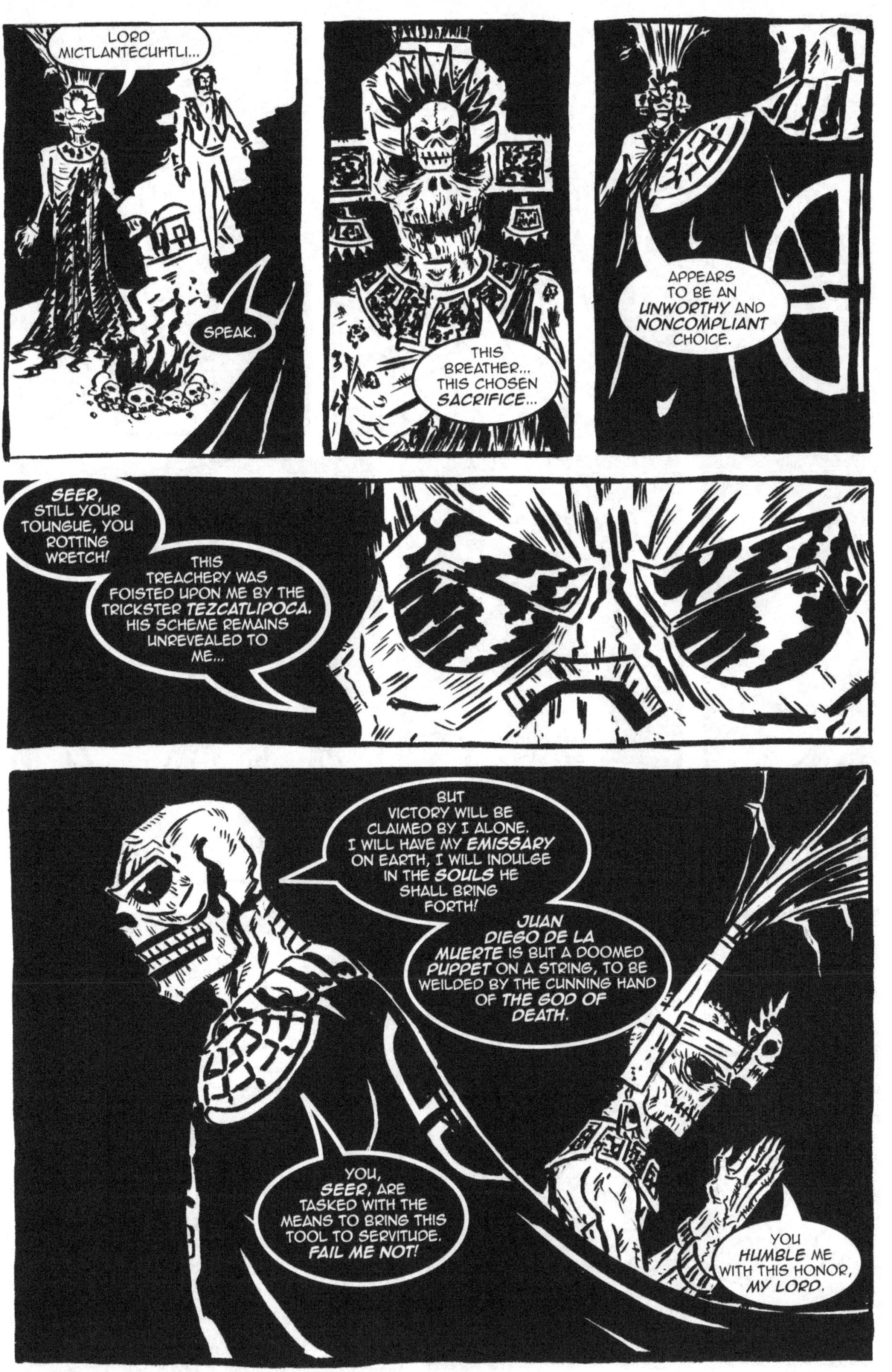
LORD MICTLANTECUHTLI...
SPEAK.
THIS BREATHER... THIS CHOSEN SACRIFICE...
APPEARS TO BE AN UNWORTHY AND NONCOMPLIANT CHOICE.
SEER, STILL YOUR TOUNGUE, YOU ROTTING WRETCH!
THIS TREACHERY WAS FOISTED UPON ME BY THE TRICKSTER TEZCATLIPOCA. HIS SCHEME REMAINS UNREVEALED TO ME...
BUT VICTORY WILL BE CLAIMED BY I ALONE. I WILL HAVE MY EMISSARY ON EARTH, I WILL INDULGE IN THE SOULS HE SHALL BRING FORTH!
JUAN DIEGO DE LA MUERTE IS BUT A DOOMED PUPPET ON A STRING, TO BE WEILDED BY THE CUNNING HAND OF THE GOD OF DEATH.
YOU, SEER, ARE TASKED WITH THE MEANS TO BRING THIS TOOL TO SERVITUDE. FAIL ME NOT!
YOU HUMBLE ME WITH THIS HONOR, MY LORD.

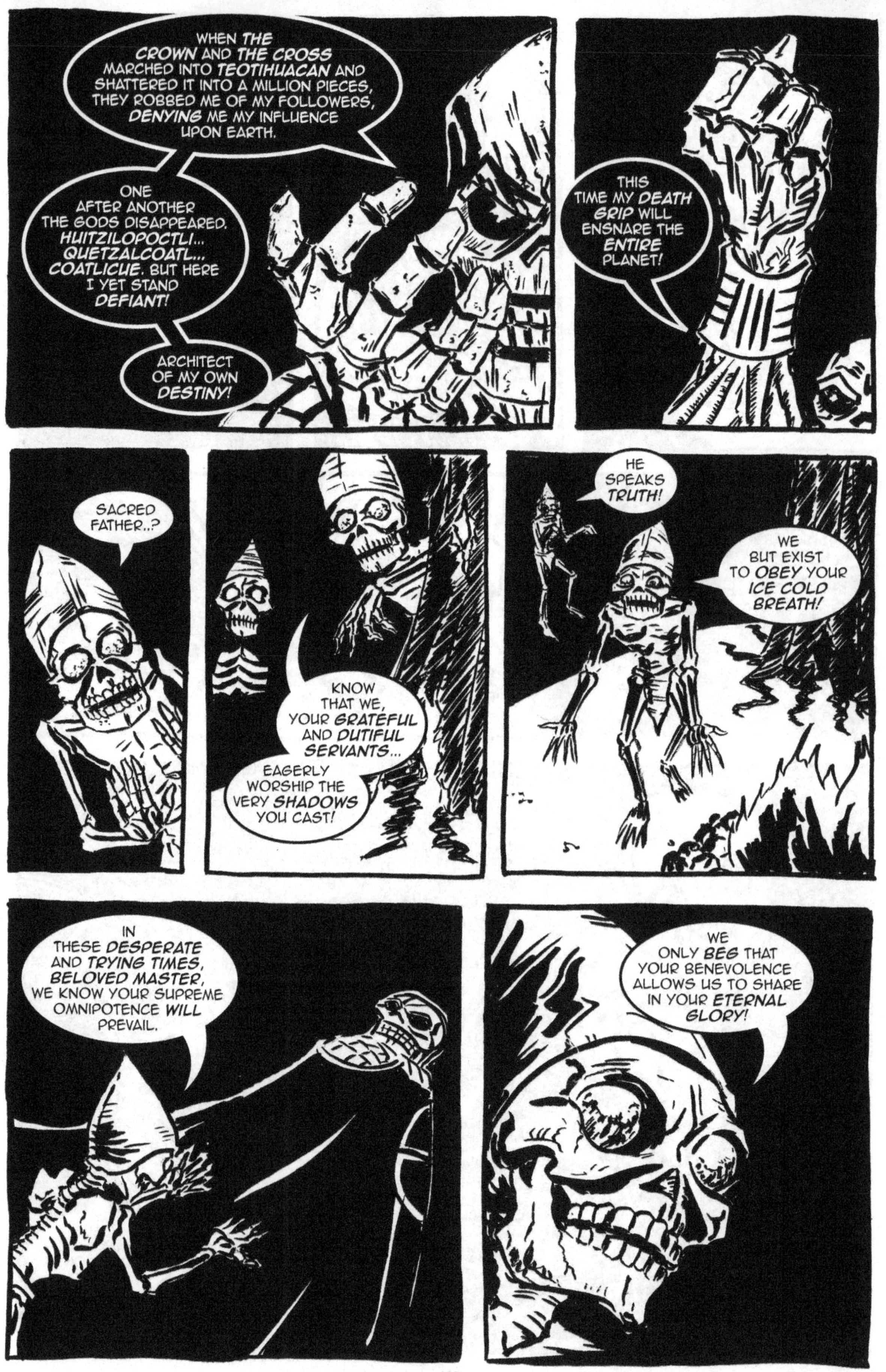
WHEN THE CROWN AND THE CROSS MARCHED INTO TEOTIHUACAN AND SHATTERED IT INTO A MILLION PIECES, THEY ROBBED ME OF MY FOLLOWERS, DENYING ME MY INFLUENCE UPON EARTH.
ONE AFTER ANOTHER THE GODS DISAPPEARED. HUITZILOPOCTLI... QUETZALCOATL... COATLICUE. BUT HERE I YET STAND DEFIANT!
ARCHITECT OF MY OWN DESTINY!
THIS TIME MY DEATH GRIP WILL ENSNARE THE ENTIRE PLANET!
SACRED FATHER...?
KNOW THAT WE, YOUR GRATEFUL AND DUTIFUL SERVANTS...
EAGERLY WORSHIP THE VERY SHADOWS YOU CAST!
HE SPEAKS TRUTH!
WE BUT EXIST TO OBEY YOUR ICE COLD BREATH!
IN THESE DESPERATE AND TRYING TIMES, BELOVED MASTER, WE KNOW YOUR SUPREME OMNIPOTENCE WILL PREVAIL.
WE ONLY BEG THAT YOUR BENEVOLENCE ALLOWS US TO SHARE IN YOUR ETERNAL GLORY!

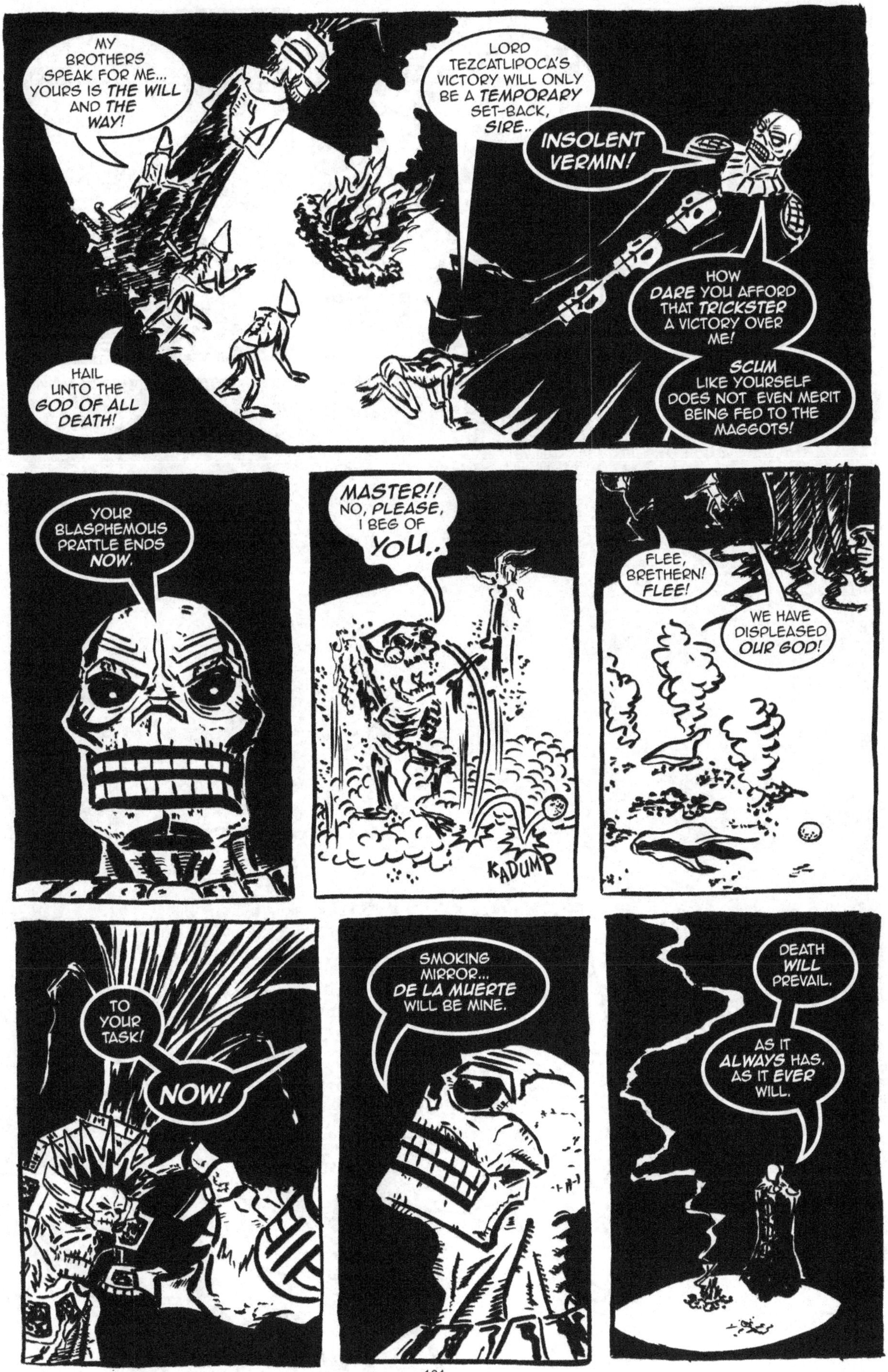

MY BROTHERS SPEAK FOR ME... YOURS IS THE WILL AND THE WAY!
HAIL UNTO THE GOD OF ALL DEATH!
LORD TEZCATLIPOCA'S VICTORY WILL ONLY BE A TEMPORARY SET-BACK, SIRE..
INSOLENT VERMIN!
HOW DARE YOU AFFORD THAT TRICKSTER A VICTORY OVER ME!
SCUM LIKE YOURSELF DOES NOT EVEN MERIT BEING FED TO THE MAGGOTS!
YOUR BLASPHEMOUS PRATTLE ENDS NOW.
MASTER!! NO, PLEASE, I BEG OF YOU..
KADUMP
FLEE, BRETHERN! FLEE!
WE HAVE DISPLEASED OUR GOD!
TO YOUR TASK!
NOW!
SMOKING MIRROR... DE LA MUERTE WILL BE MINE.
DEATH WILL PREVAIL.
AS IT ALWAYS HAS. AS IT EVER WILL.

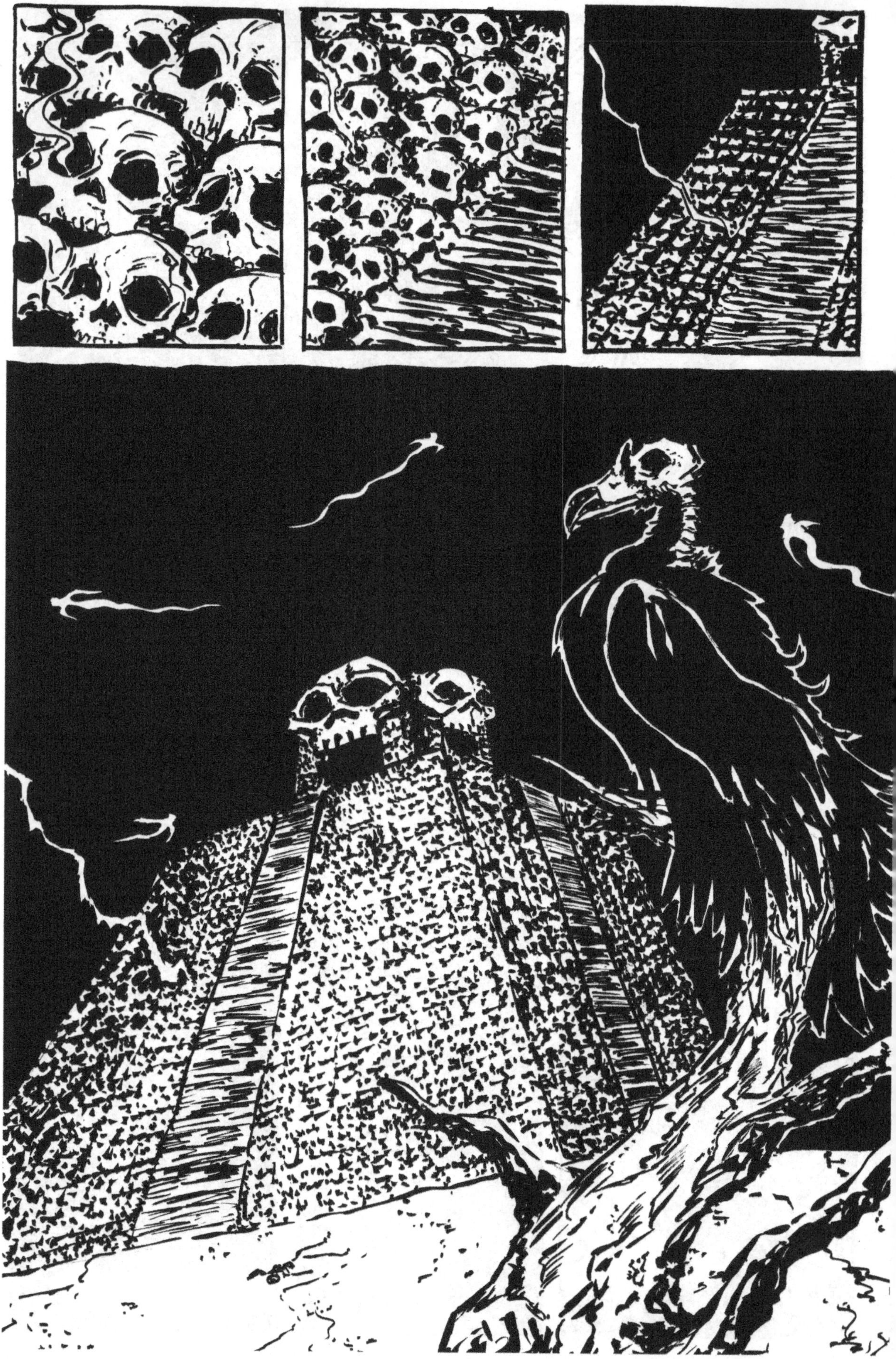

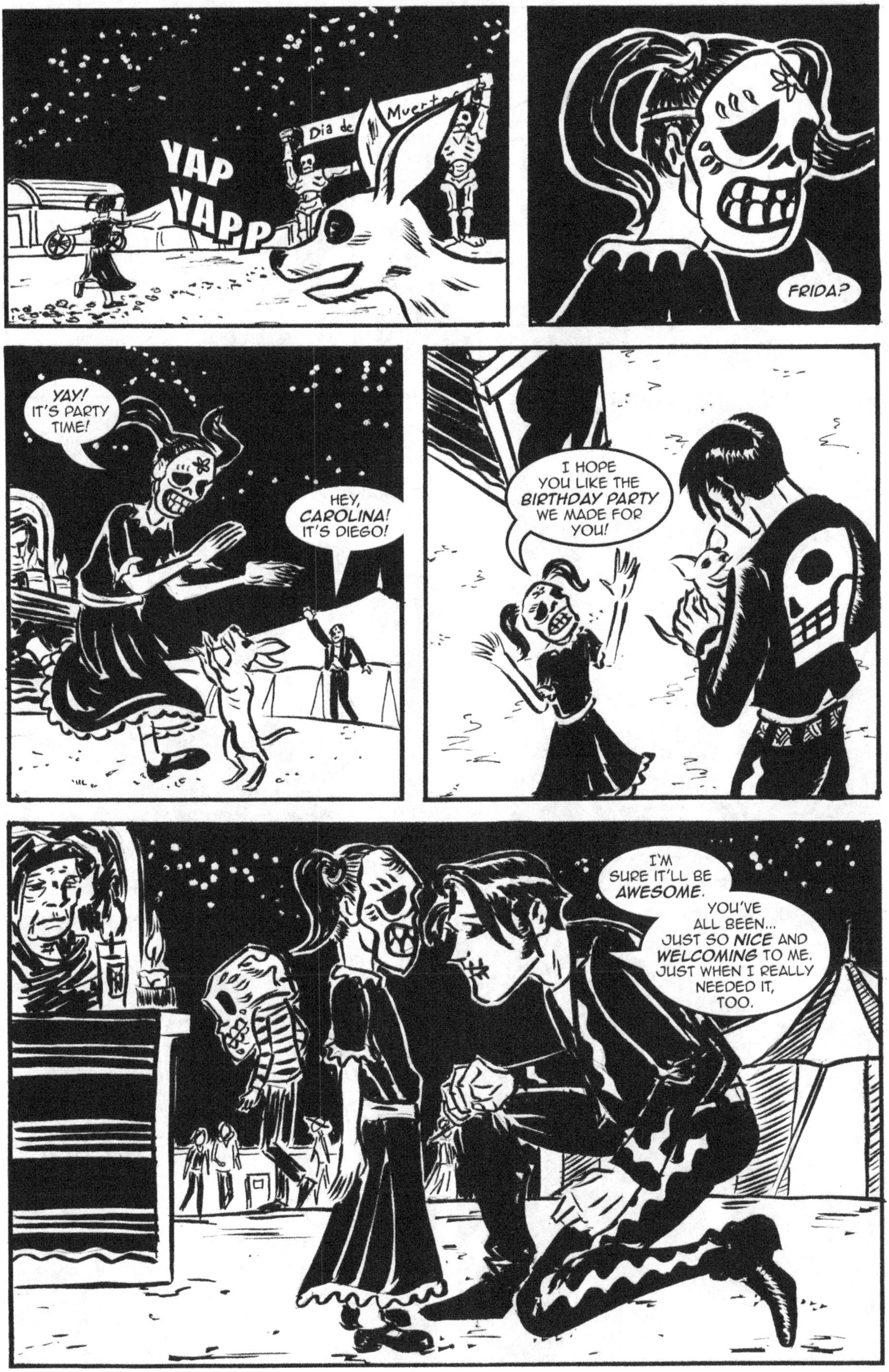
YAP
YAPP
Dia de
Muertos
FRIDA?
YAY! IT'S PARTY TIME!
HEY, CAROLINA! IT'S DIEGO!
I HOPE YOU LIKE THE BIRTHDAY PARTY WE MADE FOR YOU!
I'M SURE IT'LL BE AWESOME.
YOU'VE ALL BEEN... JUST SO NICE AND WELCOMING TO ME. JUST WHEN I REALLY NEEDED IT, TOO.

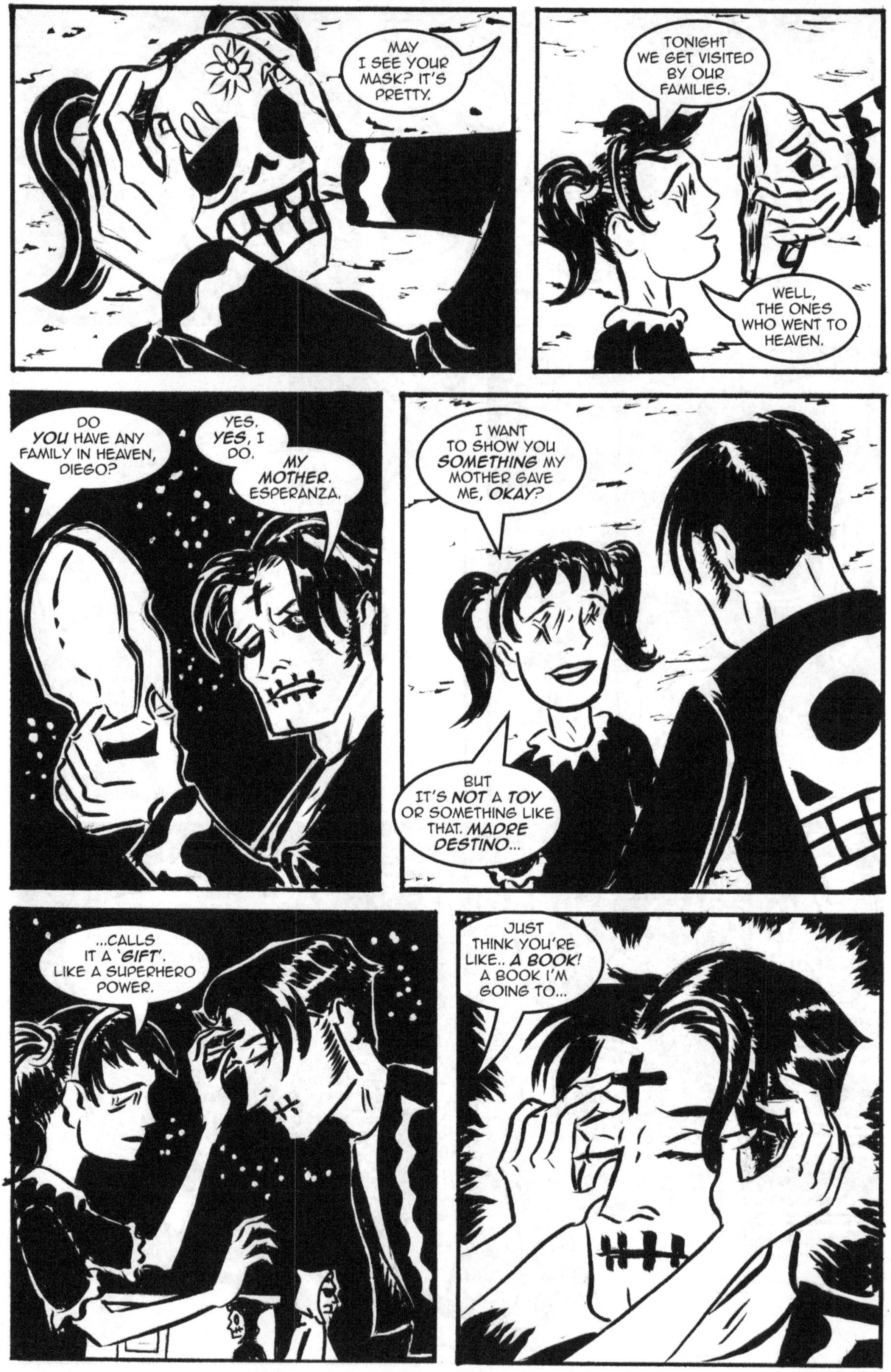
MAY I SEE YOUR MASK? IT'S PRETTY.
TONIGHT WE GET VISITED BY OUR FAMILIES.
WELL, THE ONES WHO WENT TO HEAVEN.
DO YOU HAVE ANY FAMILY IN HEAVEN, DIEGO?
YES. YES, I DO.
MY MOTHER. ESPERANZA.
I WANT TO SHOW YOU SOMETHING MY MOTHER GAVE ME, OKAY?
BUT IT'S NOT A TOY OR SOMETHING LIKE THAT. MADRE DESTINO...
...CALLS IT A 'GIFT'. LIKE A SUPERHERO POWER.
JUST THINK YOU'RE LIKE.. A BOOK! A BOOK I'M GOING TO...

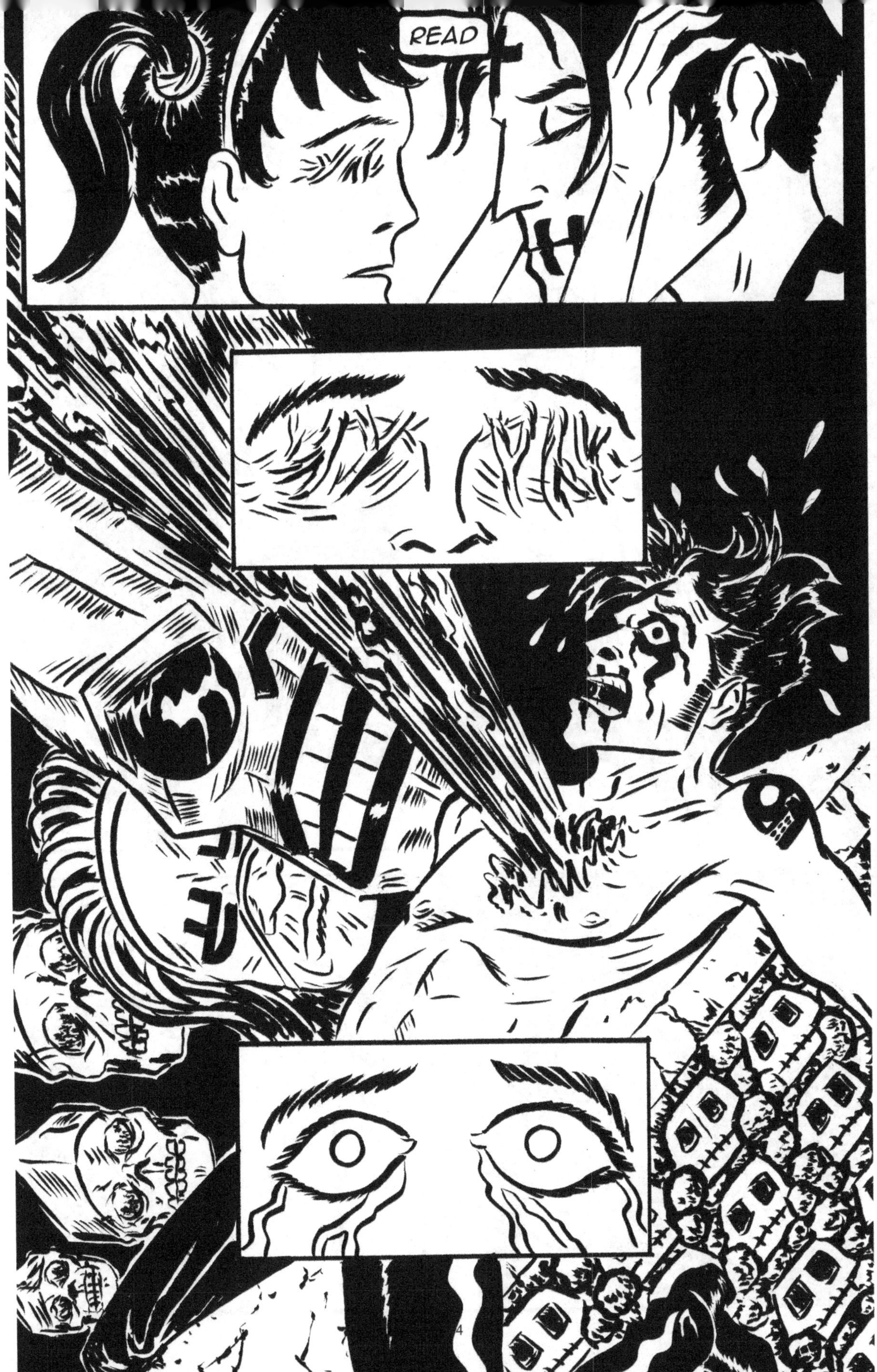
READ

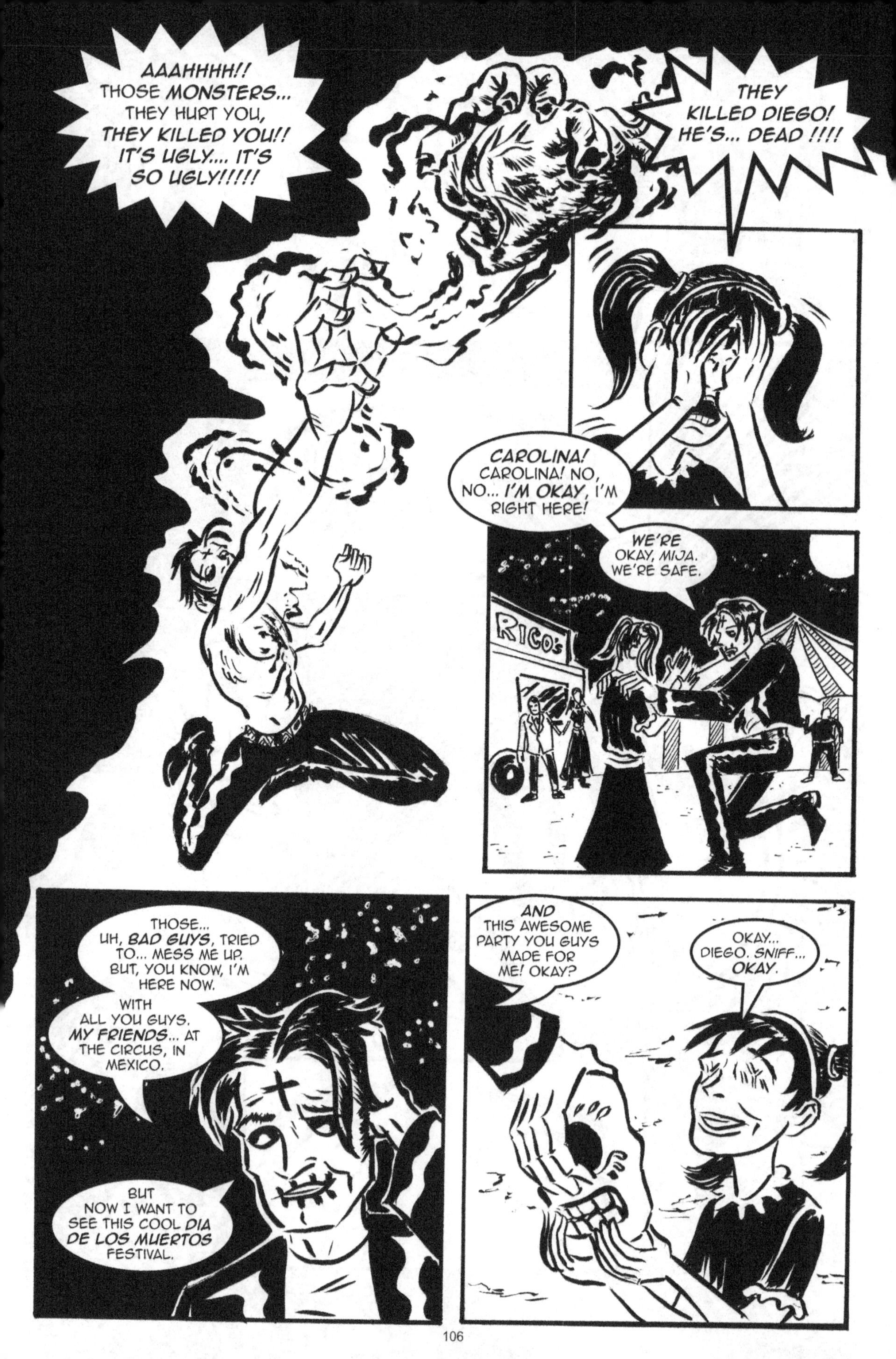
AAAHHHH!! THOSE MONSTERS... THEY HURT YOU, THEY KILLED YOU!! IT'S UGLY.... IT'S SO UGLY!!!!!
THEY KILLED DIEGO! HE'S... DEAD !!!!
CAROLINA! CAROLINA! NO, NO... I'M OKAY, I'M RIGHT HERE!
WE'RE OKAY, MIJA. WE'RE SAFE.
RICO'S
THOSE... UH, BAD GUYS, TRIED TO... MESS ME UP. BUT, YOU KNOW, I'M HERE NOW.
WITH ALL YOU GUYS. MY FRIENDS... AT THE CIRCUS, IN MEXICO.
BUT NOW I WANT TO SEE THIS COOL DIA DE LOS MUERTOS FESTIVAL.
AND THIS AWESOME PARTY YOU GUYS MADE FOR ME! OKAY?
OKAY... DIEGO. SNIFF... OKAY.

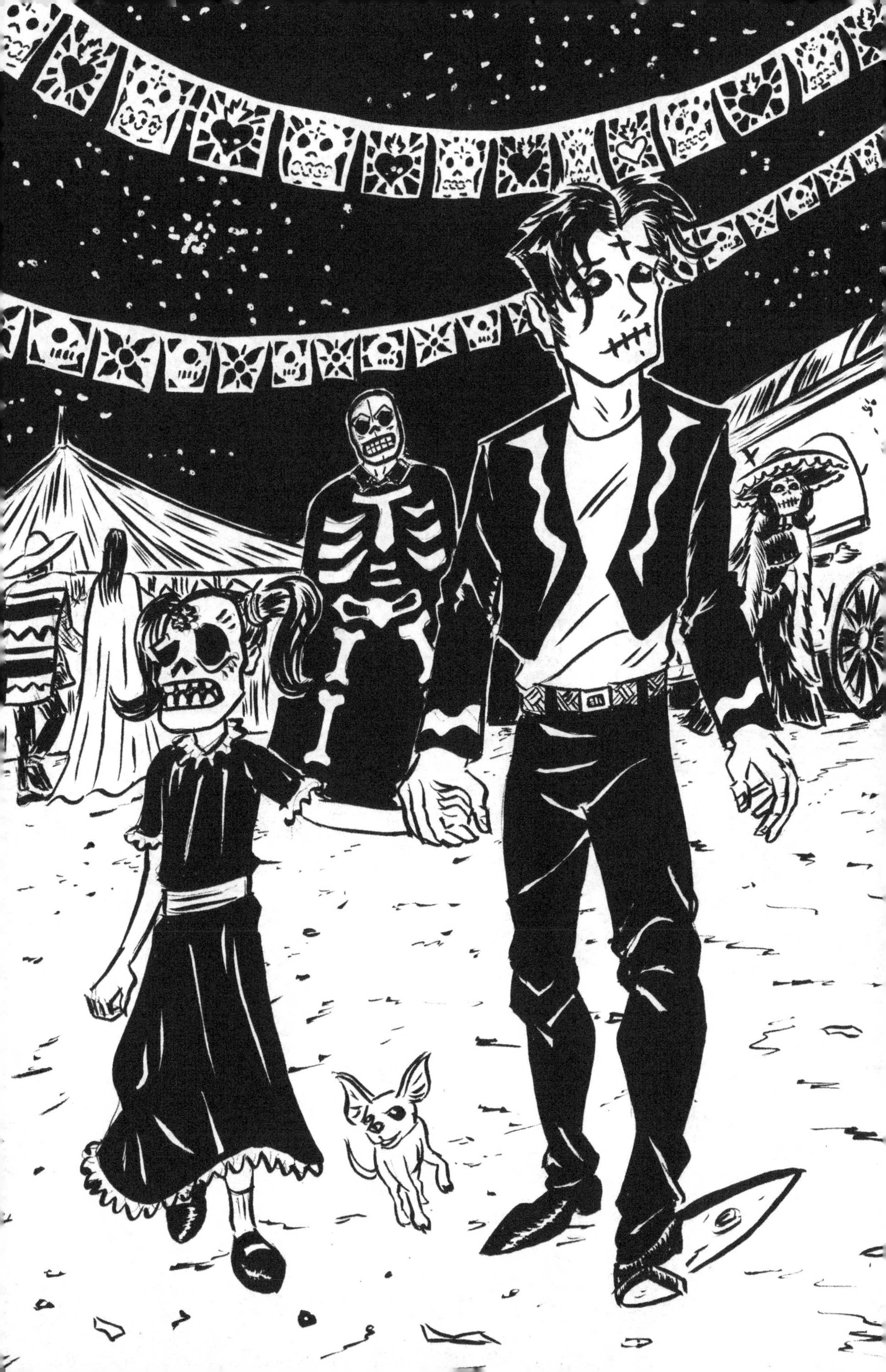

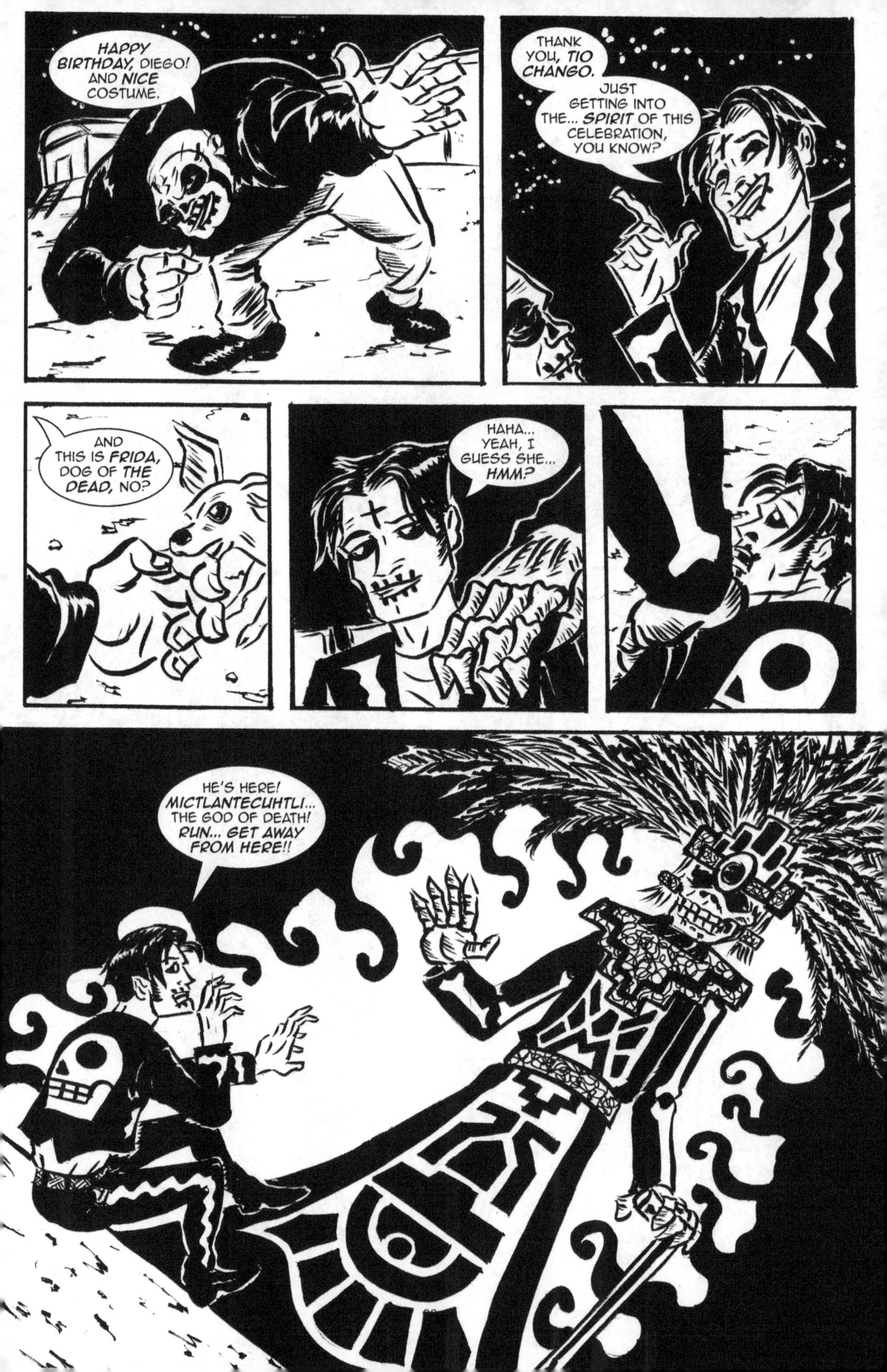
HAPPY BIRTHDAY, DIEGO! AND NICE COSTUME.
THANK YOU, TIO CHANGO.
JUST GETTING INTO THE... SPIRIT OF THIS CELEBRATION, YOU KNOW?
AND THIS IS FRIDA, DOG OF THE DEAD, NO?
HAHA... YEAH, I GUESS SHE... HMM?
HE'S HERE! MICTLANTECUHTLI... THE GOD OF DEATH! RUN... GET AWAY FROM HERE!!

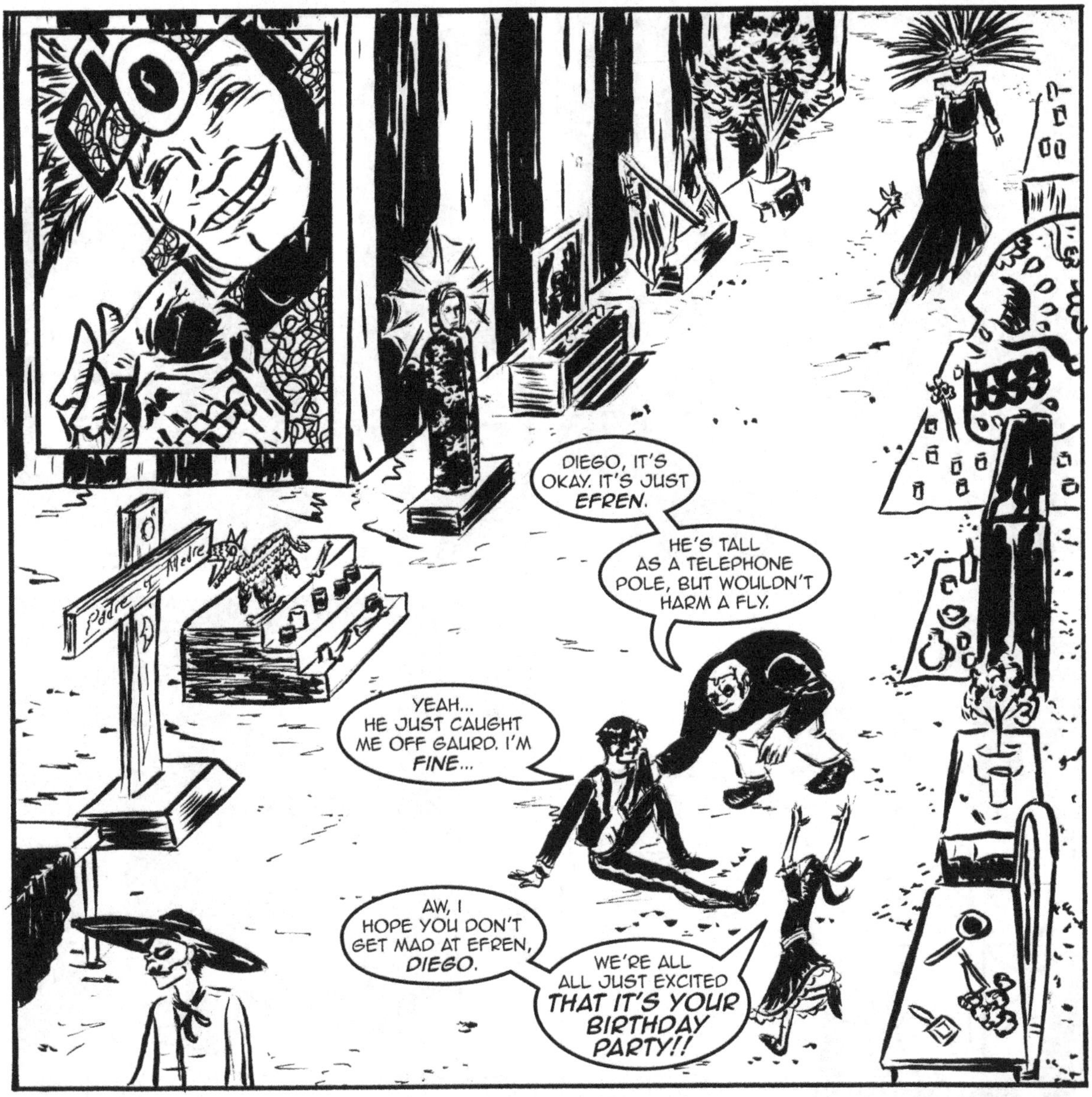
Padre Madre
DIEGO, IT'S OKAY. IT'S JUST EFREN.
HE'S TALL AS A TELEPHONE POLE, BUT WOULDN'T HARM A FLY.
YEAH... HE JUST CAUGHT ME OFF GAURD. I'M FINE...
AW, I HOPE YOU DON'T GET MAD AT EFREN, DIEGO.
WE'RE ALL ALL JUST EXCITED THAT IT'S YOUR BIRTHDAY PARTY!!

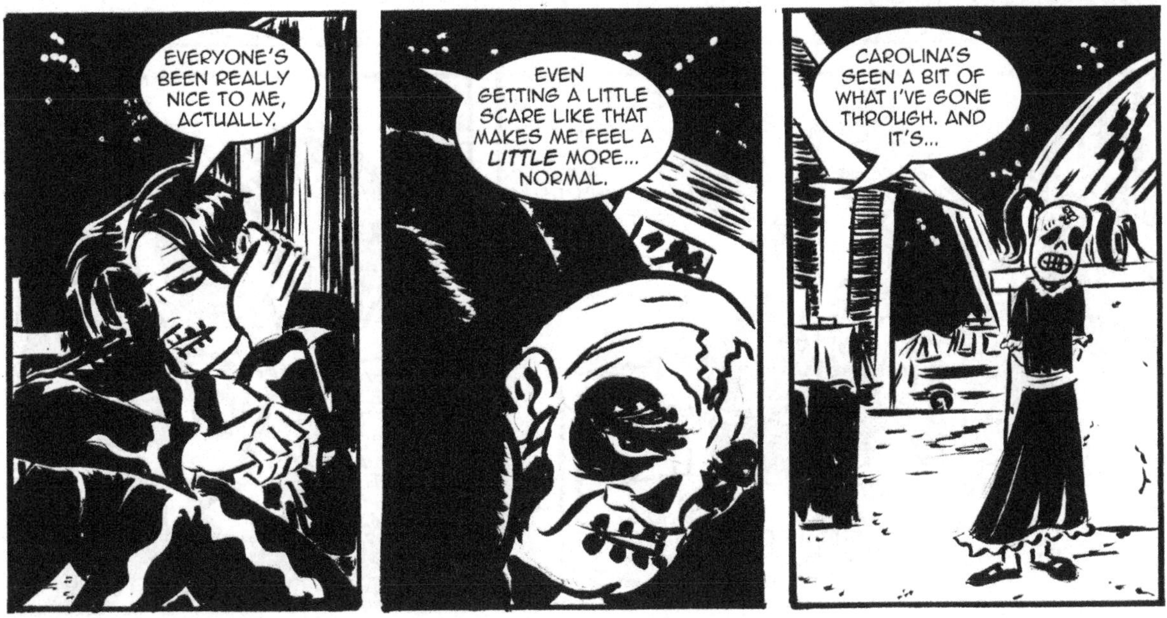
EVERYONE'S BEEN REALLY NICE TO ME, ACTUALLY.
EVEN GETTING A LITTLE SCARE LIKE THAT MAKES ME FEEL A LITTLE MORE... NORMAL.
CAROLINA'S SEEN A BIT OF WHAT I'VE GONE THROUGH. AND IT'S...

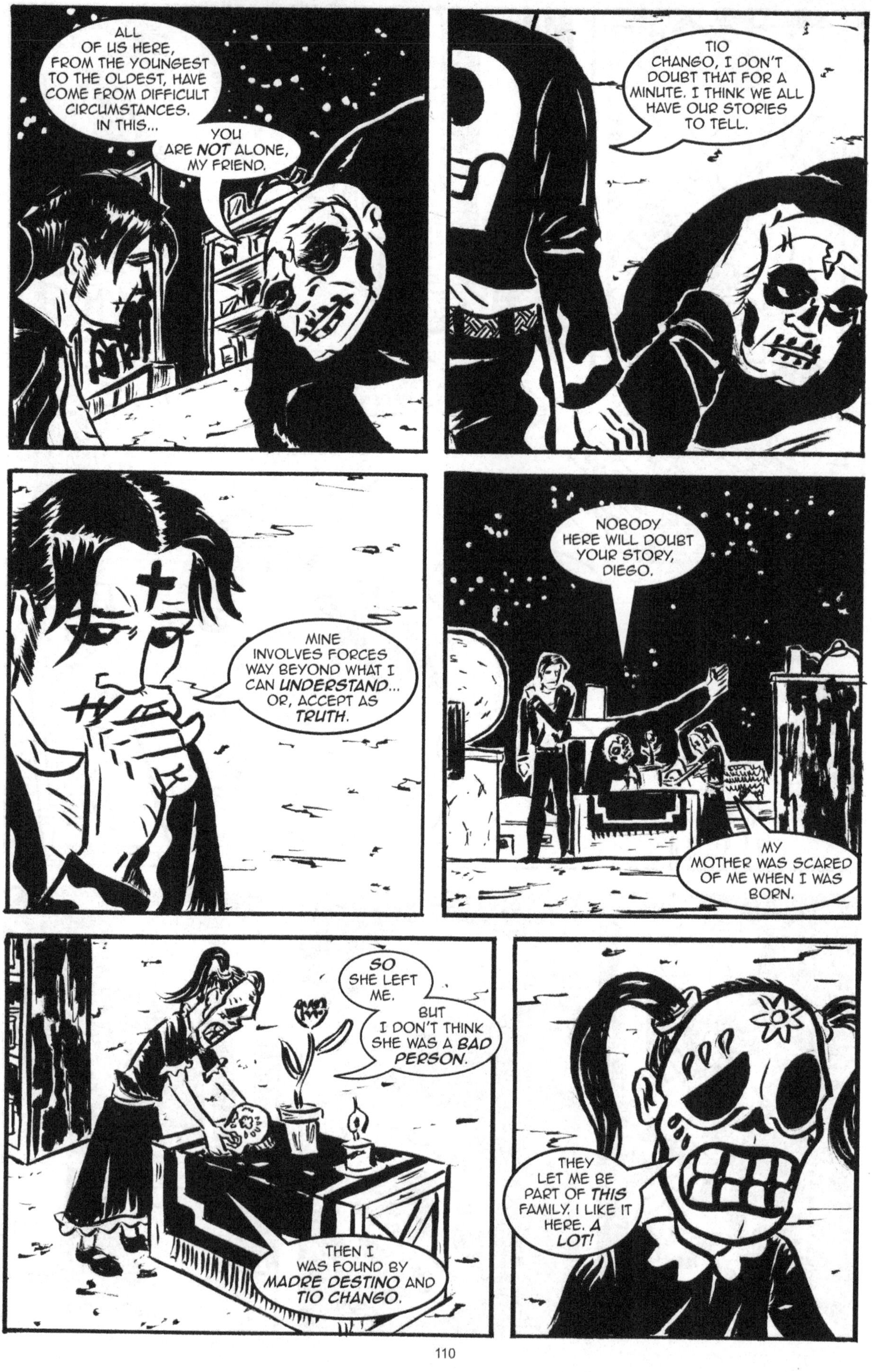
ALL OF US HERE, FROM THE YOUNGEST TO THE OLDEST, HAVE COME FROM DIFFICULT CIRCUMSTANCES. IN THIS...
YOU ARE NOT ALONE, MY FRIEND.
TIO CHANGO, I DON'T DOUBT THAT FOR A MINUTE. I THINK WE ALL HAVE OUR STORIES TO TELL.
MINE INVOLVES FORCES WAY BEYOND WHAT I CAN UNDERSTAND... OR, ACCEPT AS TRUTH.
NOBODY HERE WILL DOUBT YOUR STORY, DIEGO.
MY MOTHER WAS SCARED OF ME WHEN I WAS BORN.
SO SHE LEFT ME.
BUT I DON'T THINK SHE WAS A BAD PERSON.
THEN I WAS FOUND BY MADRE DESTINO AND TIO CHANGO.
THEY LET ME BE PART OF THIS FAMILY. I LIKE IT HERE. A LOT!

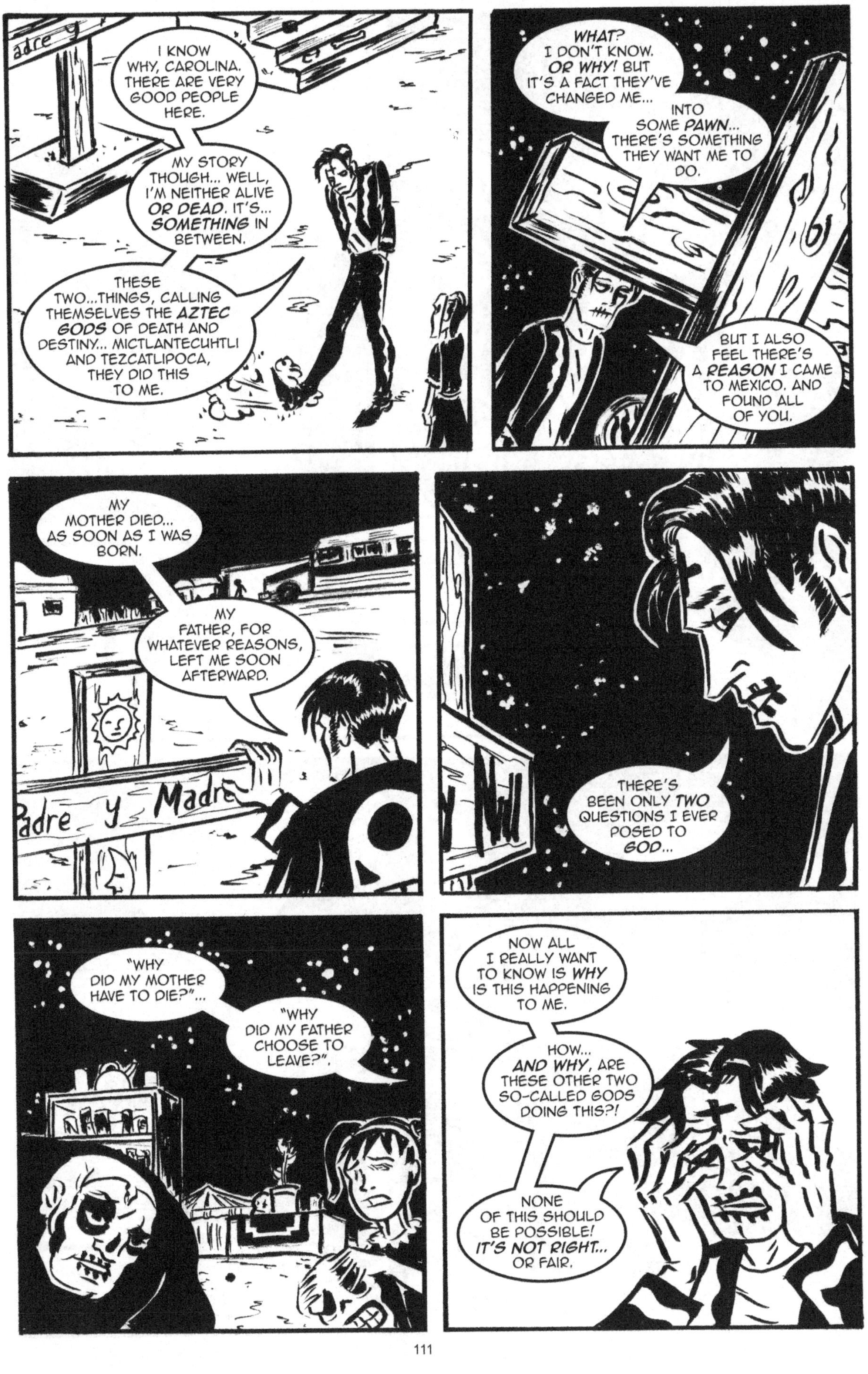
I KNOW WHY, CAROLINA. THERE ARE VERY GOOD PEOPLE HERE.
MY STORY THOUGH... WELL, I'M NEITHER ALIVE OR DEAD. IT'S... SOMETHING IN BETWEEN.
THESE TWO...THINGS, CALLING THEMSELVES THE AZTEC GODS OF DEATH AND DESTINY... MICTLANTECUHTLI AND TEZCATLIPOCA, THEY DID THIS TO ME.
WHAT? I DON'T KNOW. OR WHY! BUT IT'S A FACT THEY'VE CHANGED ME...
INTO SOME PAWN... THERE'S SOMETHING THEY WANT ME TO DO.
BUT I ALSO FEEL THERE'S A REASON I CAME TO MEXICO. AND FOUND ALL OF YOU.
MY MOTHER DIED... AS SOON AS I WAS BORN.
MY FATHER, FOR WHATEVER REASONS, LEFT ME SOON AFTERWARD.
Padre y Madre
THERE'S BEEN ONLY TWO QUESTIONS I EVER POSED TO GOD...
"WHY DID MY MOTHER HAVE TO DIE?"...
"WHY DID MY FATHER CHOOSE TO LEAVE?".
NOW ALL I REALLY WANT TO KNOW IS WHY IS THIS HAPPENING TO ME.
HOW... AND WHY, ARE THESE OTHER TWO SO-CALLED GODS DOING THIS?!
NONE OF THIS SHOULD BE POSSIBLE! IT'S NOT RIGHT... OR FAIR.

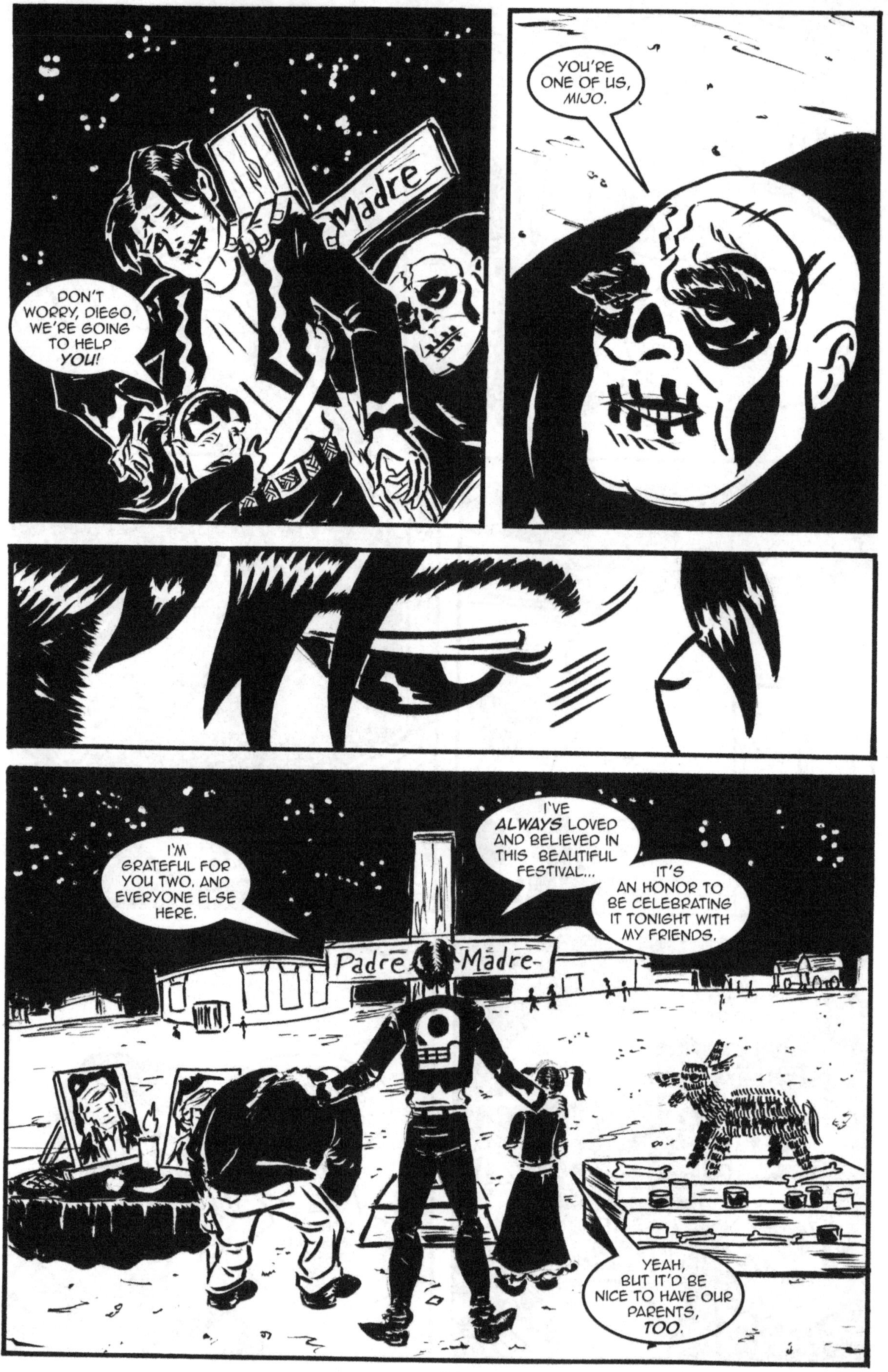

Madre
DON'T WORRY, DIEGO, WE'RE GOING TO HELP *YOU*!
YOU'RE ONE OF US, *MIJO*.
I'M GRATEFUL FOR YOU TWO. AND EVERYONE ELSE HERE.
I'VE *ALWAYS* LOVED AND BELIEVED IN THIS BEAUTIFUL FESTIVAL...
IT'S AN HONOR TO BE CELEBRATING IT TONIGHT WITH MY FRIENDS.
Padre Madre
YEAH, BUT IT'D BE NICE TO HAVE OUR PARENTS, *TOO*.

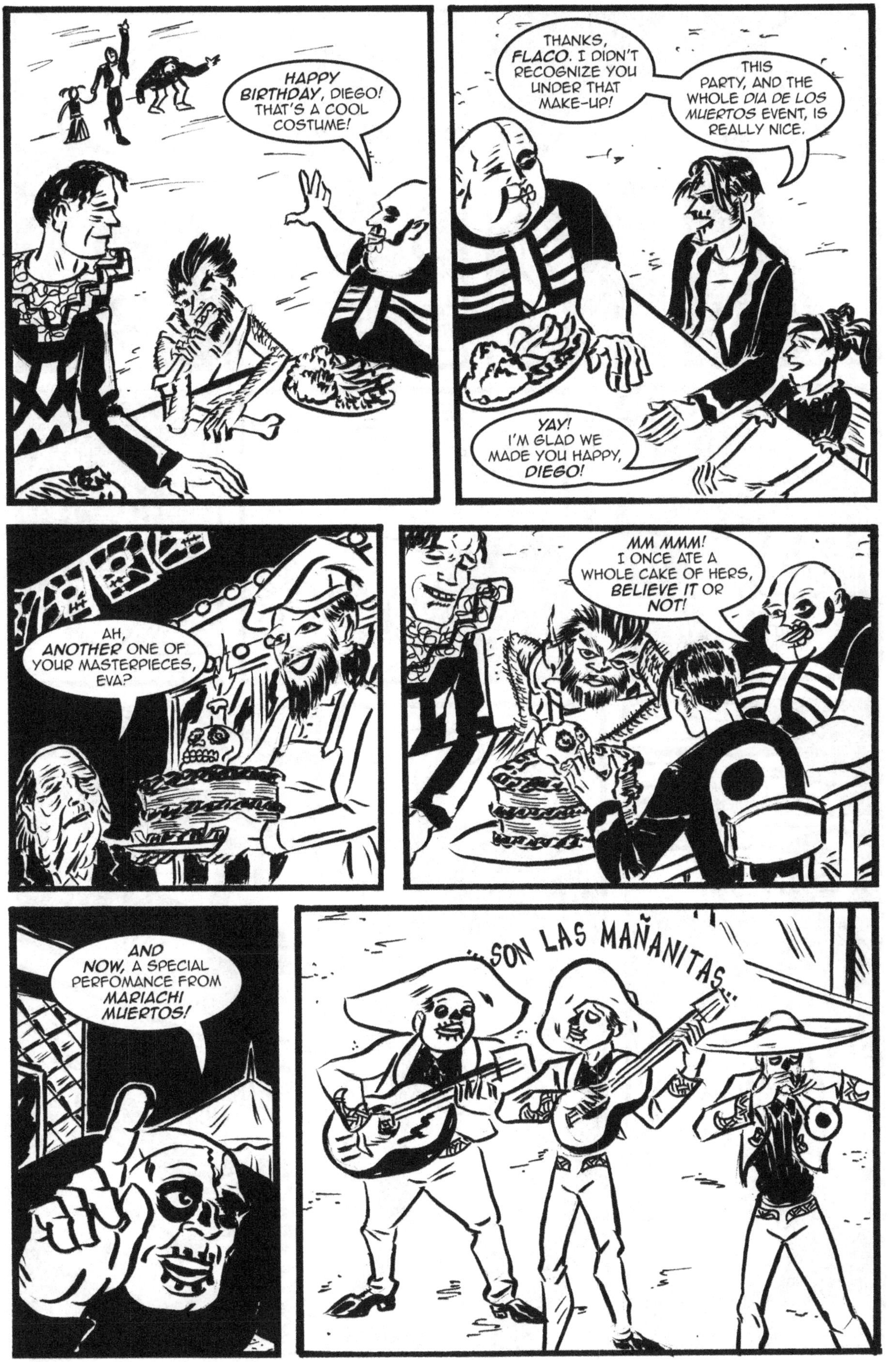
HAPPY BIRTHDAY, DIEGO! THAT'S A COOL COSTUME!
THANKS, FLACO. I DIDN'T RECOGNIZE YOU UNDER THAT MAKE-UP!
THIS PARTY, AND THE WHOLE DIA DE LOS MUERTOS EVENT, IS REALLY NICE.
YAY! I'M GLAD WE MADE YOU HAPPY, DIEGO!
AH, ANOTHER ONE OF YOUR MASTERPIECES, EVA?
MM MMM! I ONCE ATE A WHOLE CAKE OF HERS, BELIEVE IT OR NOT!
AND NOW, A SPECIAL PERFOMANCE FROM MARIACHI MUERTOS!
...SON LAS MAÑANITAS...

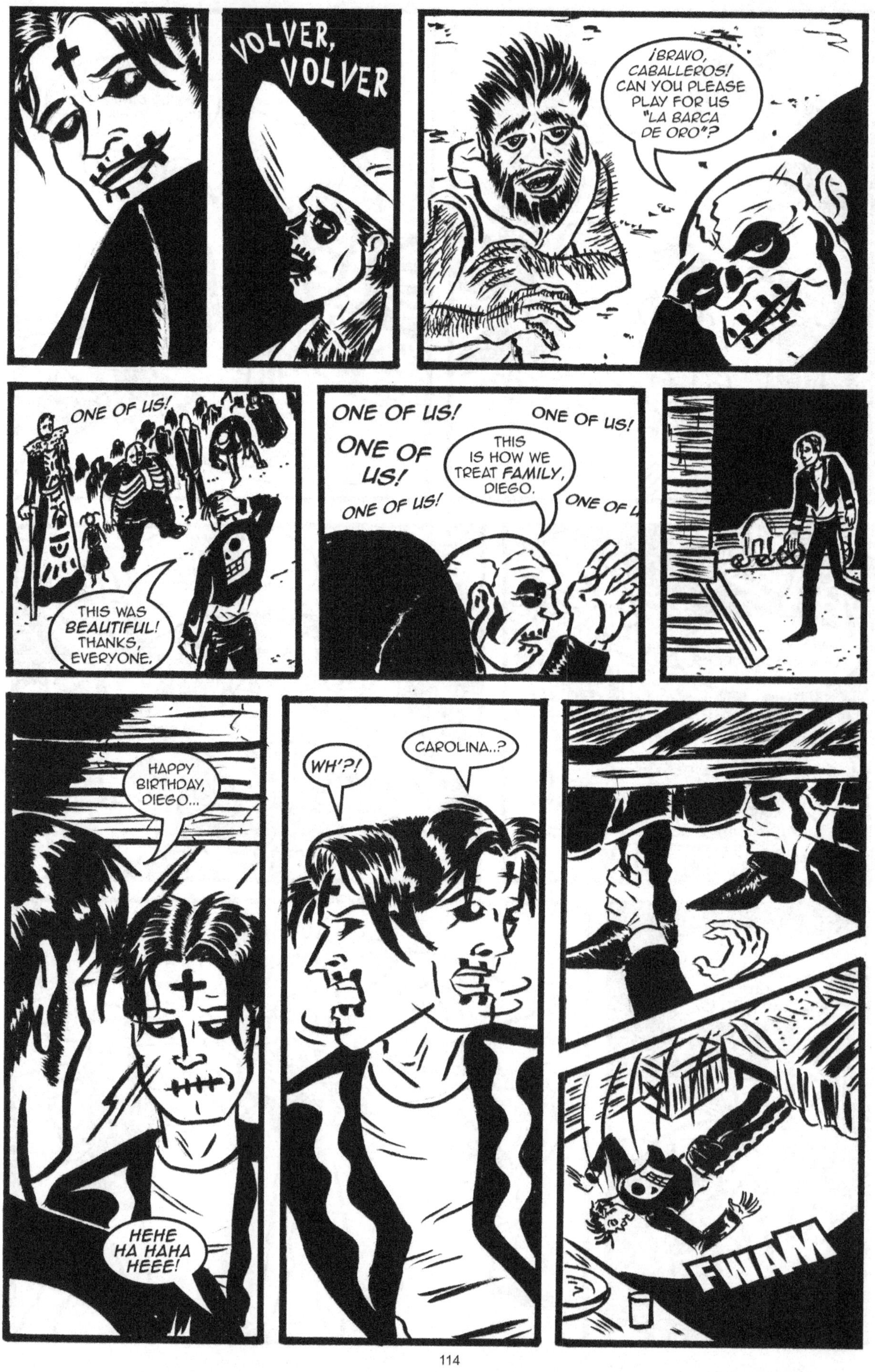
VOLVER, VOLVER
¡BRAVO, CABALLEROS! CAN YOU PLEASE PLAY FOR US "LA BARCA DE ORO"?
ONE OF US!
THIS WAS BEAUTIFUL! THANKS, EVERYONE.
ONE OF US!
ONE OF US!
ONE OF US!
ONE OF US!
THIS IS HOW WE TREAT FAMILY, DIEGO.
HAPPY BIRTHDAY, DIEGO...
HEHE HA HAHA HEEE!
WH'?!
CAROLINA..?
FWAM

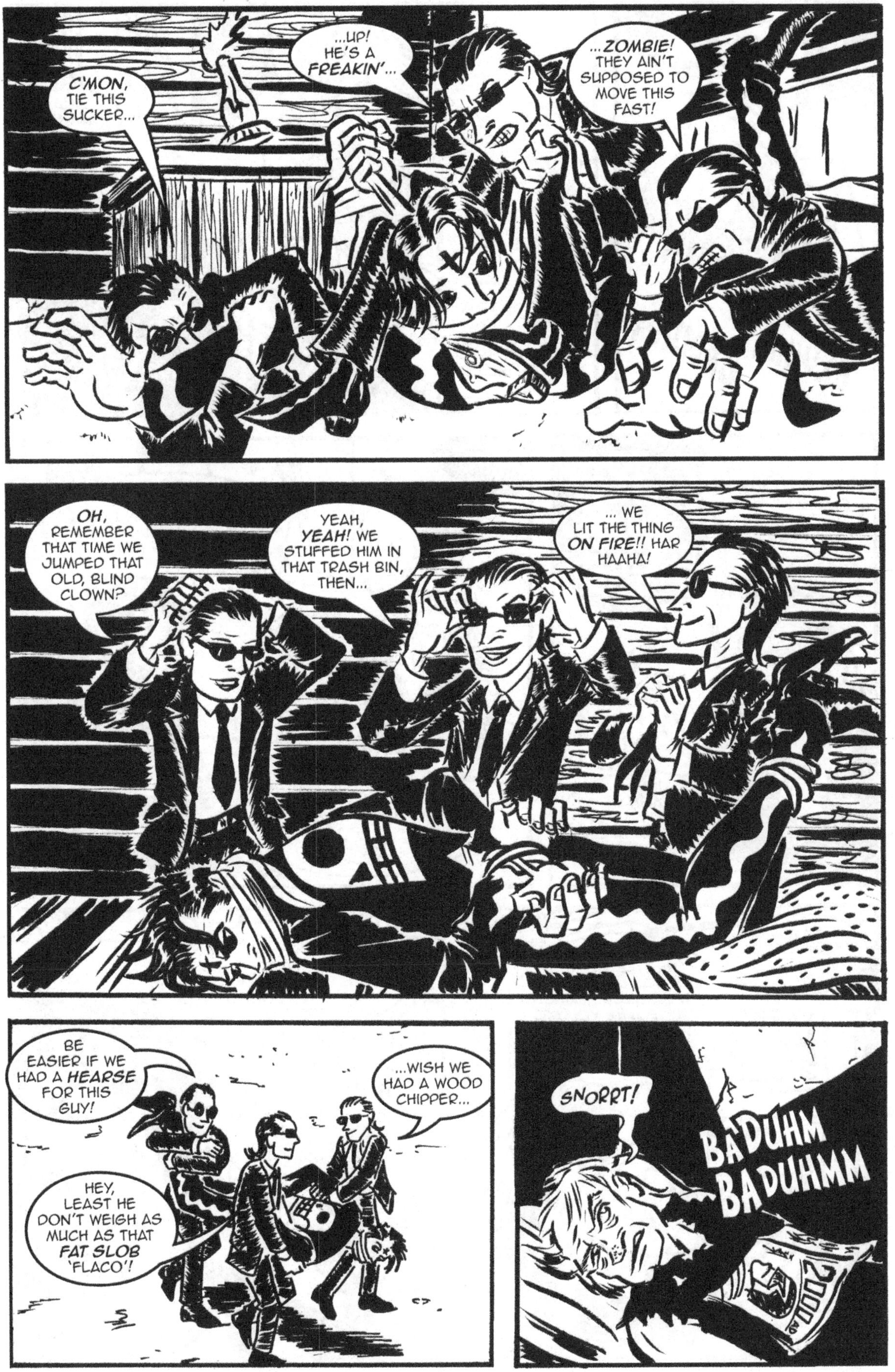
C'MON, TIE THIS SUCKER...
...UP! HE'S A FREAKIN'...
...ZOMBIE! THEY AIN'T SUPPOSED TO MOVE THIS FAST!
OH, REMEMBER THAT TIME WE JUMPED THAT OLD, BLIND CLOWN?
YEAH, YEAH! WE STUFFED HIM IN THAT TRASH BIN, THEN...
... WE LIT THE THING ON FIRE!! HAR HAAHA!
BE EASIER IF WE HAD A HEARSE FOR THIS GUY!
HEY, LEAST HE DON'T WEIGH AS MUCH AS THAT FAT SLOB 'FLACO'!
...WISH WE HAD A WOOD CHIPPER...
SNORRT!
BADUHM BADUHMM

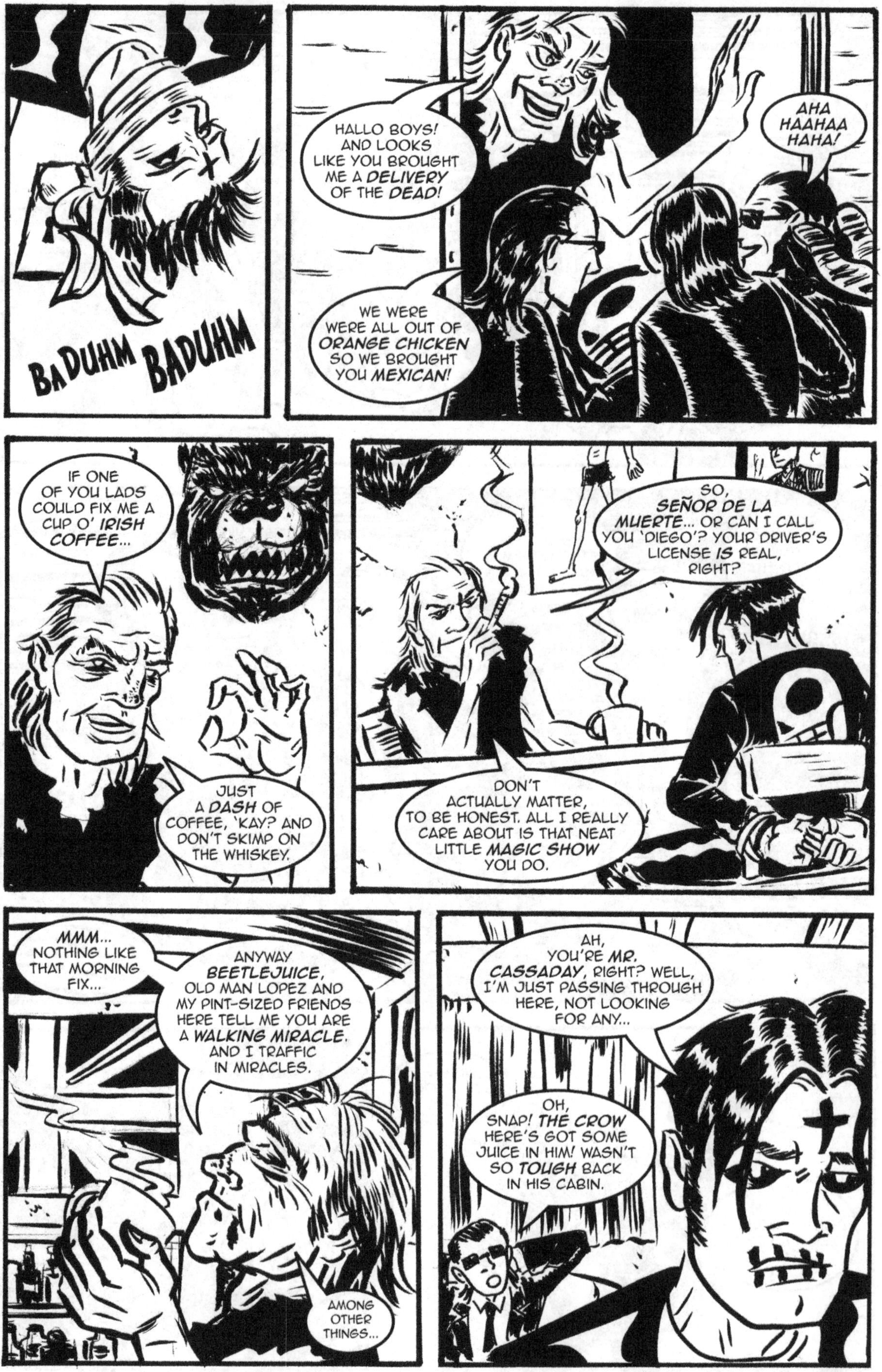

BADUHM BADUHM
HALLO BOYS! AND LOOKS LIKE YOU BROUGHT ME A DELIVERY OF THE DEAD!
AHA HAAHAA HAHA!
WE WERE WERE ALL OUT OF ORANGE CHICKEN SO WE BROUGHT YOU MEXICAN!
IF ONE OF YOU LADS COULD FIX ME A CUP O' IRISH COFFEE...
JUST A DASH OF COFFEE, 'KAY? AND DON'T SKIMP ON THE WHISKEY.
SO, SEÑOR DE LA MUERTE... OR CAN I CALL YOU 'DIEGO'? YOUR DRIVER'S LICENSE IS REAL, RIGHT?
DON'T ACTUALLY MATTER, TO BE HONEST. ALL I REALLY CARE ABOUT IS THAT NEAT LITTLE MAGIC SHOW YOU DO.
MMM... NOTHING LIKE THAT MORNING FIX...
ANYWAY BEETLEJUICE, OLD MAN LOPEZ AND MY PINT-SIZED FRIENDS HERE TELL ME YOU ARE A WALKING MIRACLE. AND I TRAFFIC IN MIRACLES.
AMONG OTHER THINGS...
AH, YOU'RE MR. CASSADAY, RIGHT? WELL, I'M JUST PASSING THROUGH HERE, NOT LOOKING FOR ANY...
OH, SNAP! THE CROW HERE'S GOT SOME JUICE IN HIM! WASN'T SO TOUGH BACK IN HIS CABIN.

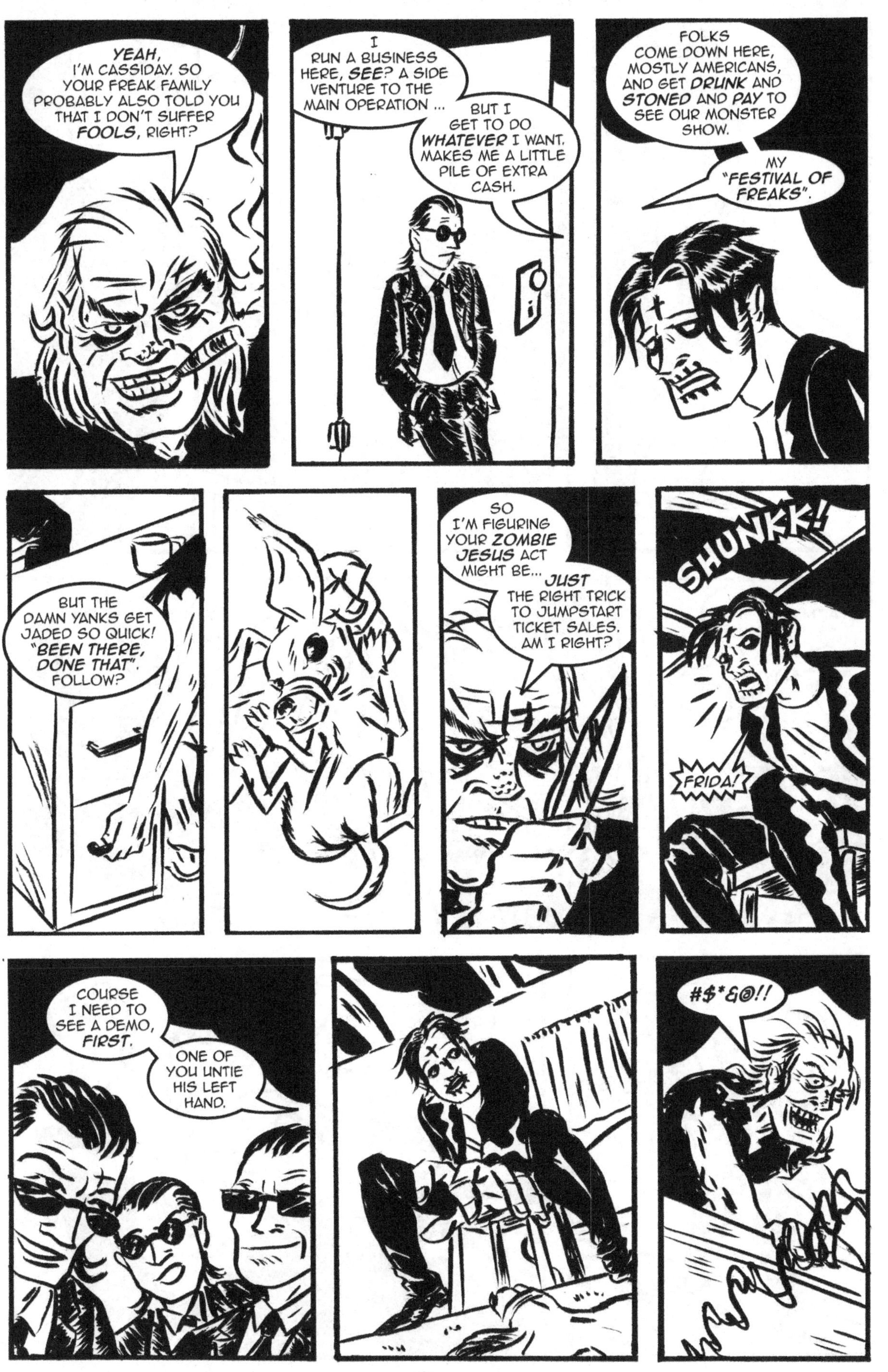
YEAH, I'M CASSIDAY. SO YOUR FREAK FAMILY PROBABLY ALSO TOLD YOU THAT I DON'T SUFFER FOOLS, RIGHT?
I RUN A BUSINESS HERE, SEE? A SIDE VENTURE TO THE MAIN OPERATION ...
BUT I GET TO DO WHATEVER I WANT. MAKES ME A LITTLE PILE OF EXTRA CASH.
FOLKS COME DOWN HERE, MOSTLY AMERICANS, AND GET DRUNK AND STONED AND PAY TO SEE OUR MONSTER SHOW.
MY "FESTIVAL OF FREAKS".
BUT THE DAMN YANKS GET JADED SO QUICK! "BEEN THERE, DONE THAT". FOLLOW?
SO I'M FIGURING YOUR ZOMBIE JESUS ACT MIGHT BE... JUST THE RIGHT TRICK TO JUMPSTART TICKET SALES. AM I RIGHT?
SHUNKK!
FRIDA!
COURSE I NEED TO SEE A DEMO, FIRST.
ONE OF YOU UNTIE HIS LEFT HAND.
#$*&@!!

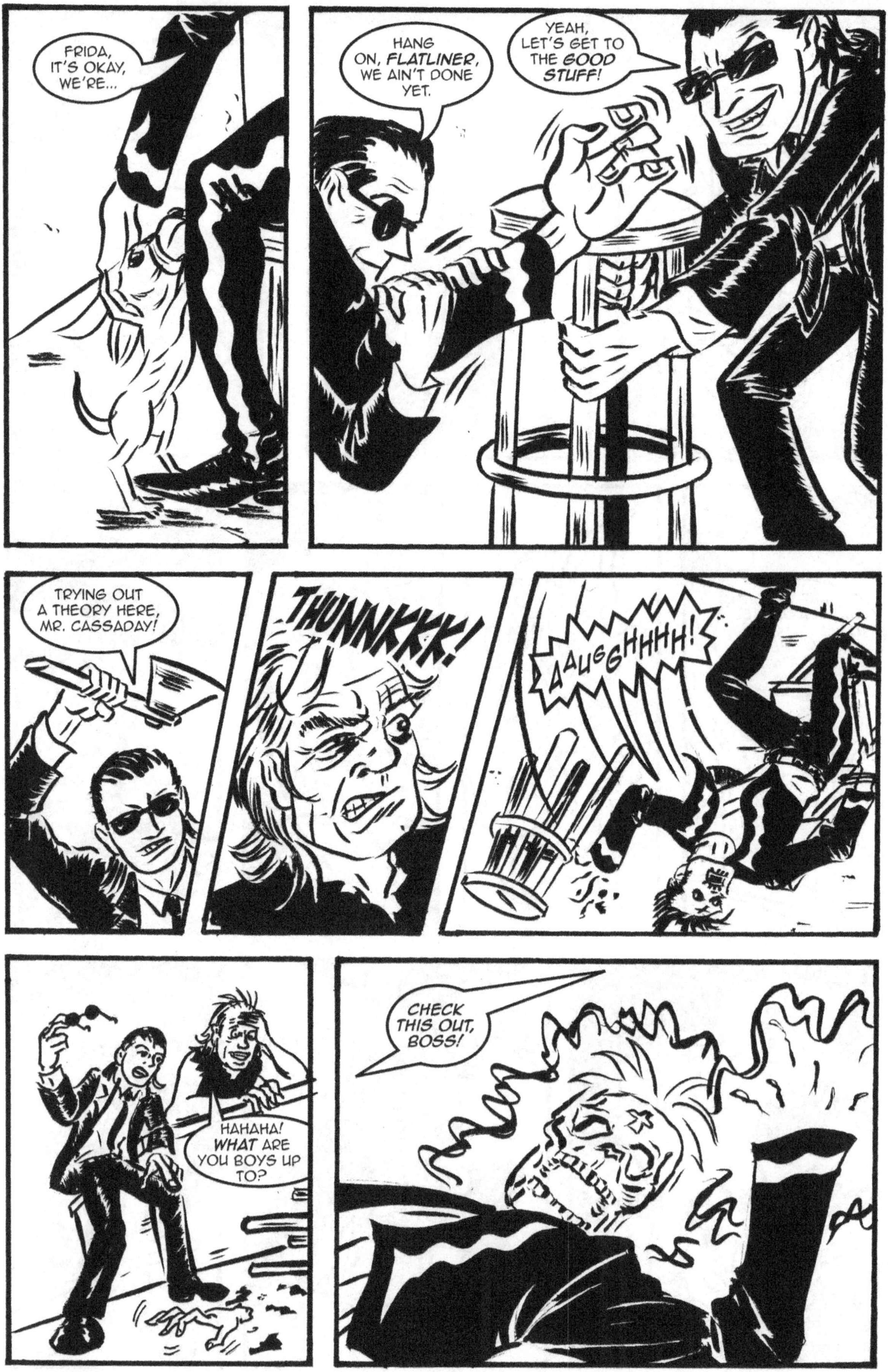
FRIDA, IT'S OKAY, WE'RE...
HANG ON, FLATLINER, WE AIN'T DONE YET.
YEAH, LET'S GET TO THE GOOD STUFF!
TRYING OUT A THEORY HERE, MR. CASSADAY!
THUNNKKK!
AAUGGHHHH!
HAHAHA! WHAT ARE YOU BOYS UP TO?
CHECK THIS OUT, BOSS!

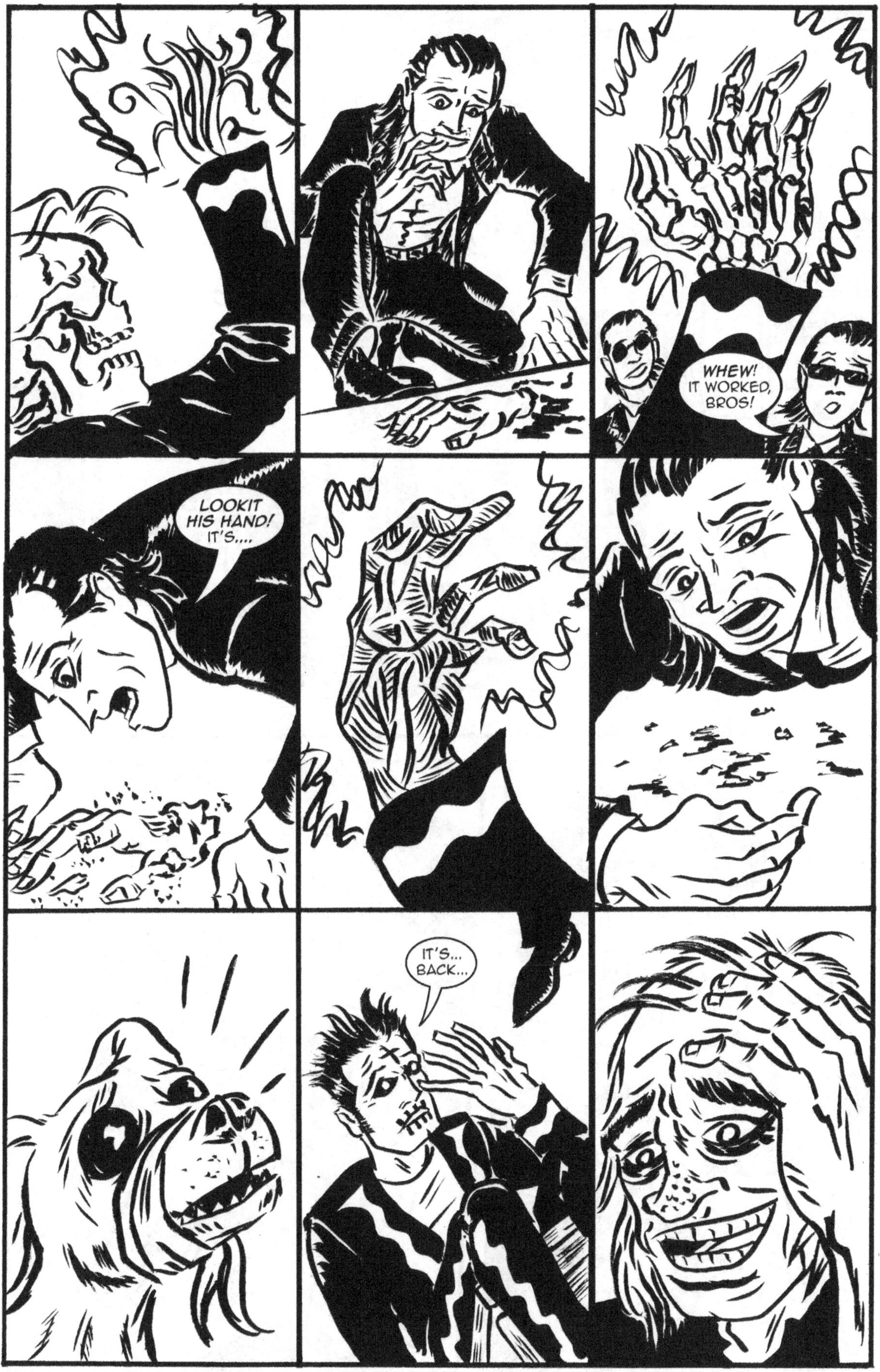
WHEW!
IT WORKED, BROS!
LOOKIT HIS HAND! IT'S....
IT'S... BACK...

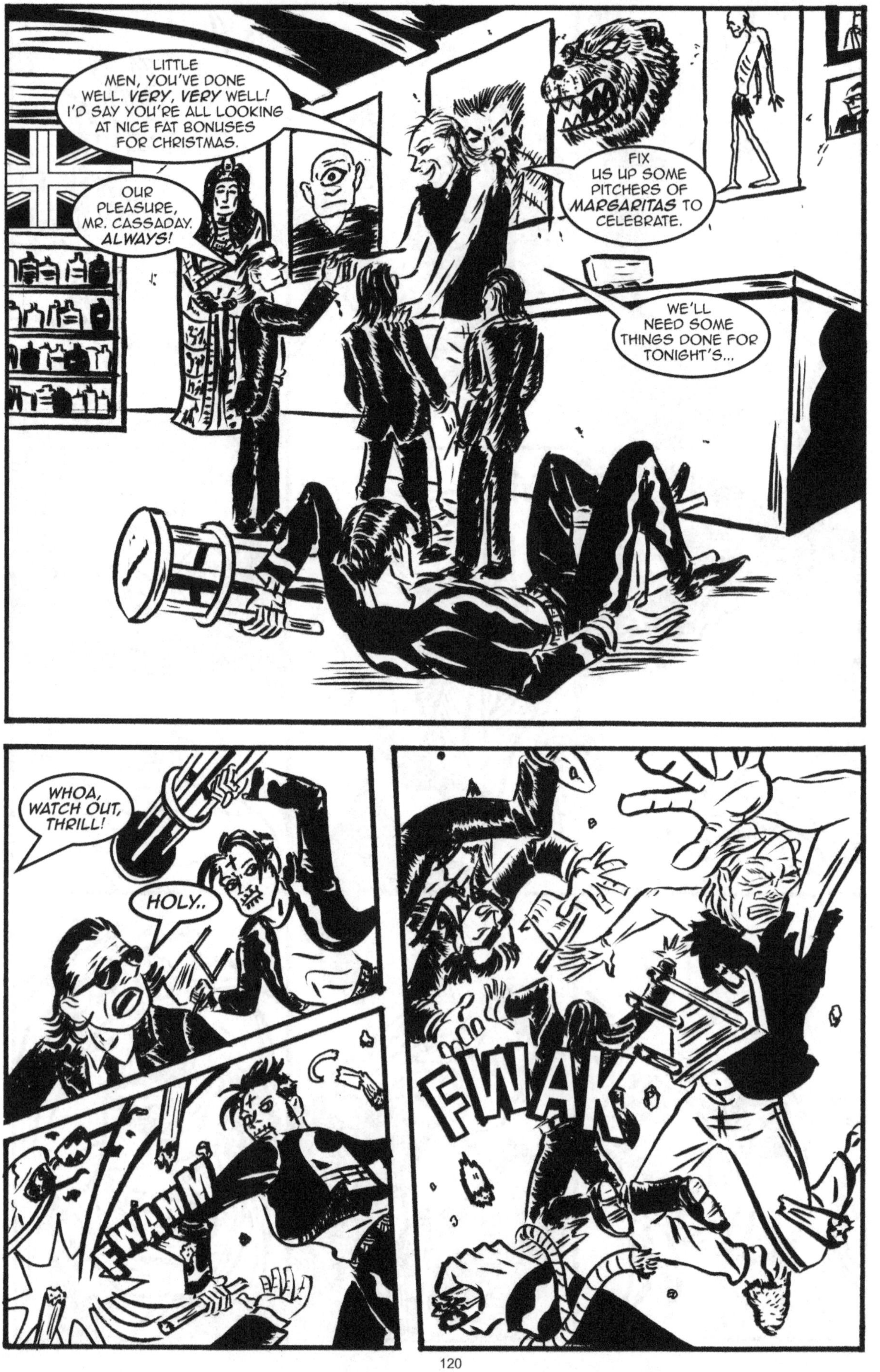
LITTLE MEN, YOU'VE DONE WELL. VERY, VERY WELL! I'D SAY YOU'RE ALL LOOKING AT NICE FAT BONUSES FOR CHRISTMAS.
OUR PLEASURE, MR. CASSADAY. ALWAYS!
FIX US UP SOME PITCHERS OF MARGARITAS TO CELEBRATE.
WE'LL NEED SOME THINGS DONE FOR TONIGHT'S...
WHOA, WATCH OUT, THRILL!
HOLY..
FWAMM
FWAK

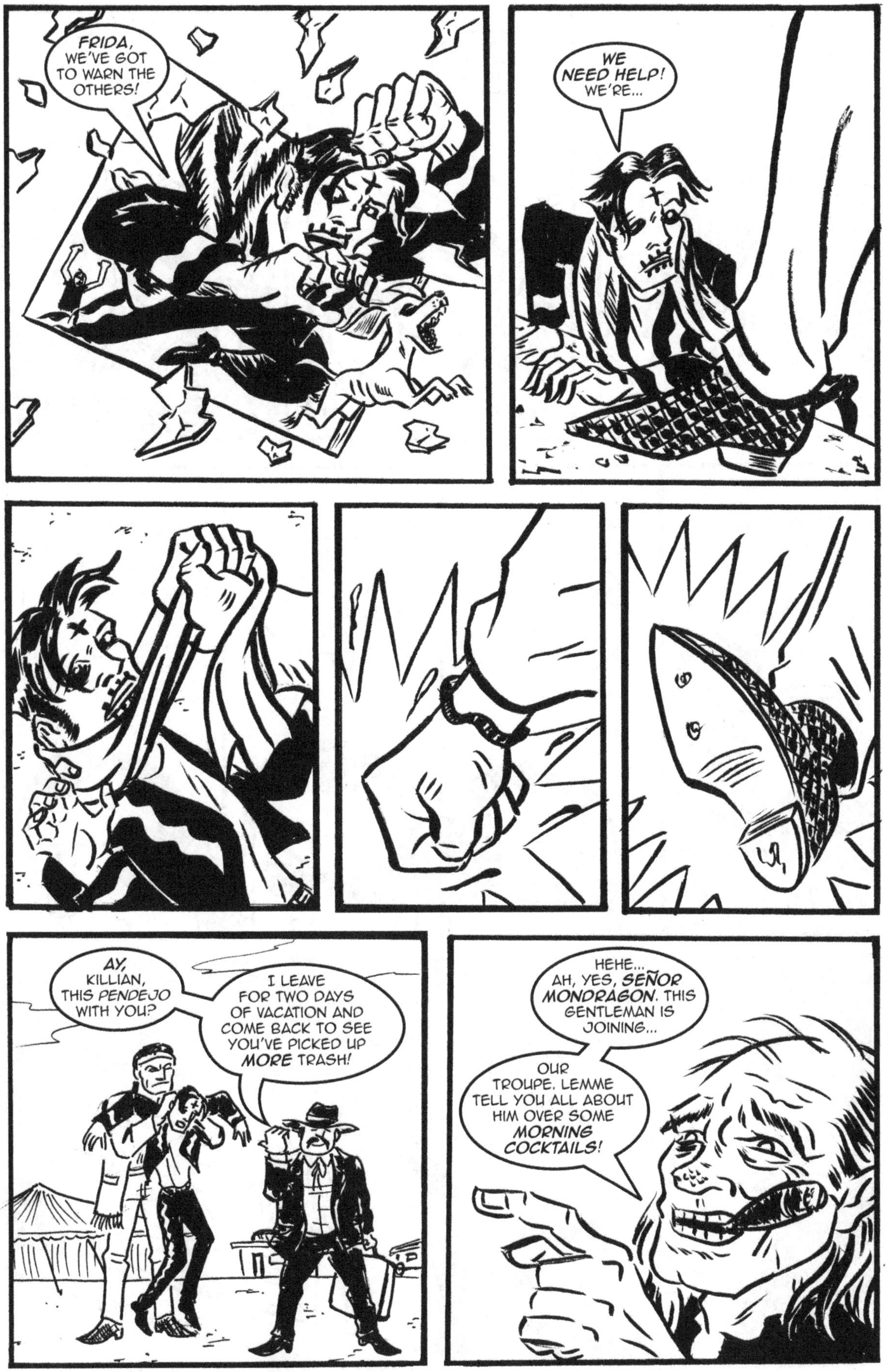
FRIDA, WE'VE GOT TO WARN THE OTHERS!
WE NEED HELP! WE'RE...
AY, KILLIAN, THIS *PENDEJO* WITH YOU?
I LEAVE FOR TWO DAYS OF VACATION AND COME BACK TO SEE YOU'VE PICKED UP *MORE* TRASH!
HEHE... AH, YES, *SEÑOR MONDRAGON*. THIS GENTLEMAN IS JOINING...
OUR TROUPE. LEMME TELL YOU ALL ABOUT HIM OVER SOME *MORNING COCKTAILS!*

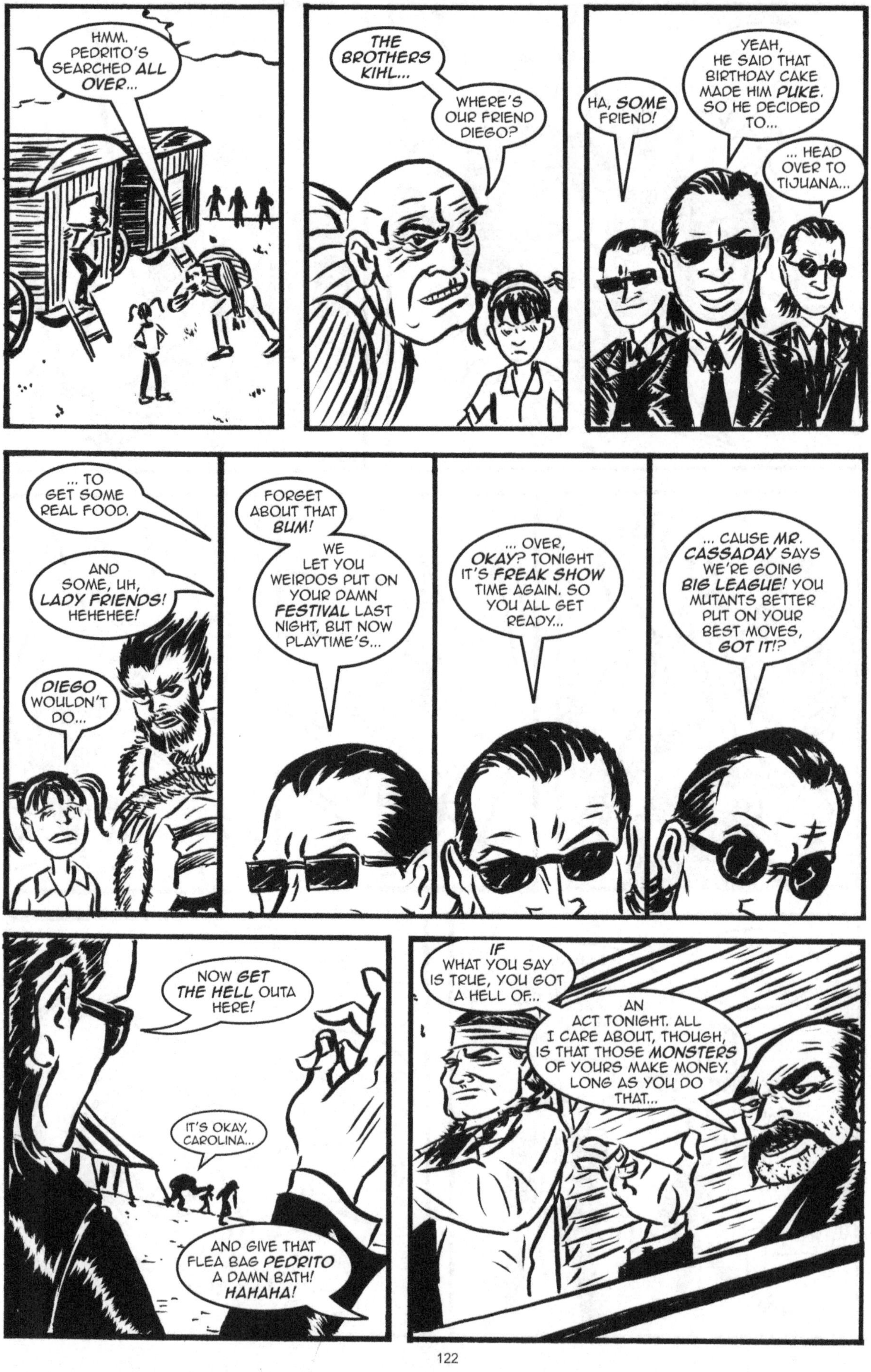
HMM. PEDRITO'S SEARCHED **ALL OVER**...
THE BROTHERS KIHL...
WHERE'S OUR FRIEND DIEGO?
HA, **SOME** FRIEND!
YEAH, HE SAID THAT BIRTHDAY CAKE MADE HIM **PUKE**. SO HE DECIDED TO...
... HEAD OVER TO TIJUANA...
... TO GET SOME REAL FOOD.
AND SOME, UH, **LADY FRIENDS**! HEHEHEE!
DIEGO WOULDN'T DO...
FORGET ABOUT THAT **BUM**!
WE LET YOU WEIRDOS PUT ON YOUR DAMN **FESTIVAL** LAST NIGHT, BUT NOW PLAYTIME'S...
... OVER, **OKAY**? TONIGHT IT'S **FREAK SHOW** TIME AGAIN. SO YOU ALL GET READY...
... CAUSE **MR. CASSADAY** SAYS WE'RE GOING **BIG LEAGUE**! YOU MUTANTS BETTER PUT ON YOUR BEST MOVES, **GOT IT**!?
NOW **GET THE HELL** OUTA HERE!
IT'S OKAY, CAROLINA...
AND GIVE THAT FLEA BAG **PEDRITO** A DAMN BATH! **HAHAHA**!
IF WHAT YOU SAY IS TRUE, YOU GOT A HELL OF...
AN ACT TONIGHT. ALL I CARE ABOUT, THOUGH, IS THAT THOSE **MONSTERS** OF YOURS MAKE MONEY. LONG AS YOU DO THAT...

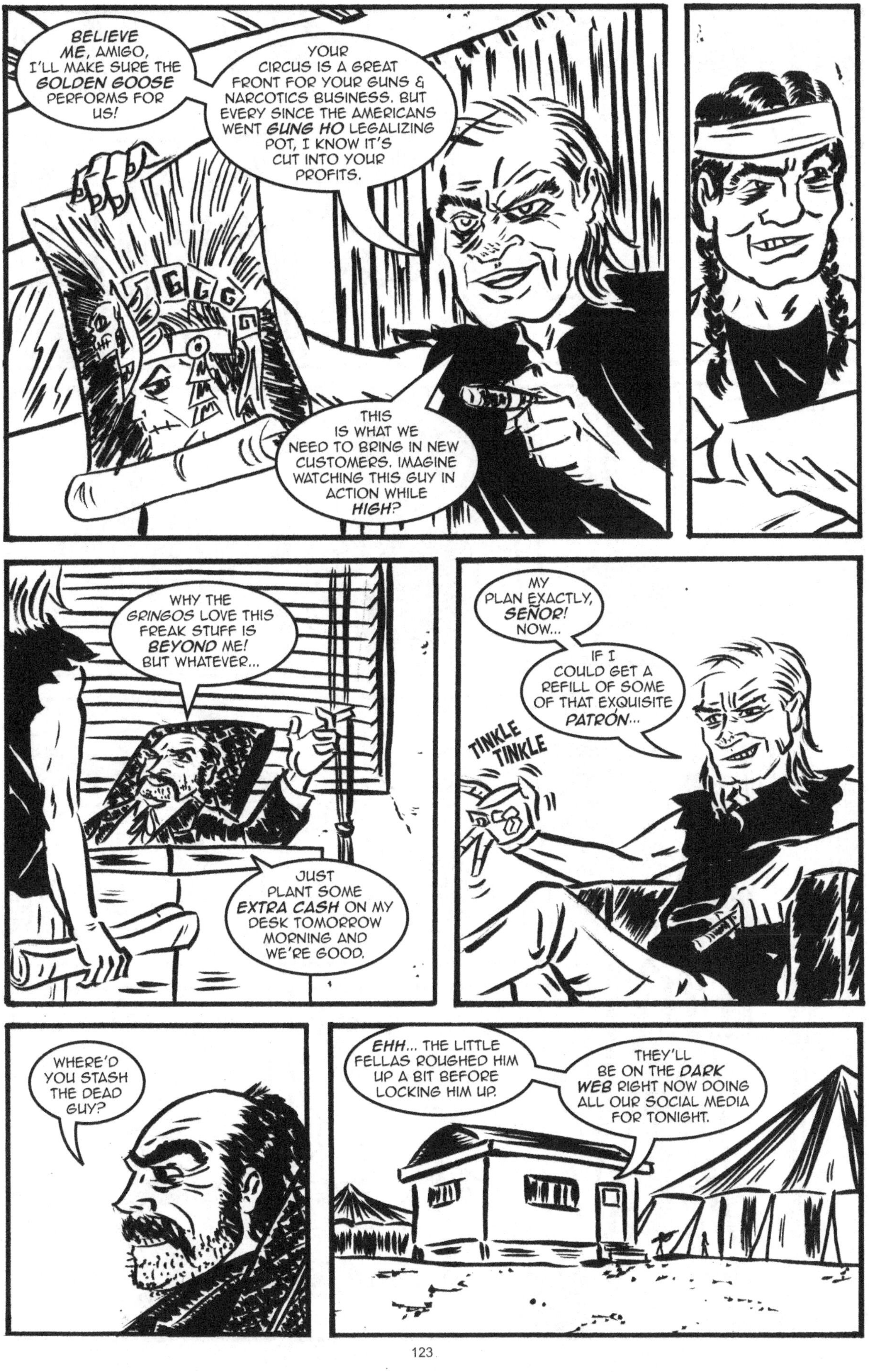
BELIEVE ME, AMIGO, I'LL MAKE SURE THE GOLDEN GOOSE PERFORMS FOR US!
YOUR CIRCUS IS A GREAT FRONT FOR YOUR GUNS & NARCOTICS BUSINESS. BUT EVERY SINCE THE AMERICANS WENT GUNG HO LEGALIZING POT, I KNOW IT'S CUT INTO YOUR PROFITS.
THIS IS WHAT WE NEED TO BRING IN NEW CUSTOMERS. IMAGINE WATCHING THIS GUY IN ACTION WHILE HIGH?
WHY THE GRINGOS LOVE THIS FREAK STUFF IS BEYOND ME! BUT WHATEVER...
JUST PLANT SOME EXTRA CASH ON MY DESK TOMORROW MORNING AND WE'RE GOOD.
MY PLAN EXACTLY, SEÑOR! NOW...
IF I COULD GET A REFILL OF SOME OF THAT EXQUISITE PATRÓN...
TINKLE TINKLE
WHERE'D YOU STASH THE DEAD GUY?
EHH... THE LITTLE FELLAS ROUGHED HIM UP A BIT BEFORE LOCKING HIM UP.
THEY'LL BE ON THE DARK WEB RIGHT NOW DOING ALL OUR SOCIAL MEDIA FOR TONIGHT.

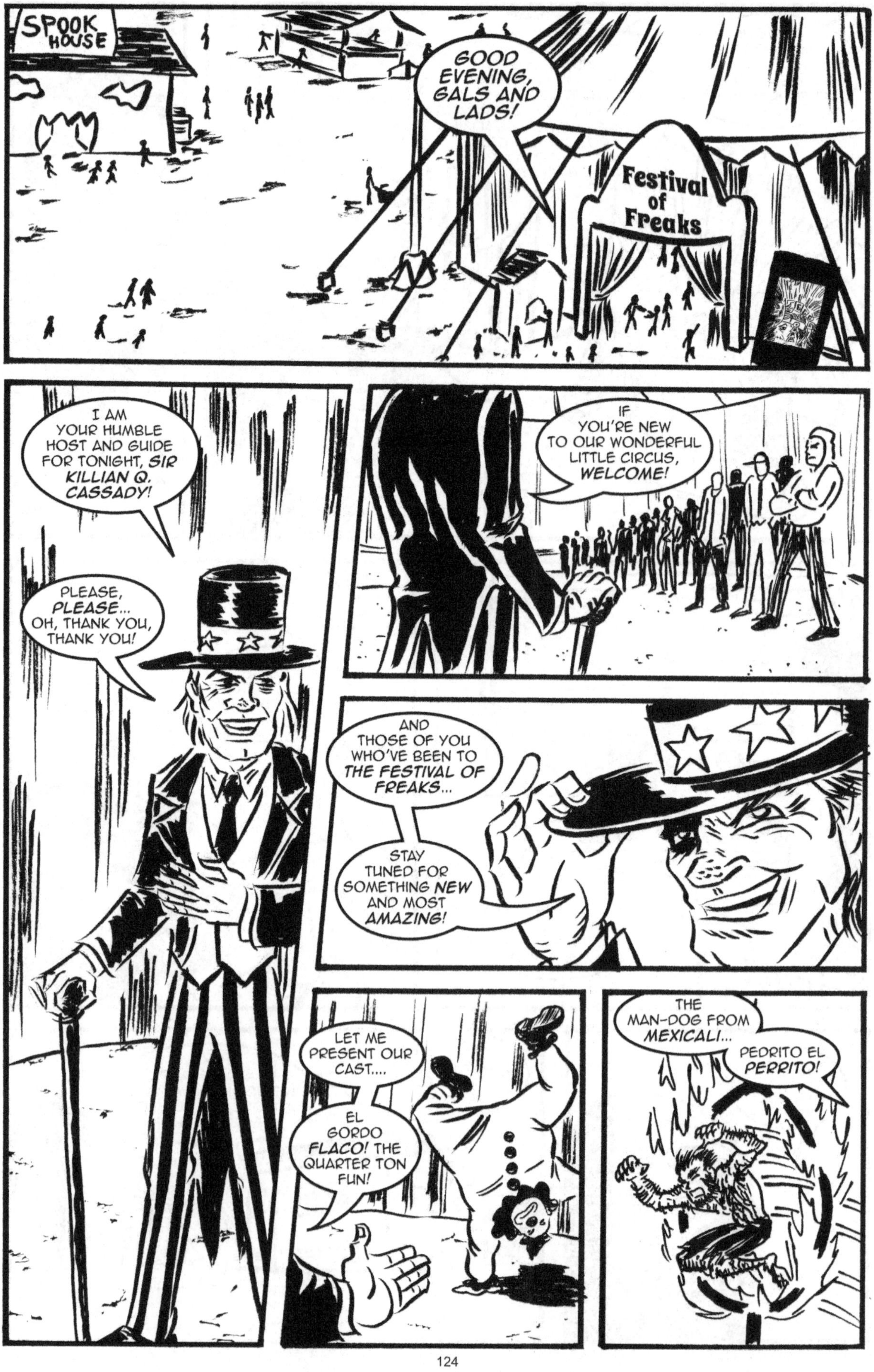
SPOOK HOUSE
GOOD EVENING, GALS AND LADS!
Festival of Freaks
I AM YOUR HUMBLE HOST AND GUIDE FOR TONIGHT, SIR KILLIAN Q. CASSADY!
PLEASE, PLEASE... OH, THANK YOU, THANK YOU!
IF YOU'RE NEW TO OUR WONDERFUL LITTLE CIRCUS, WELCOME!
AND THOSE OF YOU WHO'VE BEEN TO THE FESTIVAL OF FREAKS...
STAY TUNED FOR SOMETHING NEW AND MOST AMAZING!
LET ME PRESENT OUR CAST....
EL GORDO FLACO! THE QUARTER TON FUN!
THE MAN-DOG FROM MEXICALI...
PEDRITO EL PERRITO!

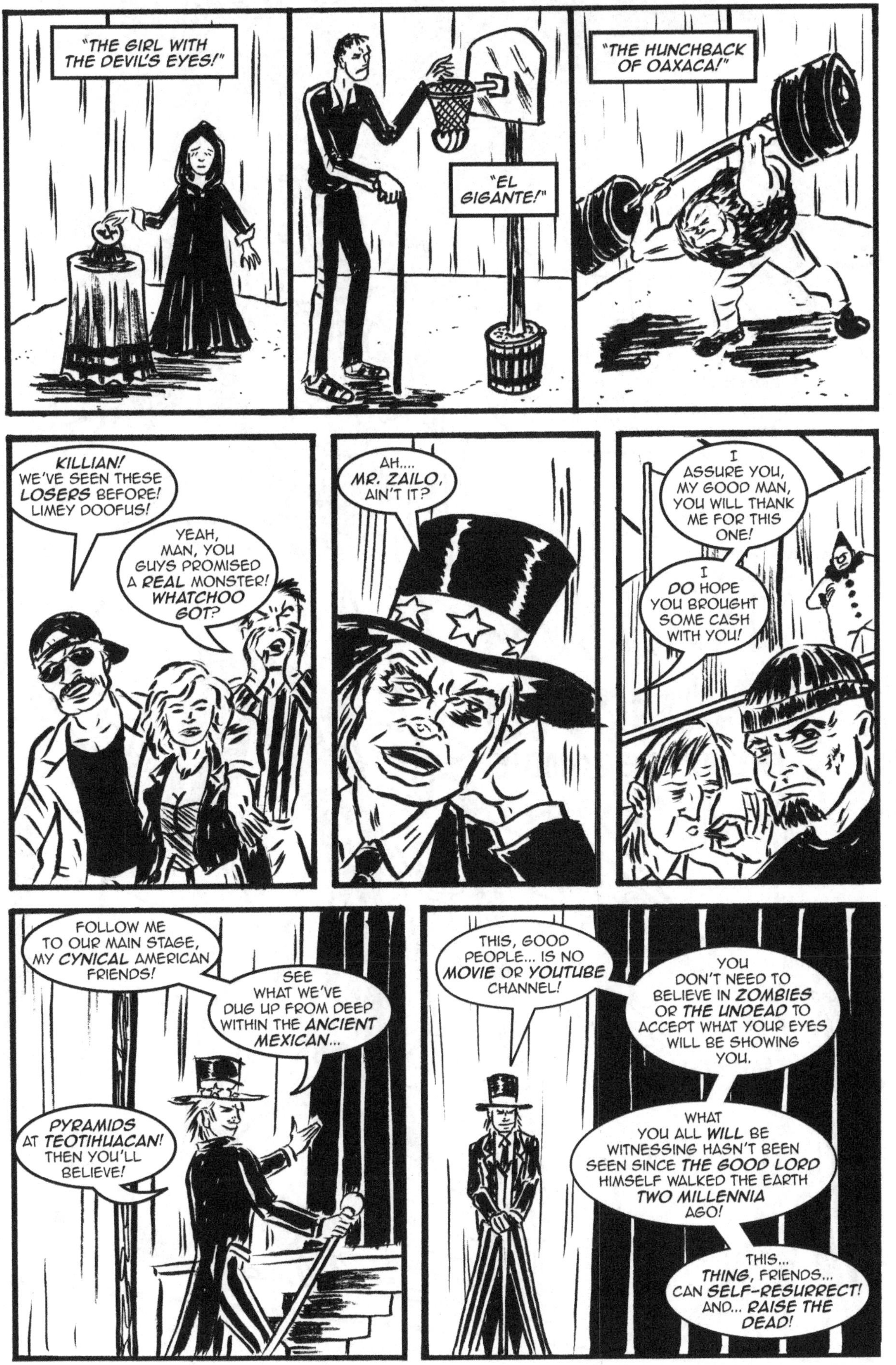
"THE GIRL WITH THE DEVIL'S EYES!"
"EL GIGANTE!"
"THE HUNCHBACK OF OAXACA!"
KILLIAN! WE'VE SEEN THESE LOSERS BEFORE! LIMEY DOOFUS!
YEAH, MAN, YOU GUYS PROMISED A REAL MONSTER! WHATCHOO GOT?
AH.... MR. ZAILO, AIN'T IT?
I ASSURE YOU, MY GOOD MAN, YOU WILL THANK ME FOR THIS ONE!
I DO HOPE YOU BROUGHT SOME CASH WITH YOU!
FOLLOW ME TO OUR MAIN STAGE, MY CYNICAL AMERICAN FRIENDS!
SEE WHAT WE'VE DUG UP FROM DEEP WITHIN THE ANCIENT MEXICAN...
PYRAMIDS AT TEOTIHUACAN! THEN YOU'LL BELIEVE!
THIS, GOOD PEOPLE... IS NO MOVIE OR YOUTUBE CHANNEL!
YOU DON'T NEED TO BELIEVE IN ZOMBIES OR THE UNDEAD TO ACCEPT WHAT YOUR EYES WILL BE SHOWING YOU.
WHAT YOU ALL WILL BE WITNESSING HASN'T BEEN SEEN SINCE THE GOOD LORD HIMSELF WALKED THE EARTH TWO MILLENNIA AGO!
THIS... THING, FRIENDS... CAN SELF-RESURRECT! AND... RAISE THE DEAD!

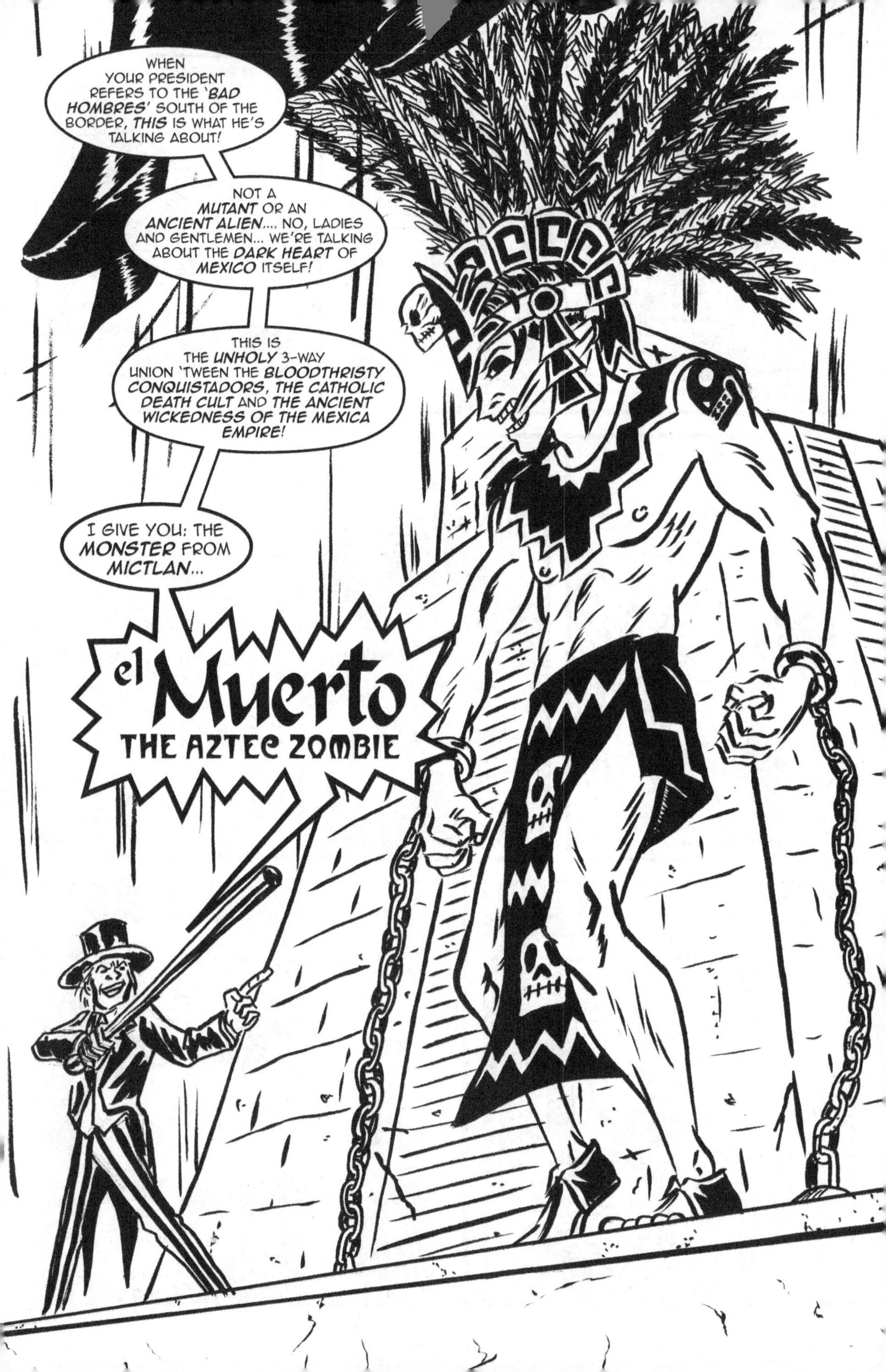
WHEN YOUR PRESIDENT REFERS TO THE 'BAD HOMBRES' SOUTH OF THE BORDER, THIS IS WHAT HE'S TALKING ABOUT!
NOT A MUTANT OR AN ANCIENT ALIEN.... NO, LADIES AND GENTLEMEN... WE'RE TALKING ABOUT THE DARK HEART OF MEXICO ITSELF!
THIS IS THE UNHOLY 3-WAY UNION 'TWEEN THE BLOODTHRISTY CONQUISTADORS, THE CATHOLIC DEATH CULT AND THE ANCIENT WICKEDNESS OF THE MEXICA EMPIRE!
I GIVE YOU: THE MONSTER FROM MICTLAN...
el Muerto
THE AZTEC ZOMBIE

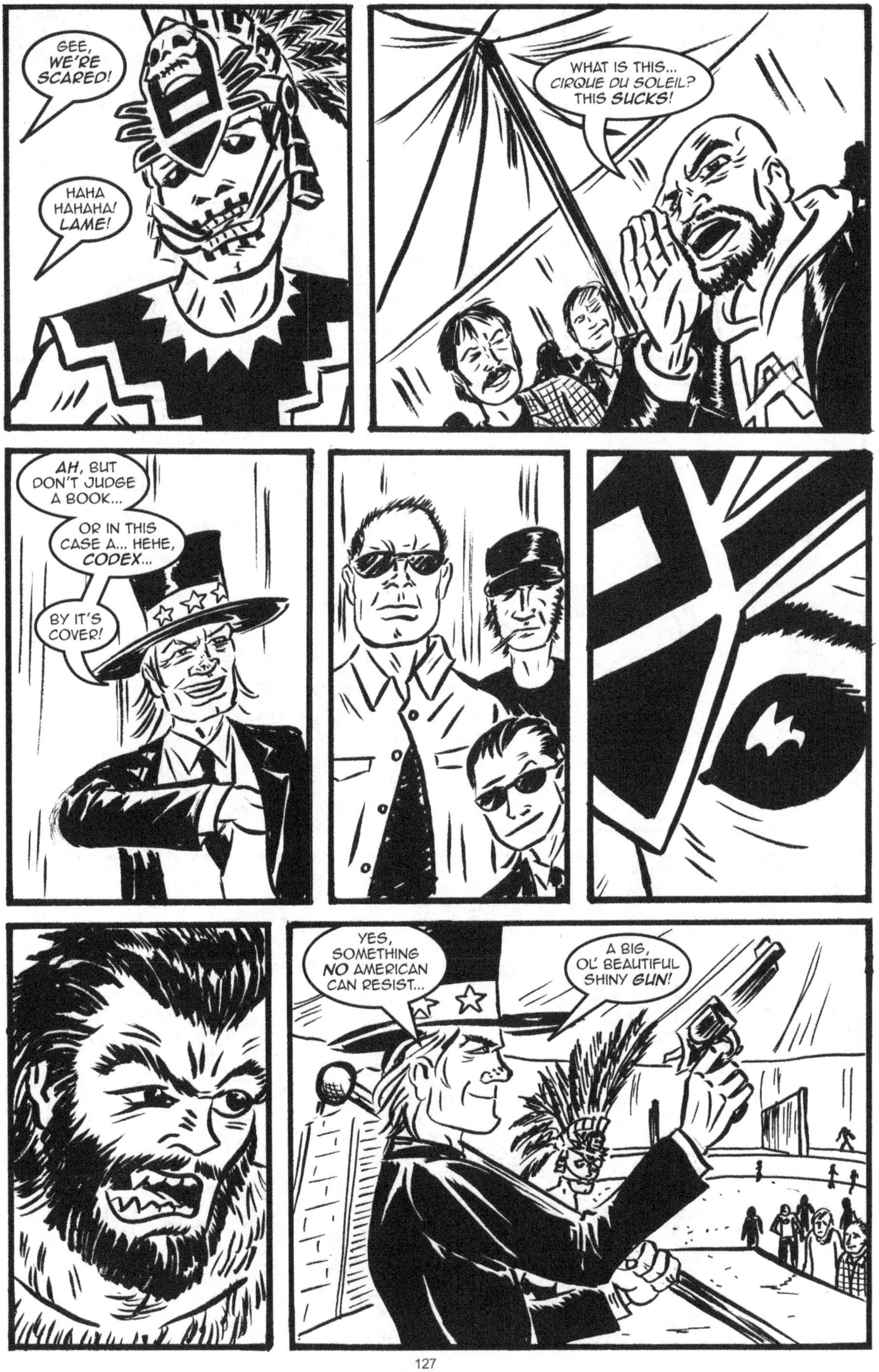
GEE, WE'RE SCARED!
HAHA HAHAHA! LAME!
WHAT IS THIS... CIRQUE DU SOLEIL? THIS SUCKS!
AH, BUT DON'T JUDGE A BOOK...
OR IN THIS CASE A... HEHE, CODEX...
BY IT'S COVER!
YES, SOMETHING NO AMERICAN CAN RESIST...
A BIG, OL' BEAUTIFUL SHINY GUN!

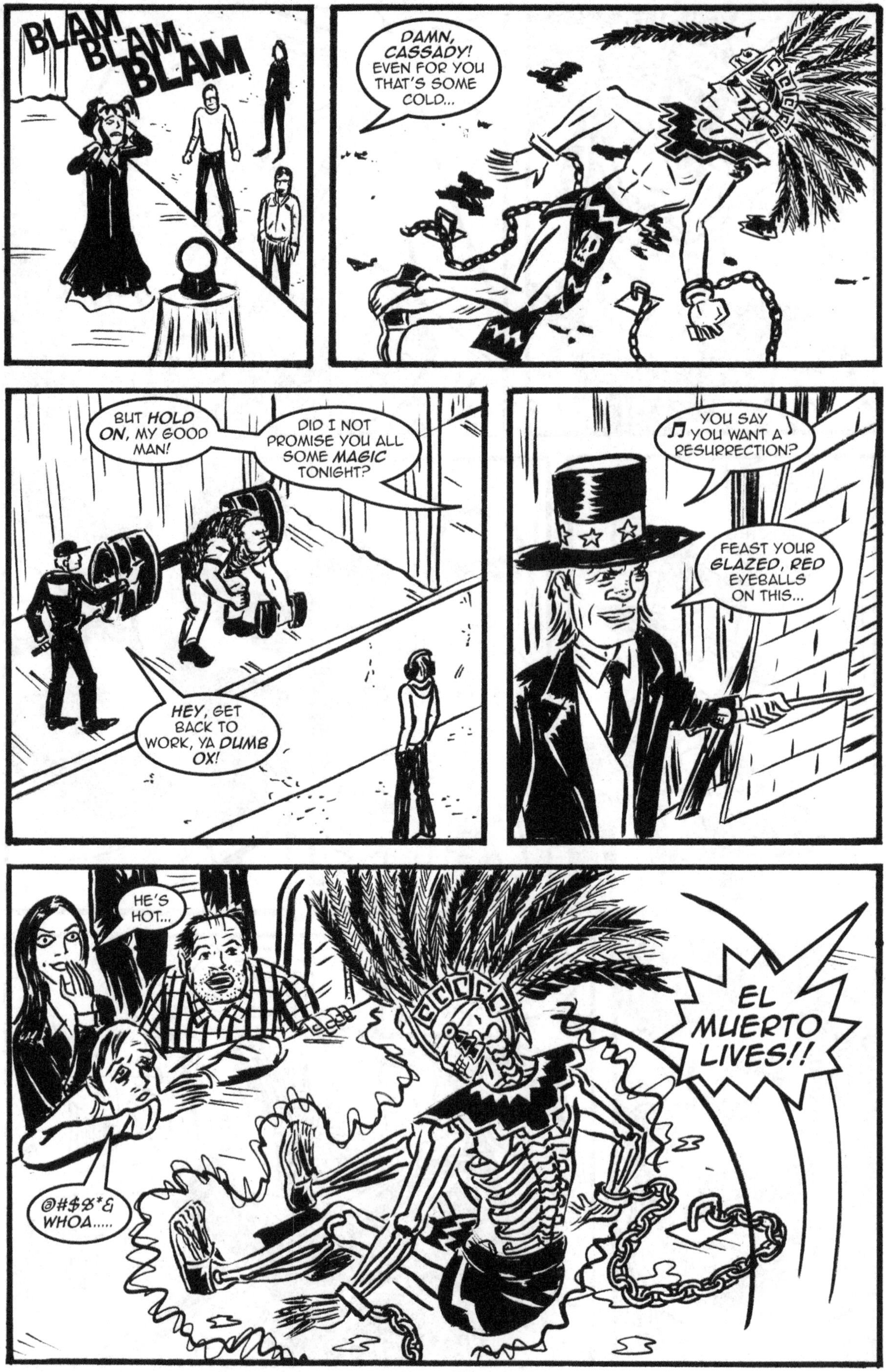
BLAM BLAM BLAM
DAMN, CASSADY! EVEN FOR YOU THAT'S SOME COLD...
BUT HOLD ON, MY GOOD MAN!
DID I NOT PROMISE YOU ALL SOME MAGIC TONIGHT?
HEY, GET BACK TO WORK, YA DUMB OX!
♫ YOU SAY YOU WANT A RESURRECTION? ♪
FEAST YOUR GLAZED, RED EYEBALLS ON THIS...
HE'S HOT...
@#$&*&
WHOA.....
EL MUERTO LIVES!!

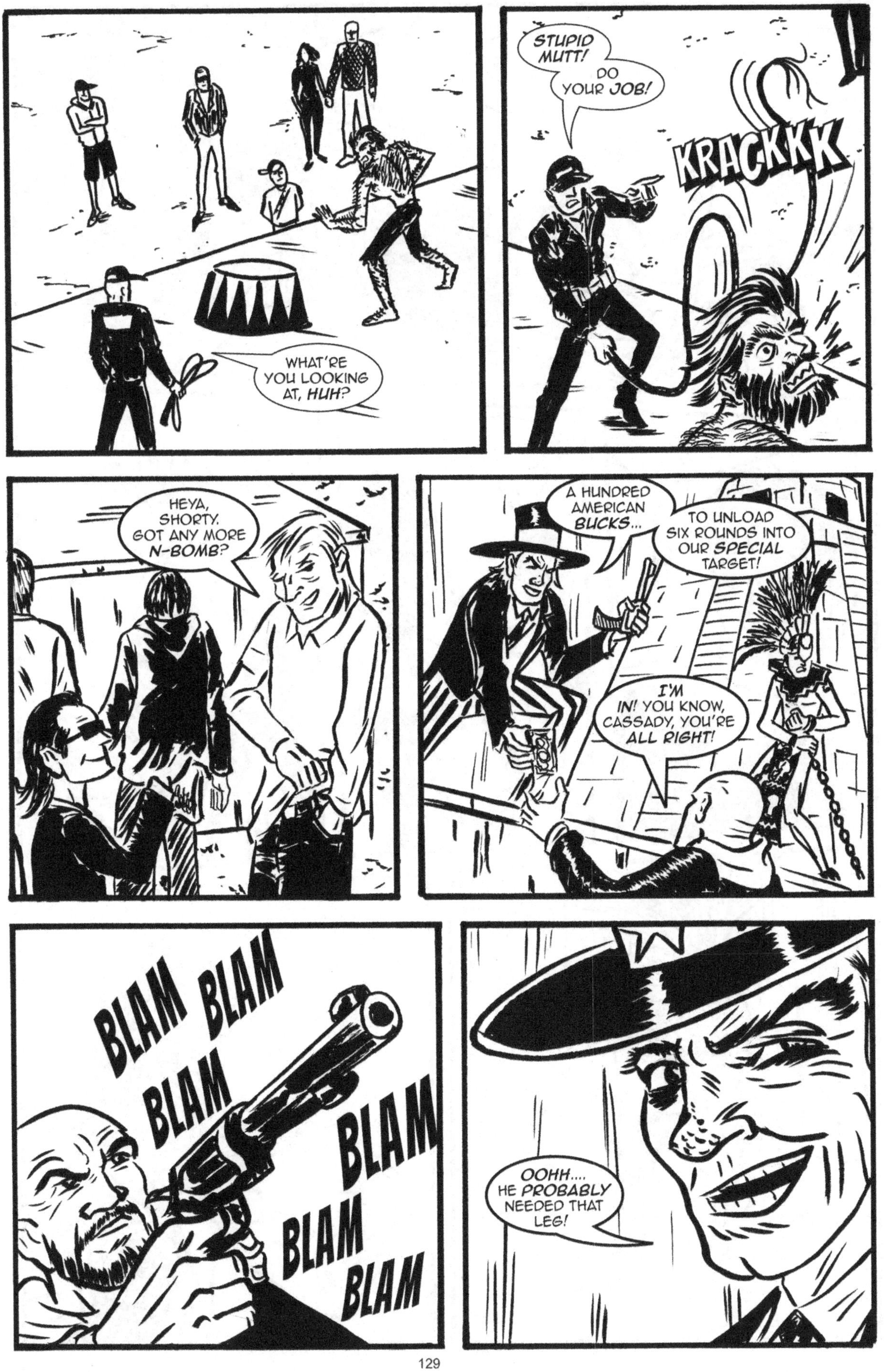
WHAT'RE YOU LOOKING AT, HUH?
STUPID MUTT!
DO YOUR JOB!
KRACKKK
HEYA, SHORTY. GOT ANY MORE N-BOMB?
A HUNDRED AMERICAN BUCKS...
TO UNLOAD SIX ROUNDS INTO OUR SPECIAL TARGET!
I'M IN! YOU KNOW, CASSADY, YOU'RE ALL RIGHT!
BLAM BLAM
BLAM
BLAM
BLAM
BLAM
OOHH.... HE PROBABLY NEEDED THAT LEG!

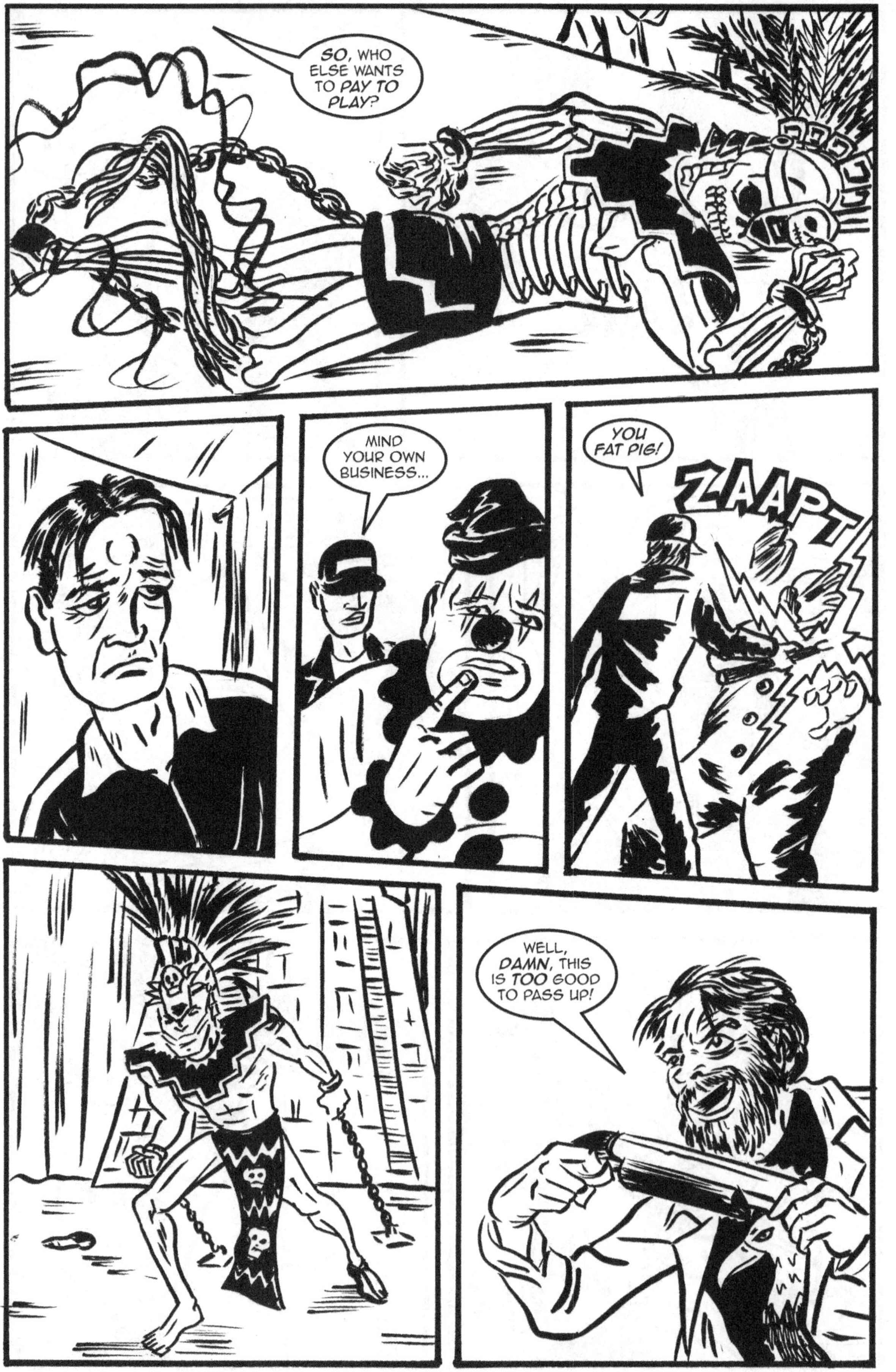
SO, WHO ELSE WANTS TO PAY TO PLAY?
MIND YOUR OWN BUSINESS...
YOU FAT PIG!
ZAAPT
WELL, DAMN, THIS IS TOO GOOD TO PASS UP!

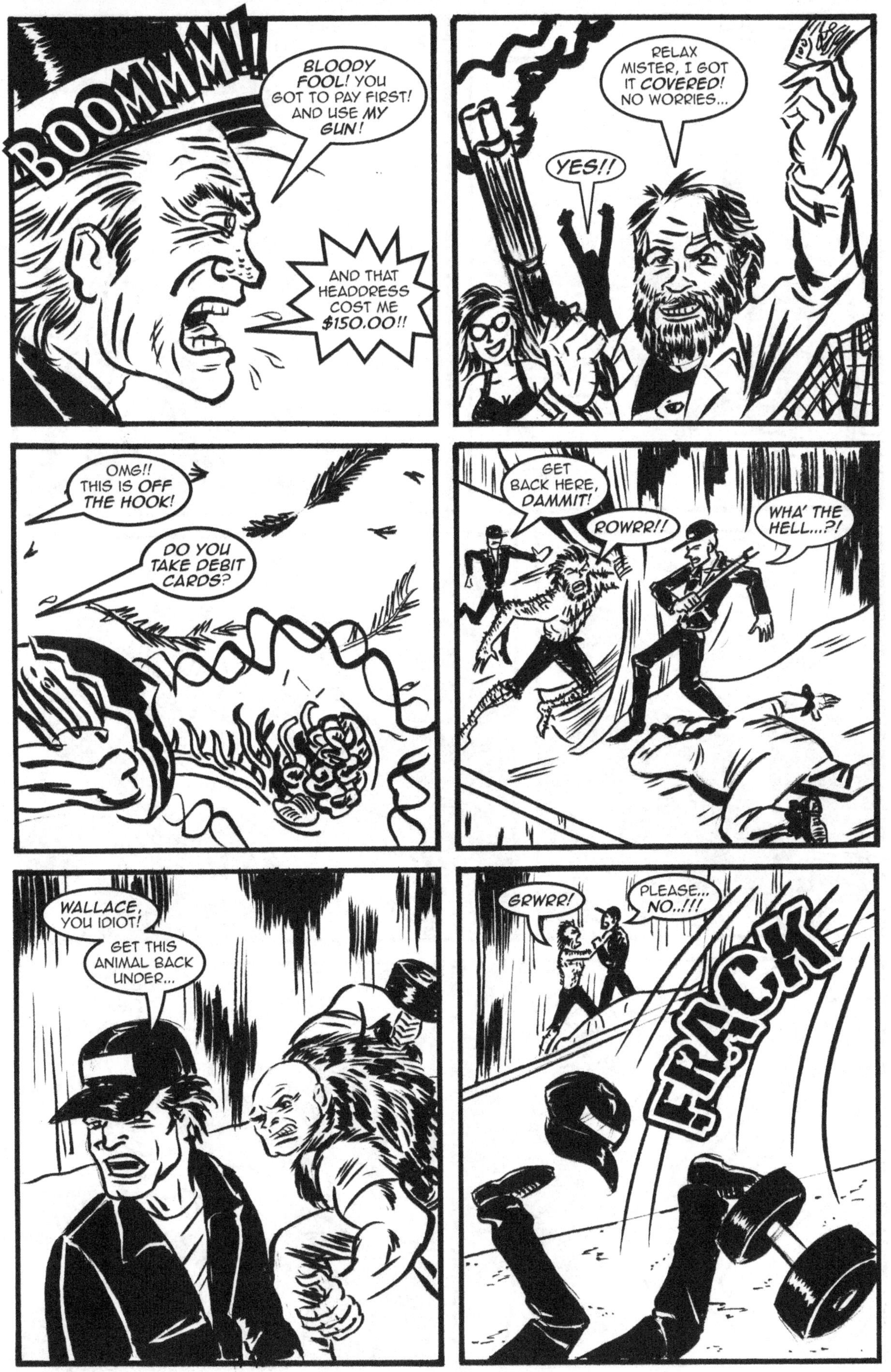
BOOMMM!!
BLOODY FOOL! YOU GOT TO PAY FIRST! AND USE MY GUN!
AND THAT HEADDRESS COST ME $150.00!!
RELAX MISTER, I GOT IT COVERED! NO WORRIES...
YES!!
OMG!! THIS IS OFF THE HOOK!
DO YOU TAKE DEBIT CARDS?
GET BACK HERE, DAMMIT!
ROWRR!!
WHA' THE HELL...?!
WALLACE, YOU IDIOT!
GET THIS ANIMAL BACK UNDER...
GRWRR!
PLEASE... NO..!!!
FRACK

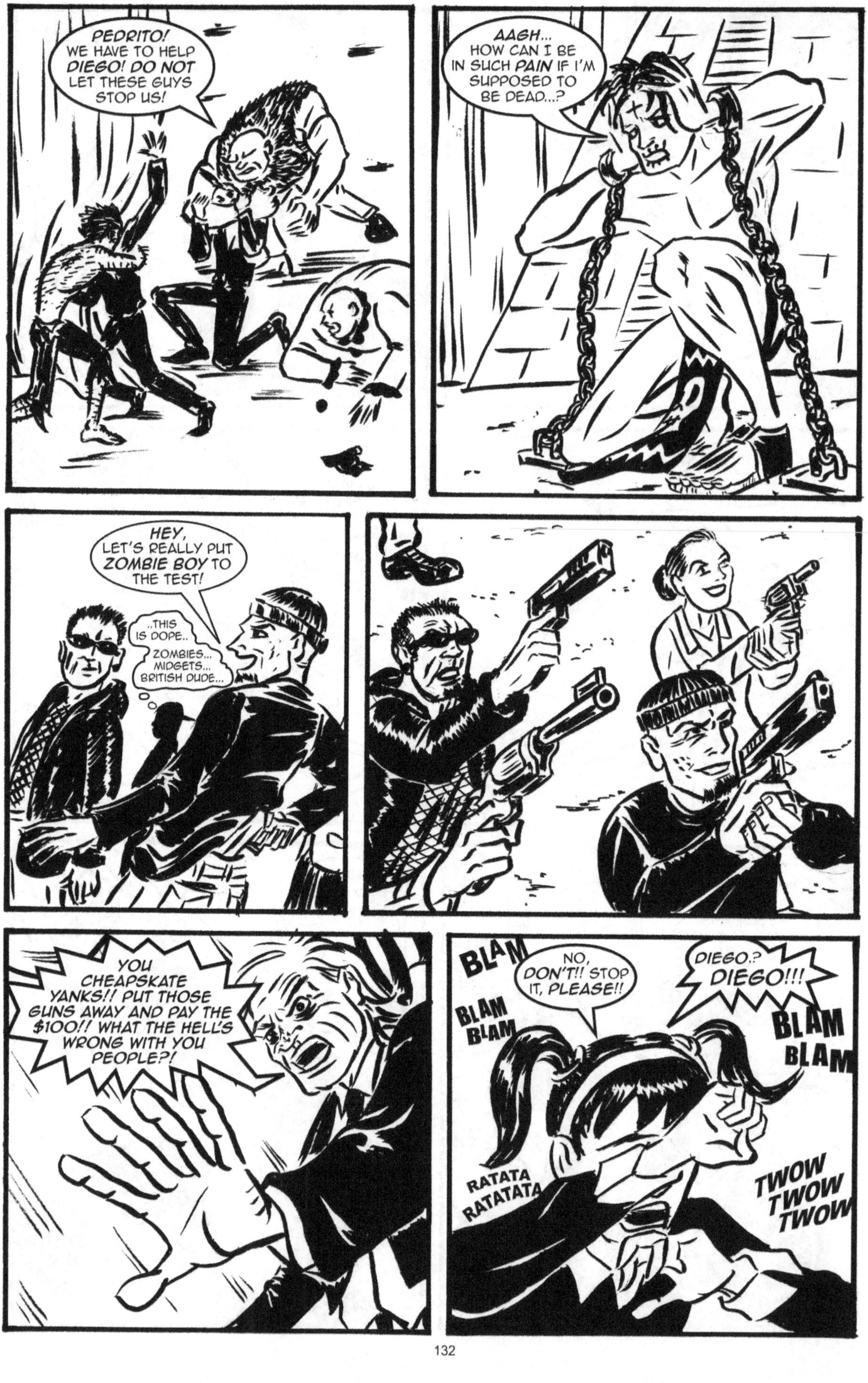
PEDRITO! WE HAVE TO HELP DIEGO! DO NOT LET THESE GUYS STOP US!
AAGH... HOW CAN I BE IN SUCH PAIN IF I'M SUPPOSED TO BE DEAD...?
HEY, LET'S REALLY PUT ZOMBIE BOY TO THE TEST!
..THIS IS DOPE.. ZOMBIES... MIDGETS... BRITISH DUDE...
YOU CHEAPSKATE YANKS!! PUT THOSE GUNS AWAY AND PAY THE $100!! WHAT THE HELL'S WRONG WITH YOU PEOPLE?!
BLAM
NO, DON'T!! STOP IT, PLEASE!!
DIEGO.? DIEGO!!!
BLAM BLAM
BLAM BLAM
RATATATA RATATATA
TWOW TWOW TWOW

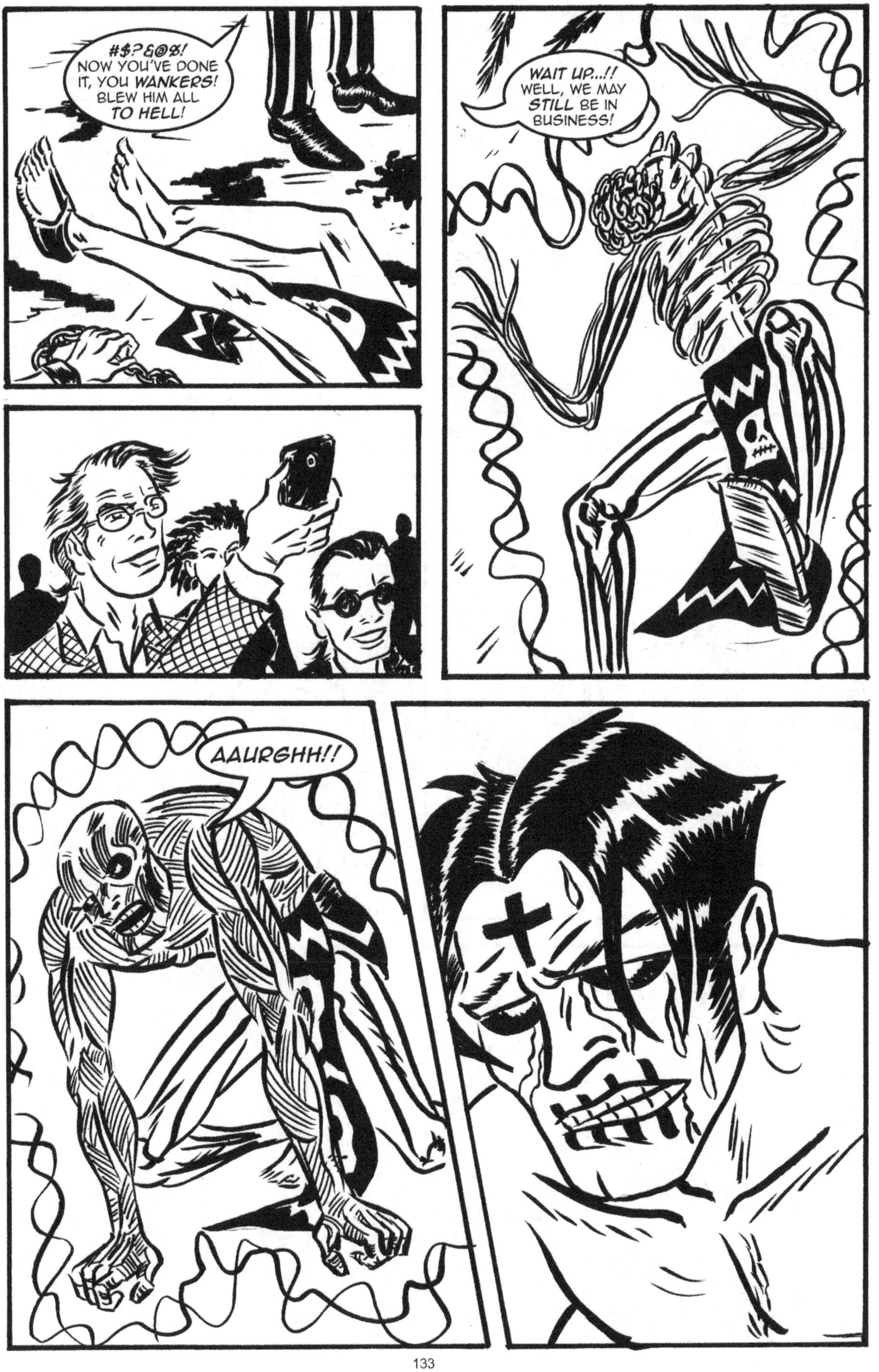
#$?&@%! NOW YOU'VE DONE IT, YOU WANKERS! BLEW HIM ALL TO HELL!
WAIT UP...!! WELL, WE MAY STILL BE IN BUSINESS!
AAURGHH!!

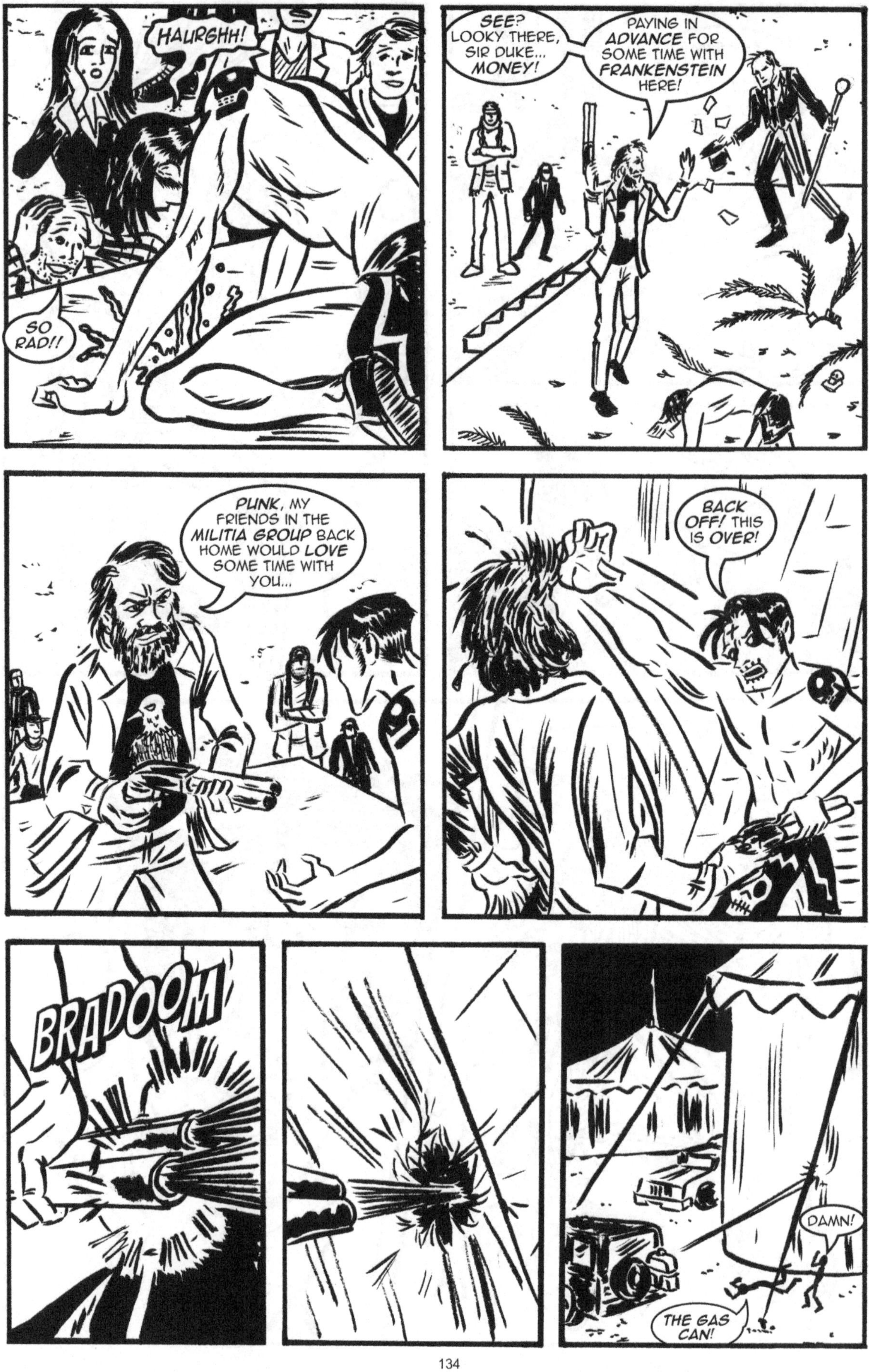
HAURGHH!
SO RAD!!
SEE? LOOKY THERE, SIR DUKE... MONEY!
PAYING IN ADVANCE FOR SOME TIME WITH FRANKENSTEIN HERE!
PUNK, MY FRIENDS IN THE MILITIA GROUP BACK HOME WOULD LOVE SOME TIME WITH YOU...
BACK OFF! THIS IS OVER!
BRADOOM
DAMN!
THE GAS CAN!

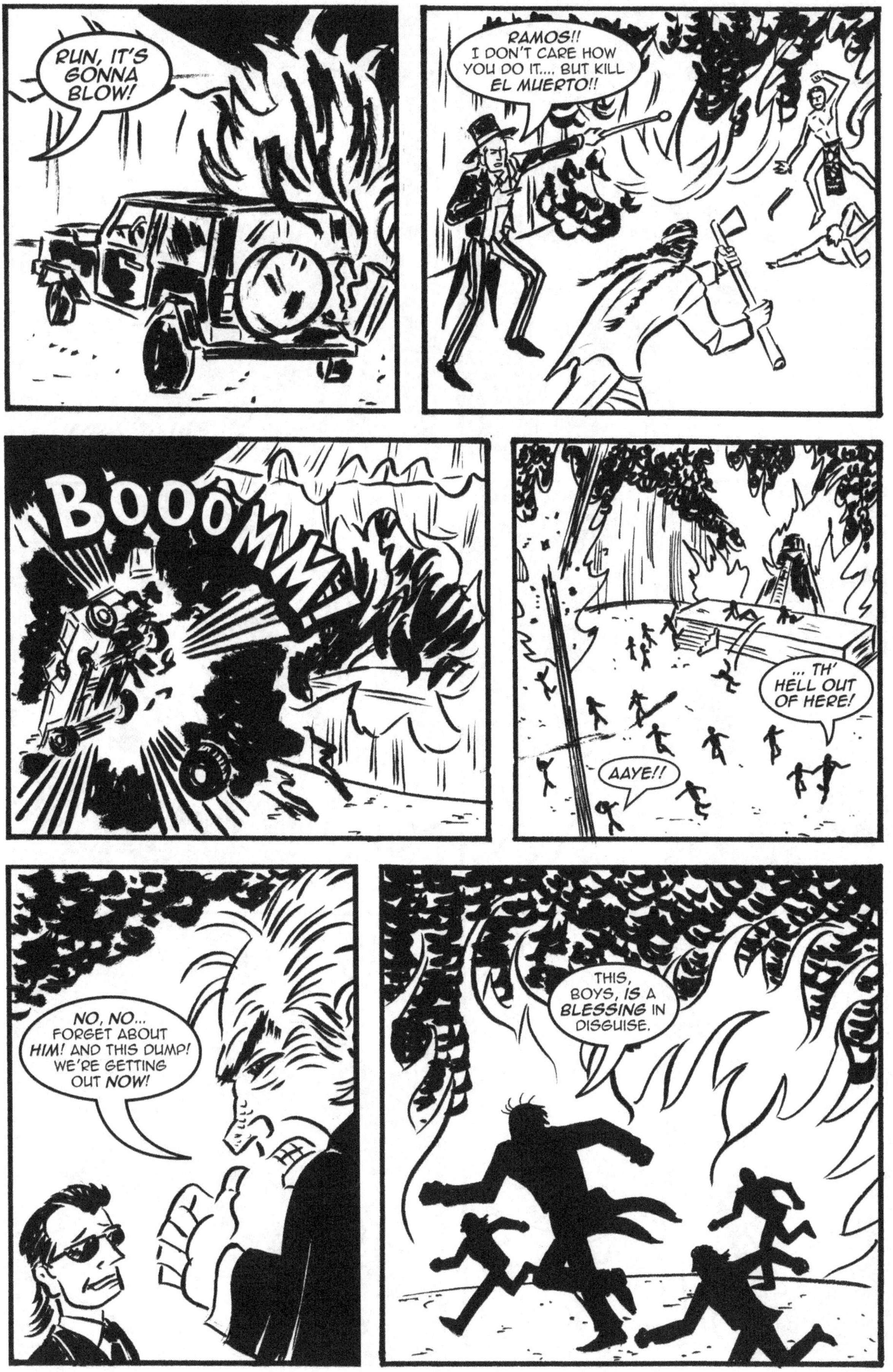
RUN, IT'S GONNA BLOW!
RAMOS!! I DON'T CARE HOW YOU DO IT.... BUT KILL EL MUERTO!!
BOOOMM!
... TH' HELL OUT OF HERE!
AAYE!!
NO, NO... FORGET ABOUT HIM! AND THIS DUMP! WE'RE GETTING OUT NOW!
THIS, BOYS, IS A BLESSING IN DISGUISE.

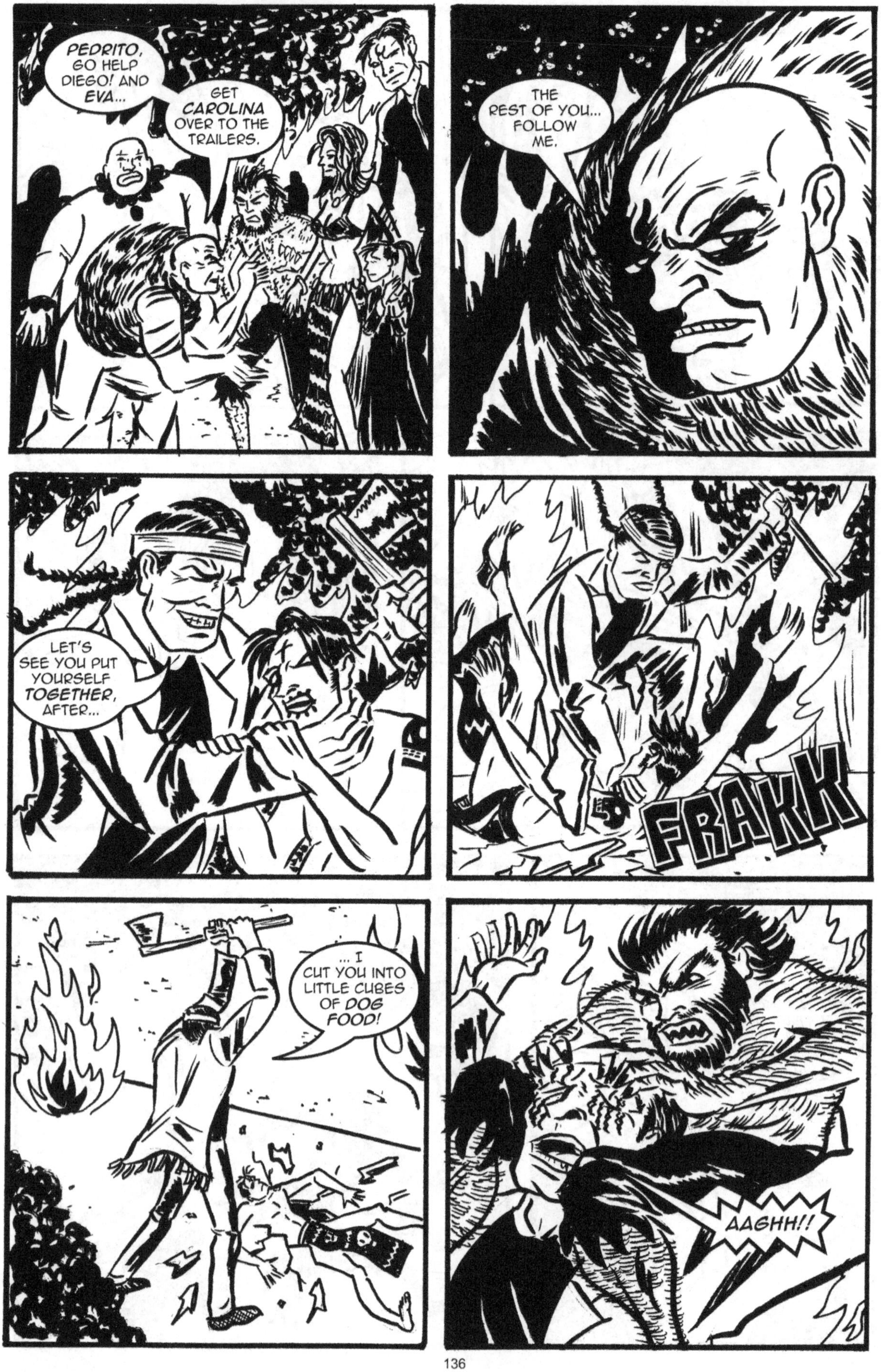
PEDRITO, GO HELP DIEGO! AND EVA...
GET CAROLINA OVER TO THE TRAILERS.
THE REST OF YOU... FOLLOW ME.
LET'S SEE YOU PUT YOURSELF TOGETHER, AFTER...
FRAKK
... I CUT YOU INTO LITTLE CUBES OF DOG FOOD!
AAGHH!!

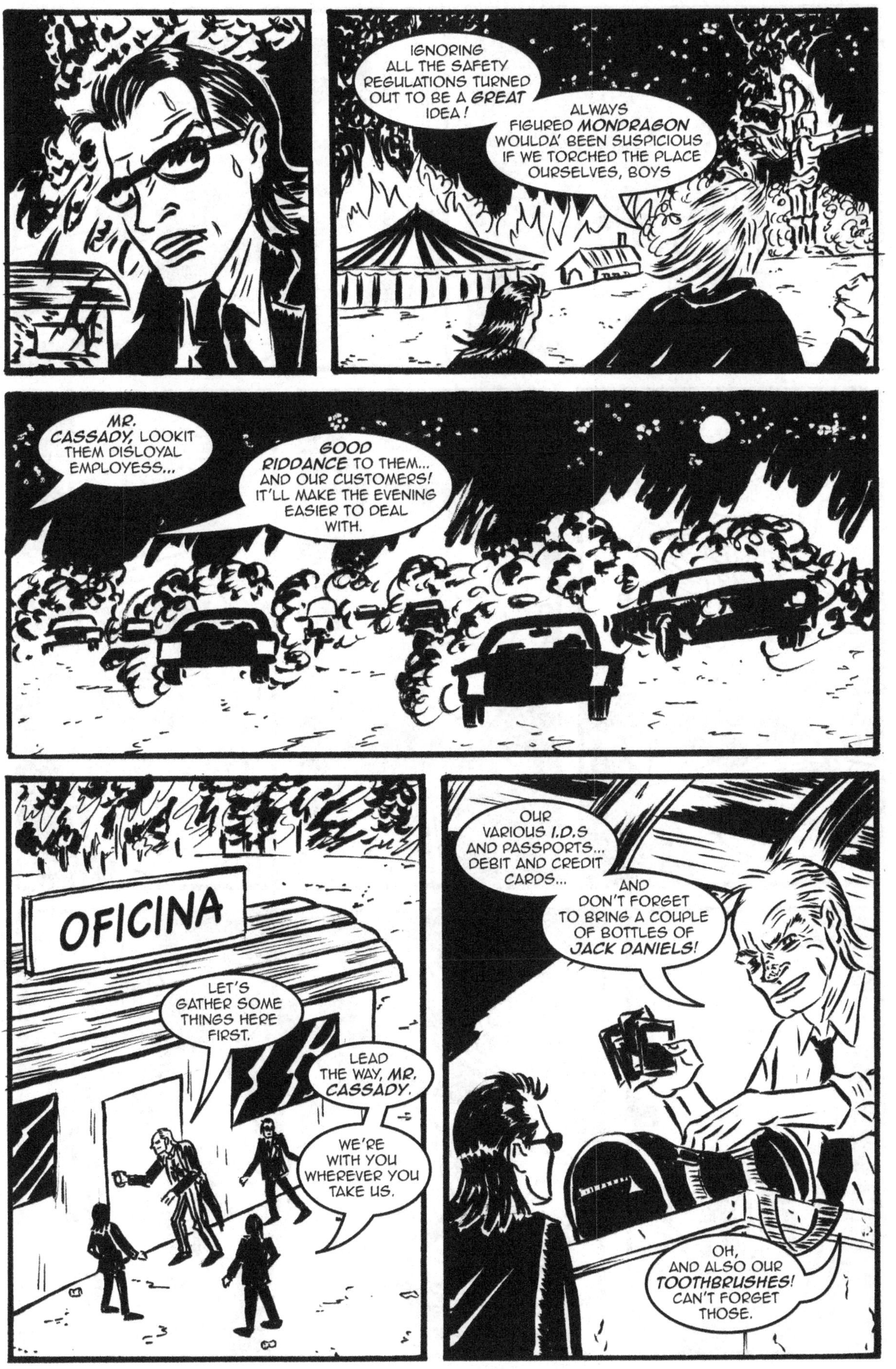
IGNORING ALL THE SAFETY REGULATIONS TURNED OUT TO BE A GREAT IDEA!
ALWAYS FIGURED MONDRAGON WOULDA' BEEN SUSPICIOUS IF WE TORCHED THE PLACE OURSELVES, BOYS
MR. CASSADY, LOOKIT THEM DISLOYAL EMPLOYESS...
GOOD RIDDANCE TO THEM... AND OUR CUSTOMERS! IT'LL MAKE THE EVENING EASIER TO DEAL WITH.
OFICINA
LET'S GATHER SOME THINGS HERE FIRST.
LEAD THE WAY, MR. CASSADY.
WE'RE WITH YOU WHEREVER YOU TAKE US.
OUR VARIOUS I.D.S AND PASSPORTS... DEBIT AND CREDIT CARDS...
AND DON'T FORGET TO BRING A COUPLE OF BOTTLES OF JACK DANIELS!
OH, AND ALSO OUR TOOTHBRUSHES! CAN'T FORGET THOSE.

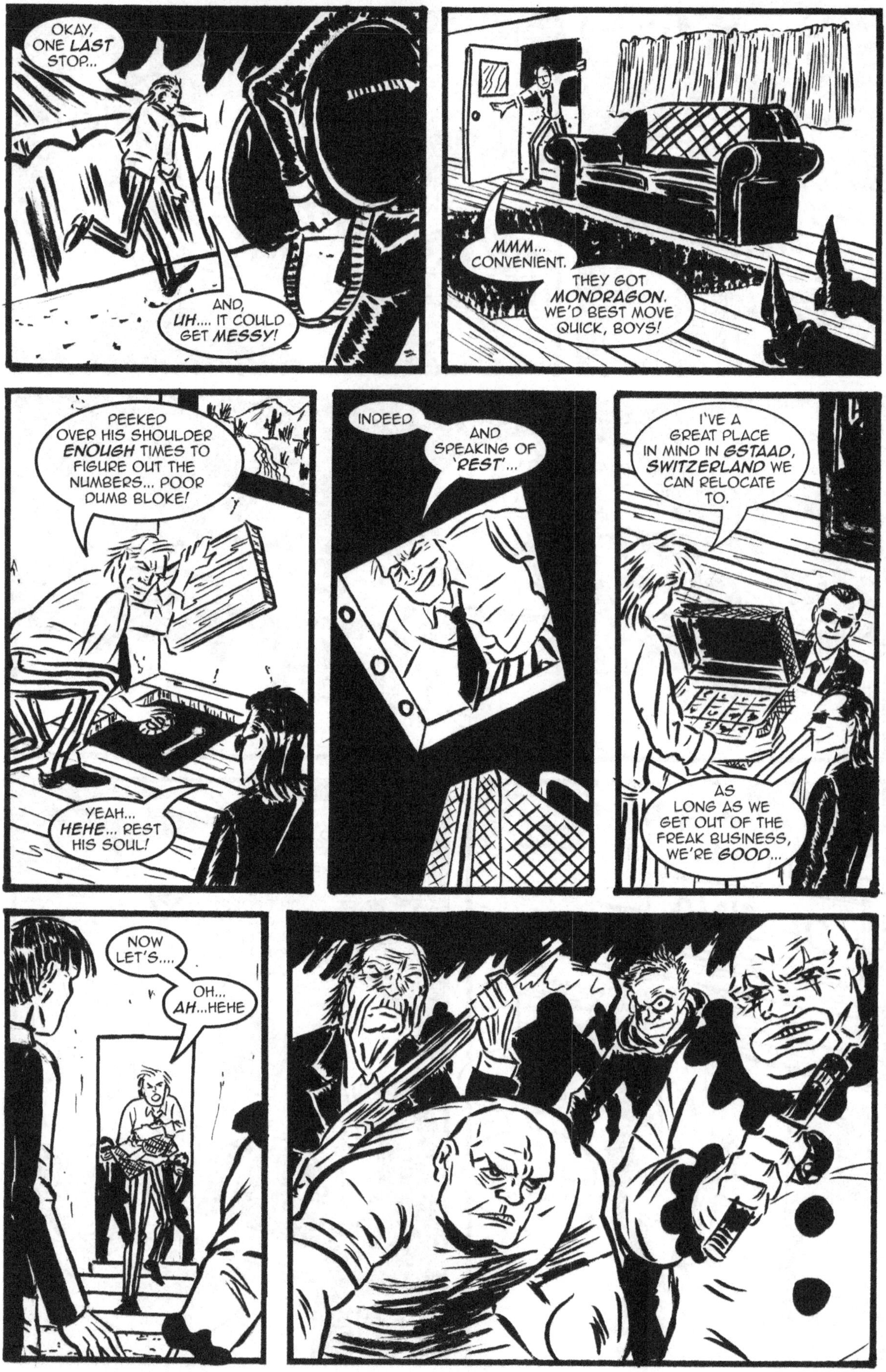
OKAY, ONE LAST STOP...
AND, UH.... IT COULD GET MESSY!
MMM... CONVENIENT.
THEY GOT MONDRAGON. WE'D BEST MOVE QUICK, BOYS!
PEEKED OVER HIS SHOULDER ENOUGH TIMES TO FIGURE OUT THE NUMBERS... POOR DUMB BLOKE!
YEAH... HEHE... REST HIS SOUL!
INDEED.
AND SPEAKING OF 'REST'...
I'VE A GREAT PLACE IN MIND IN GSTAAD, SWITZERLAND WE CAN RELOCATE TO.
AS LONG AS WE GET OUT OF THE FREAK BUSINESS, WE'RE GOOD...
NOW LET'S....
OH... AH...HEHE

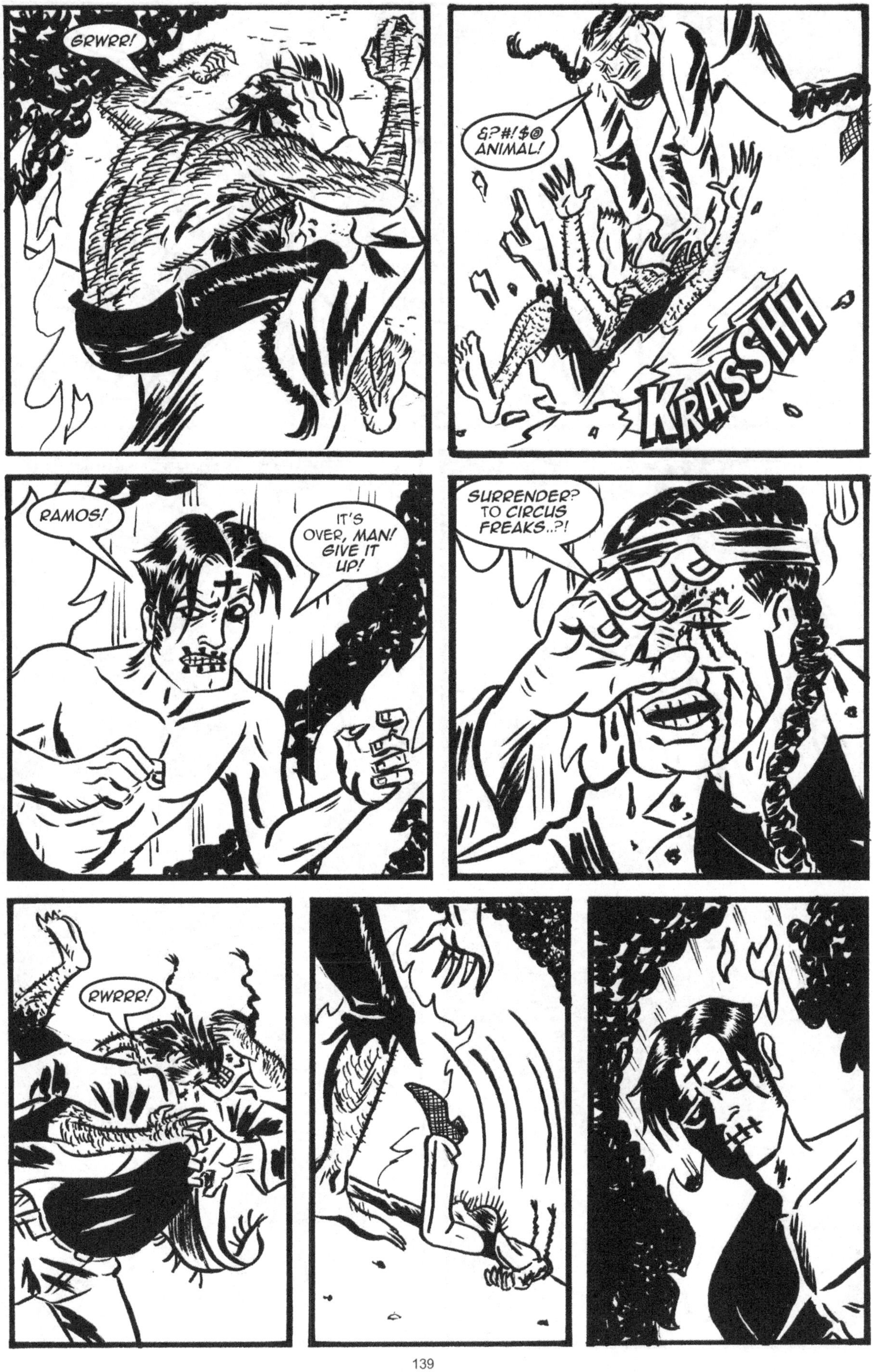
GRWRR!
&?#!$@ ANIMAL!
KRASSHH
RAMOS!
IT'S OVER, MAN! GIVE IT UP!
SURRENDER? TO CIRCUS FREAKS..?!
RWRRR!

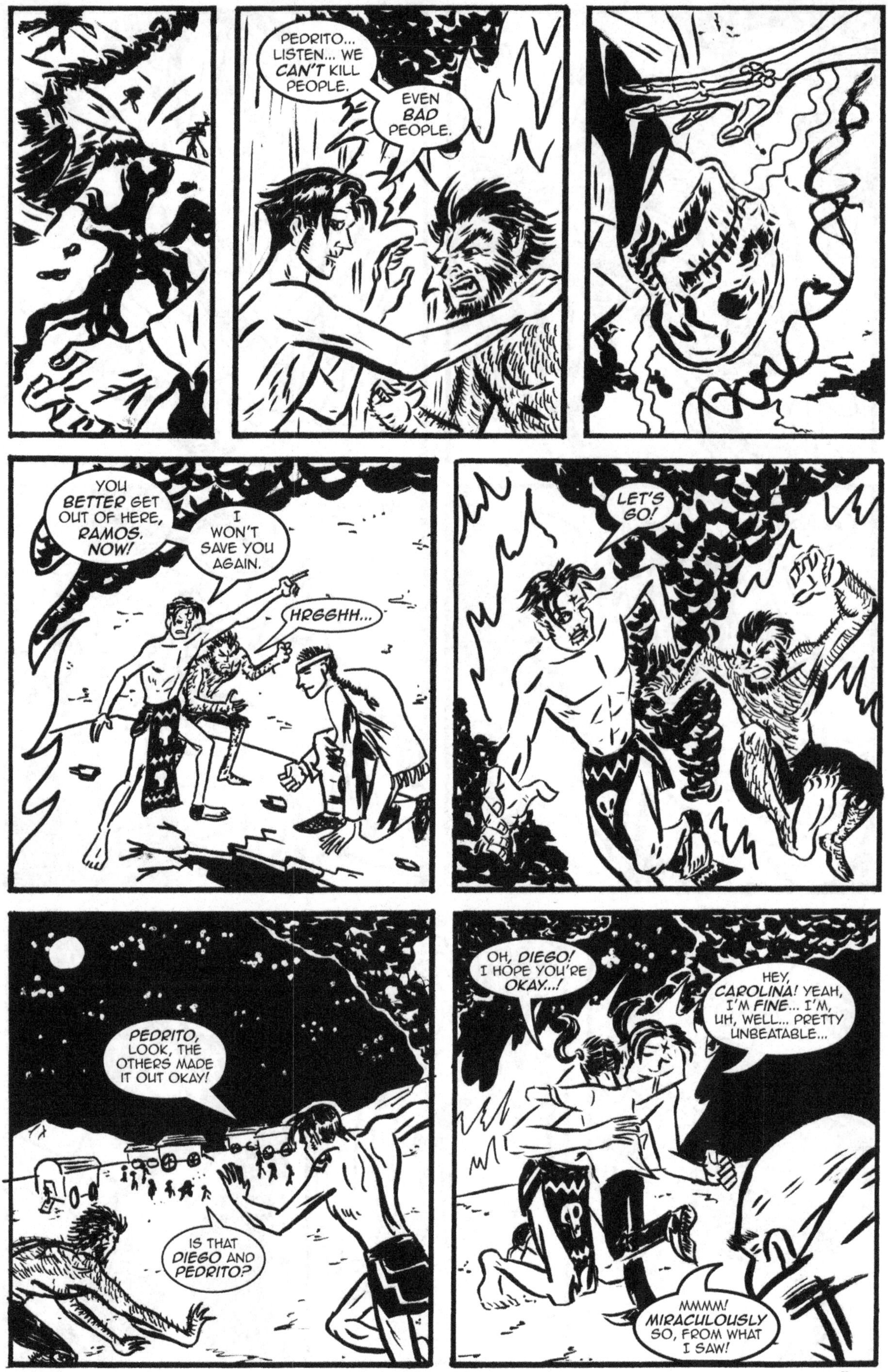
PEDRITO... LISTEN... WE CAN'T KILL PEOPLE.
EVEN BAD PEOPLE.
YOU BETTER GET OUT OF HERE, RAMOS. NOW!
I WON'T SAVE YOU AGAIN.
HRGGHH...
LET'S GO!
PEDRITO, LOOK, THE OTHERS MADE IT OUT OKAY!
IS THAT DIEGO AND PEDRITO?
OH, DIEGO! I HOPE YOU'RE OKAY...!
HEY, CAROLINA! YEAH, I'M FINE... I'M, UH, WELL... PRETTY UNBEATABLE...
MMMM! MIRACULOUSLY SO, FROM WHAT I SAW!

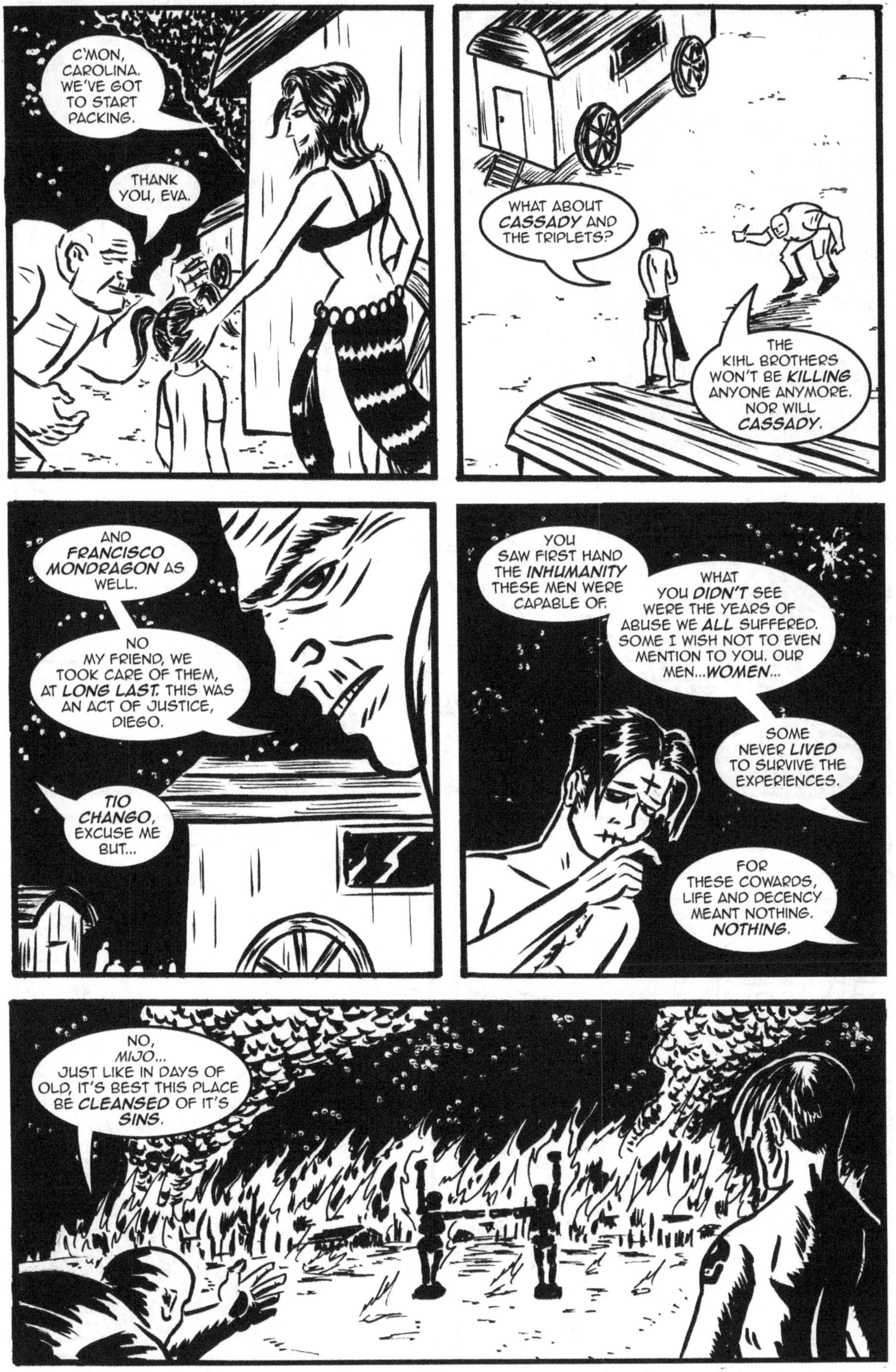
C'MON, CAROLINA. WE'VE GOT TO START PACKING.
THANK YOU, EVA.
WHAT ABOUT CASSADY AND THE TRIPLETS?
THE KIHL BROTHERS WON'T BE KILLING ANYONE ANYMORE. NOR WILL CASSADY.
AND FRANCISCO MONDRAGON AS WELL.
NO MY FRIEND, WE TOOK CARE OF THEM, AT LONG LAST. THIS WAS AN ACT OF JUSTICE, DIEGO.
TIO CHANGO, EXCUSE ME BUT...
YOU SAW FIRST HAND THE INHUMANITY THESE MEN WERE CAPABLE OF.
WHAT YOU DIDN'T SEE WERE THE YEARS OF ABUSE WE ALL SUFFERED. SOME I WISH NOT TO EVEN MENTION TO YOU. OUR MEN...WOMEN...
SOME NEVER LIVED TO SURVIVE THE EXPERIENCES.
FOR THESE COWARDS, LIFE AND DECENCY MEANT NOTHING. NOTHING.
NO, MIJO... JUST LIKE IN DAYS OF OLD, IT'S BEST THIS PLACE BE CLEANSED OF IT'S SINS.

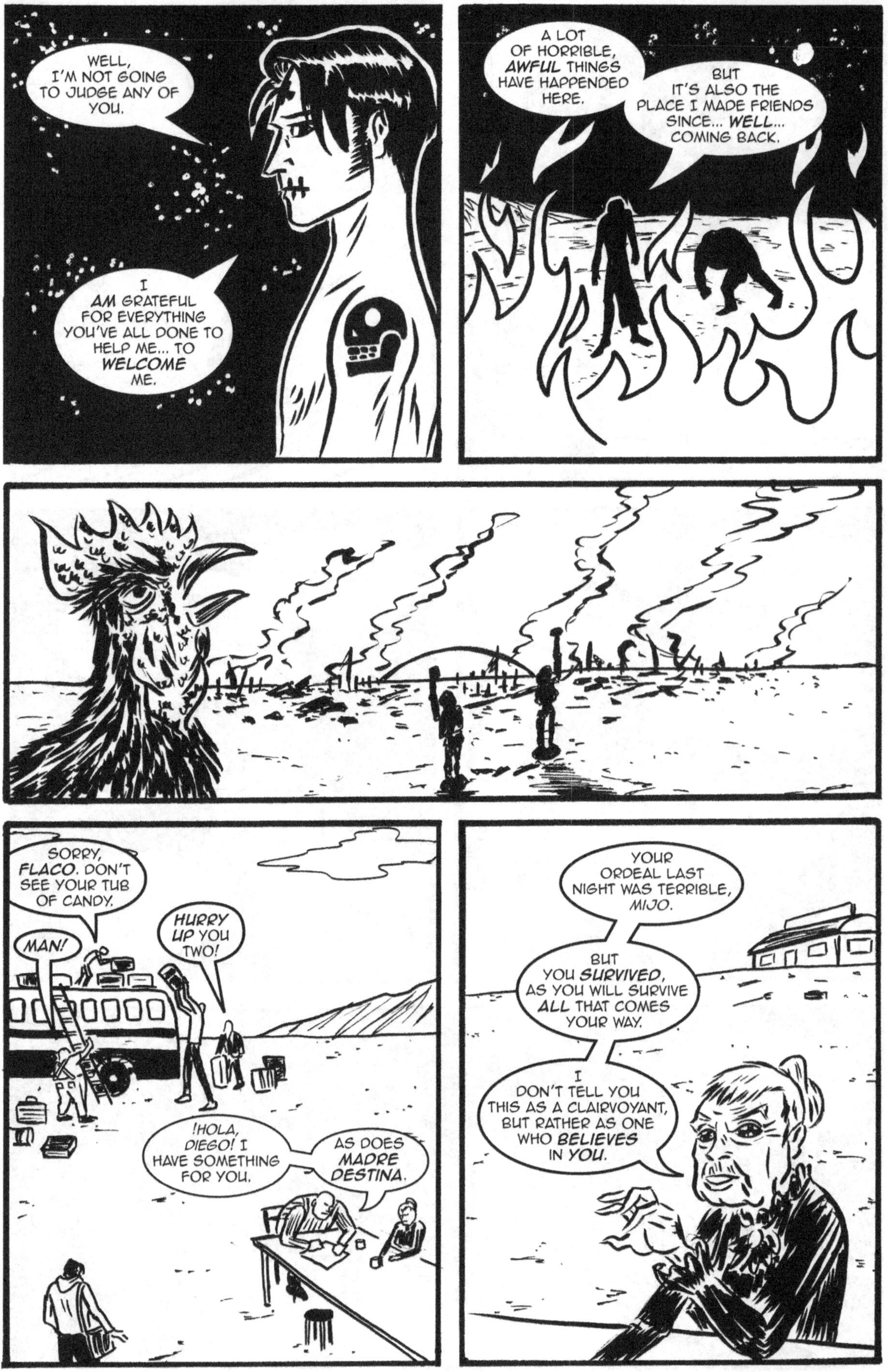

WELL, I'M NOT GOING TO JUDGE ANY OF YOU.
I AM GRATEFUL FOR EVERYTHING YOU'VE ALL DONE TO HELP ME... TO WELCOME ME.
A LOT OF HORRIBLE, AWFUL THINGS HAVE HAPPENDED HERE.
BUT IT'S ALSO THE PLACE I MADE FRIENDS SINCE... WELL... COMING BACK.
SORRY, FLACO. DON'T SEE YOUR TUB OF CANDY.
MAN!
HURRY UP YOU TWO!
!HOLA, DIEGO! I HAVE SOMETHING FOR YOU.
AS DOES MADRE DESTINA.
YOUR ORDEAL LAST NIGHT WAS TERRIBLE, MIJO.
BUT YOU SURVIVED, AS YOU WILL SURVIVE ALL THAT COMES YOUR WAY.
I DON'T TELL YOU THIS AS A CLAIRVOYANT, BUT RATHER AS ONE WHO BELIEVES IN YOU.

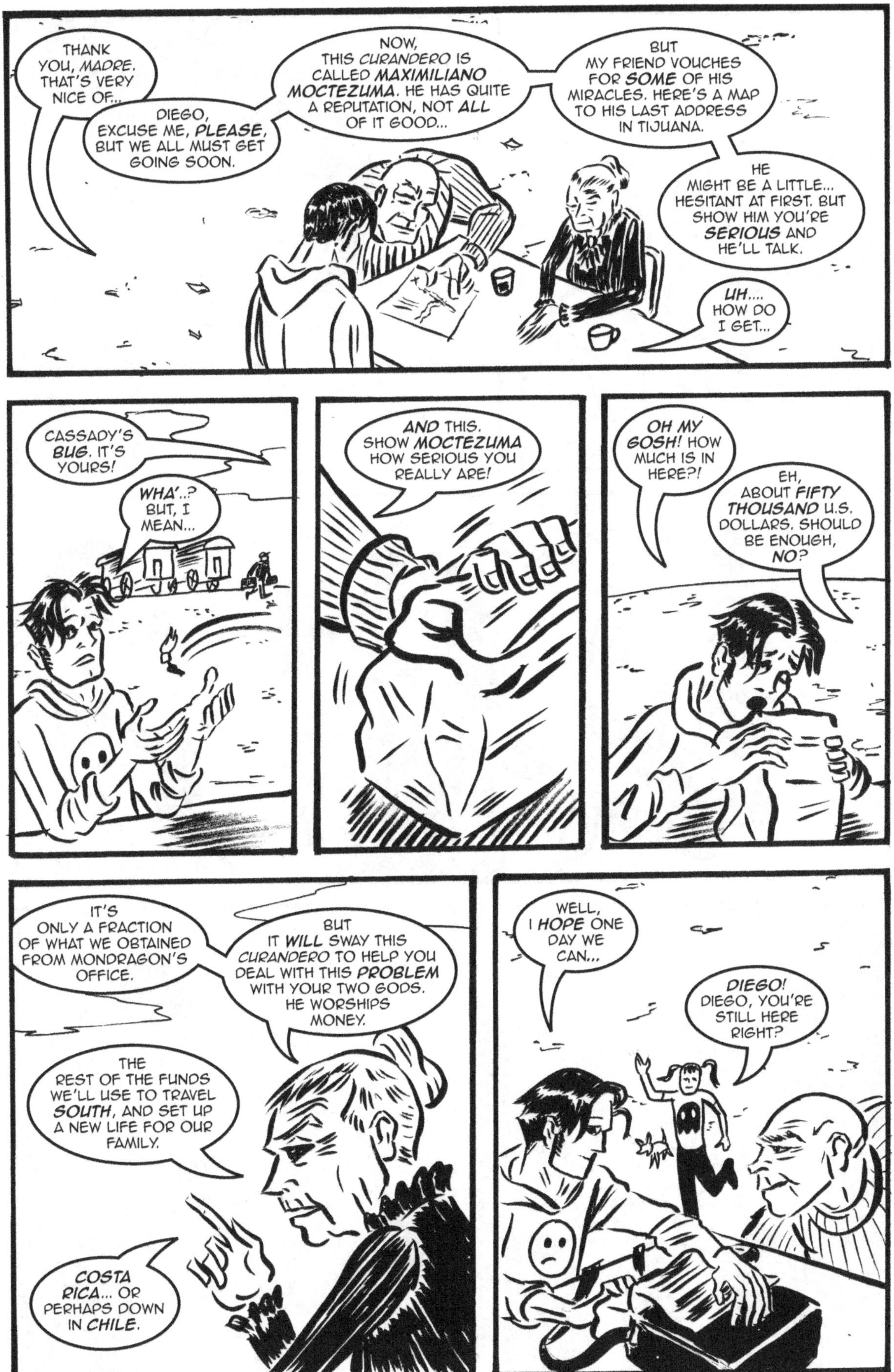
THANK YOU, MADRE. THAT'S VERY NICE OF...
DIEGO, EXCUSE ME, PLEASE, BUT WE ALL MUST GET GOING SOON.
NOW, THIS CURANDERO IS CALLED MAXIMILIANO MOCTEZUMA. HE HAS QUITE A REPUTATION, NOT ALL OF IT GOOD...
BUT MY FRIEND VOUCHES FOR SOME OF HIS MIRACLES. HERE'S A MAP TO HIS LAST ADDRESS IN TIJUANA.
HE MIGHT BE A LITTLE... HESITANT AT FIRST. BUT SHOW HIM YOU'RE SERIOUS AND HE'LL TALK.
UH.... HOW DO I GET...
CASSADY'S BUG. IT'S YOURS!
WHA'..? BUT, I MEAN...
AND THIS. SHOW MOCTEZUMA HOW SERIOUS YOU REALLY ARE!
OH MY GOSH! HOW MUCH IS IN HERE?!
EH, ABOUT FIFTY THOUSAND U.S. DOLLARS. SHOULD BE ENOUGH, NO?
IT'S ONLY A FRACTION OF WHAT WE OBTAINED FROM MONDRAGON'S OFFICE.
BUT IT WILL SWAY THIS CURANDERO TO HELP YOU DEAL WITH THIS PROBLEM WITH YOUR TWO GODS. HE WORSHIPS MONEY.
THE REST OF THE FUNDS WE'LL USE TO TRAVEL SOUTH, AND SET UP A NEW LIFE FOR OUR FAMILY.
COSTA RICA... OR PERHAPS DOWN IN CHILE.
WELL, I HOPE ONE DAY WE CAN...
DIEGO! DIEGO, YOU'RE STILL HERE RIGHT?

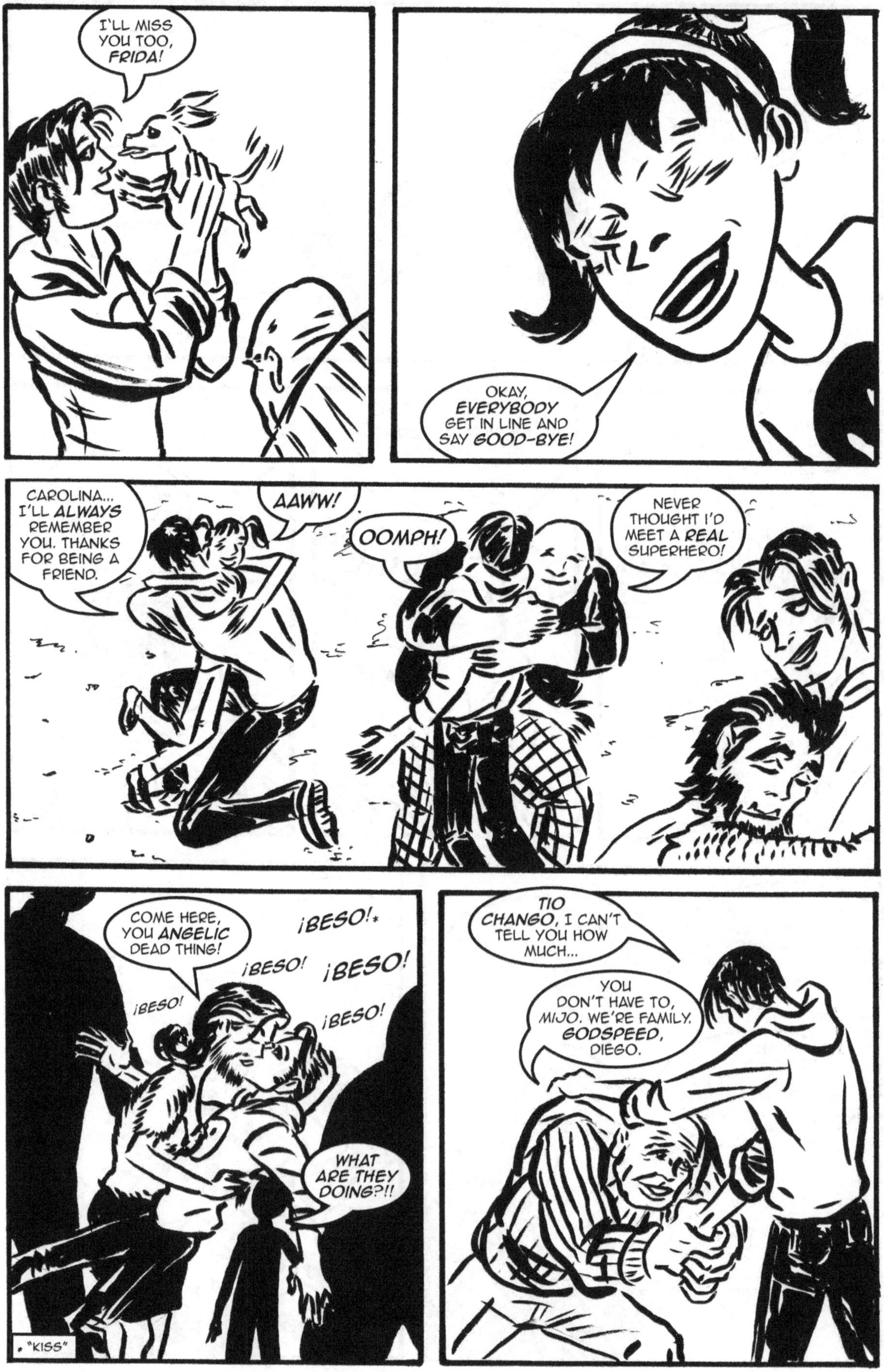

I'LL MISS YOU TOO, FRIDA!
OKAY, EVERYBODY GET IN LINE AND SAY GOOD-BYE!
CAROLINA... I'LL ALWAYS REMEMBER YOU. THANKS FOR BEING A FRIEND.
AAWW!
OOMPH!
NEVER THOUGHT I'D MEET A REAL SUPERHERO!
COME HERE, YOU ANGELIC DEAD THING!
¡BESO!*
¡BESO!
¡BESO!
¡BESO!
¡BESO!
WHAT ARE THEY DOING?!!
* "KISS"
TIO CHANGO, I CAN'T TELL YOU HOW MUCH...
YOU DON'T HAVE TO, MIJO. WE'RE FAMILY. GODSPEED, DIEGO.

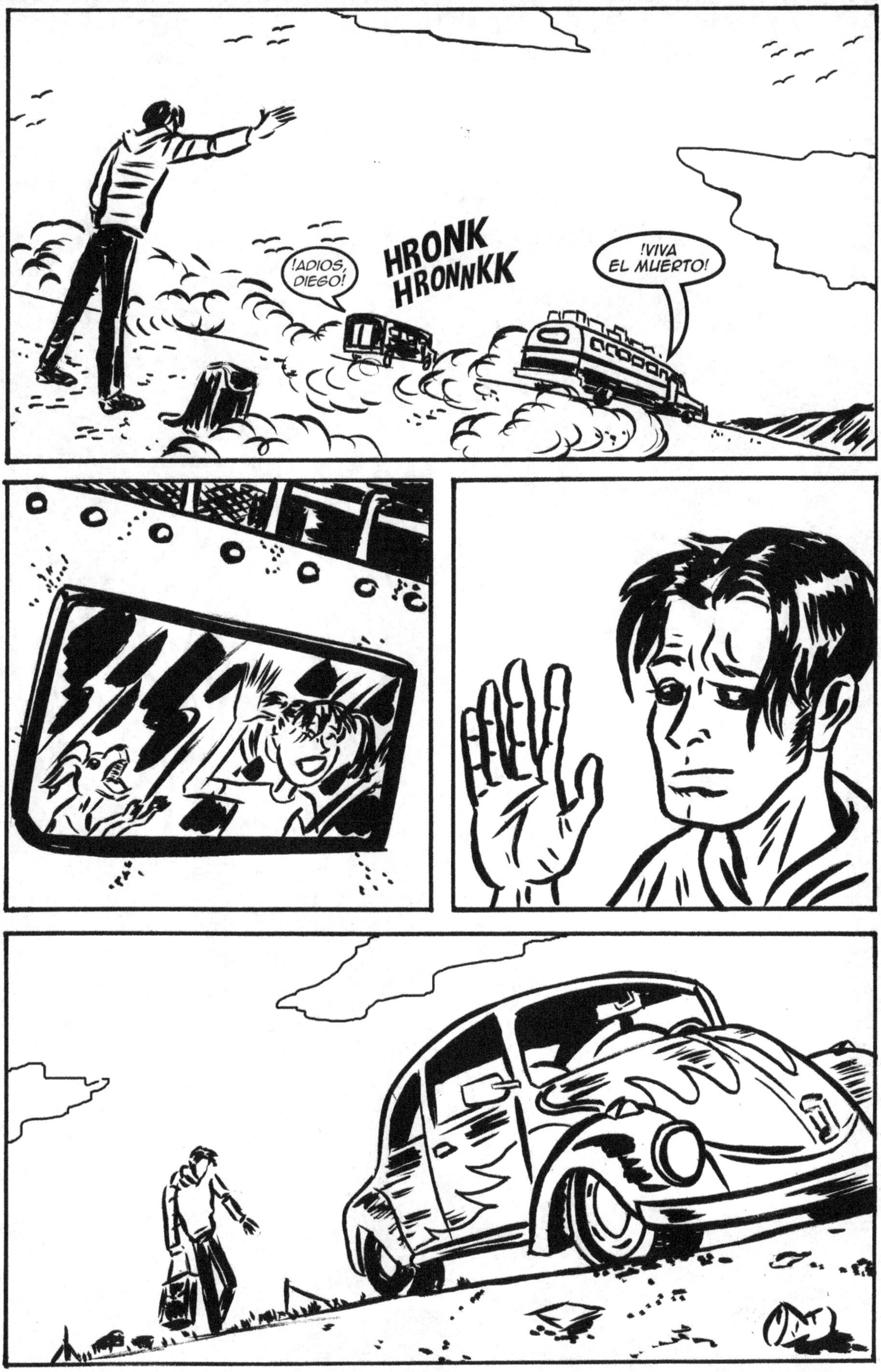
!ADIOS, DIEGO!
HRONK HRONNKK
!VIVA EL MUERTO!

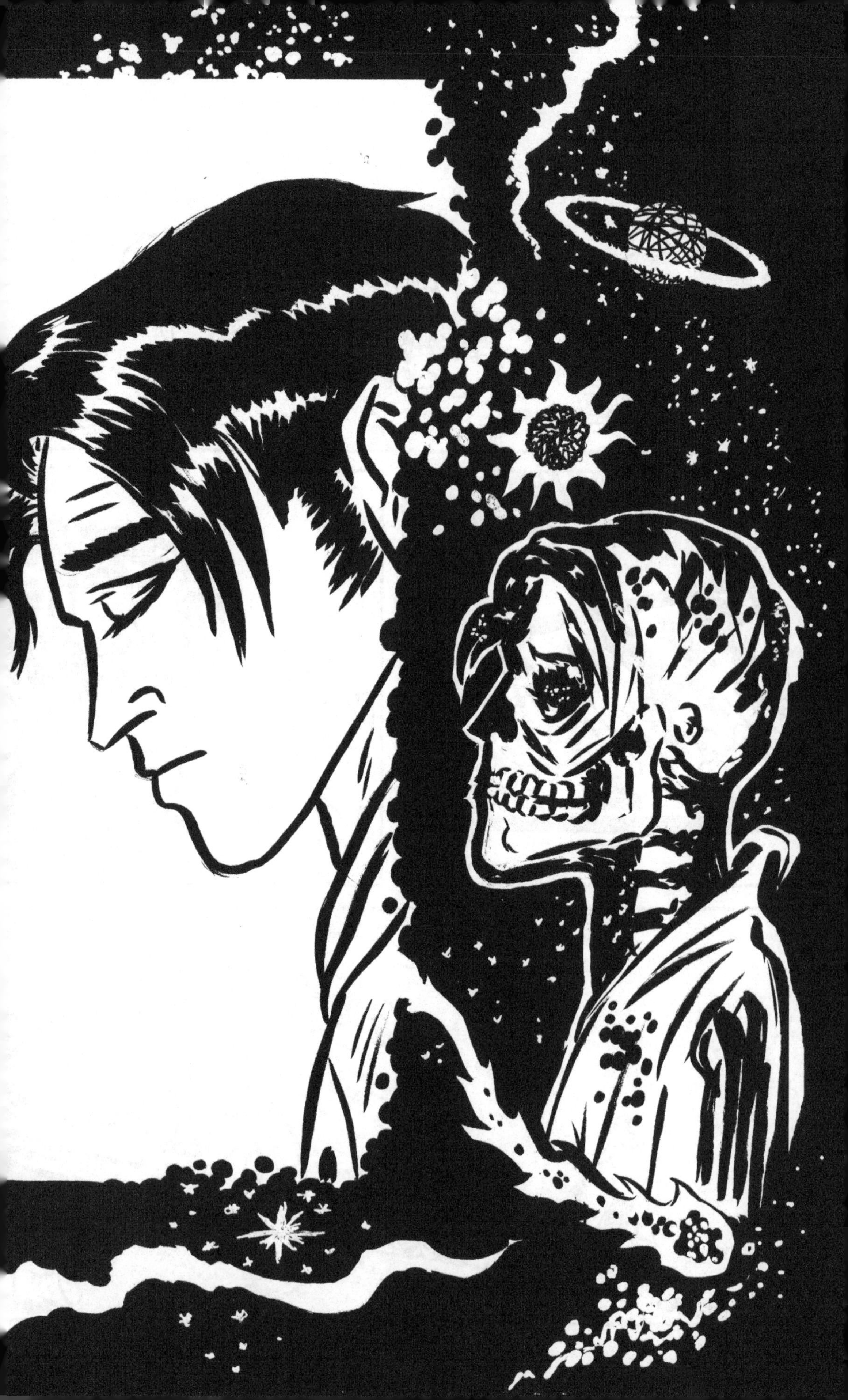

The End Of

DAZE Of The DEAD

But EL MUERTO Will Return

"Virtuosismo Etereo" written by and © Jose Iturriaga.
Used by permission. English translation by Jose Iturriaga.

I can hear in the distance
Echoes of a story
The pain of a profound loss

And I look back to
All the time that passed
And that shall never return

The melancholic notes are playing
From a universal virtuosity
The melancholic notes are playing
From a universal virtuosity
And ethereal...

Those evenings
Marked our childhood
The evolution of a friendship

The distance separated the communion
But brother, you're always here...

The melancholic notes are playing
From a universal virtuosity
The melancholic notes are playing
From a universal virtuosity
The melancholic notes are playing
From an ethereal virtuosity...

And no,
I don't want to ever say goodbye
And forget all of our memories
And no
I couldn't gaze upon you and it's far too late to cry...

The melancholic notes are howling
From a universal virtuosity
The melancholic notes are howling
From an ethereal virtuosity
The melancholic notes are wailing
From an eternal virtuosity...

I know...
That things could've been better
But wherever you are
Hear me...
One day I'll join you
And we shall smile again...

My sincere gratitude to my friend Jose for allowing me to use this very personal and transformative song in my story - Javier Hernandez

Exhuming the Series

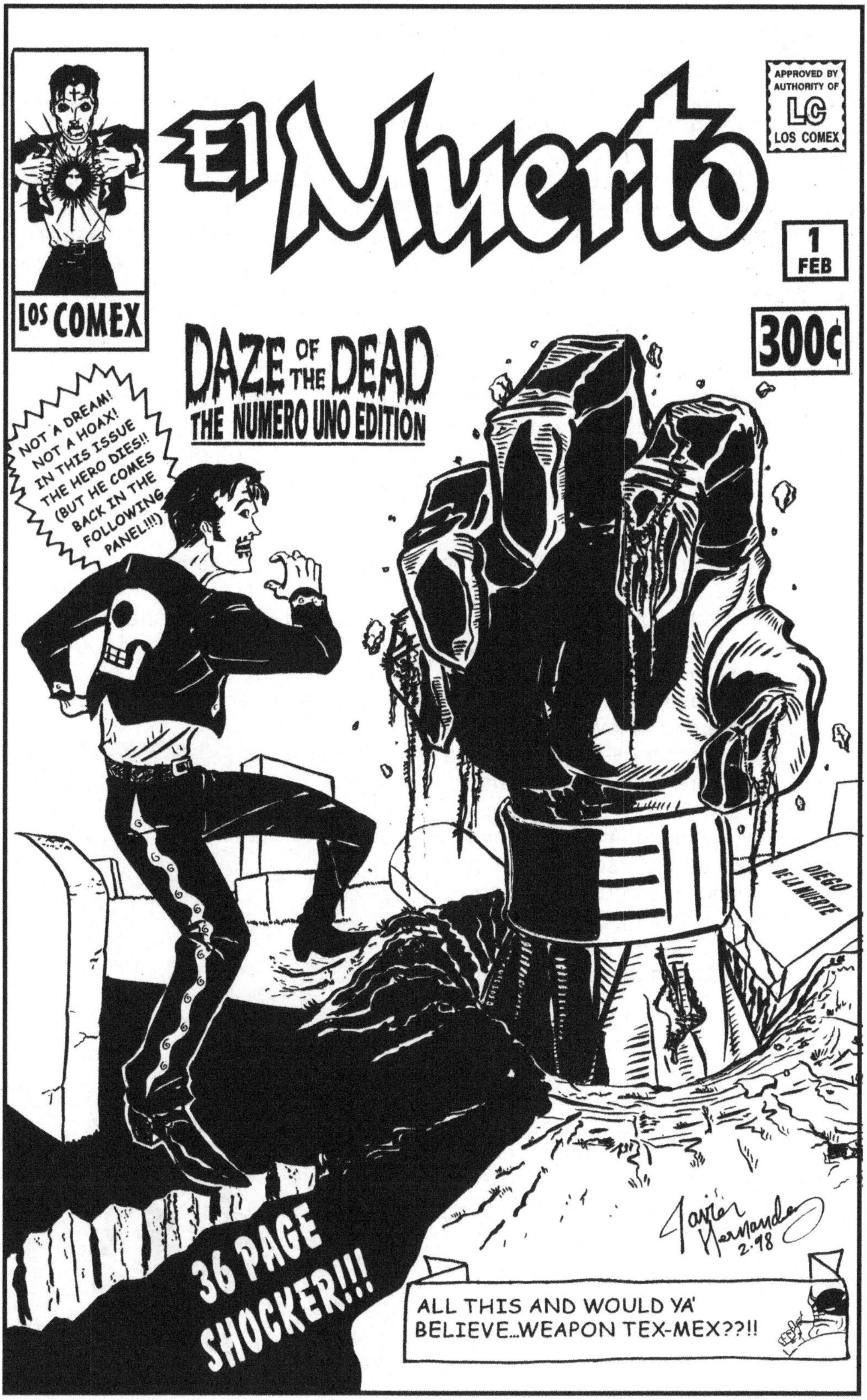
LOS COMEX
El Muerto
APPROVED BY AUTHORITY OF
LC
LOS COMEX
1
FEB
300¢
DAZE OF THE DEAD
THE NUMERO UNO EDITION
NOT A DREAM! NOT A HOAX! IN THIS ISSUE THE HERO DIES!! (BUT HE COMES BACK IN THE FOLLOWING PANEL!!!)
DIEGO DE LA MUERTE
Javier Hernandez 2·98
36 PAGE SHOCKER!!!
ALL THIS AND WOULD YA' BELIEVE...WEAPON TEX-MEX??!!

The first appearance of El Muerto occurred in February 1998 in a photocopied b&w comic called EL MUERTO: DAZE OF THE DEAD- THE NUMERO UNO EDITION. A modest little publication from an artist finding his footing in the world of comic books. Particularly self-published comics, which brings with it several levels of challenges and pitfalls.

The story you've just read, also entitled DAZE OF THE DEAD, was created over a span of many, many years. You could actually say it took 20 years to produce the final finished product! For the sake of the historical record, let me tell you a little tale of a long and winding road...

THE NUMERO UNO EDTION was the book I sold at various shows for the first few years. It was the origin story of the character, ending with him hitching a ride in the van and heading down to Mexico. Of course the plan was to continue telling the origin story, but in those early days I just wasn't anywhere near as productive as I should have been. (That's one of the pitfalls of self-publishing. It's far too easy to leave things on the back burner since there's no one pushing you to get to work on the next issue). I also distracted myself by doing an offshoot of El Muerto called Manga Muerto, which basically was my idea of reinvisioning the character as a Japanese-style hero with a giant robot! Yeah, I went down the road of doing to short stories with Manga Muerto, always telling myself that I'd get back to the regular version of the character. That's called lack of discipline mixed with generating too many new ideas at one time!

In 2002, having got the Manga Muerto bug out of my system, and also having sold out both print runs of THE NUMERO EDITON (less than 500 in total), I decided to put more money and effort behind El Muerto and reprint that first issue with a goal of wider distribution. So I invested about $2000 in a much larger run (3,000 copies) which I had printed at a local company. They printed newspapers and magazines so large orders were business as usual for them. I created a new cover, which was printed in color this time, added a few extra features and reprinted that initial "Daze of the Dead" story for a whole new audience. And this time I even had the comic distributed by a national comics distributor, Diamond Distributors, which allowed comic shops across the country to order copies for their shops. What's old is new again.

el Muerto
THE AZTEC ZOMBIE
#1 $3.95
KING SIZE PREMIERE ISSUE!
BIG
UMBRELLA

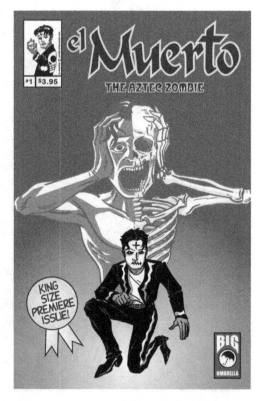

Previous page: The ultimate collector's item! Debut appearance of El Muerto from 1998. I've always claimed there were no more than 500 copies made because I did two print runs and I believe I did 300 initially then another 150. But in case I'm off by about 50, I say 500 copies in total. I only have a scant few of these left myself. But I need something for my retirement plan

Right: The 2002 EL MUERTO KING SIZE, reprinting the origin story "Daze of the Dead". This King Size edition was printed with color covers and recieved national distribution.

el Muerto
MISHMASH
$2.95
JAVIER HERNANDEZ
A CAPTIVATING COLLECTION OF EL MUERTO STORIES INCLUDING AN ALL-NEW TALE... PLUS: REPRINTING A TRIO OF RARELY-SEEN MINI-EPICS! MANGA MUERTO IN...
"YOU-ONLY-DIE TWICE"
"DEAD FOREVER"
RIP
"MAD MARTIAN PARTY"
AND, THE AUTO-BIOGRAPHICAL CULT CLASSIC:
"DOS MIL"*
WHERE EL MUERTO COMES FACE TO FACE WITH HIS CARTOONIST CREATOR!

Continuing the saga of the Aztec Zombie!
el Muerto
DEAD & CONFUSED
PART 1
$2.95
JAVIER HERNANDEZ

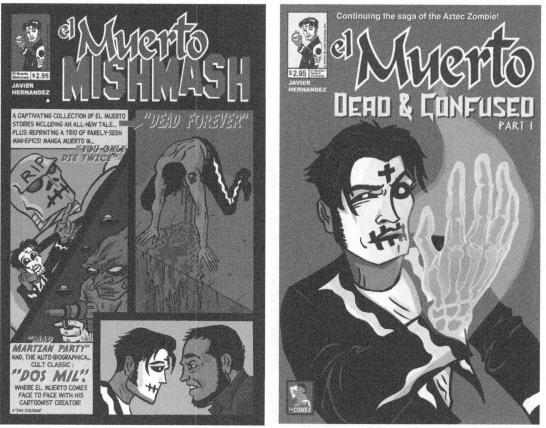

The second and third issue of the series. El MUERTO MISH MASH (2004) and EL MUERTO: DEAD & CONFUSED, Pt. 1 (2008)

By 2001 I had already been contacted by director Brian Cox regarding his interest in El Muerto. At that time I was also working as the art director for a screenprinting company, which really took up so much of my time in those days. Once 2002 came around and I had published the EL MUERTO KING SIZE, I was both being courted for a movie deal and slowly working on the next chapter of my series.

In 2004 I released EL MUERTO MISH MASH, a collection of previously published short stories, including the first Manga Muerto comic from 1999 and an autobiographic story from 2000. Also included was “Dead Forever” a new short taking place after the events of “Daze of the Dead”, as Diego rides in the van toward Mexico. This was basically a story where he’s reliving the events of his life in his head, allowing the reader to get some back story on the character up to the moment when he was sacrificed and resurrected by the Aztec gods Mictlantecuhtli and Tezcatlipoca.

I’m not going to blame the movie’s production for the slow release of the subsequent El Muerto comic, because I was a terrible procrastinator. But I did involve myself (contractually, thanks to my lawyer!) with the involvement of the Muerto movie every step of the way. Contract negotiations, then later production meetings, ran from 2002 all the way up to January 2005. Then we went into official pre-production followed by the 4 week shoot. As mentioned in the introduction, it was a jarring experience to leave the film set for the last time in February 2005 and then basically get back to working on my comic. But that’s what I did and eventually got the third chapter of the story done! EL MUERTO:DEAD & CONFUSED, Pt 1 was released in 2008 (a year after the film itself was released, actually).

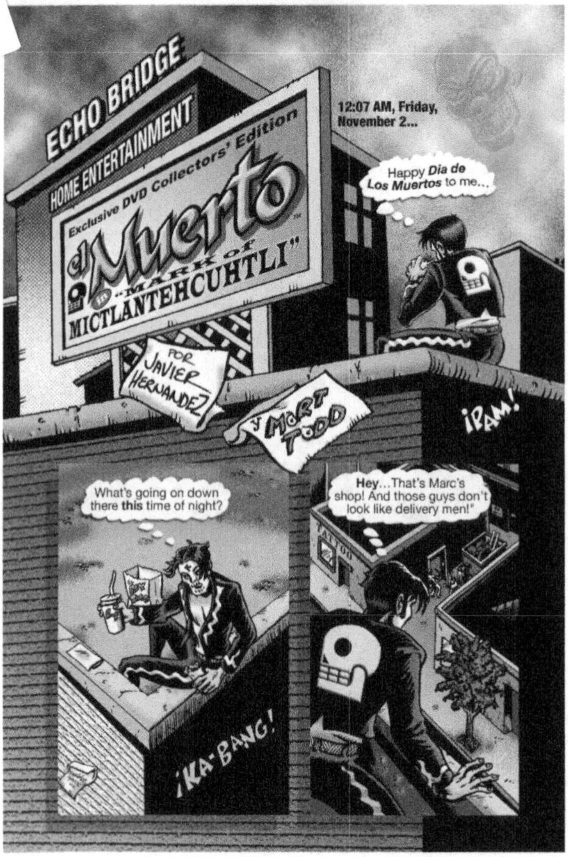
ECHO BRIDGE
HOME ENTERTAINMENT
Exclusive DVD Collectors' Edition
El Muerto
"MARK OF MICTLANTEHCUHTLI"
POR JAVIER HERNANDEZ
Y MORT TODD
12:07 AM, Friday, November 2...
Happy Dia de Los Muertos to me...
What's going on down there this time of night?
Hey...That's Marc's shop! And those guys don't look like delivery men!"
¡BAM!
¡KA-BANG!

There was a brief venture into some comic book making for me while I was involved with the movie. Once the film was getting ready for it's DVD release, I had suggested a few special features to the distributor, Echo Bridge. My idea was for a special El Muerto story to be included as a mini-comic in the DVD package. They agreed, I had my lawyer draft up our terms and price, and asked my friend Mort Todd, an accomplished and veteran comic book creator and publisher himself, to collaborate with me. I needed to get the story done quickly so bringing someone aboard was a necessity. I came up with the plot and wrote the script, as well as draw the layouts for the story in pencil. Mort inked it, colored the gray tones and lettered the 8 pages. The DVD and mini comic were released in 2007.

Part 1 of DEAD & CONFUSED finally found Diego getting out of that van after a 10 year ride! (The original comic was released in 1998). He arrives in Baja Mexico and soon finds himself amongst the denizens of Mondragon's Circus and Festival of Freaks. The issue ends as Diego prepares to visit the Dia de Los Muertos festival being put on by the family of circus misfits who have befriended him. With the story to be concluded in Part 2..

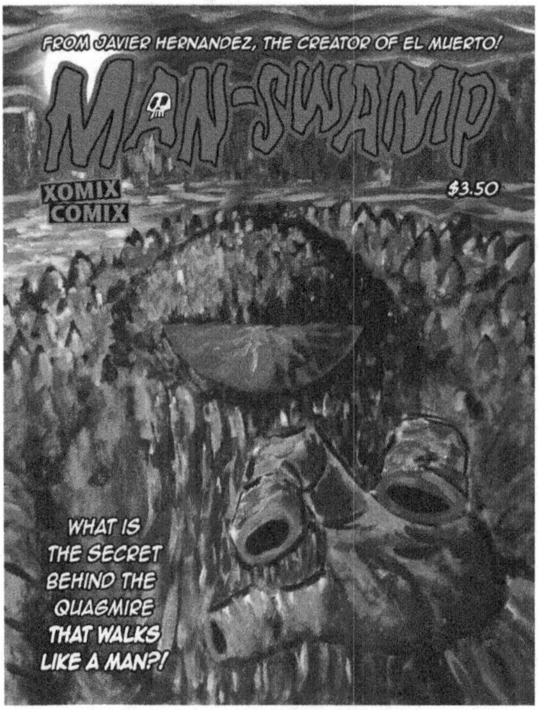
FROM JAVIER HERNANDEZ, THE CREATOR OF EL MUERTO!
MAN-SWAMP
XOMIX COMIX
$3.50
WHAT IS THE SECRET BEHIND THE QUAGMIRE THAT WALKS LIKE A MAN?!

If you've read the graphic novel before reading this, then the plots I've mentioned from these early El Muerto comics will sound familar. But you haven't been reading the original issues, or seeing the original art. After I had released the first part of DEAD & CONFUSED in 2008 I committed the 2nd sin of self-publishing (the first being taking too much time for your follow up issue): I jumped right into a rabbit hole of distraction. In 2009 I created a new comic, with a completely different character, that I was eager to get into production. MAN-SWAMP turned out to be the first of several new titles I published over the next few years! While it was always my goal to conclude El Muerto's initial origin story, I just couldn't

The debut of the Man-Swamp (2009)

couldn't resist the call to create what's basically amounted to my own mini-universe of characters.

The Man-Swamp was followed by Dead Dinosaurio, The Coma, "Comics!" and the follow-up issue "More Comics!"... A very productive group of years, at any rate. But the problem was that there was no Part 2 on the horizon for DEAD & CONFUSED. So finally in about 2014 or so I realized that the time was way overdue. I pulled out my copy of Part 1 to refresh myself and then set about drawing the concluding story. And worked on it I did for a good year or so. But as I was diligently working on the climatic conclusion to the saga of Diego de La Muerte, I was once again sidetracked (if that's the right word) with creating and producing two additional features: MANIAC PRIEST and LES VODOUISANTS! The first being a supernatural vigilante thriller done in homage to 1980s vigilante exploitation films, the latter the story of a married couple who are voodoo powered protectors from Haiti.

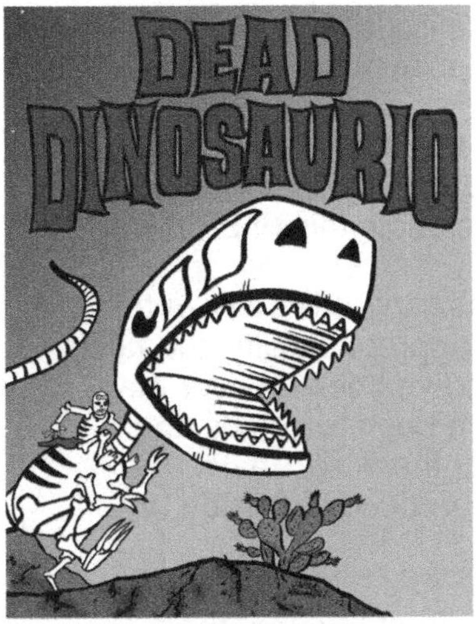
DEAD
DINOSAURIO
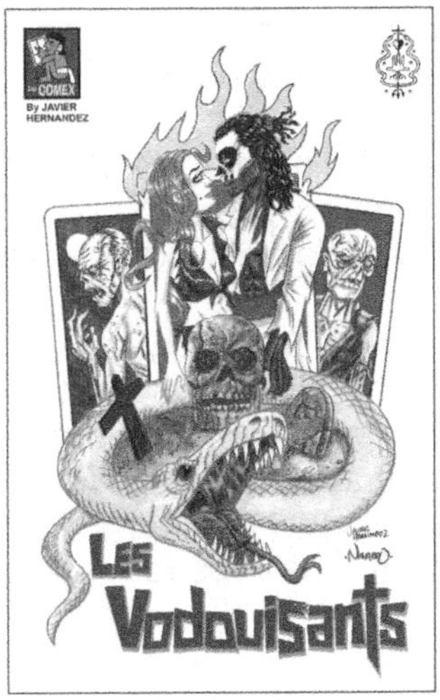
COMEX
By JAVIER HERNANDEZ
LES
Vodouisants
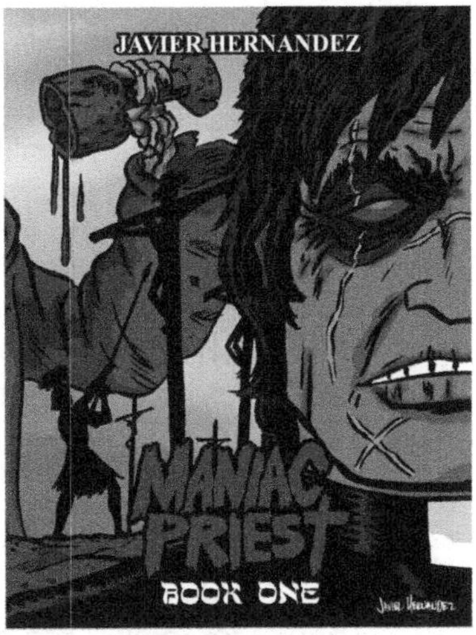
JAVIER HERNANDEZ
MANIAC
PRIEST
BOOK ONE

Three "distracting" comics projects! DEAD DINOSAURIO (2012), LES VODOUISANTS (2015) and MANIAC PRIEST (2016)

In due course though, I finished the conclusion to DEAD & CONFUSED. The plan was to collect the previous El Muerto stories, along with the newly finished Part 2, and publish it as a tradepaperback, which would officially be the complete origin story of El Muerto. However, a thing occurred to me just as I finished that large batch of new pages. I looked at the first story, from 1998, and felt, fairly strongly, that the art style and scripting just didn't match up with the new material. We're talking about the growth of an artist from a span of some 20 years, and in fact a novice comics creator producing his first published work from that time. I didn't want readers to be distracted by the varying quality of the individual issues, so I decided to redraw the entire first issue. And it wasn't just about redrawing the same pages over again, panel for panel. This time around I fleshed out the back story of Diego to showcase his childhood and introduce his hitherto unseen guardian Grasiela. I showed the courtship, romance and break-up between Maria and Diego. Some minor incidental scenes were discarded, and other scenes were created. It was very important for me to provide the reader with a much richer and more immersive experience into Diego's life, creating a more invested interest in him and his circle of friends and family. Because of the upcoming supernatural fantasy that I was about to drop him, and the readers, into, I wanted to ground everyone into the familiar dramas we all often find ourselves living out in our own daily lives.

So of course once I redrew those pages, I looked at the other two issues (EL MUERTO MISH MASH and DAZE OF THE DEAD, Pt 1) and felt the same thing: That those stories, released in 2002 and 2008, reflected a level of work that didn't match up with the new material. So I spent more time in redrawing those pages, again adding new sequences and reenvisioning other passages. Everything I did, redrawing some 70 pages of story to align up with the 60 or so new pages, was to provide a cohesive visual narrative for the readership. A compete reenvention of the original El Muerto story, with the never before seen second half. The 'new' story within these pages, DAZE OF THE DEAD, is indeed the official start of the Muerto saga for all intents an purposes.

Here's a quick aside though: There are actually 10 pages in this book that are carried over from 2008's DEAD & CONFUSED, Pt 1. Yes, those particular pages, as I examined them, I felt were successful enough in terms of quality to be intregated with new pages. I won't take the time now to reveal which pages those might be, but if you have a copy of DEAD & CONFUSED, Pt 1 then you can compare them. If anybody here wants to guess which 10 pages are the original ones, maybe I can reward you with a prize of some type?

And so, if this is your first time reading El Muerto, welcome! I hope you've enjoyed the story. If you've read any previous Muerto comics, let me thank you for sticking around for the long delayed complete origin tale of El Muerto.

It long ago occured to me that as the author of this saga, the story of this guy Diego who gets thrown into this winding road of unpredictability and fate and adventure, perhaps in some way, mirrors the one I've been on over the past 20 years. Nothing as fantastical, but certainly I've been to places and experienced things and met people I would not have otherwise. That's true for anyone who takes it upon themselves to follow a particular decision or plan of action, I'm sure.

Thanks for joining me on this 150 plus page segment of my unending creative journey. Please join me again for the next trip. There's more ahead, I guarantee it!

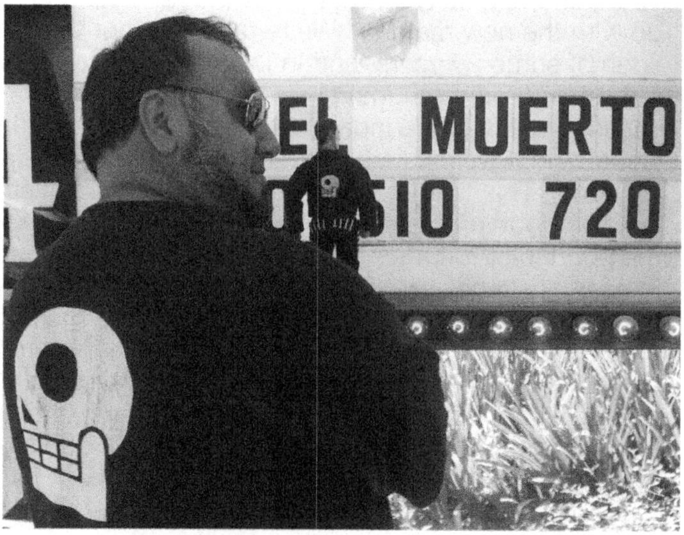
EL MUERTO
720

Taking in a movie with a little friend. EL MUERTO's exclusive one-week engagement at the Laemmle's Grande 4 Plex in Downtown LA, September 2007. The theater is reported to have closed down in 2009.

Me and El Muerto are still here, though!

Biography

Javier Hernandez, born in East LA, published his first comic in 1998 (EL MUERTO) through his imprint Los Comex, and has since produced a variety of titles featuring his unique brand of haunted heroes and heroic monsters (The Coma, Weapon Tex-Mex, Maniac Priest & others).

As a writer and artist, Javier has also produced work for a variety of publications, including The Charlton Arrow, GHOULA, Ditkomania, "Hey Kid's, Comics", Esperanza: the Journal of Latino Culture & others.

2007 saw a film adaptation of El Muerto starring Wilmer Valderrama. Javier served as the Associate Producer and also appeared in a cameo role. The film, written and directed by Brian Cox, won Best Feature at the 2008 Whittier Independent Film Festival and screened at various film festivals throughout the U.S.

In 2011 he co-founded, with Ricardo Padilla, the Latino Comics Expo, the nation's premiere convention spotlighting the contributions of Latino creators in the fields of comic books, political cartoons, animation, film and related popular arts.

✉ misterjav@gmail.com
🐦 /javierhernandez
📷 /javierloscomex
f /javier.f.hernandez

www.javzilla.com
www.elmuerto.com

In Memoriam

In the tradition of Dia de Los Muertos I'd like to acknowledge the following writers and artists from comic books and comic strips who have influenced me and my own work in varying ways.

While they've passed on, their art and legacies remain to inspire and brighten the path forward.

Charles Addams

Ross Andru

Gus Arriola

John Buscema

Gene Colan

Steve Ditko

Will Eisner

Steve Gerber

Chester Gould

Jack Kirby

Joe Kubert

Harvey Pekar

Frank Robbins

Dick Sprang

Osamu Tezuka

Herb Trimpe

Made in the USA
Columbia, SC
28 August 2019